And
Introducing in th

A history of many aspects of the British Professional wrestling scene, both inside and also outside the ring detailing the mainly Scottish Forum spanning the "The Golden Era" of the 1960's the 1970's as well as the far less lauded 1980's, which witnessed the sad demise of the long running TV broadcasts of the sport in the UK.

Ask him again ref!

Written
By
Dale Storm

(A former pro with 20 years experience in the ring)

Also included is a running glossary of the everyday but secret language, both voiced and signed plus the terminology used by those who worked in the industry.

When reading these pages it's important to remember this remarkable fact. Some of the best wrestlers the UK ever produced never appeared on British Television.

If memory serves me well all my recollections are true.

Ask him again ref!

This Opus has been described as both a "Diary" of Dale Storm's personal journey through the period and also a potted history of some aspects of the onetime vibrant, mainly Scottish based section of the Professional Wrestling Industry in the UK during the 1960's the 1970's and the early 1980's. This author is more than happy to concur with this assessment of its content and its conclusions. At 460+ pages some might find it a little long but it's taken that time to tell everybody's story. It is also a one off memoir there will be no second volume coming off the presses later on.

For
Lilian, Lara and Nicholas

Editing and additional material by Wrestling Heritage
www.wrestlingheritage.co.uk

Like my good friend Adrian Street, I too have written, proofed, formatted and published this work by myself. Any spelling and grammar errors are entirely my own.

Front Cover: All pictures are courtesy of Mr Robin Christie. (Copyright owner) The poster was promoting a wrestling show in my home town of Ayr in the 1970's. "Romeo" Joe Critchley one of the best performers ever to grace a British canvas is prominent in two action shots. The rest feature the Scottish based masked villain the Viking, another good grappling rule bender who really knew how to noise up the crowd.

Although the copyright for most of the photographs appearing in these pages has been established and credited, the ownership of older pictures has been harder to ascertain. However every effort has been made to contact and credit the ownership of every entry apologies to the owners any emissions are entirely unintentional.

*** Deepest apologies for the poor quality of some picture inserts ***

ISBN-13:-978-1492890577
ISBN-10:-149289057X

Ask him again ref!

Acknowledgements and Dedications

Firstly to my Dear Mother the best friend I ever had.

To my hardworking Miner Father, with whom I did not always agree.

To my "Spartan" siblings without whom we'd never have gotten started.

To Mr John Gourlay who tried to pass on his bodybuilding knowledge.

To my cousin Mr Billy Irvine who was always my biggest supporter.

To Wee Tam and Margaret Stevenson, for being my good friends.

To Mr George Nesbitt the Annbank Village School Headmaster.

To My Uncle Joe Wilson the Annbank Village School Janitor.

To Mr Danny Flynn, Mr Freddie Woolley, Mr Gordon Corbett.
Mr Jack Atherton and Mr Brian Dixon all mentors and promoters.

To Lara, Nicholas, Mr Jim Lee and Mr Tommy O'lone for all their help.

To all the Lads and Lassies who attended the Mossblown Gym.

To the late Mr David Simpson one of life's true gentlemen.

To my good friend the late Mr George McDonald from Elgin Town.

To Mr Alan Balmer a truly modest gentleman.

To Mr Peter Preston, Mr Eddie Rose and Mr Adrian Street good friends and great wrestling professionals. Thank you one and all.

To Mr Joe Critchley, Mr Ezra Francis, Mr Jim McKenzie, Mr Sammy Taylor all sadly gone, but now living again in Wrestling Heaven.

To "Anglo-Italian" and "Hack" at the Wrestling Heritage web-site.

To Darren, Peter and all in Kent for their dedication to the Re-Unions.

To fellow professionals who truly shared my regard for the business.

To Mr Peter Preston for very kindly, agreeing to write the Prologue.

To Mr Raymond Plunkett without whom we'd have been long forgotten.

To Jackie McCann for the informed "When Grappling was Golden" site.

To Wrestling fans everywhere this Grappling Gladiator salutes you all!

Ask him again ref!

The Prologue

This mostly factual memoir of some selected aspects of the colourful career of a successful journeyman professional wrestler in the UK during the sports **"The Golden Era"** began to emerge purely by chance during the research process into a one-man "single-hander" career based stage play about Dale Storm's twenty years in the ring.

Many readers will perhaps not be aware however that grappling on UK TV actually began when ITV first started broadcasting in 1955. Or indeed that **"World of Sport"** the Saturday afternoon magazine style programme which included many other popular sporting genres was first aired on 2nd January 1965. At which time the producers incorporated the Professional Wrestling slot into their new programme format at its then very popular time slot of 4pm.

Unlike the four hour TV sports show wrestling's tenure didn't end when twenty years later * ***"WOS"*** was taken off the air in1985. The **"Grunt and Groan"** portion soldiered on until1988 but by then according to those in change at ITV at the time falling performance standards lacked the previously displayed high levels of skill and consistency meaning the programme continually struggled to attract worthwhile commercially viable audience viewing figures.

This odyssey is based around Dale's ring career but in order to understand his total professionalism, dedication and loyalty to his art form, allied to his high regard for almost all his fellow performers and all of wrestling's innermost secrets. You firstly need to be aware of the environment into which he was born and the people who influenced his early upbringing, as it was they who instilled the values of comradeship, loyalty, meticulous preparation and the highest ideals of good presentation he always endeavoured to display when in the ring.

**** "WOS" (World of Sport) ITV's former sports show.***

Most of his peers were also working class lads and lassies from areas as far afield as the North of England, Lancashire, Yorkshire, Essex, Lincolnshire, Kent, The West Country, The North and the South of Ireland, Wales and of course Bonnie Scotland. Among the regular visitors on the Scottish circuit when Dale was starting out, some of whom he worked with back then and later on and whom he rated highly were Halifax based grapplers Bob Sweeny and "Farmer" Johnny Alan along with other sons of Yorkshire such as former miner Mal Kirk, Judd Harris and one time Joint Promotions Middleweight Champion Mr Eric Taylor.

His mentors were working class people from a small tight-knit community mostly Coal Miners, their wives or their mothers. Both his grandfathers worked in the coal industry. One was badly hurt down the pit and finished up on lighter duties and on even lower wages in the Wood Yard on the surface. The second on his father's side was a veteran of the First World War campaign in Northern Greece. He was also the very first man to operate a fully mechanised coal cutting machine in the busy Ayrshire coalfield in the 1930's when all of the local industry was still privately owned by people like the all powerful Baird of Dalmellington Company. This was prior to the formation by the Old Labour strategists of the National Coal Board in 1948. His father, older brother, most of his uncles and cousins all worked in the mines. Many school friends on leaving at age fifteen served engineer and electrical apprenticeships mostly for the National Coal Board and all would eventually get their hands and faces dirty toiling in the bowels of the earth, a place where danger was never very far away!

Dale was born into and spent his early years as a lad in a staunch old school, old socialist *"Real Left Wing"* mining community in the Ayrshire village of Mossblown, five miles north east of the town of Ayr in the rural heartland of Scotland's picturesque, history laden South West.

Peter Preston

Chapters List

It was 1980 and the month was early November, the night was cold and damp, it always seemed to be that way whenever I was booked into Hamilton Town Hall. By this time Joint Promotions had disintegrated and UK Wrestling was in a state of flux! I'd travelled the length and breadth of Scotland and beyond, even over Hadrian's Wall in far worse weather than this though, besides my young daughter and son were both happily playing a game of eye-spy in the back seat and my loving wife was sitting in the passenger seat quietly feeding me from a salt and vinegar crisp packet. Not unusually I'd had to leave Ayr immediately I'd finished work for the day, the kids had been given there tea earlier and my good lady had made me up some of her always tasty sandwiches. She'd picked me up at the appointed time and we were off up the road full of excited expectation. This was a special journey for our two kids as they'd always wanted to see Andy Robin in the flesh, ever since he's sent them both a special collectors, limited edition Hercules the Bear T-Shirt!

His opponent on the night was Kendo a formidable advisory so real fireworks were assured! It turned out to be a memorable night all round but sadly not for the reasons we'd hoped! Disaster and mind numbing pain and anguish loomed large! Really bad times were about to be visited on someone on that show but to whom? As well as being the promoter Andy was also as usual topping the bill, I was in the second favoured slot. This was effectively my twentieth year in the business and I'd mix it with a lot of the top dogs, but this time I was facing a legend in the form of the only man who'd triumphed over the rings top villain Mick McManus live on TV! This tough son of York was a pocket tank of a man, feared by many but respected by all, definitely not a man to take liberties with! The bout was going well for me and I was confident of a big career boosting win. I'd taken the first fall in the third but he'd come back strong in the forth and powered

his way to an equaliser, his vast amateur catch training was beginning to show! The fifth was just about even but I was still in the bout and I sensed he may be tiring just a little? As the bell sounded for the six and final round we shook hands in the centre of the ring and as I crouched slightly to a defensive position I could feel something wasn't right underfoot, but no chance to contemplate it further as he was on me like flash! Two rapid forearms smashes powered into my chest, he was a master of that skill, an arm roll and then another but still I'm doing ok, but crashing into the canvas from an exceptionally high, bone crushing backdrop, having been posted twice beforehand was always very dangerous and then from nowhere disaster struck......!

..

Ayrshire my home county at one time boasted three of the most popular Wrestling venues in Scotland: Ayr Ice Rink, the Dam Park Hall in Ayr and the Grand Hall in Kilmarnock all were wonderful places to work, all were different and all were unique in their own way. My grandfather, an honest hard working miner taught me a lot about life and he once told me should I find myself in a strange pub, order a pint go to the toilet have a look round and then decide whether you really want to drink the beer! One warm summer night having performed at the Grand Hall, I'd just managed to get myself in the door of the "Nuek" Public House across the road before 10pm curfew. I did as my grandfather had instructed and I ordered my pint, but on my return from having a pee I was left with no real decision to make regards the relative merits of the quality of the beer etc. Standing on the bar drinking out of my glass was a white greyhound, apparently the owner who was sitting at the end of the bar had been at the show and being a devoted follower of the rivalry between both towns he was making his point! Which only goes to prove that in life just like in the ring, as much as you may try you can't please all of the people all of the time. Thank god I hadn't paid for the drink!

Ask him again ref!

CHAPTER ONE

(Red is the Colour)

From a very early age an inbuilt mistrust of the "Gaffer" "The Tories" and the "Class Divide" were being formulated in my active fast developing young brain. The tough working man environment I grow up in instilled a sense of community and helped to make me both physically and mentally stronger. Although the badly mistaken and now sadly clichéd working class adage which heralded the fact "Real Men Don't Cry" was never far away and it served as a constant reminder that showing real emotion was considered by some to be a sign of weakness! It was regularly interpreted to mean you were very probably a Sissy, a Big Girls Blouse, a Nancy Boy, a Big Jessie or even in the homophobic vernacular of the period a Poof! In these times men had to be seen to be masculine and macho and anything else was simply not allowed to exist!
Or at least it was never displayed outwardly for fear of peer ridicule, disgrace and possible imprisonment!
Without this hard-man environment my boyhood sessions as a young boxer and my flurries into the exciting world of martial arts etc, would probably never have seen the light of day. My character development was further honed as a youth whilst living in Australia where I was constantly immersed in the close male ethos of "Mateship." Where total reliability is shown to and received from good friends and workmates on a daily basis. This added yet another solid building block to my make-up and my personality.
As a young adult my full-time bread winning day job was on the tools in large part in the motor trade. Regularly right after my normal working day had ended around 4-30pm I would often drive distances of sometimes in excess of 300 miles round trip to a wrestling tournament somewhere in Scotland. Occasionally I travelled even further afield over Hadrian's Wall to work for promoters on shows in England's heartland. After fulfilling engagements I would

immediately undertake the return journey and this usually meant arriving home around 1, 2, 3 or even 4 in the morning and after grabbing only a few hours of hopefully restful sleep, I'd be back on the tools starting my regular daytime job all over again the next morning at 8am sharp. This odyssey also includes some of the names of those I encountered during my two decades in the square, three roped ring almost all of whom earned my total respect and were then given by me the title **Mr!** Early on in what was originally a stage play writing process it soon became apparent there was a lot more going on in the pages than was required to fill a theatre time slot of around one performance hour. During the research process years of facts and memorable incidents, some good, some bad, some happy and some sad were being brought back to life. Good friends well remembered and some now sadly passed over were asking for their tales to be told by the man who was to almost everyone else included in these pages always regarded as an honest, a good, a loyal and a trusted friend. The lot of someone in the world of grappling and indeed the performance arts in general, especially for those who did not readily achieve some level of recognition could be a tough life and a really difficult learning curve. This situation is often referred to in the world of television or theatre when being repeatedly overlooked for a part in a production by the rather simple but inept phrase of "Collecting Your No's." This is nothing more than just another way of encountering rejection and dealing with it head on! There's an infamous tale attributed to Larry Olivier telling how he pushed his hand through an open dressing room doorway at the interval and gave an thumbs up sign to a fellow performer, only to then slowly turn it upside down until the digit was then at the bottom in a Caesar like you will die manner. I shudder to think what state the actor must have in after that brutal critique. Money alone to many was not always the driving force especially given the fact that in today's terms at least most nearly always received payments of ridiculously low levels of financial remuneration. All that is except for the chosen few who were gifted star and sometimes even superstar status but sadly not always because of their higher levels of expertise or their superior performance skills!

It's difficult for an outsider to even come close to understanding why these often poorly rewarded diehards chose to travel the length a breadth of the UK like the mummers and wandering minstrels of the past and usually in cramped, cigarette smoke filled cars or more often in a twelve seat promoter owned mini-buses. Niggling injuries received in the ring were always an on-going and constant threat to their earning power and sometimes the **"Villains"** could also suffer the extra indignity of being hit over the head or on the body with whatever came to hand, wielded by some of those who had paid their hard earned cash to watch their often outlandish, over-the-top even gregarious performances. Luckily I was seldom if ever on the receiving end of a blow from an unhappy punter. To put it in the more regularly used vernacular of the genre apart from the fact those who paid always seemed to appreciate my one hundred and ten percent effort, quite simply my character was what was known as a **"Hero"** a **"White Hat"** or a **"Blue Eye"** this usually meant I was deemed immune from the onslaught of disgruntled grannies wielding an umbrella, a heavy handbag or even a sharpened up knitting needle!

There are many stories in these pages but not all of them are about me or indeed the successful headliners. This totally unselfish rather basic approach has been deliberately adopted as a genuine homage to those many individuals whose undoubted contribution to wrestling's history has been sadly neglected in favour of some much lesser individuals, whose standing among the real ring men was far less lauded and applauded than it has been by the paying public. Although, I do take time to mention some of the stars of my era who were personal friends and whose biographies, photos, exploits and personal stories feature regularly on the undeniably well informed **"Wrestling Heritage"** web-site at www.wrestlingheritage.co.uk

Ask him again ref!

Another highly merited devotee is Chris on the **"Wrestling Furnace"** web-sight at www.wrestlingfurnace.com

*** *If you haven't already checked out these wonderfully well informed sites, highly rated and contributed too regularly by real wrestlers who actually worked in the business I suggest you do so as soon as possible* ***

I have chosen to give readers a snapshot insight into other equally interesting **"Workers"** who graced the business and who have seldom if ever had a mention in other publications over the intervening years. I also endeavour to give some, albeit rather limited access where possible to events and situations which before, during and after The Golden Era ended, had normally been cloaked aspects of the genre and freely accessible only to the inner circle.

Most of these men and woman performers were the characters regularly filling the lower half of the card who regularly supported the "Big Brand Name Creations" and the top of the Bill, so called "Super Star" performers?

I have also included some hopefully amusing anecdotes about others around whom the whole show was staged and the action regularly played out. These include some Referees, M C's and Time Keepers. Even some lowly Ring Seconds are singled out and get a special mention and some well-deserved and definitely well earned praise.

Promoters have also been included, mostly the ones I worked for personally, some good and some bad. I also try to expose some of the main differences and the demarcation lines which existed between the **Dark-Side** in the form of the **Independents** as opposed to the much more powerful establishment ruling order. These outsiders were largely breakaway renegade groups who consisted in most cases of smaller promoters far too numerous to mention. Some of the original leading lights were Danny Flynn and Fred Woolley, Gordon Corbett, Jack Cassidy,

Ron Farrar, Norman Berry and even Shirley Crabtree, but the biggest of these was undoubtedly **"Mr Paul Lincoln."** **Paul Lincoln Management: Often copied seldom bettered!**

TOP CLASS WRESTLING
make sure it's a
paul lincoln
Presentation
Paul Lincoln Managements Ltd.

Part of Paul Lincoln's advertising strategy

Paul Lincoln

Later rebel additions included Orig Williams and the much younger Mr Brian Dixon and both promoted widely. Whilst in the Blackpool area Mr Bobby Barron usually held sway. All these worked shows on the Scottish Circuit at one time. But they were nearly always living in the shadow of the much more powerful "Big Boys" generally referred to by most of the lads in the trade as simply **"Joints."** This operation was the biggest organisation in Britain. It had been established around 1952 and from then on it attempted to operate a UK wide cartel type monopoly and in that venture they were over time, largely very successful.

Being fortunate enough to be connected with one branch of so called "Show Business" sometimes opened up doors into other areas of the tinsel tinted crazy world some wrestlers operated in. Things of course could prove difficult on the odd occasion for a young impressionable village lad like me to keep his feet planted on terra firma and his head out of the clouds in my early career years. Thankfully my Wee Mammy Mrs Margaret "Daisy" McFedries Bryden (nee Frew) was always there with a few short but firm "bring me back to earth" words if that star struck, glazed look ever dared to show itself in my eyes. This mantle was then taken up, if a little reluctantly at first by my then young, still quite shy, but very loving wife Lilian. Sadly this proved to have far less of an effect on me at times unlike my demure, only 5 foot tall Mater. This was especially true in the early years of our eventful journey towards our now fast approaching 2020 Golden Wedding marriage celebration. Lines of autograph hunters can also turn a head and pints or the odd glass of malt whisky being sent over in bars from well-wishing fans can be another. Although always very much appreciated, well-meaning gestures like these can sometimes be a huge distraction nevertheless. Night Clubs were amongst the places always open to young wrestlers and standing in long queues was regularly avoided. Yet again that can if allowed to prevail, greatly increase the diameter of your hat size. Experience and maturity can usually facilitate an eventual rising above an ever enlarging ego. Good luck can also play a part but nothing is more reassuring than the support of a strong and loving wider family unit. What's more, fortunate young wrestlers can also be afforded opportunities to meet and greet with some very interesting individuals, luckily this often proved to be the case during my career run and for that experience I remain ever humbled and eternally grateful. My general grounding in entertainment proved invaluable and helped to pave the way into other career opportunities in later life. Among which were steady employment as Singer/Comedian and a spell as a Cabaret Compere with "The Rank Organisation" and shortly thereafter years of academic study and training as an actor afforded me several reasonably well paid opportunities as a jobbing thespian on both stage and screen for a period. Latterly I turned my hand to script writing and after a spell of further study the award of a behind the camera BA University Degree proved to be an invaluable add-on. This led me into directing short films in the genres of comedy and drama and also occasionally in the art of balanced, honest and informed documentary movie making.

Many thanks are gratefully extended to all who took the time to take care with my one-time highly toned, sweat soaked body when working with them in the ring and for all those memorable years of fellowship and heart felt long lasting friendships. I in return have gone to great lengths to bring you, the reader these almost entirely unabridged and unaltered tales every one of which has been honestly and faithfully recorded within these pages. Warts and all!

The timeline for this sometimes slightly fractious press interview out of which this odyssey developed begins in 1984. The back-story is the highly confrontational and still hugely emotive event namely the 1984/85 Miner's Strike. It must however be both stated and indeed noted from the outset that although almost all of the events mentioned in this opus are indeed true and did actually happen, they did not necessarily all take place in that particular twelve month period. They have therefore and only for the purpose of the narrative storyline and continuity all been chronicled together for both my convenience and hopefully far more importantly for the enjoyment and the fulfilment of the reader. It must however be fully understood from the outset that this autobiography is definitely not an **A to Z** expose' containing headline grabbing gossip about my wrestling friends and other grappling contemporaries. Neither is it a contest by contest, blow by blow account of whom I fought and whom I always beat! That illusion may still be created by others but that self-centred approach is definitely not for me. These pages are hopefully more of a chronicle of some of those who graced ***(or in some cases disgraced)*** both the live shows of the time and also some of the televised bills as well. Although many who were regular fans back then during The Golden Era of British Wrestling in the 1960's the 1970's might argue that things were never quite the same during the far less lauded period that signalled the start of the downward spiral which began in the late 1970's and ended in late1980's. It is however hopefully also much more of an odyssey covering many aspects of the travelling grappler's lives and their lifestyles, both inside and outside of the ring Including some events and situations which have not normally been chronicled in similar works about the "**Grappling Gladiators**" from the popular **ITV "World of Sport"** era. Every biographer who actually took the bumps, the forearm smashes, dropkicks, monkey climbs and the figure four leg locks or who sent themselves out over the top rope just to hear the gasps of the crowd and by so doing at the same time they further enhance the reputation of their worthy opponents, will have a different tale to tell and an alternative way of telling it. I am no different from any of the others who have published their stories, all I can say in my defence is this; I have done my very best to tell the truth and hopefully bring you some enjoyment at the same time.

The secret of success for many was usually a colourful costume, a particular style, a unique hold or a spectacular signature finishing move. All of these gimmicks hopefully made them stand out from the crowd and in some way helped to make them far more interesting as a spectacle. Apart from my dedicated ability confirmed in writing by none other than the great Adrian Street in the latest edition of his memoirs "**IMAGINE** What I Could Do To You" allied with my enthusiasm and my natural athleticism, I always preferred to let my love for my sport, its traditions and its history shine through when I was performing in the ring. The fact that crowds regularly applauded appreciating my efforts, my approach and my dedication speaks volumes.

I for my part always stayed true to my roots by being regularly attired in **"Red Trunks"** with my **"Red Sock Tops"** showing above **"Red Laced"** shinny Black Boots!

The opening salvo outlined in Chapter Four and also in the first part of the concluding scenario being played out in Chapter Thirty Two are hopefully structured in such a manner as to clearly serve as a "Metaphor" for a chain of totally avoidable circumstances put in place by some very blinkered individuals, who driven on by both greed and their own overblown egos then

delivered a body blow to our sport from which it was destined never to recover. These actions were in my opinion the catalyst which led to the sad and premature demise of our own once extremely popular television genre recognised the world-over as the British-style of Professional Wrestling. The scrapping of the original Saturday 4pm show signalled the death knell and Sky's introduction of their now extremely popular, instantly embraced by a younger audience satellite broadcasts, containing the glitzy Hollywood Showmanship, Over-the-top American Style are now popular and commonplace. Further consigning our native style to the dustbin of the dark and distant past!

The globally recognised organisation which runs these shows was originally constituted as the WWWF until it was shortened in 1979 to WWF. A subsequent logo ownership dispute raised in the courts in 2002 by "The World Wildlife Foundation" saw the brands initials changed once again to the format it continues to trade under today, namely that of the WWE.

And Now! Introducing in the "Red" corner!

..(Courtesy of Robin Christie)

The Masked Viking and a devoted fan

CHAPTER TWO

(Seconds away round One!)

The clearly sexually liberated British Band **"Frankie Goes to Hollywood"** were riding high in the charts with the May release of their timely second hit aptly named **"Two Tribes."** Given the large scale political turmoil which had erupted in the first quarter of 1984 in retrospect the subject matter seems to have been entirely appropriate. October's top spot **"Freedom"** from the two piece Boy Band **"Wham"** the title of which suggested the continuation of the violent struggle also seemed apt. As the months rolled by things did not improve on the picket line and during the December festive period we had the rather sad and in some ways unseasonal **"Do they know it's Christmas?"** The inspiration for which was driven by newsreel footage creating an aura of disbelief and horror which asked the question how we in a First World Western Country could stand back and watch hundreds of thousands, mostly young children die of starvation in Africa quite literally in front of a camera. Luckily the caring population of the UK spurred on by a huge concert staged by pop and rock stars at Wembley Stadium in the June of the following year and the live global TV coverage that accompanied it, helped to raise millions. Sadly and rather ironically in the midst of all this generosity and euphoria, hundreds of long established UK communities had also died after that monumental political struggle and the long term unemployment that followed helped finished them off for good. Sadly there was no large scale outcry on British TV News and no star filled Wembley pop concert raising money to feed and clothe those poor unfortunates. In this particular instance "Charity" most certainly did not begin at home!

The large scale sales of the record did however have a huge impact elsewhere as the money donated helped feed millions in Ethiopia and in the process the single became one of the biggest selling chart entries of all time.

Total capitulation and the annihilation of nearly all striking miner resistance came about the following spring, almost twelve months to the day from the time the workers first manned the picket-lines and took on the might of Thatcher's government and the Ronny Regan led Capitalist Chicago School of Economics "Monetarism" Ideology.

Rather ironically the June of that same year 1985 saw the re-release of the now famous show tune from the American musical **"Carousel"** taking over the highest chart position. Having been adopted some years earlier by both Celtic and Liverpool FC fans as their anthem **"You'll never walk alone"** It now became in the process a swan song for the end game in the National Union of Mine Workers epic struggle to keep the British pits open and the industry alive. March 1984 the futuristic year date highlighted by the publication of "George Orwell's" thought provoking novel of the same title on 8th June 1949 was now resonating loudly. During that fateful period we witnessed the final salvo in the latest long list of the UK mine-workers history of industrial actions. The climax coming after a concerted right wing press propaganda campaign heralding the use of strike breaking private haulage firms and the distasteful involvement by the government of its highly controversial policy of the blatant politicisation of normally A-Political police forces all over the UK.

Peaceful normality as far as the Tories were concerned finally raised its ugly, draconian head around the end of the first quarter of 1985. The miners and the some other Trade Unions who had openly and defiantly supported them had been quite soundly defeated by both the moneyed establishment and the fascist like national police constabularies, helped in part by the covert involvement of some specialist army units. This result heralded in a period where Britain's large scale industrial production was about to come to an end. The UK's Industrial Map and its once proud world beating industrial bases of Steel, Ship Building and Coal etc, were destined never to be the same again!

*** The threat of mass "Payoffs" "Unemployment" and "The Dreaded Dole Queue" now loomed even larger! ***

Constant anti-trade union rhetoric directed mainly at the NUM leader Mr Arthur Scargill and National Organiser Mr Mike McGahey the fulltime Miner's Leader in Scotland, had been fuelled on an almost daily basis mainly in the right-wing owned press. Led by such bastions of democracy as the Tory Party's Golden Boy Rupert Murdoch the millionaire proprietor of News International's "The Sun" as it continued to print its blatant half-truths and outright lies. [Sadly its still the UK's biggest selling daily] Just like back in the dark days of the earlier 1974 "Three Day Week Struggle" the lack of heat and light, strange to say had not effected the day to day, or indeed the night by night production of the coal being brought to the surface by "Scab" strike breakers in most areas in the UK. Especially in the deeply divided Nottinghamshire Coalfield as this area had now become not only the frontline but also the heartland of the turncoat, breakaway, sadly brainwashed bullshitting so called "Democratic Union of Mineworkers!"

Those living in big towns and the cities who were largely unaffected by the strikes and who still had some money in their pockets continued to pursue avenues where they could escape the everyday worries and frustrations generated in mining areas by the sometimes biased TV news coverage. Uppermost among these popular diversions were the touring professional wrestling shows which continued to be promoted nationwide, thankfully provided at least some small level of wages for some members of my miner by day wrestler by night family!

Wrestlers travelling in mini-bus groups etc, largely in the Kent/Essex areas [Dartford Tunnel in particular] and almost as often in other areas such as in Yorkshire, Lancashire, England's North East, Nottinghamshire and also in Central Scotland were regularly pulled over by police officers. Where they and the public at large were then roughly challenged in a Gestapo like fashion as to where they were travelling to and why? [Some of the actions regularly adopted by the police were challenged years later in the UK courts and found to have been totally and utterly illegal]

Part of the continued support for this sporting genre was due mainly to the success of the long running ITV "World of Sport" programme whose older 4pm original slot lit up the long winter months every Saturday afternoon.

This action-packed Sports Magazine programme was hosted by **Dickie** "Mallen Streak Hair" **Davis**. [The Mallens being a very successful drama series which ran on the BBC in the late1970's and early 1980's written by the celebrated author Catherine Cookson. The whole family group stood out because of their white streaked front section hair do, Yorkshire born actor John Duttine played the starring role of the illegitimate son Donald Radlet]

Dickie Davis World of Sport's long serving Presenter

The informed commentary was usually provided by Cairo born, son of a British Colonial Service Finance Officer Mr Kenneth Walton Beckett better known to TV viewers as the presenter **"Kent Walton."** This former posh school "Charterhouse Boy" joined the "Royal Air Force" at the outbreak of The Second World War in 1939 thereafter he attended London's Embassy School of Acting before pursuing a thespian career. Between times he hosted as a radio Disc Jockey-Presenter and occasionally as a stand-in commentator during National Lawn Tennis Association Tournaments. [Kent Walton sadly left us in the year 2003]

The television wrestling shows regularly pulled in huge audiences with viewing figures in the millions every week. Its fan-base ranged from hero worshiping children to swooning housewives, as well as the overly excitable and often very dangerous Granny's from Hell Bovver Brigade!

The Alter Ego personas of these ring performers were every bit as well known as the top sports stars and professional footballers of their day. Even the TV Soaps got in on the act when Ian Campbell the bearded Scots ring villain appeared in a contest on "Coronation Street" when he took on challenger and TV character "Stan Ogden." Eventually falling foul of the much tougher Milk Stout drinking, hairnet wearing, anti-hero "Ena Sharples" played by Violet Carson. Had he been even more unlucky and come up against henpecked Stan's spouse the equally formidable Hilda Alice Ogden [nee Crabtree, no relation] played by the nations favourite Jean Alexander the shame may well have forced him to retire prematurely. Nevertheless this whole incident only enhanced wrestling's appeal even more but unlike today's lust for so called "Celebrity Status" where any so called talents aren't always immediately obvious, grapplers were blessed with ability in abundance. Their talents set them apart from most of today's shallow "one week wonder" celebrities who live out their petty fantasies spurred on by the red top press. Whilst attempting to fulfil a hunger for that now regularly misquoted "Andy Warhol" statement "In future everyone will be world famous for fifteen minutes!"

These largely unsung sporting heroes were mostly hardworking, dedicated athletes who travelled the land largely underpaid and sadly undervalued by more than a handful of those who put together the weekly shows. Nevertheless they were always completely skilful individuals, totally and utterly dedicated in the main to their very popular, sometimes extremely dangerous art form.

Within the confines of their sport these worriers communicated by way of secret coded messages occasionally using **"Touch"** or sometimes **"Signs"** and also some **"Key Words."** These were nearly always referred to by those in the know as **"The Strength."** Another term was **"The Script"** usually applied to what was about to transpire in the ring during the bout itself, at other times regards key words the one most often used was **"Queens."** This was a reference to the uninitiated who were to be kept in **"The Dark"** at all times. Queens referred to the football team "Queens Park Rangers" specifically used during conversations which might involve strangers, thus alerting the other performers in the immediate vicinity to the fact there were **"Strangers in the Camp"** who needed to be kept in **"The Dark"** therefore the use of rhyming slang became second nature and a regularly spoken second language by everyone "in the know" in almost all the areas of the grappling business.

The methodology did however change somewhat when we were in really close proximity to an opponent in the ring. Codes were then transmitted through the medium of the **"Grip"** nearly always referred to by fraternity members as the **"Squeeze!"** This consisted of a series of coded messages transmitted purely by touch, a grappling form of the Braille language if you will.

A vitally important example might be when a villain felt the crowd hate factor was approaching fever pitch, in other words **"The Heat"** level threshold. He would then transmit this fact to his victim by means of "the squeeze" this would be a signal to his opponent to make his **"Come Back Moves"** and take over as the leading figure in the contest. Hopefully this timely change of tact avoided the unwelcome and unwanted intervention of the fired up, baying for blood audience. Thankfully only occasionally bad timing and bad luck meant the comeback occurred too late. Inevitably this usually meant "Mad Mental Mayhem" sometimes ensued.

The setting for this episode is the **"Eldorado Stadium"** in Leith. A busy dockland area and former whaling fleet hub adjoining greater Edinburgh. Incidentally this is the venue where I [Dale Storm] made my very first pro appearance in Scotland under the banner of **"Joint Promotions."** It took place during a Tag Team Tournament and my partner on that night was my older brother Billy. [This was not his ring wrestling name] Our opponents in the ring that night were two very popular well established fellow Scots, Glaswegian Mr Jim McKenzie and Dumfries born but Leeds based Ian Gilmour. Another of the relative rookie teams appearing that night also consisted of two sibling brothers; they were "The Clarke Boys" who were occasionally referred too by some as "The Boston Poachers" from Lincolnshire.

Bill the older brother went on to forge a glittering career under several ring disguises, prominent among these being the **"Red Devil"** and the enigmatic **"King Kendo"** both were of course masked personas. The younger Ron like the rest of us pursued a workman like career but he didn't reach the same heights of notoriety as his older sibling.

Sadly the Eldorado Stadium was totally destroyed by fire and then later demolished. That same year 1988 coincidentally saw the end of UK TV Wrestling. The building itself was old and dingy having been converted from its original use as an engine shed for former owners shipbuilders Hawthorn. It was located in Mill Lane just behind the old State Cinema later to become a Bingo Hall. The "Eldo" as it was known to the locals was situated between the main thoroughfare of the A900 (Leith Walk) and a narrow river/canal flowing behind the building known locally as The Water of Leith. It also sat in close proximity to the busy industrial Harbour and Port area. As well as hosting one of the British Isles most popular pugilist sports the other end the building also boasted a very popular Dance Hall. Prominent among those who played there regularly was the internationally acclaimed Edinburgh outfit "The Tommy Sampson Orchestra." The complex itself was owned and run by a local resident and successful entrepreneur by name of **Hugh Magourty.**

The Eldorado in Leith is gutted by fire in 1988

The Wrestling Promoter was rather unusually, given the fact both he and his siblings were all sons of Yorkshire, a somewhat dour individual. In his day he too had been an accomplished ring performer in his own right having had at one time a physique akin to the proverbial Greek Adonis. His name was....................................**"Max Crabtree."**

........................**The story continues in the year 1984.**

Max had spent the last few years slowly manoeuvring himself to a position where he'd eventually become head strategist and organising coordinator taking over form the one time overarching ruling business consortium which in the main controlled almost all the larger seating capacity venues. These in turn regularly generate the highest earning bums on seats returns of most halls UK wide.

Some of those reading this might well be asking themselves what possible qualification, expertise and experience Dale Storm might have for making any wide ranging comments about any of these wrestling promoters!

.... **"Who the hell does he think he is?"**

Let there be no one under any illusion regarding my pedigree and my hard earned wrestling and general entertainment industry knowledge and expertise, all of which was gained whilst serving a hard but enlightening apprenticeship both inside the ring and also outside it as well in varying capacities. These included front of house, the real art of fly posting; easy some might say! Yes maybe but they have to be in the correct place to accrue maximum effect from minimum numbers displayed and definitely not on sites where you might fall foul of the local authority, these are to be avoided at all costs. Prosecutions and fines cut into your profit margins, also gained was a complete working knowledge of bill poster design, layout and presentation as well as other various stage craft techniques which also proved to be a must. During this time I was privileged to be fully enlightened as to the science of the theatre, entertainment, performance ethos and the workings of the minds of those who paid their money at the box office, all of which I utilised to the full both at the time and over the passage of the years. I then adapted this new found knowledge for use in several other entertainment genres. Most of the expertise gained on the Ring Craft side was under the tutelage of one the best wrestlers ever to turn Promoter, who even after all these years still stands tall in the annals of the history of British grappling. He and his friend **"Mr Freddie Woolley"** were two wrestlers who had been former Joints employees. They'd broken away and formed one of more successful Independent outfits ever. Following the untimely death of my mentor Salford based operator **"Mr Danny Flynn"** in the second half of the 1960's, I gladly took over the running of his most popular Clyde Coast summer tour venue **"The Rothesay Pavilion."** Initially this was only done as homage and a tribute to the man who had started me off in the business. Its secondary purpose however was to stop any of the now growing group of interloper outsiders from taking over and spoiling this popular jewel in Danny's Scottish crown. In total I promoted almost constantly for a period of approximately ten years. These ventures largely featured in holiday camps, private social clubs, large hotel function suits and town halls in the Central Belt and in the South of Scotland. Other outdoor seasonal work involved my village gym trained lads headlining at annual Agriculture Shows as well as Rotary and Round Table Fundraisers. There was also the usual round of guaranteed easy payers known as **"Bill Money Jobs"** (Work done for a fixed fee for someone else) where they then stood to make the potential bigger profit or sometimes even a loss. These deals were popular among all promoters as they guaranteed a small profit with no chance of risking your own money. Losing money on a show was almost always referred to in the slang language of the profession's promoters as **"Doing Your Bollocks."**

One or two good "Bill Money Jobs" meant an extended run away from base giving the younger lads on the circuit a chance to sample the ups and downs of the social life outside the ring, where with a bit of luck they shared the delights sometimes eagerly provided by those of the female variety who just adored the new young flesh on display. Put rather crudely the "Grappling Groupies" couldn't get enough of those fit young men they worshipped and adored both in and sometimes out of their tight fitting ring costumes.

Being the owner of the British television wrestling franchise meant you wielded a lot of the power in the business and with it came total control over the setting up of the industry trends and the featured personnel, including the creation of all the championships belts and the champions who wore them dutifully festooned around their usually athletic waists. Equally importantly it also gave Joints almost total control over all of the content being portrayed not only on the box on a Saturday afternoon but also subsequently on mid-week late night shows as well. This influence extended into almost all the live performances which were also being generated by this now even more popular sporting genre. The public just couldn't get enough. Professional Wrestling was now one of the undisputed television top dogs.
Collectively this uneasy and sometimes fractious alliance was made up of former rival promoters who had agreed to divvy up the UK into smaller individual areas to suit their own profit making purpose. As previously stated they were now known by the collective name and corporate title of Joint Promotions and they were incorporated on 13th March 1952 in London under Registration Number 0505419. They were also part of the Europe wide "Alliance Europeene De Lutte De Combat." All their Champions were accredited and recognised under a new set of rules drawn up in Committee Rooms of the House of Commons under the Chairmanship of The Admiral Lord Mountevans in 1946.
The promoters; many of them characters in their own right were all powerful and were sometimes very manipulative individuals. Prominent among the independents north of the border and working under the umbrella of a revamped new version of the original **"British Wrestling Federation"** logo was Welsh born Orig Williams. Paul

Lincoln had been an original member of the ***"BWF"*** set-up. The reworded version now read; "Wrestling Federation of Great Britain" Lincoln himself achieved almost legendary status in both the UK capital city and also in the home-counties. One of his regular shows at that time was the very popular Saturday night bill at the Metropolitan Theatre on the Edgware Road London. He also worked in Scotland's larger population centres in places like the ever popular east coast venue of the Murrayfield Ice Rink.
Globetrotter Williams also operated in his native Wales again largely unopposed and also very successfully in what was at that time the biggest of the available venues on the Isle of Man **"The Villa Marina."** It had at one time been demoted to the number two draw for a few short years when the **"Summerland Entertainment Complex"** was opened in 1971. It was forced to close after it was gutted by fire just over two years later in 1973 never to re-open. The twisted hulk was demolished in 1975. Joints also ran in other places both in Douglas and in other Manx towns as well prominent among these was "The Palace Ballroom." Orig "El Bandito" Williams had according to his own publicity machine become the top dog indie operator by that time. He had very probably set himself up in a very flexible company structure sometime in the early part of the 1960's? Although I have no solid information regards actual start dates or official registration numbers etc. It's also been alleged by some he could be a very secretive and selective when he wanted to be and further alleged he even went to the extent of inventing a factious partner whom if my memory serves me correctly was often referred to as Mr Greco. I can vaguely remember being asked on the odd occasion when I phoned to find out what work I had for the next month, if I wanted to speak to Mr Greco.

In the land of St George the Indies main man was now, the much younger northern lad who in many ways was a much more astute and a clever operator coming originally or so I'm told from the Birkenhead. He started promoting officially

around the summer of 1970 initially under the banner advertising **"Wrestling Enterprises"** this was later changed to **"All Star Wrestling Promotions.**" It's still owned and run in one form or another by the likeable Englishman **"Mr Brian Dixon."** Latterly he and he alone went on to trump the remnants of Joint Promotions big style, something former top associates like **Paul Lincoln** and even **Mr TV Jackie Pallo** never achieved in full. He successfully promoted as an indie in the ultimate venue which was **"The Albert Hall"** once the exclusive preserve of the Joints Group under their Brixton based associate Dale Martin. Having broken the monopoly mould he then went even further by finally defeating the socially out of touch entrenched views of some openly sexist bureaucrats. Politically correct gender altering trends and the rise of the Feminist Movement forced them into allowing the staging of the first **"Ladies Contests"** in that iconic Capital space. [On 24TH April 1987 it also became the host venue for his wife Pat's [Mitzi Mueller] farewell, final wrestling contest!]
Although I almost certain I'm correct when I say the tough pioneering Yorkshire lady pro **"Ms Sue Brittain"** [Marge Farrar] was actually the first female wrestler ever to work under the jurisdiction of the ***GLC*** at the Wimbledon Town Hall. Her opponent on the night was "Jane St John" the time scale was August 1979 she [Sue] had taken a head-on stance against their post war ban on woman performing in their local authority halls, I'm very glad to say she won. [Sue passed away in April 2013 she's sadly missed RIP]

Back on the television operators front just a few years later Max Crabtree [mentioned earlier] due to the fragmentation of the Joints Monopoly in the late 1970's eventually achieved his long held ambition of rising above everyone else to become the new, all-powerful UK wrestling "King Maker." He continued in top slot until TV broadcastings subsequent catastrophic collapse in the late 1980's! It's perhaps also important to note that he [Max] didn't entirely have it all his own way all of the time, mainly due to the fact

Brian Dixon latterly also secured part of the ITV Contract for himself. It ran from January 1987 until the late autumn early winter of 1988 at which point this Saturday afternoon Iconic British Institution "The Wrestling" suddenly ended!
So having taken over by buying out most of the Joints originals with the exception of The deRelwyskow organisation; "All Star Wrestling" the Crabtree family were now the custodians of a re-vamped and re-branded organisation called **"Wrestling Superstars Limited"** Company Registration Number: 02893820 formed in 1991 and dissolved only a few years later in or around 1995
It will however forever remain a mystery to both myself and the others in the business whose livelihoods now depended on Max why the moneymen original owners and their now mostly comfortably well off families: Folks like **Dale Martin**, **Morrell and Beresford, deRelwyskow and Green**, **Bill Best and Arthur Wright** ever allowed a situation to be set in motion which given the passage of time, only a few short years later almost certainly culminated in the largest single event which brought down the once proud and very successful "British Wrestling House of Cards!" This was of course the seemingly unbridled, large scale, full blown, unprecedented and unashamed promotion of the ultimate folly. The introduction of the bigger, the lethargic, the sedentary, the huffing and the puffing brigade known collectively in the business as: **"The Bigger Belly Bumpers!"** This was perhaps the biggest single slap in the face to the really talented, crowd pleasing, textbook, hardworking time served established ring men stationed UK wide. Although some totally innocent unsuspecting members of "Joe Public" fell for that large lardy-arsed bullshit hook line and sinker, many more didn't and they began to turn off their TV sets! Sadly British Wrestling's "Die of Death" had now been forged and sadly there was now no way of turning the clock back! Up to that point only one of our lads had been gifted a slot on the very popular "This is Your Life" iconic television show and deservedly so. He was of course the

one and the only **Mr TV Jackie Pallo.** Born in Islington in London's East End on January 12th 1926, he was later billed as coming from Highbury. My old buddy and fellow pro **"Mr Eddie Rose"** once told me a story about a time when he was booked to go on with Jack. It concerned the way he was greeted by Pallo when entering the dressing room on that particular evening. Not in a nasty way you understand, it was more about the language used; the actual words as Eddie stepped through the door were; **"Hi Fodder!"** Jack went on to explain his remark like this; "You're good fodder for the likes of me Eddie because you're a good safe worker, you die well and most importantly from a promoter's point of view you're cheep!"

Rather sadly even the wonderful Wednesday night illusion of peace, love and comradeship which had helped raise Pallo's personal profile even higher and at the same time greatly enhanced the profile and the reputation of our sport a further one hundred fold, had now been infiltrated and was about to be totally undermined. A Fifth Column type influence was new busily working in the business. Through this haze of nationwide success a rather cunning and sadly sycophantic plot was at work which was about to unashamedly shatter all that had been achieved previously in an industry whose image up to that point had been very carefully nurtured and built up over preceding decades.
Enter the blatant introduction by the Family Crabtree of their overweight out of condition sibling, this meant "Big Shirley" became only the second and always perhaps rather predictably the last wrestling recipient of the now fondly remembered "Big Red Book!" Rumour has it the big lad had absolutely no idea he was being set up. Conversely it's really hard to believe the ever sharp publicity seeking "Mr Pallo" would have been entirely in the dark when his name was first mooted as a possible celebrity target back in 1973. He was always far too astute not to have been pulling at least some of the strings from the backstage area. Self-promotion was his great art. Well

done to you my son you were always well ahead of most of the pack. [It's also very interesting to note that during the presentation of the actual show later on after the initial "sting" as the line of wrestlers filed into the studio. One of the first onto the TV screen after Mr Andrews and Big Shirley himself was Kendo Nagasaki minus his mask. A well built, youthful, dark and curly mop topped Peter W Thornley can be seen casually taking his seat among the wrestling background artists]

Pallo and his son JJ had plans to stay well ahead of the curve when in the 1990's they formed a company called W.A.W. **"Wrestling around the World."** Their plan was to film wresting shows and then sell the footage on to European, Japanese and American cable channels. A far better idea might have been to have formulated that plan a decade earlier. [Jack died on 11th February 2006 in Ramsgate Kent. He was survived by loving wife Georgina "Trixie" [nee Wilson] and their grappling son Jackie Junior. RIP Jack .you were always a great showman. More information about Georgina is covered in another chapter]
Shirley's new found fame caused acrimony among large sections of the fraternity although it must however be stated unequivocally it was actually another of Joints promoters **"Mr Norman Morrell"** who was the original driving force behind the revival of the "Busby" wearing, so called former Guardsman's career, raising it from the ashes of its demise some years earlier under its then Indie banner and rather inexplicably breathing new life into it around 1972. [Norman Morrell passed over in the year 2000] It was not in fact until 1974 that brother Max now almost the Capo de Capo very enthusiastically also jumped onto the now fast growing "gravy train of the misguided" who also mistakenly believed "Big was Beautiful!" Although The Crabtree's Dynasty and their blinkered and unbridled involvement cannot be blamed for the demise of the mid-week late-night grappling slot. [It had been withdrawn in 1976 and they were not in complete control until much

later] On the other hand they have little wriggle room regards the sad demise of the Saturday Wrestling Show. Disaffection with the scheduling of a much earlier time slot and far more importantly the public rejection to the boring rapidity of some lacklustre, rather mundane performers and the ever growing gap in the UK talent base resulted in a continual drop in the audience figures month on month. This inevitably meant the writing was on the wall Big Time! [The axe finally fell in late1988 bringing to an end (33) thirty three years of television wrestling's "Grunt and Groan" wielded with merciless haste by **"Greg Dyke."** He was at that time both Head of ITV Sport and also the Director of Programming at London Weekend Television. We were later informed that decision had been taken on purely commercial grounds the rational being due to the lack of real jobs and the low spending power available to its predominately working class audience, many of whom were at that time among the Three Million Unemployed. It was felt those watching having very little cash in their pocket were of minimum benefit to the corporate world of the Monetarist Global Economy which was being driven relentlessly forward by Margaret Thatcher's vision for a Free Market Economy. Typically this flagship Tory policy had been formulated by Sir Keith Joseph Minister for Social Services and Science and a devotee of Milton Friedman and the US Chicago School of Economics]

Once again Big Business their Accountants and Advertising Agencies ruled the roust, Saatchi & Saatchi the real driving force behind Thatcher and the Tory Election Campaigns were now a leading the "Yuppie" driven live for today Posh Bastard Economy! Together the unholy British sibling triad of Max, Brian and the first born big brother Shirley exercised an overarching power which they used both selfishly and at times rather ruthlessly to great effect. During their blinkered stewardship they would make, sometimes break and regularly alienated some of the biggest crowd pullers and crowd pleasers in the business. Many of whom due to their success and their notoriety had almost to a man become instantly recognisable, hugely popular household names and the real stars of wrestling. Some top performers were quite rightly rewarded and were moved higher up the "Ladder of Success" whilst many others were sadly and wrongly elevated to the status of TV Superstar where some of them become overly americanised in the process. Rather sadly to such an extent that their constant overuse of microphones and loud entrance music, especially the sadly overrated and mournful "We Shall Not Be Moved" become the over-the-top" nauseous norm. Some others whom in this authors opinion were always **"Stiff Workers"** [Not a joy to work with, nearly always dangerous and all elbows and knees, upstaging and self centred] and who were never close to me personally began more and more to use the system, unashamedly to great effect, largely to promote only themselves, whilst all the time establishing links which would get them relocated across the Atlantic. Not that there was anything wrong with wanting to get on in life, ambition of itself is no bad thing. Where this particular situation fell down however was the blatant use of our system and the sport to move their careers onwards and upwards, whilst at the same time damaging the British TV image to such and extent that they helped doom it to its eventual extinction? This of course was not the case for those who'd already left Joints and who had given many years of faithful service to UK wrestling. Others of course having a lot less longevity and whom were fairly new in terms of time served in UK pro wrestling were simply selfish and self-promoting, and they cared little, if anything at all for our sport, its history, its traditions and its long established pecking order. But they were after all from a different generation and they had become Thatcher's children. They were part of the yuppie culture of the "Have's" or maybe it would be more appropriate to say the "Going to Have's" as opposed to our generation the "Have Not's." They wanted more and more and because those in charge of the new system allowed it, therefore they could take it, and they did! Or conversely was it me who cared far too much for the business that had taken me under its wing all those years before? Should I have adopted a completely different approach? Should I have joined them and only considered myself to the detriment of all others and everything else? Personally I don't think so, except to say if I'd only taken the opportunity to return with my family to Australia as had been on the cards in 1978, then perhaps things might have turned out a lot differently? It could have been the start of a new life for both my wife and our young family and just maybe then I could have avoided that painful career ending injury! Who knows what might have been? Que Sera, Sera!

In complete contrast back in 1967 a group of three good and true men which included the now Legendary **"Gentleman" Jim Lewis"** along with **"Red Callaghan"** and **"Chick Elliot"** had at that time tried to formulate what for all intent and purpose could have been legitimately called **"A Wrestlers Trade Union."** Where Guaranteed Minimum Wage levels of £6 per bout for bottom of the Bill, £8 supporting and £10 for Top of the Bill were being offered and largely paid out over that period. The one proviso seemed to be you had to work for this group of individuals and I assume a small alliance of their favoured contemporaries. That was all well and good as far as I was concerned but sadly this utopia was destined to fail. Some Indie Promoters and also the much larger all powerful Joint Promotions were totally opposed to the paying out of flat rates of pay negotiated by Trade Unionised Collective Bargaining. Especially as they were far in excess of the sometimes £3 and £4 they preferred to hand out to dedicated, hardworking bill filling grafters. Some however did join a union, but mainly in secret, more about that later perhaps? As for the term "Reasonable Expenses" it too was seldom on the radar of many either, although to be fair given I myself never worked in London I am however reliably informed by those who did, that most of the

Capital's Promoters not affiliated to Joints were always well ahead of most of the Northern guys when it came to both wages or legit expenses and again most importantly subsistence or digs. It would be remiss of me not to mention that Joints Brixton based Dale Martin outfit mostly used "Martinos" to accommodate their wrestlers and at pre Decimalisation prices the cost had been 7Shillings and 6pence B&B for many years! Any affiliation I had with Dale's was only through Jack Atherton their northern associate. I was never at anytime booked directly by them.

...............Now getting back to the Crabtree Brothers!

The sibling brothers' ego trip can be adequately summed up by the fact they allowed, through their mistakes and egocentric illusions many of the Top Men to drift away from under the umbrella of what had been regarded as the number one Pro Organisation in the UK; namely Joint Promotions. Sometimes rather childishly after some petty, non-discussion barriers had been erected and almost always by the threesome following requests by headline performers for a legitimate, inflation driven wage rise amounting for the most part to sums of only a few more pounds sterling.

Over that period large bums on seats crowd pulling favourites including handsome young Heavyweight Hero "Tony St Clair" left the fold; as did "Adrian Street" "Jackie Pallo" "Les Kellett" "Peter Preston" "Andy Robin" "Ian Gilmour" and ultimately even their Top Man, Arch Villain and ace television star **"Mr Kendo Nagasaki"** also relocated. Personally I remain unconvinced however that "The Crabtree Mafia" could ever recognise, let alone freely admit they were in large part directly and ultimately responsible for the sad demise of our beloved genre. Had it been managed with far more care and had those who thought themselves bigger than the sport itself been taken in hand and had their antics been nipped early on. It could in my opinion have continued to fill our television screens for many years thereafter, still holding down its spot as the undisputed top draw definitely still the "Best Show in Town"

When all is said and done some might refer to those who followed their dreams, hopes and aspirations and who successfully made their way reasonably regularly employed between the lower and the higher echelons of the Professional Wrestling business, as the Grunt and Groan Gladiators of their day, because most of them were undoubtedly just that and usually far more besides. I myself prefer to think that some of us including the likes of: Danny Flynn, Freddie Woolley, Adrian Street, Jackie Pallo, Kendo Nagasaki, Bob "Blondie" Barratt, Lord Bertie Topham, Dave Shillitoe, Gentleman Jim Lewis, Jimmy Breaks, Mark "Rollerball" Rocco, Mark Wayne, Eddie Rose, Joe "Romeo" Critchley, Crusher Mason, Ezra (Zulu) Francis, Dwight J. Ingleburgh aka Sam Bets, Peter Preston, Al Marshal and of course Mick McManus were all at heart really just a bunch of strutting peacock overly frustrated Rock Singers! I know I was and I still am and like everyone mentioned above I loved every minute of my time in this wonderful business of ours.

(Courtesy of Mr E. Caldwell)

Eddie Rose Aeroplane Spins Mark Wayne

CHAPTER THREE

(The Action)

This encounter takes place in a dressing room especially created as "A Homage" to one of Britain's most popular and at times Wildest Wrestling Venues **"The Eldorado!"** It was situated in the Port of Leith on the River Forth adjacent to Scotland's Capital city of Edinburgh and I was a venue that came to life with a vengeance on a Tuesday evening. For the benefit of the reader the scene and the dressing room layout have been set thus: As you enter through an old fashioned four panelled wooden door immediately to your left is another wooden door marked Showers. On that same side is a rack of wall mounted metal coat pegs, some clothes are hanging there. There's a mirror on the opposite wall to your right. It has a short low voltage strip light fixed to the wall above it. Benches run the length of both the walls. The room is of average size being approximately fifteen feet square. A solitary shade free florescent strip fitting is built into the low slung ceiling. The décor is sparse and Spartan and the remnants of a couple of really old wrestling posters hang discoloured from the wall facing the entrance doorway. Two round backed wooden chairs occupy the centre of the room.

It is however not a truly accurate reconstruction of the original dressing rooms set-up in this very popular venue. It has been structured in this way to suite the narrative, characterisation and this particular situation

A now greying marginally overweight man with twenty years experience as a full-time pro wrestler sits on a bench busily preparing as best he can for the fray. Tonight he is listed in the Top of the Bill Slot a place he has occupied on and off over recent years, having long since established a regularly enthusiastic and loyal fan base of both the young and the not so young. He's consistently maintained his popularity over the intervening years and is well liked and respected by both fans and his peers alike, particularly in Scotland. He has however been seen less regularly in halls in England since entering the sport as a youth under both the Joint Promotions banner, less frequently, than on bills under an Independent promoter.

Visits to the land of St George were usually for folks like former top pro and Joint Promotions associate **"Mr Jack Atherton"** in halls operated by him and also on other bills structured by fellow, very supportive, Promoters such as deRelwyskow and Green in Lancashire and Yorkshire as well as many appearances on the original Sir Billy Butlin owned Holiday Camp circuit located around the UK for their regular weekly personnel provider **Best/Wryton.**
Self preservation and the need to both earn better wages and at the same time promote his ever expanding profile further afield have seen Dale moving back to the top organisation whenever a slot was offered. Testing the waters and trying out the ever changing opportunities with several branches of Joints was a fairly regular occurrence for those, who like him preferred to work in the much looser framework on the far less regimented Independent circuit!

Moving usually meant starting once more on the bottom rung of the ladder again and again. Filling the lower slots on many of these shows was always a constant source of frustration and disappointment for most of the already seasoned men, mainly due to the occasional poorer quality ring craft and performance skills shown by many of their inexperienced raw opponents. Resulting in yet another shorter tenure stay than had been hoped for. Carrots of better and more regular work dangled under his nose by some promoters on both sides were often less than honest and on some occasions failed to fully materialise. The most southern part of the UK along with London and the Home Counties have sadly never ever been graced by his clever and athletic presence in a paid performance, although some fact finding trips sussing out the situation in the Capital City and in other southern areas early on in his career showed some promise but were never followed up.

Most of his more memorable top half of the bill slots during these raids over the border so to speak were impressive if a little limited, among the bigger names encountered during this period were the likes of Adrian Street the popular Welsh welterweight, Ian Gilmour, Jeff Kaye, Peter Preston and fellow Yorkshire-man Lee Sharon, and more than one usually hard fought contest verses Scottish Lightweight Champion Jim Mackenzie. Adrian's, Peter's and Jim's warmth and their genuine friendship are rated very highly among a whole raft of fond memories from that time on the Joints Promotions side of the grappling fence.

Strangely yet another supporting contest against the new and up and coming, very highly talented **"Mr Marty Jones"** for Jack Atherton at the Drill Hall in Dumfries proved to be yet another watershed moment. In as much as young Marty's career path rightly led him onwards and upwards to top billing and some well deserved TV superstardom moments and Dale's led him back to where he felt most at home and better regarded by fans and some promoters alike. Despite this setback he still worked regularly for the supportive gentleman matchmaker Jack for years after that night

On other occasions contests involving good friend and former Joints Middleweight Champ Eric Taylor's two athletic sons Steve and Dave saw Dale working quite regularly with these youths whilst they served part of their apprenticeship on shows put together by Orig Williams and occasionally Brian Dixon. This grounding eventually saw both these lads beef up and blossom under the Joints banner before they also moved over the pond to the USA.

Among other very popular workers regularly encountered

were Johnny Saint, Catweazle, Les Kellett, Jackie Pallo, Bill Turner, Bill Ross and Len Ironside all of whom shared a ring in several halls with Dale for promoters such as Max Crabtree, Morrell and Beresford and the afore mentioned deRelwyskow and Green. In such places as Leith's Eldorado, Kilmarnock's Grand Hall, Kirkcaldy's Town Hall and Falkirk's equally busy Town Hall respectively. He also appeared regularly in Perth, Aberdeen, Stirling and Caird Hall Dundee and also in the white hot heat of Hamilton's Town Hall in particular. Again disillusioned at the lack of real appreciation for his popular crowed pleasing profile by the Crabtree's in particular and the unfriendly disposition shown by some of the Scots born bill fillers, who'd hardly been in the business but a few short years meant Dale invariably drifted back to a far more comfortable place once again and rather inevitably on the Dark Side. Sadly it has to be honestly stated that his talents were consistently much better appreciated outside the TV Organisation. Top Slots were always much more regularly available to him over on the Indie side. For instance a European Title winning contest being just one of many championship contests allotted in several weight divisions over the years, this one against Ian Mackenzie [No relation to fellow lighter-weight Jim Mackenzie] Ian was fast and skilful but nevertheless he was always very generous in the ring.

Luckily following the abandonment by many Joints stars of the now steadily sinking ship that was once the unshakable TV Kingpin in the direction of the Indies helped reawaken old rivalries with such greats as: Adrian Street, Les Kellett, Jackie Pallo and once again Peter Preston. Culminating in the shroud business opportunity seized with both hands by his fellow Celtic worrier, which at that particular time helped to salvage Dale's career from near disaster! This move by one of the son's of Stirling **"Mr Andy Robin"** proved to be very fortuitous! It came at a time when another "Bandit" like cowardly and unscrupulous performer sought to end his [Dale's] career prematurely and all from afar and mostly

from behind the popular Scottish wrestler's back!
Although even at that same time all was certainly not doom and gloom as thankfully his clever skills and dedication had been instantly recognised some years earlier by The Master **"Mr George Kidd"** one of Britain's and indeed Europe's top performers, a man who'd also lived worked and promoted his own shows under "Matsport" in London in the 50's, before agreeing a Joints tie-up in the early 60's regularly used Dale on his top class Caird Hall Dundee shows! **"JA Promotions"** [Jack Atherton] had over the years also used Dale in halls he had been associated with.

The action starts in the dimly light Leith dressing room, the muffled sound of the crowd enjoying yet another supporting contest can be heard coming up from the packed to capacity auditorium downstairs. Seated on a bench Dale pulls on a pair of brightly coloured tights then opening a small pill box he places two in the palm of his hand. He then drinks them down helped by the contents of a large glass "Irn Bru" bottle. One capsule consists of a strong painkiller and the other is an equally potent anti-inflammatory. Picking up a newspaper he then moves to sit down on a slightly more comfortable chair and starts to read it. After a few minutes the relative silence is broken by the sound of a knock at the door. Dale continues to read, totally ignoring, the person on the other side of the wooden divide. Seconds pass, once again there's a knock on the door, still it gets no response from the person studying the black and white print. A third and much louder attempt at gaining someone's attention finally entices a grudging reaction for behind the paper barrier. Reluctantly he acknowledges the unwanted interruption although he still does not lift his head. Nor does he shift his eye-line from the printed page.

And so our Diary of a Pro Wrestler's Odyssey begins.

CHAPTER FOUR

(The Metaphor 1 Genesis: (Part Two & Part One)

Dale Storm, ego battered and face blooded makes his way along a backstage corridor towards a dressing room. He is well aware of the now slightly diminishing noise of a hostile crowd as they make their way out of the auditorium. The faint sound of a female voice calling after him cannot be distinguished through his now throbbing and damaged ear. The cauliflower condition of the right one has long since meant the loss of its sharpness, as for the other one it's recently damaged drum aches terribly, whilst being slowly lubricated by hot free flowing blood, making it very difficult to discern that he is not alone. As he turns the door handle and enters the darkened empty space, suddenly he feels the touch of a hand on his shoulder! Even angrier now he ducks slightly, whilst in the same instance spinning round on the ball of his favoured right foot, fist clenched. His mind has now switched from a mood of silent melancholy to one of rage and near madness! Through a rapidly closing damaged left eye he is just as suddenly brought back from the land of supposed fakery and rather abruptly catapulted back into the realms of the real world by a rare vision of a smiling, almost angelic faced female form standing before him. Her right hand already outstretched in a saintly Madonna like pose, rather endearingly she then hands him his now badly torn, dishevelled ring jacket. The natural motion of her moving slightly forward, forces him backward just a little to a position where they are now both being silhouetted in the doorway against the dim light of the corridor. Do I know this girl? Have we met before? God I can't remember! He mutters to himself struggling to recall a name. Given both his physical and emotional state at that precise moment, allied to his now

thumping headache and a reluctance to engage in any small talk, nevertheless he nods just a momentarily appreciative acknowledgement of how grateful he is to have had his property retuned to him. Through the overarching pain and the deep seated embarrassment now manifesting itself as feelings of both, disappointment and rare frustration he plays out in flashback pictures in his head the ego shattering disappointment of the totally unexpected events of the last few unbelievable minutes. His pride along with his sheer professionalism and his devotion to the ethos and the integrity of this largely closed shop business which has given, both him and his contemporaries regular employment for a long time now has just been shattered. Done to death by the epitome of an ever growing totally self-serving arrogance that's just been blatantly exhibited in the ring by one of the next generation! Sadly some of these new brooms have somehow been wrongly permitted to regularly bestow the totally undeserved and in many cases grossly unwarranted titles of would-be "Super Stars" rather arrogantly and rather unashamedly on themselves!

(The Genesis: Part Two) * In a real time framework *

Giving the young stranger an inquisitive look Dale asks her a question. Sorry, but who are you? Where did you appear from? Somewhat confused her reply is short and to some extent not what he was expecting.

Where you told me to be, you brushed passed me just now at the top of the stairs. Don't you remember?

Leaning forward Dale takes the jacket from her outstretched hand, he looks really shaken now. Thanks for returning this I'm grateful, I've had it for a long time now. He then attempts to close the door but the reporter stands firm making it impossible for him to do so.

Ask him again ref!

I thought this kind of stuff was all fake, just a load of old posers, huffing and puffing and having a girly go at each other like a couple of old grey granny's with handbags.

Pointing to his face Dale gets a little angry. Its all fake is it? See this damage to my face well it's all just smoke and mirrors, just some make-up, some fake blood and a whole lot more besides! Its all just make believe! It never really happened it's all just an elusion. Or in my particular case a really bad nightmare!

Really, well you could have fooled me.

Job well done then, at least we got something right tonight! Anyway, I won't be in need of your help anymore. Thanks for this you're a star.

Brushing him aside the young lady charges forward, now fully in the room, taking his towel from off his shoulder she wipes away some blood from Dale's ear, then handing the towel back she speaks again.

Well some might argue with you there mate, me for one. Look at the state of you! You're a bit of a mess. You dropped your jacket as you crushed past me and you didn't even notice, it's lucky I was there to pick it up again. Sadly that was only after it was ripped to bits by a couple of lunatic punters!

Look I don't want to seem ungrateful and I am glad you rescued my stuff but I'm ok now, I'm just a little battle scarred that's all.

Battle scarred is it? The Christians in the Coliseum got off lighter than you did sunshine, you wouldn't look out of place in any Casualty Unit! Your bloody nose and that eye will be closed in no time at all. Take a good look at that once brightly coloured costume of yours, it really stands out even in this low light adorned in that wonderfully fluid red tint!

It's just a bit of **"Claret"** it gets used in our business from time to time but this time the blood belongs to me and it wasn't prearranged. Usually you get some notice and some instruction beforehand. Some people may tell you the **"Blade Job"** concept was imported from American, that's not quite proven but their audiences seem to love it! It has however been used as **"A Flash"** in the UK for many years now. It can be a bit of a hit or a miss in the UK, too much blood can have a strange effect on an audience. That's probably why Shakespeare and other Play-writes in his day employed brightly coloured red handkerchiefs to signify the result of a stabbing or the end product of a swordfight on the stage. A really good idea don't you think?

[Claret is a term used in the grappling business to describe blood false or genuine. Sometimes, it would be a fake blood capsule or on other occasions, real blood. It, having been induced to flow by some creative slight of hand when using a "Blade" This consists of a small corner of a broken down razor blade. Folded a few times and then wrapped up in some flesh coloured, sticky medical tape. Leaving just a hint of the tiny sharp edge exposed. It was usually palmed by the referee or hidden in a Sock Top or in a waistband by the villain. Most of those instructed to use it however, preferred to do the cutting bit themselves. As an over zealous, hyped up opponent could on occasion get it all wrong! Sometimes this resulted in a near total frontal scalping fiasco]

It's alright don't fuss! It's nothing my wife's old "Hoovermatic" twin tub and a few scoops of "Daz" washing powder won't be able to fix.

What about all those rips in your vest? No amount of

Ask him again ref!

accomplished needlework is going to put that right, is it?

Listen, I'm grateful and I'm not in the mood to argue so let's part on good terms shall we? Anyway, do I know you? Have we met before, because I really can't remember! Did I say that earlier? God what's happening to me? Dale stands there silent for a moment. He's in a bit of a daze.

Sounds like a concussion very probably.

Anyway this area is off limits to the public. I did tell you that earlier, didn't I? If it's the toilet you're after again, the public use the one in the foyer.

Strange how you remember that part from earlier, Freudian Slip perhaps?

They're on the right hand side as you come in at the front door, Ok.

Toilet, what for the second time in just over an hour? Well actually no, and then again maybe yes. Oh and the answer to your question just then, is yes. We did have this conversation before. Earlier on, don't you remember? Are you sure you're OK? Your speech is a bit slow and your memory doesn't seem all that great either. Could really be a concussion, how's your head? Thumping is it? Feeling sleepy or nauseous maybe? Oh about the toiler offer. It wasn't uppermost in my thinking earlier, but with all this extra excitement well maybe? You know what I mean.

Looking at her rather strangely Dale says nothing for a moment or two he just stands there looking quite lost. Into the silence eventually he speaks. OK it's the least I can do but be quick will you don't want anybody getting the wrong idea. Pointing to the door marked showers. It's in there.

No, after that sermon on second thought maybe not?

Ask him again ref!

Good God! Make your mind up will you. How old are you anyway?

Oh a lot older than you seem to think. You're clearly having trouble getting things into perspective now aren't you? I'm really getting worried maybe you should see a doctor?

I'm fine, stop fussing will you? It's nothing I can't handle I've had a lot worse but not for a long time now, in fact you'd have to go back to when I stated in the business. Back then I was as they say "Paying for my learning."

Before I go maybe you could do something more for me?

Steady now, as I said earlier this is a private area and you're just a kid. Wrestlers only, no public allowed in the dressing room area under any circumstances that's what the sign at the end of the corridor says. Anyway it doesn't pay to go upsetting the promoter.

No, no, you misunderstand me I just need a little more information that's all, given what's just taken place I may need to revamp my notes slightly.

Sorry, but I really need to get cleaned up, you don't happen to have a couple of Aspirin tablets in your bag do you? Autographs at the Stage Door after the show and if it rains you can usually get me and most of the other lads in the pub over the road, might cost you a pint though.

No, I really need to speak to you again especially after this awful distraction. The whole incident is more than a little bizarre.

Look I'm trying to get undressed here, I could really use a hot soothing shower right now might help clear this bloody headache? Some ice would be great as well I'd really like to get the heat out of the bone around this bloody eye socket before it starts to swell up too much.

What about the St Johns Ambulance people? They're bound to be in attendance here for every show?

I haven't got a clue but if are they'll be long gone by now. I don't need them anyway all I want is a wash and a good rub down. I don't want to be left with a strain or something now do I, pulled muscles can cost you work and we all need the money especially nowadays given the way the British economy is heading under this lot!

More anti-Tory rhetoric is it and at a time like this considering you're a bit frail at the moment. Anyway that's all we get from the Trade Union side where do you get all this venom from? Reading the Daily Communist maybe?

No, I buy a Tory paper!

A Tory paper you're having a laugh, which one?

If you must know its "The Daily Express"

And why is that?

Simple! And for two reasons really; one I like to get a more detailed football perspective and the "Daily Record" is a bit narrow and a bit one sided for me, as for the other my old grandfather always told me "If you can't get The Daily Worker then get the Daily Express read it from cover to cover and then do the exact opposite politically speaking!

That's pathetic and really narrow minded!

It's alright for you to say, although I think you're wrong but right now I do have far more pressing matters. I'll sum it up in few short words for you shall I. Don't trust any of them, I never have and never will and neither should you young

Ask him again ref!

lady. Mark my words the Print Trades will be next to go!

Sorry but I'll have to disagree completely, my feeling is this, the present government is very progressive. Take the leader for instance she was the Education and Science Secretary in the Heath Government of 1974. She's a woman and that's important, although, back then she was new to high office but she's doing a grand job this time around and she doesn't come from Money, nor is she Posh born, her father owned a local grocer's shop!

You're winding me up hen! You're definitely not helping my situation.

Mrs Margaret Hilda Thatcher is a champion for the feminist movement everywhere!

Don't be daft. I will concede however she has a larger set of Balls than any of her male Cabinet colleagues!

Well don't go holding your breath because she's a very determined lady.

She's a bloody bully and a man hater to boot. It's always her way or it's no way!

Not at all, she's making her mark for woman's rights and that's what's important here.

Well politics has always been a man's game, especially in the Tory Party, come to think of it there are very few woman including working class folks in Westminster either. So you mark my words she'll never last! Dale gets lost in the moment he starts to stare into space once again.

Are you ok, you seem to be just a little lost again?

I told you earlier I'm fine, couldn't be better. Let's drop the

Ask him again ref!

subject shall we?

I'm sorry I'm just concerned about you. That's all!

No need for you to be apologising to me. I'm just a little confused right now, it'll pass.

No offence taken, that's what I was trying to tell you earlier, in lieu of recent events maybe I just need to tie up the possibility of an alternative ending for the Dale Storm story. Won't take long, maybe once you've had a wash? You haven't forgotten our long chat earlier have you? Dale gives her a vacant stare. *Now I'm really getting worried maybe I should make that ambulance phone call?*

Forgotten what chat? When was that did you say?

God you are bit wobbly, aren't you? Oh and I will use the toilet if you don't mind if the offer is still open that is?

You didn't watch that in there, you didn't really see what happened did you?

Well actually no, I decided I would and then I changed my mind. It was getting a bit warm in the auditorium so I was on my way out of the front door heading over the road to the Café to have a milkshake and a wee read at this book.

Taking a copy of "The Female Eunuch" from her handbag, the reporter holds it up for him to see.

That's when I heard all the commotion, then the lady in the Box Office went running passed me in an awful hurry so I came back into the hall. Everything went a bit mental after that. I did see some of it but only the tail-end of the proceedings. Anyway as I told you earlier, before you got into the ring I'm not really a fan, I'm just a Reporter. Surely you must remember our chat. We spoke at some length.

Ask him again ref!

Opening her handbag again she takes out a rather dog-eared note pad. *Please tell me you've not forgotten? Are you sure you're alright, you've gone a really funny colour, surely you must remember when I tried to speak to you earlier at the door of the dressing room at the start of the evening. I was told initially if I came back later, after the last contest then you might have shown up by then. But thankfully that misunderstanding got cleared up earlier on.*

Pointing to the Shower area, be quick is Dales only reply. They're usually off limits. Exiting the dressing room the reporter enters the Toilet area.

(The Genesis: Part One) Flash-back 90 minutes earlier!

Dale Storm continues to ready himself for his forthcoming contest. He preens himself a little applying some eyeliner etc. He then grabs hold of a small set of Dum-Bells, one in each hand. Sitting down on the edge of a bench he pumps a few slow reps on either arm. Placing the weights on the floor he pulls on a pair of brightly coloured trunks up over his equally bright coloured tights! Then picking up a local newspaper he settles back into a chair. He starts to read it and as he does so there is a knock on the dressing room door, at first he ignores it completely. Then after another attempt at trying to attract someone's attention, next comes another tentative verbal inquiry. Finally he (Dale) answers, but still his eyes and his focus never waver from the week old newsprint.

Eh Hello! Sorry to bother you but I really need to speak to one of your wrestlers please, a chap called Dale Storm.

Without looking up from the newspaper Dale rather grudgingly replies. Sorry, say again?

Ask him again ref!

Dale Storm, is it possible to speak to him please? Least ways that's how my Editor referred to him, he's on the Bill.

Never heard of him and who might you be anyway?

I was told he was booked here tonight by a work colleague he's a fan. He hails form the same town as Mr Storm, Ayr I believe. I'm a local journalist and I'm looking to write a story. Just a few column inches and I'll be out of here. It won't take long. I contacted him requesting a meeting. I sent him a letter via the Venue's Management Office.

Well he didn't get any letter! Anyway he isn't here at the moment why don't you come back after the main event he might have turned up by then.

I'm really sorry but I don't suppose I could use your toilet could I? I'm bursting.

Pausing for a moment Dale thinks about continuing to read the paper but changes his mind. Instead he picks up the weights again. Ok just this once in you come but be quick they're usually off limits. After a slight delay the door handle slowly turns and a young lady enters. Without really raising his head much Dale signals with a nod to the door marked showers**............................And be quick mind!**

Looking tentative the young female visitor moves quickly into the toilet area, a few minutes later as she re-enters the dressing room. Dale is still working with the Dumbbells again placing them on the floor he addresses his visitor.

By the way, sorry about all the cloak and dagger stuff earlier you have my apology it's me you're looking for. Well you never know these days, do you? A young girl turns up out of the blue banging on the dressing room door asking to speak to you and all that. What's a guy to think? We live in a different more litigious world now you know.

Ask him again ref!

So you're Dale Storm, you never are I thought you'd be much younger and a lot taller! Oh and by the way, I know exactly who my father is so you can relax!

Sorry again but these things do happen, you read about them all the time in the Sundays particularly.

Point taken, I understand you've been a Wrestler a long time now, so you've got to be a whole lot tougher than your slightly effete looking costume suggests.

That'll be the proverbial back-handed compliment will it? I probably deserve that, is that why you didn't bring a photographer with you?

No, didn't need a camera guy it wasn't necessary, maybe another time?

Pointing to his face Dale expresses his opinion. Then again maybe not at this moment maybe all this make-up tends to hide the real me anyway.

As the reporter shakes his hand he beckons her to sit down, using his towel he wipes a chair. Pleased to meet you, by the way as I said earlier I didn't get any letter. So no new album photo that's a pity, posing is something I'm quite good at and if anyone asks you were never in the toilet area OK? Now pull up a pew. Oh a minute just before we get started Press Card! Can I have a look please, can't be too careful these days. A card having been produced it's duly examined. Right that seems to be in order; Miss Jean Armour-Burns interesting name, no relation I assume? I'll just have to hope you're as creative with your words as our world class poet was. Rabbie was a good man and another lowly born son of Ayrshire. You're not one of them prying News of the World types I hope? You'll appreciate I'm sure there's an obvious need to keep outsiders in the "Queens Park" about the grappling game.

Ask him again ref!

Its wrestling slang for being in the "Dark" Get it, Park and Dark? Placing his finger to his nose Dale winks, god knows they've tried to dish the dirt on us several times over the years. Did you come in the front door or did you nip in the back entrance?

The front door, why?

So you paid then? That's good it'll help keep me in a job!

No I didn't need to open my purse that's when having the Press Card comes in very handy.

That's nice always a pleasure to help augment your salary levels. Smiling slightly the reporter just shakes her head. Dale continues. Did you happen to notice who I was on with?

"Texas Cowboy" Bull Brown am I to assume he's an American?

Yes you're correct he is an American, very perceptive. Still that's your job isn't it? Dale then breaks the enforced awkward momentary silence. Sorry, I really shouldn't be taking my frustrations out on you please forgive me. If my old mother was alive she'd have slapped me round the side of the head for speaking to you like that. Another easy night for me then, he's as slow as a week in the jail. The poor man has an ongoing alcohol problem sadly he's seldom sober he should've retired years ago.

Has this poor man always had a liking for the hard drink?

Actually no, used to be he hardly touched a drop. He picked up a niggling back injury some years back, strong pain killers and alcohol can be a lethal cocktail but he could work well back then. Believe me sometimes that's not always been the case for most Yanks who've came over here. "Ricky Starr" and "George (Catalina) Drake" being two notable exceptions, "Billy Two Rivers" "Gordon Nelson" and "George Gordienko" are three more. [Gordon Nelson created the very successful persona of The Masked American Outlaw in the mid to late 1960's. [Sadly he passed over to the other side on 16th December 2012] But then again they are all Canadian so they've probably got some old Scots Mountain Man whisky drinking ancestry hidden away in their past somewhere. Anyway where do you want me to start?

At the beginning would be good. Tell me about your career how you first got started in professional wrestling, all that sort of thing.

Well I go back the best part of twenty years now and I had the honour of being the youngest Pro in Britain when I first started, I was only just seventeen that was back in the summer of 1964. I'd served my apprenticeship Down Under in Australia in the amateur ranks at the Randwick Recreation Club in Sydney it's near the Racetrack and not all that far from the city's International Airport "Kingsford Smith." It's in the Mascot district and it's named after a couple of famous Aussie aviators. I was a whole lot fitter back then with a lot better muscle definition. You needed to look at your best back then believe me, have you ever seen pictures of those bronzed Life Savers on "Bondi Beach" well that was the level to aspire to back then. I was competing in the Greco-Roman and the Freestyle mostly they're the Olympic disciplines. Freestyle is my preferred genre its better known in Britain as a kind of Catch-as-Catch-Can. You could say it's a mix of both styles. In Greco-Roman holds are not allowed below the waist and in "Catch" almost anything goes. In its simplest form it's a kind of no holds barred free for all. I never got selected though for the top contest, no flashy Perth Western Australia British Empire and Commonwealth Games medal for me mate, although another Scot James Turnbull did win a Bantamweight Bronze. I was probably too young but you never know do you or maybe it was because I was a Scot and not a naturalized Aussie? If truth be told I really wasn't good enough! Unlike the other immigrants back then if you were born here in the UK you didn't have to become a "Digger" if you didn't want to but for everyone else who came off the boats it was compulsory; Cypriots, Yugoslavians, Greeks and of course the Italians. The two wrestling styles in the Olympics games are the natural disciplines of nearly all who come from Southern Europe, the Eastern European Countries and of course the Indian Sub-Continent as well. Then there's Highland Games and the Cumberland & Westmorland styles and that's how some of the other lads got started. Scotland's **"Power-Lock"** Heavyweight Hero "Andy Robin" is one but more about him later perhaps? Deciding to show off his Antipode connection Dale reverts into his Aussie accent. "G-day my name's Bruce I'm a Fair Dinkum Australian from Down Under mate. What's your favourite colour Blue? And what's your name Sheila?"

So you've still got some of the old boyhood patois then?

The Ities [Italians] as they're affectionately referred to back in Oz, oh and racial abbreviations and boxed stereotypes are commonplace in Australia and believe me no one takes any notice or indeed any offence. They get every bloody where them bloody blokes and they always take their Mafia pals with them. As for the Hellenic [Greeks] speakers their biggest centre of population now domiciled outside their native land is in the antipodes, it's in the city of Melbourne!

Sorry I didn't realise that was the case that's quite interesting Melbourne really? I'm told it rains a lot there.

It can and it does when I'm there I prefer Sydney. Sorry, it's a lot of information to take in. I hope I'm not going to fast?

Ask him again ref!

No, no carry on I'm listening.

Of course classic wrestling has been around in an organised competition format since the early Greco Olympic days way back in 708BC and probably even further back beyond that. Then came the modern era of the Olympic Games and thankfully back in the county of its inception Greece, although the original idea came from a clever Frenchman. Before that time from about 1889 you had the likes of the really powerful body building specialists men like **"Eugen Sandow"** the Prussian. He was the first guy to turn the genre into a theatrical art form closely followed by "The Russian Lion" although he was actually born in Tartu Estonia in 1878. He was in every way the master of his trade and his name was **"Mr George Carl Julius Hackenschmidt."** He elevated the whole thing onto a whole new level where both he and his muscles took on the world! Undoubtedly he originated the financial forerunner of what we now lovingly refer to as the Professional Game back in 1896. Coincidentally that was the same year the first reconstituted modern Olympics took place in Athens Greece. He cast off his amateur status mantle and taking on all comers in1902 in Liverpool he defeated "Tom Cannon" on September the 4th to claim the European Greco-Roman Heavyweight Championship belt. Three years later after beating the American "Tom Jenkins" in New York on 4th May 1905 he could then legitimately lay claim to being a global participant and the first undisputed World Wrestling Champion! The Yanks being what they are couldn't stomach a Russian holding the title so they put forward yet another challenger. He emerged in the form of the win at all costs, uncompromising, bend the rules hard mat man **"Frank Alvin Gotch"** Their first match took place on April 3rd1908 at Dexter Park Chicago sadly it ended with Hackenschmidt covered in blood from illegal head-butt injuries from some underhand roughhouse, bully boy tactics by Gotch. The Champion had no choice but to relinquish the title, leaving the ring late in the savage contest, therefore avoiding more of the blatantly cheating antics and the added danger of even more permanent injury to his already badly damaged legs.

................Enter the very first of the Big Return Bouts!

Perhaps the first and the biggest contest **"Gee"** [Grappling term for a big build-up] ever to take place indoors or outdoors took place in Chicago on Monday the 4th of September 1911 in the home ground of the now world famous Chicago White Sox Baseball Team in present day Cellular Field. Back then it was known as Comiskey Park. Named after its then owner Mr Charles Comiskey sadly it was closed in 1990 and was demolished a year later in 1991 to be replaced by a completely new stadium built on the old sight. Perhaps this first day of the week event was the catalyst for America's obsession with their Monday Night Sports format? An exceptionally large crowd of around 30,000 meant the gate receipts were more than $87,000 Dollars an astronomical amount of money for the period, sadly having sustained yet another bad knee injury whilst in training for the second contest "The Russian Lion" the sport's first "Blue Eye" [Wrestling term for a hero] failed to roar. Nevertheless in no way wishing to disappoint his rapidly growing army of loyal fans he went ahead with the contest regardless, he lost for the second time (2) two falls to (0) zero to Frank Gotch, on whom the title of the rings first "Villain" could rightly be bestowed [A character portraying a particular ring persona which as expected the public loved to hate.] So disappointingly for most fans the "Bad Guy" retained the World Title Crown. Frank Gotch was in many ways a blatant cheat, his motto was clearly "Win at all cost!" He would regularly oil his body before getting into the ring and continued to add more from the reserves stored in his large mop of dark hair during the contest. This practice was clearly against the laws of the sport but what might seem even stranger to most neutrals was the fact he got away with it. What does that tell us about the standard of the people who were appointed to referees his contests? He regularly used the head-butt to hurt and intimidate opponents, again illegally. It would seem his handlers and management team were not averse to rewarding others who damaged opponents like The Lion in training when their man was signed up to meet Gotch in the ring. $20.000 was Frank's share of the gate money plus a further $1,000 for training expenses from the Second World Title Contest. The loser limped away with $13,000 plus $100 for training expenses. The amiable, ruggedly handsome European wrestler continued with his new found fame and his new found show business career undaunted after he returned across the Atlantic to European soil. [George Hackenschmidt "The Russian Lion" died in London in 1968 he was aged 90]

Hachenschmidt and Gotch battle it out a second time for the World Championship in Chicago in 1911!

Comiskey Park Program 4/9/1911

First Contest at Dexter Park 1908

Old Comiskey Park

Ask him again ref!

That's a pretty comprehensive breakdown of the early history of your chosen sport.

Yes there's a lot to remember but it's my own personal labour of love. I've got nothing but total respect for all its history and all its traditions, that's why I'm in the business.

And you're doing a grand job you're obviously well read.

Thanks it's really nice of you to say so I am when I'm on a wrestling theme. I'd do you a cuppa but we've no kettle and we can only get water from the shower room sink and this is the main dressing room. Still it could be worse if it had been ten years ago during the Heath Government fiasco when electricity was rationed during that god awful Three Day Week we could have been sitting in here basking in the warm glow of low candle light. I've got a pal who was still working in my old game the Motor Trade at that time we still keep in touch regularly. He tells me back then during half the working week, they weren't allowed lights on in his place of work so he and everyone else had to lie under the cars with a small lamp hooked up to a battery in one hand and a spanner in the other now that's bound to kill your eyes after a time, don't you think so?

Definitely and it was dangerous as well. He's probably wearing glasses by now, the caused was the escalating cost of imported crude and the Middle Eastern troubles!

I'll concede you the oil shortage situation but nothing else!

It's criminal and rather a pity we can't all get along together, although you could be forgiven for thinking those individuals given the best of all possible starts in life, most of whom having benefited from a Public School education could have come up with a better plan to help the UK out of the economic doldrums than that load of old nonsense!

Ask him again ref!

Those power cuts really were badly thought out, some might have argued it's alright for that lot, at least they and their class are always guaranteed employment in places like "The City" or a job somewhere in the "Banking Sector."

Why can't we all be pulling in the same direction for once?

Politics and the privilege of class designed to keep the workers down. Oh by the way when I was taking about the men who helped mould our industry earlier I forgot to include a famous Scot. He's a bit of a legend to many his name was **"Donald Dinnie"** he was born in 1837 died in 1916 and rather strangely in of all places the same city as The Russian Lion, Old London Town. Many are now saying he should be internationally recognised as being without doubt the Nineteenth Centuries Greatest Athlete. His time and his career spanned fifty years, during that period he set up hundreds of records. The Balnacraige and the Birse areas near Aboyne in Aberdeenshire's rural heartland are part of the area where he was of born and grew up and they can be rightly proud of his remarkable achievements.

And yes it is ridiculous I quite agree, petrol is getting far too expensive but strikes and all this trade union power in the country aren't the answer either.

Sensing a situation he can't win Dale changes the subject. The shower room in here is quite nice I must say and it looks like I've got my pick of the sprays, although very strangely it's the very first time I can recall having it all to myself. All the others are sharing the other suit, now that's very strange! I've no idea what that's all about? You know it can sometimes be very hard to get noticed in this business, like most things in life you really need to be in the right place at the right time to get the breaks. Although for others the best thing is having a relative in the business and having a performing father seems to be the pathway of choice for some. To most of the purists that seems to be infinitely far more acceptable than having your mother in the game. Don't you think? He! He!

That's a sexist remark and quite frankly it's not really funny.

Sorry couldn't resist it. Anyway **"Jumping Jim Hussey"** has a lad who's doing well only he calls himself Rocco **"Mark Rocco"** [Jim Hussey who was without doubt one of British Wrestling's best ever villains passed away in 2009. He will never be forgotten by all true wrestling fans]

"Dave Finlay Senior's" boy young Davie he's in the business as well and the old stager **"Francis St. Clair Gregory**" is yet another he's got two sons earning a living Roy's the oldest and the younger slightly taller sibling is Tony. They've both dropped the Gregory name though.

"Roy Bull Davis" [Charley] has his kid in the ring as well but he doesn't use his father's ring surname either. Sometimes his handle is **"Steve Young"** and at other times he works under the name of **"Skull Murphy."**

"Les Kellett's" lad also makes a wage from the ring, working under the stage name of **"Dave Barrie"** he's a lot lighter than Les and he has a completely different approach. [Rather sadly Dave Barry passed over to the other side in 2000. Les his tough old dad left us in 2002]

Even the promoters are in on the act. "Ted Beresford's" offspring by name of **"Steve Clements"** used to get a regular slot with all the promoters and he usually had quality opponents as well. He was a natural welterweight and a good looking young lad with some talent, he regularly tagged with **"Mike McMichael"** as **"The Yorkshire Terriers**" He moved over to the Americas for a time and when he came back from working in Mexico he'd beefed up and was carrying an extra three stone in weight. He also based himself in the USA for a time, whilst there he worked under a mixture of different guises, one being the monocle wearing Sir Dudley Clements. That's when he managed "The Green Brothers" Al and Don they were the original "Heavenly Bodies" in the early nineteen seventies. Later on during 1973/74 he moved franchises and had one of the last spells representing a much later version of the original top of the bill performers "The Fabulous Kangaroos" who by that time were made up of Al Costello and Don Kent under the WWA banner in Indianapolis. They originated with and were long serving members of Stu Hart's Stampede Promotions in Canada. They were also former World Tag Champions. [Steven Geoffrey Clements (Beresford) career was cut short prematurely aged 28 years by a tragic road accident which sadly proved fatal. He and a fellow pro Jim Bernard [Working under the title The Brute] had both appeared earlier that same night on a bill in St Mary's Ohio and once again Steven was on Management duty. The date was April 21st the year was 1976 the place was Mercer County Ohio, Steve had been a front seat passenger. Apparently the car left the road and struck a concrete abutment, Bernard suffered a broken arm, damaged ribs and lacerations, his passenger died in the collision. RIP Steven God bless]

"George deRelwyskow Junior's" very likeable nephew got his first start on his uncle's promotions although he has at lot to live up to given the historical wrestling dynasty that particular family have built up over three generations now. His nom de plume so to speak is **"Barry Douglas."**

Danny Flynn's lad **"Dennis"** was in the business as well and he worked really hard and being Danny's lad he too had a lot to live up to. I'll have to come clean at this point and admit I started three siblings of my own in the sport and just like me two are good hard working journeyman mat pros and the other was at one time a very handy referee/MC. God when I started I got no help from anybody especially on a Joint Show. I was regularly so far down their programme I was often referred to as simply: "And introducing one other lively Supporting Contest!" Bloody Hell what chance has a bloke got I ask you, still that was then and this is now, it's changed days I'm glad to say. It's been really hard for a lot of these young guys, especially the ones whose fathers are big names. Some find it an almost impossible task to fill their Pater's boots. Oh by the way the other sprinklers and spare dressing rooms are all down the hallway on the right. I don't suppose you'll be wishing to see them, will you?

No thanks, I think I'll pass.

Good girl well said given the questionable habits of some of my sad contemporaries that is probably a good thing. Let's put it this way and I'm quite sure this also applies to all dressing rooms everywhere in the world, even including the famous Albert Hall! If you ever come across a half empty pint pot sitting there looking rather innocent for God's sake don't go anywhere near it! Penny to a pound it's definitely not Lager!

Quite! Just what I really needed to know, so is it safe to say you've enjoyed your career then.

Total mileage Ayr to Edinburgh and back: 165.2
Time taken for the full journey: 3 Hours 34 Minutes

George Kidd

Jim Moser

Billy Two Rivers

CHAPTER FIVE

(Careers Come and Careers Go!)

Have I enjoyed my career? Hang on a bloody minute mate it isn't finished yet! Please tell me you're not freelancing part-time for those harbingers of impending doom "The Four Horsemen of the Apocalypse!" Well are you now?

That's a bit over dramatic don't you think?

Of course I'm an actor! How old do you think I am? I've got a few good years left in me yet besides if I want that nice wee Bed and Breakfast place I'm after I'll need to keep working for a year or two yet. I've been eyeing up a place in Scarborough it's really nice down there. Yorkshire is just so beautiful and the breeze coming off the North Sea is quite invigorating, it's a country all on its own with great beer, really friendly people, nearly all from good working class stock, they're salt of the earth folks just like me.

Self praise is no real compliment.

I was brought up in a small Coal Mining Community in South West Scotland, money was always tight but when I was a kid we never wanted for anything, although if you weren't able to pay your way outright then just forget it!

That's a bit old fashioned nowadays don't you think? What about Hire Purchase or a Credit Card?

Debt! It's the Devil's work! Too much debt can ruin even a good and an honest person and probably the county's economy at the same time. If you can't afford it at the time, then work hard and save up until you can that's the way I was brought up to think. So I'm just trying to sort out my future and the legacy I'll be leaving my kids when I'm no longer around. Do you know a lot of wrestlers especially those who were the headliners, when they've retired have usually bought their way into a nice wee hotel or sometimes a pub? And then they bore their customers almost constantly with the stories of their ring exploits for the rest of their natural. That's not for me and I just need another couple of thousand and I'm well sorted.

You could always apply for a Bank Loan.

No, I don't want a Bank Lone! Have you been listening to a word I've said so far? Debt and The Devil ride together that's the way my old hard working grandmother always saw it. Anyway most of the other guys fly off to Spain, but then again they're the type who could never live without their Sun Bed or a Sun Tan anyway. As for the others well usually they get themselves the odd job on the box playing a heavy, why bother that's what I say, I just don't get it. Right enough they're mostly the ones who live in and around the London area and that's where most of the bigger Production Companies are based. There's a bit of a mistaken perception here in Scotland and in the North of England about them living south of Watford being a bit softer than us. Actually that's not quite true because there are a lot of lads down in the "Smoke" in London who're as hard as nails and I mean really tuff, Jack Ernest Gutteridge being one, he's TV Jackie Pallo to his fan base. He's a member of the famous London Boxing family born above a Gym in Islington. It was managed by his dad at the time. Jack performed well as a young amateur boxer and again like me, he too had been employed as a motor mechanic. He turned pro in the Grunt and Groan business aged twenty six. He used to give a lot of his time for free just like his father before him to the same schools teaching local boys boxing. His cousin Reg. is another famous Gutteridge, if you follow the fights on the box you're bound to have seen him he's a commentator on ITV. He really knows his stuff as well, trimmed moustache, glasses and he always wears a blazer and a shirt and a tie.

Ask him again ref!

Sorry! I've never heard of any of them, but I'm no expert.

Mimicking Jackie's mannerisms Dale pretends to be leaning over the top rope shouting out at the punters; "Init a bleeding long to drive to get up here? Why do I put myself through all this, coming all this way just to entertain a bunch of losers like you lot. Have you bought my new record yet?"

He likes to talk a lot then seems to be a common trait for you people.

Dale misses her point completely and carries on regardless still imitating Pallo. "Oi you there! Yeah you who else? Am I talking to myself here or what? I've just bought a castle up here. What's that you say? I don't know where mate, do I."

And is he making enough money to do things like that?

What buy a castle? No definitely not in the ring he doesn't but he does do films and television as well and they generally pay much, much more. Dale continues his story. "It's somewhere in the Highlands?" Say's Jack. "What's that? Don't ask me mate speak to my accountant it all looks the bleeding same to me this country. All blooming multicoloured mini skirts and tartan material covered pig's bladders. Bunch of bleeding Pansy Potters and as usual they'll be some idiot going all red in the face blowing into it! Anyway, how would you like to come and haunt it for me, my castle that is? Oh suit yourself then, see if I care!"

Still doesn't ring any bells, but it's quite funny! Keep it up.

Jack and JJ were on the Bill at the Kelvin Sports Arena. JJ is Jacks son Jackie Pallo Junior he's a nice lad but not as good a worker as his Dad, but given time he might be? Anyway, the youngster starts in on the promoter giving him some serious rabbit, little realising perhaps that he's one of

Glasgow's finest, one of the Golden Boys of the Scots Boxing fraternity. He's none other than the former British Empire and one time European Bantamweight Champion and he's also one of only a few outright holders of a Lonsdale Belt. **"Mr Peter Keenan"** was his name. Sadly he'd had a bad night and he'd as they say **"Dropped a Bollock"** [He'd lost some money on the show or so he was telling everyone he had] "It's been a bad night boys" was his tail of woe. I kind of felt for Peter because clearly is hadn't been a sell-out, but if you walk away with a full wallet in the really good nights then its only fair you should also shell out for full wages and genuine out of pocket expenses on the not so good nights as well. Sadly some promoters don't seem to see things in those terms.

...And then it happened!

There was a bit of a disagreement over the London Duo's travelling expenses, one word bothered another and then the shit hit the fan! Well it's perhaps much more appropriate to say something hit something! Jack junior wrongly calls Peter a name, the word is a little to indelicate for your young ears then he starts swinging punches leaving Peter with no real choice but to smack him one but only once mind. Bang! Straight on the chin and then just like in those kid's cartoons he's seeing stars and he's licking the shine off the lino. So naturally old Jack steps in to defend his lad and takes one of the ex-Camp's haymakers smack on his chin as well. Stumbling backwards more than a little stunned, Jack shaking his head to clear it as every schooled fighter should do halts proceeding and buys himself even more time by bending down to help his son up off the floor. Thereafter and very slowly he starts to remove his gold watch then he hangs his jacket up on one of the numerous pegs on the wall. All the while buying many more head clearing seconds. Well the room fell into a deathly hush and what followed next was like something out of one of those Chaplin type Silent Movies; some clever footwork here and there followed by a head swerve or two from both guys, then with hardly a serous punch landed by either man the culmination of the pantomime work-out resulted in; Peter spark out and on his back slowly sliding along the deck and only coming to rest when his head hit the opposite wall with a thud. Jack senior then walks over picks him up and slaps him gently awake. Then he sits himself down again and carries on getting himself ready to perform for the paying public. Utterly amazing, but still he never ever got paid the full amount for petrol money etc that his lad JJ had been demanding. The best remembered facts of this story and the way it really went down have become somewhat blurred over the intervening year although they are still regularly discussed when grapplers get together to talk about old times. They even get a further mention in the fifth edition of Adrian Streets autobiography; **"IMAGINE** What I Could Do To You**"** For most who were actually there on that fateful night in Glasgow's West End what I've highlighted was how these events are best remembered and chronicled.

It's really hard not to like Jack although he's a cocky old bugger, he loves his tea though and he's even got me addicted to the stuff now and yes you've guessed it, like him I drink it by the bloody pot-full as well. He's a bit choosey who he shares his car with though, it's a SABB.

A SABB! I expected a Mercedes or at the least a Jaguar.

Actually it's always a Saab, he's got quite a few now, he seldom trades them in and he never scraps them. He just parks the older models along his driveway at his home where they stand like soldiers at attention on parade.

Then there's his wife Georgina she's a wee smasher, they're both so in love with each other. She's a really nice person and she's well liked and well respected not only by the wrestling lads, she's also quite well know in other entertainment circles and she does a lot behind the scenes to make sure our sport is always well represented and publicised whenever she gets the opportunity.

Jackie took me to one side a few months ago and in his usual cocky manner he paid both me and the Scots nation the very best of compliments, but that's not exactly how he phrased it. Leaning in he reeled it off something like this. "Right you Storm and of course the rest of you bleeding Scots! We all know you probably are the best nation in the world, right! The only problem seems to be you all bleeding well know it! Cocky buggers! Oh and I must tell you this have you noticed that green and gold sequence covered jacket he wears when he first enters the ring? Well it's a really a "Donkey Jacket" and it's still got the name Wimpy emblazoned on the back. You must remember them they're a huge construction company, it's printed on an Orange background in black lettering across the shoulders and the whole jacket has been covered over with material.

The reporter is less than impressed by this story she tries to say something before being cut off by Dale.

No it is honest, but please don't print this and don't ever mention it outside these four walls ether it'll be our little secret, you can keep a secret I hope? Some will tell you he's hard to get alone with but I don't agree, I'm very happy to say he seems to tolerate me and we've roomed together occasionally over the years, as well as clocking up the road miles. Others might say he's tight with his cash but that's nonsense as well. Its probably a rumour started by a guy whose nick-name to some is **"Niggly"** among other things he works in the Dale Martin Promotions Office in Brixton.

Who works for this Dale Martin in the office?

Niggly does!

Ok I've got that part now.

He's their main matchmaker it's him who puts most of their shows together and he's nearly always in the Top of the Bill slot. He's also a partner in the printing business which does most of the Wrestling Posters for nearly all the shows the length and breadth of the UK and there's a lot in the business who don't like him for these very reasons, that's unfortunate but it's a fact of life nevertheless.

Surely that's a bit harsh to dislike a person just because they've taken advantage of a good business opportunity.

Your point is well made and yes there's an element of jealousy in there somewhere and the word "Advantage" sums it up completely. Maybe if they were in his shoes some would probably have done the same thing? On a personal level I wouldn't be manipulating the system in that way and that goes for all my close friends in the business as well, we're not made that way, we were brought up to be inclusive not exclusive so for us it's not about the promotion of self and neither should it be. It could just be a London thing there is a perception in some who live there that life's all about making money! Rumours also abound saying he won't travel up to the North of England or even come up to Scotland unless there's a big pay packet in it for him. I've no idea if that's true or not although I suspect it probably is. Personally speaking apart from sharing the odd dressing room over the years I don't really know the guy all that well, in fact not at all and I've never had the opportunity to ply my skills against his in the ring either. I've no idea why. He gets accused, again by some of continually pulling **"Strokes!"** [Working a situation to get the most advantage out of it for him self] Sometimes in wrestling that's refereed to as a **"Moody!"** [Meaning its bent, not real, not a truthful situation] Get it? Its just more rhyming slang but that's the name of the game. Anyway we all like to get our own way sometimes don't we, but unlike him we don't always get the chance to engineer it. At the end of the day it's probably just part of the big North and

Ask him again ref!

South of the river rivalry thing going on between him and Mr Pallo, It works well for both of them though, in terms of a bit of needle being added in an already high profile business, well nobody wants empty halls do they? So it's all good for business. It's a wee bit like the Rangers and the Celtic situation and it definitely sells lots of tickets only it's got nothing to do with religion. But just like the football when it really comes down to it, its all about placing bums on seats and generating notoriety for both himself and also Jack and of course a lot more of the most important thing.

And what might that be?

Even more cash profit for the Promoters! Deep down it was always a lot more about the public's perception of a big rivalry between the man from Dale Martin's Office and Jackie Pallo. Again it's a wee bit like the gangster turf wars between The Kray's Firm and The Richardson Brothers who were both busy empire building on either side of the river Thames. East End verses South London now that's real violence not like the pyjama pantomime stuff we peddle. More than one of the grappling lads has earned some extra cash working for both those crews at one time and another. One Scots guy in particular springs to mind and to see him in the flesh all baby face and all sweetness and light, you could be forgiven for thinking butter wouldn't melt in his mouth. Well you'd be wrong he may have the boy next door TV image but whatever you do don't get in his way when he's on an extra earner errand, as you may well get the shock of your instantly truncated little life!

And he's Scots you say?

Yes born and bread in Scotia but he's lived in England for many years now.

And you're not going to give me a clue, who he is are you?

Ask him again ref!

How right you are, the bare bones is all you're getting.

So he really is a nasty piece of work sometimes?

That would be putting it mildly, then again there's a bit more money to be had from using a Cut-Throat Razor or a Meat Cleaver on some poor unsuspecting geezer's face, now that's a real "Claret Job!" For that cowardly act you'll get paid a lot more than the pittance we get for risking life and limb every time we pull on our boot and our trunks.

On a completely different tact it's sometimes even more of a risky situation for the Ring Villains who regularly throw no more than some harmless water from a plastic bottle at some overly enthusiastic female punter armed with an umbrella, but then again the criminal penalties if you get caught doing all that nasty physical harm mischief are far more severe than getting Black Listed or Suspended for a short spell by a Promoter for blatantly over stepping the entertainment value index with a stroppy punter. Especially if he [The Gaffer] has had to shell out for a dry cleaning bill or purchase a replacement for a slightly ripped shirt!

Believe you me that Old Bailey Court Case might have caught up with The Twins and put then away for 30 years and the rest but it didn't end the violence, no sir not one little bit. I met one of them once, well if truth be told I was actually standing next to him at the bar for just a few short seconds and that was well enough for me. He looked me up and down you know the way some folks do when you're a stranger in their camp. Something like: "What are you doing in my bar and why are you standing in my place? Mate! We were in a club, as it happens in Islington, it was owed by the Teal family. Three brothers one of them I think his name was Bobby had a bit of form and as it turned out he was a pal of Reggie's. The Twins used that gaff as their second home for a time although as some of us were out of town, non Londoners we didn't know that at the time, but others did! Later on that night in they came but too no big fanfare so I was none the wiser. Another lad in our company he was London born let slip they were The Firm. That signalled it was drink up time for us mate, especially me. I was out of there sharpish like a shot out of a gun!

....**Bang!**

What were you doing in London and why were you in there of all places?

It was a "Wembley Weekend!" England verses Scotland International. The city centre was really busy and we wanted to get some quiet time, it was the local lads that had taken us out there, they were well known in the area. The Twins liked to mingle with the show business element. We'd won 3-2! Maybe it was the Scots accent that seemed to noise him up? A few grapplers have "Worked the Doors" of properties owed or protected by them and sometimes they ran other little errands and capers as well but that's another story perhaps best left for another time and a different day. Maybe if I'm really struggling to finalise the "Dosh" for my wee retirement venture? Well you never know do you? I could always get a Big Pay Day Brown Envelope from the likes of The News of the Screws. [Slang name for The News of the World Britain's oldest Sunday newspaper] for dishing the dirt if I've a mind to. Only joking there's no chance of me doing anything like that, and that means not ever! But if I did, I can see the headlines now. Exclusive! Former Wrestler Spills the Beans Big Time! **"DALE COOKS UP A STORM!"** Now is that good or what? Are you all right hen you've gone a funny colour? Was it something I've said? Was I being too graphic? Sorry, I'm getting carried away with myself again his really isn't what you came to hear.

No it is, just that bang fazed me a little, please carry on.

What did you say? Sorry, say again my hearings gone a bit

duff too many of old Les Kellett's slaps, boy can he hit you a dull one and it's usually bloody painful!

Getting back to your original point who is this Niggly chap?

Ah sorry again I should have said already. You'll know him better as the huge TV Star by name of Mick! That's **Mick McManus"** you must have heard of him, the whole of Britain knows who he is. He's "The man they all love to Hate!" Nutty Old Jack once **"Jumped the Ring"** [A ploy sometimes prearranged to wind up the audience] on him during a live TV Show at Wembley way back in 1962, for which he got a severe dressing down from Dales [The Abby's] if you prefer the real and original family name. Quite simply because he didn't follow the **"Script"** [He didn't do what he was told and he didn't ask permission before hand to do what he did] you're always going to be on a sticky wicket if you openly challenged one of Joints **"Star Men"** especially if it's live on television. There was however an upside to the whole matter and as it tuned out it was the making of both their careers **"A Grudge Match Bout"** [A big Geed Up well hyped contest] was quickly and cleverly arranged it took place live during that football season on FA Cup Final Day TV Show. Some have reportedly said it drew an even bigger audience than the Cup Final itself, although I for one find that highly questionable but you never know do you? Everything seemed to change slightly after that and although most Saturday afternoon shows were still live, up to and around 1972, portions of World of Sport Bills were then pre-recorded for short episodes of late-night mid-week viewing.

Really! On whose orders was that done?

I'm sorry I can't answer that question even if I knew the answer which I don't.

But which is it really? You don't really know or you're not going to be telling the likes of me?

All I can say is that situation happened live and in front of an awful lot of viewers but it was what happened around five years later which became an even more talked about live incident! Strangely it also involved Mickey Mac and he would argue on the day he was really **"Double-Crossed!"** Peter has always stood by the fact that he did as he was told and no act of treachery was carried out by him! So after that act of what some at Joints saw as gross misconduct almost all the TV stuff was given a make-over and it was then mostly all pre-recoded. Apparently in the dressing room before the bout he [Mick] had not an inkling anything was untoward [He was completely in the "Dark"] and therefore he had no prior knowledge of what was about to unfold. He would later on whilst in the ring quickly realise at one fall down he was in fact now deep in the shit put there by an up-and-coming rough and very tough young Northern Grappler for Yorkshire's Bradford area.

His name was:.............................**"Mr Peter Preston"**

That ground breaking incident was live on the Box as well and again it was on a Saturday afternoon and god did that one caused even more of a furore! A lot of serious questions were then asked about the outcome right at the top of the Joint Promotion's Tree. It's remained a talking point ever since! In fact there will be, even now, after all this time hardly a night in a dressing room somewhere in the UK when it's not referred to in one form or another.

Although Peter seized hold of his main chance with both hands and continues to be loudly applauded for his actions in most quarters especially in the Midlands, Lancashire, Yorkshire, the North of England and by almost everyone in Scotland as well. To his great credit he has always totally refused to speak frankly to anyone regards all of the facts surrounding the real story in the run-up to that fateful day. Only a very, very few carefully chosen confidants have been privy to even the very smallest of near clues to what actually happened in the lead-up to that Winter day in1967.

It was a memorable year in other sporting circles also being a period when the underdog did very well all round. Also-ran "Foinavon" won the Grand National at 100/1 and Scotland's Celtic FC against all the odds became the first UK team to win Football's Big Prize; The European Cup. We also beat England 3-2 at Wembley Stadium! Denis Law, Bobby Lennox and Jim McCalliog were the scores.

Rather strangely as this monumentally idiosyncratic contest began to unfold the transmission of the end game was inexplicably cut short in the south of England, but what was even stranger it continued in its entirety around the rest of the UK regions. [A situation that after all this time has still never really been fully explained by the TV people of the day] Clearly it took both the director the producers and ultimately McManus himself right out of their respective comfort zones. It was perhaps especially difficult for the TV crew to deal with technically when not being fully aware of what was about to take place and all under the watchful eyes of millions of live television fans. Given Peter's tough northern amateur background and also his Rugby League training allied to his speed and phenomenal reserves of stamina and physical strength, it's really hard to see how his opponent could have taken him on in a real, honest **"Shooting Contest!"** [A contest where there is no TV style ref breaking you apart it's all in and the last man standing is the winner] McManus is the great TV Showman of that there is no doubt and especially in the eyes of the paying public he is/was deservedly held in very high regard, although it continues to be more of a "love to hate" relationship. Ultimately he was totally lost and out of his depth on that fateful day in the "Hard-Man" stakes and his almost total humiliation was for the most part happening live right there in front of over excitable kids, their parents and their grannies sitting in their cosy wee living rooms.

Looking back now after all these years it could be argued that this whole sorry incident could just as easily have delivered a serious body blow to the future of the business and its continued position in the hearts and minds of its loyal armchair admirers but luckily it did not do so! In fact it had the opposite effect on an all round business footing for most promoters especially in the North. They'd never had it so good and the bums on seats money making business opportunities went ballistic, a fitting tribute to the craft and the workmanship of the "new young pretender" perhaps?
It must however be stated in his [Peter's] defence maybe it should never have had to happened in that way or indeed should never have happened at all, but it did and clearly some in high places were taking this opportunity to settle old scores. None of which were instigated first hand by the always very likeable, kindly Wee Man from Bradford. I like to think at the end of the day and in the long term it served as a wake-up call and was a good thing for the future direction and the rational of the business as a whole.
After that fateful day at The Lime Street Baths on 14th January 1967 brother Preston's new found fame and notoriety was then used primarily by promoter Norman Morrell [A major driving force behind all that was good in UK wrestling] to fill halls in Yorkshire and elsewhere to bursting point, time after time and why not? The name of game more often than not is about "The Gee" [The blatant promotion of coming events] engineered in its entirety to make more money by seizing the moment. Norman's undoubted loyalty to those he rated would, I feel, have ensured the wee man who made it all possible received a share of any extra financial rewards. Shortly afterwards Peter tuned up at St Georges Hall Bradford little realising those queuing round the block were there to see him!

Initially he'd been summoned to Morrell's office in Bradford at very short notice when it became obvious there was an injury vacancy for the forthcoming show. On arrival Norman informed Peter he'd have to test him out to see if he was good enough. The **"Pull-round"** would be right there on the carpet in his office. As the furniture was being stacked along the walls, the well meaning Ernie Lofthouse Norman's Road Manager, who also worked in the office, enlightened Peter that Mr Morrell had a dodgy right knee. I can only assume in doing so he was anxious to avoid the Promoter sustaining further damage to his long term leg injury. Naturally he thought Peter would not use that privileged information as in so doing he would be gaining an unfair advantage over his employer. Bad mistake; after that there was no holding Peter back and his target was now the failing leg joint! The contest was over almost before it got started and young master Preston got the job. Other Northern Promoters also followed suit and helped fill the Bradford grappler's date book. None of them or indeed their Bank Managers ever regretted that event on that historical day in North London. For a long time after that many other household names especially those in the Home Counties feared they might be next. Especially some slow to acknowledge the dogged determination and sheer physical power of this Yorkshire Terrier but they had little or no need to worry, although it's fair to say it was a real wake-up call for some in the game. The look of sheer terror on some faces thereafter slowly changed to a persona of calm relief after locking into the opening hold at the start of the contest to be greeted with those magic words direct from Mr Preston's smiling lips:

........*"No you're ok, it's not happening to you tonight!"*

This situation was of course for others not directly involved a source of almost constant amusement, some were even seen standing in the wings giggling to themselves at what might or might not be about to unfold in the ring, but for Peter's advisories it was clearly a very welcome relief.

Anyway, getting back to the original thread; Jack did the ring jumping thing entirely on his own volition and initiative without asking anyone else's permission, as it turned out it was the further making of both their TV careers and later when summoned to appear, old Jack argued his corner forcefully in the Dale Martin's Head Office in Brixton, but I'm not sure Mr Pallo ever got any of the credit he truly deserved for his clever, on the spot decision to perpetrate that free publicity making masterstroke. The Dracula styled hair look-a-like [Mick] hails originally from the area of New Cross where he was born, it's on the south side of the river and its quite close to The Den, Millwall Football Clubs Ground or so I'm told. I've never been there myself some say it can be a bit rough on match-days. William, George, Mathews. (McManus) was born 11th January 1920. He trained at the John Ruskin Amateur Wrestling Club. He had been a Physical Training Instructor in the RAF so his fitness was never an issue. It's quite amazing the number of people who did well in the business who were ex-RAF. Some have said he actually had his first bout in Australia in 1945 when he was stationed out there. Others will tell you he made his professional début in Britain in 1947. He was sometimes billed as "The Dulwich Destroyer" [Mick passed over to the other world on Wednesday 22nd May 2013 aged 93 years in Brishing House a home for retired entertainers. It's been widely reportedly he died of a broken heart following the sad death of his long time beloved wife Barbara in January of 2013. RIP Mick]

Do you follow the football? Stupid question of course you do you're a Scot. So which team do you support?

Wrong sport I don't have a favourite soccer team my boyfriend plays rugby. He's a prop-forward.

Nonsense! You can't come from Scotland and not come down on one side or the other of the religious divide when it comes to Fitbaw! No, on second thoughts don't tell me. It's got to be "The Old Firm" Celtic probably, not Rangers or maybe an English football team. Manchester United maybe? They've got some really big rivalries going on down there as well, United and City, Liverpool and Everton, Spurs and Arsenal. So maybe it's the Man City Super Blues then? They've not been all that good of late, nothing like they once were. They'll be back but God knows when?

Well in that case it's probably Partick Thistle, I like the look of the scarf it's got some lovely bright colours.

Now who's having a laugh! Eh? The dressing room banter is momentarily interrupted by announcement from the internal Tannoy System.

"The Second Bout has just ended; a six round, hard fought one fall each draw Ian Gilmore verses Johnny Saint. John says to tell you he'll meet you across the road, your usual will be on the bar around 9-45. We'll be having the obligatory fifteen minute Interval, then your on next. Did you see that wee lassie, the one who was looking for you earlier? She's far too young for you, you're more her mother's age group."

Embarrassed by the crude comments from the announcer Dale tries to make light of his comments. Ignore that clown! George Bernard Shaw was correct when he said "Youth was wasted on the young; Anyway they're good those two lads, well turned out with great wrestling ability, especially the Saint! He's always got the prestige of the business in the forefront of his mind. There are a lot of really good lightweights, welter and middleweight guys around at the moment. People like Zoltan Boscik, Jimmy Breaks and John Cortez plus Vic Faulkner, Bobby Barnes, Jack Dempsey and many others including the gifted, prank pulling Mick McMichael. They're all English based but we've still got some good workers up here in Scotland. Folks like Jeff Bradley, Scott Thomson, Lenny Ironside and Bill Turner, others who were born in Scotia who are now household TV names include Clayton Thomson, Ian Campbell and Chic Purvey they all took up residence south of the border years ago now. Oh and lets not forget our own top Scots based top Tag Team **"The Fabulous Harlequins"** Although just slightly heavier now than they were when they first started they're just as agile as they ever were. They've got a similar style to the highly acclaimed London based team the Cortez Brothers. Those boys Peter and John came into the business through Paul Lincoln's stable I believe. Other popular teams include **"The Eagles"** but the most popular team as far as the TV watching public are concerned are **"The Royals"** That's Bert and his younger brother Vic, they're very colourful. Vic's much cleverer when it comes to single bouts though. Bert for me personally has more of a staccato style it's not everyone's cup of tea, but as I said we can still hold our head up high because we've definitely got a lot of real talent on this side of the border right now. Collectively far more than there ever was in the past and although it's blowing my own trumpet just a little! I've got to say the Mossblown Village Gym has got to take the lion's share of praise for the work it does in helping to bring on the new breed of properly grounded, properly versed in the history of the sport next generation of Scots ring men and woman.

Of the younger lads who work regularly **"Big Ian Miller"** tends to stand out, he's a good honest worker and he's been on the mat since he was around twelve years old and he debuted in the paid ranks age sixteen. He's a really useful young Heavy Middleweight and rather immodestly I have to admit I taught him almost everything he knows. Then there's **"Bruce Welch"** he's one of the founder members of our fraternity and he's a good all round pro with a lot of experience. He's working in the Light Heavyweight bracket. I may tell you more about him later?

Another promising new comer is **"Young Starsky"** he's a really clever lad, fast in the ring and strong in the hold but away from the ropes he's really quiet shy, a bit of a deep thinking lad. I fist met him when I was employed for a short time in the same garage environment in which he served his apprenticeship. He's always been he's pretty good with a spanner in his hand.

Obviously by what you were telling me earlier, a lot of these guys make a living continually winding up the paying public and all from the relative safety of the ring.

That's the name of the Game. The baddy big guy bashes the little goody guy then the downtrodden goody guy makes a ring "Come Back." [Turning the tables on the bad guy] and right there and then in front of the punters eyes a minor miracle unfolds. Crash, bang, wallop the bad guy is then defeated and all is well with the world! Make no mistake without really good ring "Villains" such as McManus, Jimmy Breaks or Jackie Pallo they'd be no real reason for all action "Heroes" to come riding into the fray to rescue the oppressed! Without that entire collective they'd be no future survival for Grappling as we know it either!

One of our older office cleaners attends almost every week, but by all accounts she goes absolutely bananas! She tells me she's gets herself up at the ringside at every opportunity. Surely that can't be true?

Why not? If she's getting involved even in a small way then it all adds to the overall performance. It's all part of the show and it helps to pays all of our wages.

So are you're trying to tell me a lot of equally overly excitable fans turn up at other venues who're equally nutty!

Before we go any further can I ask you what might seem a rather stupid and rather obvious question.

Well if you must!

Have you ever actually been to a live wrestling show?

Ask him again ref!

Well not really, I did tell you that earlier, remember? Obviously I must have been taking to your deaf ear.

So you've never ever sat in the audience.

No but I'm a journalist, a professional I've got a trained eye well capable of covering an entertainment enigma like you.

So I'm an enigma now am I? Well that'll look good as my new billing on future poster.

Anyway I've watched a couple of late night TV broadcasts. Not the Saturday shows. I'm far too busy shopping and there's no chance of me giving up a Gossiping Lunch and a catch-up with the girls just to watch a bunch of silly, grown men running around in Lurex tights, make-up and multi-coloured calf high leather boots.

Giggling the reporter continues; *I think I've just described a Floor Show in a trendy Transvestite Revue Bar.*

Tuning his deaf ear Dale ignores the derogatory comments; Ah Ladies who Lunch how utterly fascinating. Now listen up and you might learn something about some of the other type of so called ladies who will sometimes go to any lengths, short of throwing their knickers onto the mat to get what only they consider to be their monies worth! They will use anything at their disposal to exact some vengeance on those whom they may feel have taken unfair advantage over their always willing to die for the cause, whiter than white, blue eyed ring heroes.

I'm all ears, fill me in.

OK, I will. Better hold on to your hat girl!

Total mileage Ayr to Aberdeen and back: 300 Miles
Time taken for the full journey: 6 Hours 36 Minute

Mike Eagers

Jim Breaks

Peter Keenan

Pete Lindberg

Buddy Ward

Billy "The Master" Riley. Spot the "Catch" Wrestlers

CHAPTER SIX

(Mad Punters and Puncture Marks)

Lady punters out to reek vengeance are not a pretty sight and sometimes they get quite dangerous! Under normal circumstances they're usually quiet law abiding citizens who pay their entrance fee and then occasionally they proceed to take over the performance, perhaps an extreme case of the fifteen minutes of fame syndrome? Or it may well be an outing of domestic tensions borne out of the frustrations of an unhappy marriage that seems to turn these normally friendly ladies into serial men haters when the rings limelight floods over their drab lives. Some are so well known in certain regions of the UK they've almost achieved legendary status. Believe me I kid you not.

There's a regular attendee in the venues in Scotland's South West who is notorious and she can be a bit of a handful. She's been entitled by her many victims with the name Mad Maggie although no one has ever been brave enough to call her that to her face. Actually away from the ring ropes she's a really lovely person, very polite and very mannerly. In fact she's a real lady but once the contest starts look out all who enter here, Villains that is thankfully.

Her full name is Mrs Margaret Deans and she hails from Muirhead, it's a largely working class area in Troon Ayrshire. She's been employed almost all her adult life in the hotel trade in the kitchen and she's been resident at "The Klylestrome Hotel" in Miller Road in Ayr for years now. In the culinary sense she's a very talented individual but her alter ego can pop up and pop out at anytime and on any given night. It's at that moment she metamorphosis into a "Mad Genie" who's finally broken free and is now flexing her muscles outside the confines of her bottle like prison. Her night off seems to be fairly flexible so she can appear at anytime. She's also quite well known for her deliciously tasty pastry creations some of which she brings along and gives away to us **"Blue Eyes"** [They're the clean cut heroes of the ring] Cream Cakes for Dale. Lovely!

She's particularly infamous for her knitting needles and she can be fairly creative with them but not in a part-time cottage industry Fair Isle Jumper sense! She uses them to stab your buttocks and even your bare back and her stand-by weaponry includes a Large Leather Handbag and a big multi-coloured collectable Royal Troon Golf Club Members umbrella! Well being a resident in the area of one of the worlds top eighteen hole courses what else would she carry around with her? Besides it rains a lot down her way.

What else in deed?

When she's in her "On the Moon" faze her language is reminiscent of a drunken Ship Yard Worker, only her's is ten times worse. [Maggie as she was known to her friends passed away in the early 1980's she's sadly missed by former close friend and of course all her wrestling victims]

There's a like minded equally sneaky contemporary of hers in Oban, come to think of it they could even be related. Oh no heaven forbid! Let's hope not because if those two ever formed a Tag Team they would take the World Title in less than ten minutes taking on and beating all comers!

Anyway lets move on to a story involving a former trainee and a good mate of mine "Big Arnold" No actually I've changed my mind I'll get back to him a little later. Let's set the scene first by talking about his misses "Our Auntie Betty." That's how she's very affectionately known among the lads, she has a very loving and a very generous nature but don't ever cross her, that's when her "Protective She Lion" determination can kick in. Especially if you're messing with either her man or any of her young family! So being on a short spring break she was travelling with hubby on a Highland getaway tour. She was sitting as usual a few rows back from the ring busily engaged in following a printed pattern and clicking away at her knitting needles. Must be a history repeating itself thing, she was similar to that "Madame De'Farge" lady proudly perched by the steps at the Guillotine in the centre of Paris France in that classic writer Charles Dickens' famous novel which is set during the French Revolution entitled "A Tale of Two Cities."

So as the Betty Lady sits there laughing to herself at the reactions of the paying audience, the love of her life was going about his business and not very gently as far as the audiences perceptions were concerned, busily battering lumps out of his opponent. Somewhat predictably right on cue Arnold got attacked and was duly administered a healthy doze of comeuppance by this local Amazonian who flailed away with her heavy umbrella at him. She swung it like King Arthur's famously magical sword Excalibur.

And did this Our Betty, did you say, not jump in to help out her battered husband?

Well that's what we thought might happen, in fact we were all willing her to join into the affray. Make a welcome change, us watching them how would that be for turning the tables? Us sitting in the ring watching them perform? But it was not to be sadly she just continued to knit one, purl one, although she did call out things a couple of times.

And what did she say exactly?

Oh quite mundane stuff really, things like "You're wasting your time there Misses! I've been battering him for years and it's done me or him any good whatsoever. He still nips out that front door whenever he feels like it, up to that Miners Club for a few pints of Guinness and I'm left sitting there in the house on my tod with the weans." [A Scots word meaning children] "Then he'll appear back home at some ridiculous hour, misguidedly thinking I'll be grateful for his soppy drunken sexual advances. He's got no chance!" "Thank god for my "The Peoples Friend Magazine" it's always been the ideal passion killer for me"

My mother reads that one! Is that why she buys it?

Well who knows? Might explain why you're an only child.

Unimpressed by his last remark the reporter draws Dale a look, then she continues. *She must have said and done a lot more than that surely?*

Who your mother?

Enough already! We're just not going there ok?

Sorry, relax I'm just having a laugh. Am I forgiven?

No you're OK it's me who should be apologising, I'm sorry, family is a touchy subject. It's been a long day, carry on.

She did say a lot more, things like; "Hit him harder! Hit him again! Thump him even harder next time. Again! Even harder but don't draw any blood because if you do he'll be washing and ironing his Ring Gear by himself, daft clown!"

Sounds fascinating!

Fascinating, well that's one way of putting it and yes it's all good for the game and its public persona, but when it gets out of hand it can turn very nasty. One time, and I don't want to be nominated for a medal or anything, you understand. I'm just telling you what happened alright? At a show in the Perth Ice Rink Bill Clarke and he's a big lad got caught in the middle of "No Man's Land" [A sporting expression meaning he got ambushed when out of the ring in a part of the auditorium where he was furthest away

from the safety of the dressing room] by a bunch of nut cases hell bent on causing him some serious harm. Only by luck I had gone out there to sign a few fans autographs books and I watched the whole ugly episode unfolding in front of my eyes, boy was it scary. Naturally I was in there like a shot. The big man who was wearing his usual Thermos [A hooded mask, sometimes it's referred to as a Bonnet] was just so very obviously badly disoriented. He'd clearly lost any sense of direction and probably because of the numbers of people surrounding him and the many punches and the Doc Martin clad booted kicks which were flying into his body. Jumping in among his attackers I pretended to be a punter as I took him in a headlock. I then gave him **"The Squeeze"** and backed that up with a not so loud word in his ear that everything was going to be ok. It's me Dale Storm follow me! We then set off like a Party Conga Line threading our merry may through the irate natives. Luckily I managed to manoeuvre him through the bodies all the way back to the dressing room corridor. Because of the size of these places a safe refuge in all Scots Ice Rinks was always far too far away from the ring. Conversely on the up side the size of these places makes for a real Stadium Show atmosphere which just can't be beaten or replicated in smaller venues.
If unlike me you've always been a regular villain you are therefore always in danger of running the gauntlet of hatred and danger whenever and wherever you performed.

I will however always remember being wrongly billed as one of the bad guys on a show in "The Corn Exchange" in central Edinburgh, it turned out to be the first and I think the last outing ever organised in that venue by Orig Williams. And as far as my long standing "Blued Eyed Boy" "Mr Clean" reputation was concerned it was not my finest hour. Apart from what I'm about to tell you my only enduring memories of that night are some very cleverly executed aerial manoeuvres on my part and an equally memorable really well worked finish by my opponent. The rest of the contest just came and then went almost in the same breath. The set-up on the night was an American Style "Rubble" involving six guys, one of those last man standing things and in my opinion a complete and utter waste of time and effort. I'd never been involved in one before and strangely he never repeated that pattern of bout anywhere else in Scotland after that night. I wonder why?

The process of getting down to the last two men was for me quite mundanely boring, but it was smattered with times of real physical struggle especially involving folks like a "Stiff" local, but likeable lad called Andy Bremner. Among the other four there was also a former son of the same city recently returned home after years of residency on England's southern coast. At least he could work and he was very light in the touch and was not at all dangerous.

The elimination process finally completed two men we're now going head to head for the **"Main Prize"** that turned out to be me and my old mate Jim Mackenzie. Wee Jimmy was nothing short of one of the most popular men I've ever met, both when outside and again inside the ring. The fans just love him and so too did his contemporaries including the likes of me, but as that's the way the dice had fallen so on with the show, the entertainment, and the **"Big Finish!"**

This as it turned out was his very first bout under the big Welshman's banner, Jim having been another brought over and away from Joints with promises of higher wages and more regular work. A familiar carrot but unlike some Jimmy would I'm sure have made certain all the promised hype was made good. Time always allows for some deeper reflections of life's situations and thinking back now that night may well have been one of those often talked about life changing moments, a pre-determined and a totally engineered episode! A let's use this time to put this ever growing in popularity Dale Storm guy in his place and back in his box, a place where I Orig the gaffer, have even more control over him. I've really no idea why Williams was adopting this attitude after all the years of comparative harmony between us. It wasn't as if I didn't always work my socks of for him, I had always made it a rule to give of my very best on every performance night for all the people who gave me employment. Strangely I was never allowed to get too popular with the punters on the ex-footballers shows. Maybe he didn't like to be overshadowed and if you actually do a head count of almost everyone else who'd built up a good following in his ranks they'd all moved on. Why was that? And why, rather strangely was I being cast as an out of character for one night only villain? Would it continue to be for one night only? Things were getting very, very strange. Good pros always gave of their best for those who paid our wages and that included our best and purist armature shoot style stuff as well, but all to no avail. They who shall be obeyed the audience were screaming for more and they wanted blood, as I was the junior man I had to be the fall guy. Well Jimmy wasn't about to change horses in mid stream after a lifetime of building up his good guy persona now was he? Apart from being as hard as nails he was just far too nice to bend the rules so I'm your man. I just got steamed in and moments later the bout really took off and the **"Heat"** went off the scale! The action went backward and forwards and the punters were up and down and over and out, it was like the battle of Bannockburn, Stirling Bridge and the Alamo all rolled into one! Only we were in charge, not them! We just let them think they were leading the line. We kept a tight hold in a manner of speaking, not something good pros would normally do but the ring was placed right up against the high stage. So the punters were very close and were looking right in on the action from only a few feet away.

The build-up to "The Finish" was fast approaching and I'd thrown Jimmy out onto a smart looking blonde's lap on the stage, then I followed him out and in grabbed hold of him, in the same instance I also helped myself to a generous handful of rather large breast belonging to the lady who broke his fall! He must have notice this and his high moral values must have kicked in? The wee bugger then turned the tables "Arm Locking" me! He then invited said blonde to slap me across the face in reparation for my foolish indiscretions and she duly obliged. Whoosh! In my rather helpless position I was left with no choice but to grin and bare it. To her credit she **"Sold it"** well and the baying crowd loved it. Jim then followed that up by head butting me in "Full Glasgow Kiss" fashion sending me flying over the top rope back into the ring. I might add I had to twist in mid air twice in order to get my body set-up for the bone crushing touch down bump! Bearing in mind, as I mentioned earlier the ring was well below the stage. My under carriage came down none too soon and a successfully trimmed landing was well executed. I had just relaxed momentarily and was just about to congratulate myself on a great job well done when out of the corner of my eye I could see what Hemmingway might have described as "a majestic ocean going Albatross, floating wings fully outstretched" above me. Only on closer inspection I could just about make out what it really was as it landed at a great rate of knots on top of me. It was Wee Jimmy! What a great way to execute a finish! Magnificent! The crowd went wild and if it hadn't been for the fact I had to play out my part, staying in character right up to curtain fall waiting for the bout winning obligatory count of three from the referee. I'd have thrown off my now heavy breathing, sweating profusely human duvet and clapped him myself. It was always a great pleasure to work with the man who was by far the best lightweight in Scotland. That's of course excluding the legendary, long standing World Lightweight Champion Mr George Kidd because we don't count him in the ranks of the mortal he's on a much higher plane. In our sporting Hall of Fame he's nothing short of God like!

Is he really that good?

Ask him again ref!

Yes he is of that there is no doubt but let's get back to the job in hand even if on this one occasion I'd had to change hats from White to Black for the good of the show then why not. That's what we should all have been doing each and every time we pulled on our boots, if that's what the bout required. I stated this story line talking about mad, mental folks who regularly attack wrestlers. Let me give you another example and its far more serious. My old pal Peter Preston was stabbed with a sharpened nail file whilst he was getting out of the ring after yet another victory, and the whole incident also happened in a Scots Ice Rink. The puncture wound went in really deep! He was very lucky because that act could have cost him a kidney!

Enough of all this stabbing and injury stuff! It's depressing.

Ok here's a change of subject then, lets talk about some of the other lads who've come into the pro ranks through the conveyer belt of my gym they're all good unselfish pros who were taught in the correct and proper manner.

Firstly there's **"The Viking"** he's really strong and very, very powerful. He's a villain with a big shinny bronze coloured helmet, side horns, a double sided hand axe and lots of real fur leg add-ons and attachments, and guess what he loves to ride his Motorbike to and from the shows.

Motorbike, so he'll be a Hells Angel then?

No he's not a bloody Hell's Angel, nothing of the kind they're a Bunch of Loonies! He's quite the opposite in fact out of the ring he's a bit of a pussy cat and very ordinary. He brews his own beer, smokes a pipe, plays guitar sings Country songs and he does his best to take care of his aging mother and father, he's almost totally conventional.

Then there are the "Isdale Boys" brothers actually and both are very clever. Jim's the youngest "Jumping Jim Farrell" he served in the RAF Regiment and the older sibling Bobby "Bob Bell" has a mobile grocery business. They're a really close knit family. Oh God, I've just remembered I've completely forgotten our original topic of conversation Big Arnold, it must have been the Edinburgh connection? I've been away at a tangent a wee bit like another of "Auld Reekie's" [A Ye Olde Scots name for Edinburgh] favourite TV sons Wee Ronny Corbett. Sorry! You should have said it could help keep me on subject if I go of piste again. OK?

So back to Big Arnold and before you ask no I'd never cross his misses, no bloody chance. Like a few others on Indie Bills he fills in as "The Outlaw" [Originated and portrayed by the Canadian powerhouse performer the undefeated Gordon Nelson] now and again but he's also a very good, solid worker in his own right. He's a really big powerfully built lad well over six foot tall and very strong as well. Works underground in the coal pits. He's good but he's no Nelson, another very capable performer who works in The Outlaw Mask is the Yorkshire born and another Charley Glover trained worker Carl Dane. Fred Hill from down St. Helens way also worked that character and also the Kurt Stein persona for a number of years. My lower jaw is still more than a bit ropey due to a misdirected forearm smash I received back in the 60's form Freddie. He's also a very powerful man who toured on the Indian sub-Continent with the likeable and very popular Dwight J. Ingleburgh aka **"Sam Betts"** [Likeable Carl Dane sadly died in April 2008]

Arnold's hard to beat and he's developing his own following and his own style. Given his size he may well finish up at Joint Promotions some day. Then you've also got John "The Farmer" not to be confused with the Yorkshire's legendary Farmer John Allan, he's in the same weight division though and unlike most of those who use that particular handle, he does earn a living from the land, it's been in his family for years. He's a good lad really but he's quite infamous now among his peers, usually during the

Christmas or the New Year story swapping interlude at parties. Primarily because of being put in the position of being a last minute stand-in when one of Adrian Street's scheduled opponents had an unfortunate call-off injury

Big John, that's his proper Christian name kind of stole a lot of Adrian's moves from around the start of the fourth round during that encounter, not that he was intentionally taking the piss you understand. The real reason is far more plausible than that. The thing was he'd simply ran out of ideas of his own, prior to taking that job he been used to finishing his fights off with a knockout in the third or maybe just into the fourth round. So he hadn't logged up a whole lot of ring miles by then and was quite limited moves wise. He's a big lad though but Adrian was always far too good and far too clever to get caught up in any of that power play shit. You should have been there it was quite entertaining. I'm not so sure the man from the land should have done that though, it's never the best policy to be using another wrestler's stuff especially when he's in the same ring and standing right in front of you. The Scots Farmer paid the price for his indiscretions with more than a few bruises. Let's just say it wasn't his finest hour. [The original "Farmer" John Allan left us for a better place in January 2013 he was very popular with colleagues and is sadly missed] That brings us rather nicely on to another guy who can rightly claim to be a really powerful performer: He works under the guise of **"The Sheik"** or simply Robin to those who know him better. He's a tall good looking young man with dark haired and warm dark eyes, but he has a well paid day job in a popular hotel chain where he's a top chef and he's deeply in love with a really wonderful long term girlfriend name of Alisha. They're saving up to get married soon, bless them, so although he's working out regularly on the mat he's not been seen in the paid ranks as often as I and other like-minded folks would have preferred. At his present rate of power development I'd give it around twelve to eighteen months and he'll be just about ready to make a challenging for the British Heavyweight Title. Among those who've worn that belt are Albert "Rocky" Wall, "Steve Veidor" "Gwyn Davis" **"Tony St Clair"** they've all shared the use of the Title Belt for a few years now, but former 1967 to 1970 Champion **"Mr Billy Robinson"** with no disrespect intended toward all the others previously mentioned is the real Yard Stick! Although Billy Boy's been knocking them off big time over in the USA, his return to the UK if it ever happens would be the tour I for one would like to see. Young Robin one of the New Kids on the Block measured up against the Top Dog! I'd even buy a ticket to be there and of course there are a couple more who could legitimately call themselves real contenders. Maybe they are, and then again maybe they're not but we'll leave them out for now shall we? Anyway at the end of the day who'd bet against the legendary Billy? Probably not many, if I really think about it not me either!

Why might that be?

Simply because I hate losing money! Watch this space! Scotland can best boast a lot of classy lighter weight contenders. I think I alluded to some earlier, didn't I? And among them we've got The Little Master himself Dundee's Geordie Kid might you be thinking of interviewed him?

No not yet but after this one I might do a series of articles now that I've started, I'll see what my editor thinks.

You should get yourself up there to Tayside and quick he's got a lot of great stories to tell, he's been all over Europe. Are you sure you're warm enough you look a bit chilly?

No I'm fine thanks.

Your colour has gone a bit white. Do you feel a bit shivery?

I'm good thank you. What about some human interest

stories. Tell me more about some of other lads. Oh, and don't forget the lassies as well.

Total mileage Ayr to Stranraer and back: 100.2 Miles
Time taken for the full journey: 3 Hours 14 Minutes

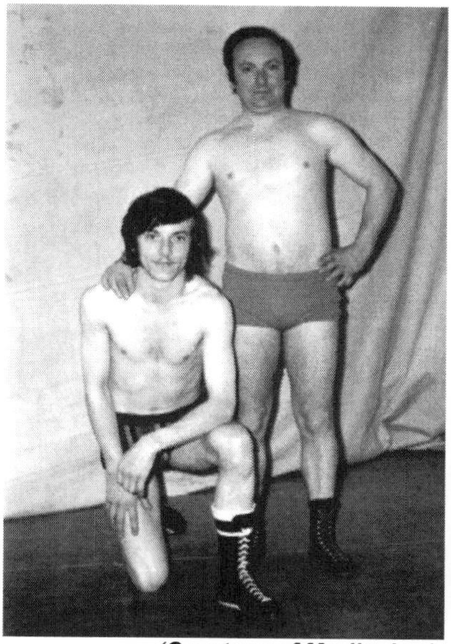

(Courtesy of Mr Jim Lee)

The Isdale Brothers

(Courtesy of Robin Christie)

Big Robin as "The Sheik"

(Courtesy of the late Mr Andrew Bryden Senior)

Sometimes "Outlaw" Big Arnold and Oor Aunty Betty

CHAPTER SEVEN

(The Lads and the Lassies)

The Lassies! Lady Wrestlers! We're getting more and more of them coming into the business everyday now, some are mostly over zealous young ladies hell bent on cashing in on their so called emancipation but what the hell. Some have come over from places like Australia, they're mostly blonde, natural and otherwise, well built and boy, are they shapely. Thankfully we've not yet inherited any of those posing, enhanced plastic boobs large cleavage Yankee Birds so you won't see any of them or indeed any other ladies on any of the Joint Promotions Shows. Although don't be surprised if you do someday soon. Things can't continue the way they've been going into the 1990's! It'll happen! Politically Correct pressure will be brought to bear.

Is their a hidden meaning here? Are you trying to tell me something I should know?

You could say that yes, if I'm being honest there are some ladies out there who are streaks ahead of some of the males who're on the box. ***"We're having none of that Woman's Lib stuff here"*** used to be the call from some in power and it seems like that's still the rational on at least the Joints side of the business I wouldn't want to be accused them however by putting words in their mouths. Although their Television contract and their governing body's rules might well not have allowed them to include woman wrestlers bearing in mind the rule changes in the 1940's. I think you'll find there is no provision in there that allows the matching up of two ladies in a contest? Then again it may well be just a strong church influence? It's all powerful politically even in present day Britain when it comes to the Laws of the Land. The House of Lords is full of Bishops and the likes so there may well be a bit of a Wesleyan type influence going on? In fact it's even worse than that in some other places like in the Islands off the West Coast of Scotland for instance and especially on a Sunday! Then you've got the Welsh Baptist Chapel stuff as well, it's like a kind of a modern day Cromwell Puritan Regime if you get my drift. God that's a laugh in this business of ours! Don't lose your head. Eh! Get it? Don't lose your head, funny or what?

No it's not the least bit funny.

Oh suit yourself! Let's call it a potted history lesson: King Charles 1ST Verses Oliver Cromwell. I'll just prattle on here for a bit, shall I? Maybe you can stop me if something comes up that's of interesting to you. Ok?
There have been some great stories and some really good contests involving some members of the female side in the ring, if I can find the time I'll give you a rundown later. Crowds are really mostly all the same in all the halls up and down the British circuit, although most of us have tended to avoided going over to Northern Ireland for a long number of years now, it's "The Troubles" you see. The Province has of course got their own home based workers and some of them like Dave Finlay Senior promote as well. Things have been getting steadily worse especially since 1969 which saw a split in the long established IRA, that caused the formation of the break away group calling themselves the Provisional IRA. "The Provo's" to me and you, but you'll already know this stuff a lot better than I do.

Then there was the "Bloody Sunday" incident back on 30th January 1972 when the British Troops, mostly The Para's were accused of unlawfully killing 14 people. [After a government lead enquiry announced its findings in 2010 it's now been generally accepted these casualties were totally innocent civilians] in the City of Derry. This has for varying reasons now become a recruiting flag for even more killings. Allegedly that mindless act has only added to an already festering mountain of hatred and resentment where sectarian knee capping, shootings and beatings as well as a raft of other everyday indiscriminate bombings have now become commonplace. These acts of violence have left an ongoing legacy which rather sadly still exists today. I've no idea if things like this have affected the always totally enthusiastic local crowds in places like The Ulster Hall in Belfast. Hopefully it still pulls in good numbers? It had a fantastic atmosphere but over the piece especially back then it was the getting into the city and the getting out again safely that became the biggest worry.

The South of Ireland is however normally a totally different place, it's a real shame about the Six Counties situation but hopefully someday it will all sort itself out? Because if it doesn't, I fear for the future and the solidarity of the rest of the UK as we know it today. Still they've got some top pro performers of their own over there so they have, men like **"Mr Eddie Hamill"** he's very clever very fast and very agile. You've also got **"Billy Jo Beck"** he's been doing some jobs for Joints off and on for a time now. When things got really tough in the Provence and the Independent work started to dry up they stated to drift over here to the mainland, Wales mostly where they had a tie-up with and got steady work from a Welsh based promoter. Long before that Joints had others folks from the Emerald Isle on their books, lads such as the likeable **"Dennis Savage"** he used to base himself in Leeds. Perhaps not the most polished performer but just like all the rest who helped fill the card he did his very best to make the victor look good. He was a smashing accordion player though. [Sadly Dennis died in a car crash in 1970 he was on his way home from a short wrestling tour]

"Dave Finlay Senior" as I indicated earlier is another from over the water, he's a very popular chap and he's got a son, wee David. He [Dave Junior] has been developing at a phenomenal rate. Billy Joe and others had been working on a circuit set up by Dave senior, Eddie worked on it as well but they too had to leave and seek fights on mainland Britain. Young Dave started off his pro career as a late replacement in a Tag Contest, when he was barely into his teens. Although he'd been trained by his father and entered lots of "Catch" contests as he grew up, his career has really taken off since he went over to the Joints camp. He's as "Fit as a Flea!" Older Dave has been a very capable and confident armature stylist for many years now. Brother Hamill is generally quite quiet, but sometimes in the Province its better not to say a whole lot anyway as you never know who might be listening. Eddie has a background and training in the Martial Arts it's been a good **"Flash"** for him and he's made a success of it.

Good God! Sorry I almost forget about the comedic Wee Leprechaun fellow **"Mr Michael O'Hagan** he's lovely and he's very funny as well. The last time I was talking to him, when I could get a word in that was, he mentioned he'd bought a new car. I can't for the life of me remember the model now but it was green coloured with fancy white upholstery and it was one of those classical European designs. The one's with the Big Bug Eyed Headlamps. Anyway, he was telling me he'd been home to visit his old dad in Donegal. [An area on the West Coast of Ireland belonging to The Republic although it's in the north of the country geographically speaking, but it's not part of Ulster] His old-man couldn't believe his son could afford such an expensive set of wheels and to tell you the truth I had trouble figuring that one out for myself. Especially on the kind of wages we get. I don't bloody think so! Anyway the thing that really stuck in my memory was his dad's comments regards the big headlamps, Michael put it this way. Dale attempts to do Michael's native accent:

"Be Jesus Michael those lights are so big you could see right out of sight with only the one o' dem, and probably a lot further besides. In fact right over that big hill up ahead there and down the road a ways on the other side with the

likes of two of them big lamps. I'm telling you now me boy! You could do that very thing and more and that's for sure. And you're all the luckier because you've got the two o' dem tings, one on the right and one on the other side at the front of that big new fancy cost a lotta money car of yours!"

Whether that tale is true or not I don't know, but you've got to admit it is quite funny. Although he'll try to tell you every word was in fact gospel, but that's just the kind of chap O'Hagan is and he's also very clever with it. His countryman "Kevin Conneally" is another motor-mouth performer he's equally as funny. It's been my experience that it's a bit of myth about the Irish being thick or stupid because they most certainly are not, it does however suit their purpose and their mission in life I'm thinking. He really does look at certain times just a little bit like a wee caricatured Leprechaun, he really does honestly. I get a bit freaky though when he starts talking about the IRA. [Irish Republican Organisation originally constituted by both Catholic and Protestant founder members. Their aims and ideals were probably formulated around the time of the Irish Rebellions of 1798 and 1803] A few years back I used to carry my extensive toolbox, jacks, axle stands and spares around in an older, well used Bedford half ton van. One day I answered my door bell, only to be greeted by a rather shifty looking guy with a Dublin accent. He wanted to know if I would consider selling him my wheels, I liked that old van it was kind of rusty in places but I could park it anywhere without fear of getting another dent or another scratch, so I declined his offer. Some days later I read in a newspaper the police had issued a warning to the public to be vigil if approached by anyone of Irish decent offering over the odds cash money to purchase vehicles in the UK. Apparently some bombings had been carried out with cars sold in good faith by honest unsuspecting owners in Britain. I've no idea if it was a genuine attempt to buy my van or a terrorist group looking to transport explosives or just somebody O'Hagan had sent round to wind me up. I've often thought to myself I really hope it was the latter. Michael sometimes teams up with Teddy Bear Taylor for Tag Matches, that's a strange and potentially explosive hook-up though given the fact Ian, that's his Christian name is a die-hard No Surrender Orangeman! [A strong supporter of the Protestant faith especially in the North of Ireland and in the West Coast of Scotland] Hence the Glasgow Govan area football club handle; the "Teddy Bear." It's a name given to the Glasgow Rangers Football Team and its loyal supporters. He's another solid performer and like his side-kick he too can be equally hilarious. He probably won't like me for saying this but the Taylor boy well he's kind of cuddly looking. I'm only talking about his rounder shape you understand, nothing more than that. Round and cuddly! Another aspect of them being in a team together is it's a great example to those on both sides of the religious divide that everyone can get along if only they'd forget old scores and distant historical events and work together more. Probably in the paying public's eye though, the funniest guy in our fraternity would have to be **"Mr Les Kellett"** he's got to be one of the Top Dog Showman but if he gives you one of his crowd pleasing slaps then you may have been truly hit and bloody hard and you may be in a bit of pain. You might even, as has happened to others be short of a bit of a tooth! He's been described by some as a bit of a bully and believe me there's a lot of good men who are not all that keen on upsetting him. He used to live on a small Yorkshire farm in the middle of nowhere. Maybe he still does? I'm told it had no running hot water and definitely no electricity supply either. So maybe it's no bloody wonder he's such a tough old bird. Outside the ring though he's a very private man, loves the odd glass of Whisky although he'll deny he touches a drop and he's also very particular about whom he shares a room with when he's on tour. I'm one of the lucky ones because he seems to like me. Although he's woke me up once or twice in the middle of the night, usually when he's been fighting with the furniture. He's got a particular liking for wardrobes and he's even been known to Pee in them on occasion! Allegedly! Funny maybe but nevertheless very strange, although I'm sure he wouldn't want to be reminded of it. So for God's sake don't print it! Well actually come to think of it that's maybe its not all that unusual; my younger brother used to come walking into the living room in our house when I was a kid, at the strangest of times in the evening, Sleepwalking! Then he'd Pee on the open hearth Coal Fire, not really very complimentary when you're the offspring of a hard working Miner. Good god did it smell but he was only about five or six at the time. Maybe even at that early age he was determined to make a comment about where his own social loyalties lay and where his true political leanings would end up. Bloody Snob! Les has got a style his own although even he'd have to concede a lot of his comedy element has been used to good effect previously and by one of his former Tag Team partners **"Mr Joe Critchley."** When Joe eventually left Joints it was then all too easy for some who stayed on to then steal a lot of Joe's stuff. Things like putting his fists up in an old fashioned boxer style or allowing his false teeth to suddenly jump out of his mouth onto the canvas when you had him in a body scissors and you'd swung he up into the air and then bounced his arse down onto the mat again!

Rectum!

No, but if I'd been a little less gentle it I could have done some serious damage to his Piles!**............Funny or what?**

Oh forget it!

He was also known for his own peculiar brand of facial expressions or his constant Stage Whisper type comments to both opponents and colleagues alike during a contest. Most of which sent the audience into convulsive laughter. The same kind of stuff is done now by Kellett and I would argue the bases of most of those ideas came from being around Joe. It was also all too easy for him to break your hand hold when you lent back with a foot on his stomach when your intension was to throw him head over heels. He'd just break you and then go for a walk around the ring laughing to himself or just stand there hands on hips shaking his head leaving you prostrate on the canvas.

The Dumfries Drill Hall has always been a great venue. Jam packed full with hard working farmer types, all strong young guys and some really good looking young lassies as well. The front row on the left hand side of the auditorium was always dominated by a really tall guy. He must have been around seventy years of age and very probably retired. He was well made with hands like goalkeepers gloves, craggy faced, kind of weather beaten you might say. You know the type, worked on the land from dawn till dusk six days a week as strong as an Ox. Always wore a flat Harris Tweed cap, probably attended faithfully at his Church every Sunday without fail. A good and Godly man!

I was sharing the top spot with a real pro, one of the best Thermos operators since the now legendary master "Dr Death" retired. The Doc was a guy called Paul Lincoln an Australian but if you don't mind we'll just call this other chap Bill for the moment, is that alright?

Bill or Paul what's it to be?

No Paul was the other guy in the other Mask, he's the Aussie! OK? He's the one I mentioned firstly by name.

So the guy you're on with, his real name may not be Bill? You're just saying that's his name.

Yes that's what we're calling him for now. He's the second other guy.

Which guy is the second other guy?

Ask him again ref!

He's the guy I'm on with that night. Got it?

So this Paul is the first other guy?

Yes that's correct, he's the first other guy. OK?

So who's this Bill chap then?

He's the other guy who's not Australian born.

So if he's not Australian what nationality is he then?

You're not getting this are you? He's King Kendo and he's English, remember?

This is the first time you've introduced an English nationality.

Oh is it? Sorry I should have made that clear from the start. He's the Big Thermos wearing guy, the one I'm in the ring with and if you'll give me a minute I'm going to be telling you what happened when we were in there.

That's the very first time you've mentioned a King Kendo as well! I'm not the one getting mixed up here! You're the one who threw this Bill guy into the mix. Remember?

You're right I'm really sorry again, King Kendo was my opponent in the ring that night we were sharing top billing. I was sure I'd talked about him before.

Not that I recall. In fact you definitely did not!

Well maybe I didn't say, anyway, are we clear now?

Yes almost.

OK so the penny has finally dropped.

Ask him again ref!

Getting there but the penny is dropping very slowly.

Sorry Hen. [A Scott's slang saying meaning girl] I was starting to confuse myself. No! No, don't be writing that down, not yet it might still need an edit. He used to have an office in London's Soho area. That's us back to Paul now, he used to run his own shows years back, mostly in the City and around the Home Counties, but he did travel much further afield if the audience demand was there. It was never a good idea to go about getting yours truly into any promoter's bad books back then, in fact nothings really changed they are still all powerful. So that's where some discrete editing might be required? Do you get my drift?

As I said it's a bit slow, and there's one more thing.

Oh were not going back there again are we it's really quite easy. Bill equals King Kendo and Paul he's the other one and he's not British, he's the Dr Death guy and he used to have the London office. They're both different masked men and two different people from two different eras. So are we sorted now?

Yes, as I said earlier I'm almost there.

You don't happen to have an Aspirin in your handbag do you? I think I'm developing a migraine.

Yes probably, I'm a woman we cover every eventuality.

Ok, so let's try a different tact shall we? If you're into the History of British Music, the Pop stuff at least and I'm sure you will be. He's the guy who started a lot of those young Rock and Rollers off on the road to stardom in the 50's and early 60's, he gave them a place to play. That's the Paul guy not the Bill character, anyway, folks like Tommy Steele, Cliff Richard, Marty Wild, Wee Willie Harris and Terry Dene. Most people don't really remember Terry it's been said by some that he went a wee bit strange in the head. Allegedly! Paul also gave stage time to The Rolling Stones in fact to almost everybody except The Beatles! Strong rumour has it that Bruce Welch; rhythm guitar with the Shadows was once a ring builder on Lincoln's shows!

Oh I love the Beatles. Who doesn't?

Well that's nice to know. Anyway he owned the 2i's Coffee Bar in Soho's Old Compton Street. Oh and I'll explain more about the term **"Thermos"** sometimes referred to as being a **"Bonnet"** later on, is that OK? Must crack on remind me later. So one was a former top ring man the best guy in his field till he retired, the other still works as a Heavyweight Wrestler now that's important, so bear it in mind!

Why have I got to remember it? Why is it important?

Because all the bigger guys always get paid the better money especially those who donned the "Lone Ranger" [A reference to the Saturday matinee Cowboy hero's black mask] type headgear now bare that in mind as well. Remember I said earlier I'd be coming back to this subject a little later on, hopefully.

Back in the ring in Dumfries all hell broke loose in the fourth round. The bout had been going well up to that point, well for me at least. I was on top form I just couldn't put a foot wrong and I was now murdering one of God's top doppelgangers. God in this particular case being the legend that is now the real Kendo! He's been back on the scene in the original masked persona for a few years now having been totally unmasked voluntarily with a lot of pomp and ceremony live on TV. It was performed by his manager at the time George Gillette in Wolverhampton's Civic Hall on 20th December 1978. For some inexplicable reason he then disappeared from both the halls and our TV screens around a year later. **"Big Peter William Thornley"** had,

had his mask ripped from his head by Shirley Crabtree in a televised bout in 1975 but he'd practically coved his face with his hands to try and escape detection. Then having recovered his wits he got up from the canvas to inflict a humbling defeat on his opponent. Thereafter immediately covering his identity again, having been handed another "Bonnet" by his manager who'd entered the ring whilst the winning announcement was being made by the MC.

Bill is a very capable Copy-Cat look-a-like and his performances are always a credit to the high standards displayed by the main man of the oriental masked mystery genre, although sadly some purists don't take that view.

Copy-Cat! Is that allowed?

Well its not officially encouraged but it does happen. The big man [The real Kendo] continues to be less than enamoured by the doppelganger false flattery and he's also been known to jump the ring occasionally on other unscrupulous promoter's shows on a mission to claim back his own good name, his personal persona and credibility!

That must be an embarrassment experience for the others.

Frightening is probably a more appropriate word I would have thought, Eddie Hamill has done the same thing and quite rightly so "Kung Fu" as a ring wrestling character was first created by him. So strictly speaking in that regard it belongs to him, he's even been known to take a knife to some of the other imposters ring gear ripping it up in the dressing room in front of them! The question still remains as to how good some of these imposter doppelgangers really are at giving a good and a credible performance? At no time could anyone, not even the original guy Peter ever argue that Big Bill doesn't always give the audience a really top notch show and a good rendition with his King Kendo take on the Japanese Samurai Worrier theme.

But from a paying punter point of view they are never the real thing and neither were those who ripped off Eddie's persona either. However I'd have to defend both Bill and one or two of the others whom I worked with personally when they were doing both their versions of either Kendo or Kung Fu. I for one didn't really like the fact they were doing it but that's down to crooked promoters. It had nothing at all to do with the likes of me. Some of the Kung Fu culprits who should have known better were none other than Ian Gilmour, Al Miquet and in Scotland Bruce Welch in particular. There were others elsewhere in the UK and I must state however right from the off almost all of them were put up to the deception by one or two underhanded promoters. In Eddie's case in particular he'd actually worked with and indeed for the main offender before he moved over to Joints, taking with him his very popular masked character. That particular promoter in both the masked "Rip Off" instances was in fact the same man. He was Welsh. Maybe I'll tell you more about him later?

The Big Peter fellow was born on or around the 19th of October in the first half of the 1940's most probably in the Stoke-on-Trent area but I've been informed he spent his youth and his formative years with his family on the top half of the "Penn Road" in Wolverhampton, where his father operated a local Coach Business. The young Peter worked for the family concern and during this time he started to develop an interest in eastern martial arts, mysticism, Japan in general and maybe the possibility of a career in show business and in particular the world of Professional Wrestling. He entered grappling's close fraternity in the 1960's but it was considered by the powers who ran the sport at the time that his particular persona was not at that time suitable for our TV screens. It would be many years before he made his small screen debut having gained a lot of local wrestling hall notoriety which were then followed up by regular television exposure. After that he gained a huge following during the process although rather inexplicably thereafter, as mentioned earlier he then staged his own unmasking and then equally strangely he then disappeared from both our screens and the pro scene shortly afterwards in the late 1970's. Eventually he re-appeared only few years later in 1981 after donning once again his distinctive "Thermos" but this time around it was under the banner of the top Independent promoter Brian Dixon. A series of bouts were then undertaken against "King Kendo Clarke" these were a hard hitting winner takes all arrangement where the loser was expected to unmask. He also re-appeared several times on television during that period but mostly in Tag Matches where he was usually paired up with Bob "Blondie" Barratt "The Rock and Roll Express" [Nagasaki eventually re-appeared back in the Civic Hall Wolverhampton the scene of his memorable and in some ways bemusing and bizarre 1977 TV ritual unmasking!]

The contest took place some thirty one years later in a specially arranged high profile contest on 29th October 2008, supposedly he wanted to take his revenge for a defeat a few weeks earlier, after which some people had reportedly disrespected both his record and more importantly his wrestling ability. Audience figures of around 850 turned up on the night. The promoter was Sanjay Bagga of LDL one of the new-wave larger companies operating primarily in the South of England. According to a local newspaper a return "Gee" Grudge Match contest had been arranged after Kendo and Tag Partner Blondie Barratt had been beaten some three weeks earlier by the Championship Belt holder Yorehos Christototoulas and his partner. On that occasion Kendo had refused to unmask! This time around the much younger Champion had put his belt on the line in a straight one on one showdown but he insisted that should he be on the victorious side again, then this time the man of mystery would have to agree to definitely unmask. On the big return night in the Civic Hall Wolverhampton again according to the press report, there was a delay in proceeding which didn't impress the paying punters. Allegedly Kendo had refused to come to the ring insisting he would only take part in a return bout Tag Team Contest. The whole thing seems to have gotten more and more bizarre after that! The referee apparently banned Christotoulas from the venue but the reasons behind this action according to the journalist who wrote the article were not made wholly apparent on the night. Thereafter a Tag Contest was hurriedly arranged consisting of two opponents from a previous contest facing Barratt and Kendo. The win was fairly easily achieved by the former TV men as they rather easily overcame both opponents. The latter losing to a classic move performed by Nagasaki! It was a Catch **"Suplex"** this can sometimes be quite difficult to apply and is most definitely a very dangerous hold to administer but this time it t was expertly executed by the enigma in the stripped facemask. Its also been well documented he once owned and ran a Property Development Company among who's portfolio was a Home for Disabled Youngsters. Some folks have even speculated the reason behind that particular project was most probably because his sibling sister was said to have had some acute medical problems as a child. [It's also a matter of public record Peter spent a lot of time over the years raising charity cash faithfully and unselfishly for a local young people's charity in the Midlands area. Where he used to turn up year on year, standing there patiently in full ceremonial regalia happily helping to fulfil the dreams of anyone who wanted a memento and the privilege of having their photo taken standing alongside one of the biggest pro ring draws of all time in the history of the sport in the UK]

You can of course check him out anytime for yourself. Can't you? Newspaper people know all the angles. You can get him in the phone book under Nagasaki maybe?

Really! Well that's handy.

No I'm only joking, my apologies even I can see this might

be getting a bit over involved now, just stay with me please and in good time all will be revealed, I promise. So he's the real as I've already stated **"Kendo Nagasaki"** character. So Just in case we're getting sidetracked again let me reiterate. Bill, that's **"Big Bill Clarke"** he's from Lincolnshire and Paul, remember that's Paul Lincoln he now lives in London**.............So are we're all clear now?**

Yes totally!

Great! Well now add Peter Thornley, are you still with me?

You've just said he's the top man called Kendo Nagasaki!

They could form a bloody singing Trio how does this sound? Peter, Paul and Bill well you've got to admit it does have a bit of ring to it. Get it?**.......Ring as in ring the bell!**

A first name trio of men, yes, yes how very droll!

And hopefully a little bit Hippy as well. Perhaps I could manage them and make a few good few pounds then I can retire. I could have my B&B Business up and running far quicker. What do you think?

But Kendo already has a manager!

Who Gorgeous George Gillette?

Yes if you say so.

He has but I sometimes find myself wondering why him? In my opinion he [George] adds little or almost nothing to the overall performance. There's a painted clown element which is completely juxtaposed, but then again that may be exactly what the big man wants? Him standing there all serene and magical with his Eastern aura and his Samurai Worrier costume and his faithful servant, a "Sancho Panza" type figure alongside who's willing to do whatever it takes to ensure his master looks good at all times. It's a very American concept having a Manager although I do realise he [Peter] does not want to talk and I fully understand his reasoning for playing out that particular show business type aspect. He clearly thinks it helps his persona but his assistant isn't all that good, his voice is not suited to a microphone most of the time, mainly because he's far too close to it and he nearly always shouts into it! He's never learned how to use it properly and his diction is not good either. Although I will concede on that one particular occasion when he performed the official unmasking ceremony he had an awful lot to remember and in a particular order and he did do a really difficult job in very trying circumstances, whilst also coping with being live on television, he handled it perfectly. His make-up was as usual well over the top and he didn't really suit the blue satin gown but his use of the microphone was excellent on the day. He took his time, he didn't shout, his diction on the occasion was almost perfect and he most definitely enhanced the proceedings. Ten out of ten mate! If you compare his usual audible performances to that of a proper PA educated MC such as the likes of impeccable **"Mr John Harris"** for instance then you'll clearly see what I getting at. Then again I'm biased as I'm totally opposed to the regular overuse of a microphone just for the hell of it by quite a number of the next generation of wrestlers.

Peter might well have had even more of an impact if he'd maybe had a big buxom female fronting him. [Although not one who was as heavily made-up as his mouthpiece on his follow-up 21st Century appearance in Wolverhampton] Preferably one with huge breasts thrusting out in front like two large Japanese Suns anxious to take over the world, or perhaps a couple of chalk white faced colourfully dressed Kimono clad Geisha Ladies? Now that's a real flash!

Big Peter usually drives himself to and from bookings and

his soul mate sits in the front seat alone side him. If you're a passenger then you're destined to spend the whole journey on the back seat. Apparently like a true and dedicated professional "The Big Man" will always don the now famous stripped "Bonnet" when he's about five miles out from the venue and he will only remove it again after the performance and even then only on his way back home when he is once again around the same distance away from the venue. That's another reason why he's considered to have a lot of presentation class by most of his peers and that includes yours truly. We're talking about a man who is such a great performer and is always the consummate professional. Now that some of the other old school stars have either left the UK for America or are no longer seen on our television screens, he has almost singlehandedly among the ranks of The Second Wave of TV Grapplers ably supported by the likes of top man Marty Jones, Dave "Fit" Finlay and Mark "Rollerball" Rocco etc have been instrumental in keeping up the best traditions of the business going forward in the correct manner and in the correct direction. Especially during these hard times as far as the lower TV viewing figures have been concerned. Without these four and of course those who regularly died [Not literary] to make them look good, our business would be all the poorer and far less interesting to the spectator.

On the subject of those who "Died". [Meaning to look like you're the weaker less effective opponent or even sometimes weaker Tag Partner] The man who fills that role more than most in the highest of profile bouts has to be **"Mr Bob "Blondie" Barratt"** given the fact more often than not he's usually Nagasaki's Tag Team partner. In the grand scheme of things he is the man who takes most if not all the "Bumps" in that duo, and in so doing he may well be storing up some long term skeletal problems. That's not to say he has a weakness and would be found wanting in a singles contest, quite the contrary in fact. He's well capable and well trained. He may however just like the rest of us encounter some problems in later life, things like arthritic knees, dodgy hip joints, shoulder as well as elbow joint pain but Bob never one to complain, takes it all in his stride. He loves the business and he shows it respect. He's a good pro and a top performer having come up through the ranks serving an apprenticeship. He looks good with all that flowing hair. Some have said he resembles a younger although a lot less muscled version of Adrian Street.

It's also been widely stated that brother Thornley has himself repeatedly started misinformation rumours and innuendo to keep everybody guessing as to his real identity as did another masked superstar before him. He's also the same person whom many feel closely mentored Kendo to some extent during the early years of his development.

..................**His name is Jeff "Count Bartelli" Condiffe**.

The initial connection between the two might well be transport and the motor trade given The Count had interests in that particular industry as well. The misinformation and speculation has up to now worked a treat having deflected almost totally those wishing to know more about him and it has stopped them getting close to "The Enigma" that Peter as now become. That's the way I see it, so now let's get back to The Drill Hall Do, shall we?

Maybe King Kendo had just been having as much of an off night as I was having a good one. Everything I was throwing at him was coming off. Drop Kicks, Flying Head Scissors, and Back-Flips off the corner posts everything was going great guns. Well I was a little younger then and quite a bit fitter and lighter too, in fact I was going around that night at a hundred miles an hour and he couldn't catch me. God was he mad, he was seething! Anyway I was one score to the good having caught him with a sucker fall, a beauty over the top rope from the outside the ring. It was fully justified and perfectly legal in a manner of speaking after the flash bastard, oh sorry again hen, the nice gentleman in the mask had thrown me out into the crowd. Crash, Bang, Wallop! Luckily I was not seriously hurt but as I got back up onto the ring apron he tried to "Forearm Smash" me back into the paying punters once more but I ducked and then "Head Butted" him in the stomach through the ropes, then grabbing the top one I pulled really hard which launched me up and over his head and down his back locking in with my legs under his arms and catching hold of his waist on the way down I was then able to pin him to the mat with his shoulders on the canvas for a legal count of three. My excitable Camp Followers went ballistic!

The chap I mentioned earlier from the Emerald Isle Mr Hamill has quite regularly appeared on television under his character name of **"Kung Fu"** wearing the suitably brightly coloured Judo suit garb and a "bonnet." He used it to disguise his true identity just like many others but unlike most bonnet jobs, he in this styled garb maintained the persona of being the "Good Guy" fighting the good fight and defeating the "Bad Guys" one by one. Until he too decided the public needed to know that it was in fact him under the disguise. There must be something Freudian going on with most of those who've donned the "Mask" in as much as just as they've fully established themselves as a top draw putting a lot of bums on seats, they then kill it off to some extent by removing the mask in the ring and sometimes live on the Box! Why is that I ask myself often and still I struggle to work out an answer. There have been others of course but not many like Australian Paul Lincoln. Remember I mentioned him earlier, that guy and his Mask created one of the best and longest lasting covert villain jobs ever and to the best of my knowledge over a long period he never felt the need to kill off the "Goose the laid the Golden Eggs." Until forced to do so late on in his career in exotic places like Hull. [Sadly James McDonald [Paul] Lincoln passed away on Tuesday 11th January 2011 at the good old age of 78] George Kidd most folks agree gets the credit for inventing Paul's magic masked persona.

Incidentally Eddie might well be contravening some kind of

law regards international copyright by using that TV characters handle, who knows, but only he can do that trick where he runs along the top rope barefoot. He's a very clever lad sadly I could never have mastered that trick. Diversion over once more, now back to the matter in hand, three rows back from the ring was where I finished up when Kendo flung me out that first time but as luck would have it I landed on top of a smashing big girl and I mean a big girl. You know that phrase "Life begins at Forty" well it doesn't really it begins at 38 Double DD and I should know mate. Surprisingly the big bugger did me a favour that night as I got doubly lucky on that occasion, so later on the night after the contest had ended after only "Two Leg Openers."

How is that done? It sounds like a very complicated move.

No sorry it's not a wrestling hold its slang word for a Can of Special Brew Lager! The leading candidate for "Groupie of the Year" and myself thereafter got settled into the back of my car in the dimly lit car park round the back of the hall.

Do you sometimes use music to enter by and if so what?

Come off it that's far too kinky for me! What, like with the car stereo on and something you like playing loudly when you're getting down to the business in hand? Sorry I prefer my sex the same way I like my dinner and that's the plain "Meat and Two Veg" way of doing things just like she did!

No not that kind of entry! .Now you're embarrassing me.

Oh Sorry forgive me. I beg your pardon obviously I've got hold of the wrong end of the stick again.

I meant a theme tune used to get you into the ring.

Right got you now why didn't you say that the first time? **"Cock of the North"** no pun intended. It's a great wee tune but I only use it for title bouts or maybe if I'm on with the odd Top of the Bill draw! If I'm lucky enough to be on with a headliner it's good for creating lots of emotion, gets them going and it works every time especially when it's being played on the Bag Pipes and really loudly! She was hot to trot and I was just as eager, only me and her mind, just the two of us no Tag Team tactics being employed here. Joe and some of the other lads were playing cards in the Snug Bar next door she wasn't that accommodating. She stayed the night in the digs and I never slept a wink!

Female fan conquests are clearly an important talking point over a pint for you macho males but can we get back to the real story please? Unlike you I'm not a kiss and tell girl!

Sure thing girl anything you say just one addition to the Michael O'Hagan car story before I forget it. His car had French plates on it, that way he never ever had to pay a penny in road tax here in the UK and he wasn't the only one to come up with that dodge either, others who travel over to the continent on a regular basis continue to pull that stroke most of the time, especially if they have a vehicle that was manufactured in France like a Citroën, a Renault or something the similar. What happens over there is you get issued with a set of French Plates the very first time you buy a car and you apply to register it in your name. It's a completely different system from the one we've got here no wonder we pay so much for ours! You keep that registration number and those plates for the rest of your natural unlike in the UK. That's one of the elements that make it simple to dodge the UK System. Some folks even got hold of foreign plates, how I don't know. Then they placed them on their car maybe that's what he did? Remember what I said earlier about the Irish as a nation?

....................................They're definitely not stupid!

Total mileage Ayr to Dumfries and back: 116.6 Miles.
Time taken for the full journey: 3 Hours 4 Minutes.

"Joker" Les Kellett

(Courtesy of J Critchley)

"Romeo" Joe Critchley

"The Classy" Tony Charles

(Courtesy of Mr E Caldwell)

"Amiable" Ian Wilson

Ask him again ref!

CHAPTER EIGHT

(Back to the Action)

So as I was saying the crowd were going bonkers in the Drill Hall. I was in top form and then the roof caved in and in more ways than one. Firstly the big fellow from the front row, the farmer guy, I told you about him earlier he's up at the ringside where he used to be quite often shouting and waving those big hands of his and I'm thinking to myself it's just as well I'm a Blue Eye. I was of course in that camp almost all of the time back then, it's sometimes referred to as a "White Hat" You'll already know White Hat equals good guy and conversely Black Hat equals bad guy, equals a Villain. It's just like being in a Western film, Tin Star good guy Sheriff versus baddy Outlaw it's all the same principle.

So I've had a rush of blood and I too got carried away and I've tried out a new move which I'd not quite perfected at that stage and yes you guessed it, I came a cropper! I did a **"Ricket"** [Made a costly mistake] so I landed in a heap on the mat dazed and somewhat breathless.

Mea Culpa!

Mea who? What's that when it's at home? Is it Gaelic [A Scottish derivative of a Celtic language] or something?

No its Latin and it means: "My mistake" or "My Fault!"

So you are a Celtic supporter then? Anyway no need to rub it in.

No its Latin and it forms the basis of the world's languages, well almost all of then at least.

I thought that was the more about the Tower of Babel! Anyway, so then he picks me up nice as nine-pence.

Ask him again ref!

Who does, the farmer chap?

No my opponent, then he places me across his shoulders face down.

So that's his Big Finish?

Now you're getting into it, yes it's his Big Finish, well done.

*And that'll be **"The Kamikaze Crash!"***

So you do know a bit about him, I'm impressed he will be pleased.

Well yes, if I'm honest I have seen him on the television.

How come you never mentioned it before?

Actually he's my favourite wrestler, he's really handsome.

Handsome! He wears a bloody mask!

Yes but I've seen a picture of him without his mask on.

No way, you're having a laugh!

No I'm not a colleague on one of the Daily's put a picture of himself and Nagasaki in the gym on the wire. It's done the rounds in the newspaper business. He's got a great physique and a really curly mop of thick dark hair as well.

Well I'm not aware of any picture, I've been sitting in the same room as him and he never takes his mask off, not even in front of us pros. Clearly you weren't listening to me.

Well I know what I've seen with my very own eyes!

Let's not go there again. OK? So now I'm really shitting

myself, well it's a long way down to the canvas from up there. This guy is over six foot tall and it's a particularly hard ring the one in that hall. Anyway King Kendo is strutting around the ring probably trying to select the most vociferous section of the crowd so he can wind then up even more before launching me into the canvas. Then it happened! Talk about the agony and the bloody ecstasy!

The Old Guy in the crowd is up at the ring side and he's gesturing furiously, but he's overheating big-time!

So did that mean it was even more dangerous for you?

No, No forget about me, anyway I get paid to take the risks, well maybe not enough to be taking those kinds of risks but what the hell its our duty to entertain them.

So the Old Guy he blows a gasket and then he collapses! Poor man he just keeled over and dropped down onto the cold hard concrete floor right there in the front row! "A massive heart attack" at least that was what I was told the article had stated in the local press the week after. Bloody hell, I felt so sorry for his family.

And what about the Masked Marauder how did he react?

Funny you should ask that, it was all very strange he just sat about the dressing room after the bout for ages in what could only be described as a stunned silence.

So he was full of remorse then? Surely he didn't blame himself did he?

Is that what you're thinking? Well he probably did to some degree. In fact knowing the big man as I do, I'd say he definitely would have but he wasn't to know what was about to happen. People attack the ring all the time its part of the set-up and the audience like to play their part. Any remorse from my opponent must have come later though, remember we'd just been in the thick of all that heat. We'd just been "In the Moment" as any acting coach will tell you. Stanislavski talks about it in his books on the performance arts. As a real stand up pro I'm sure and only from a show biz point of view Kendo would have been angry as hell given how abruptly the contest ended! Somebody had brought all the house lights up not long after the poor punter went down and that stopped the contest. I'll resist saying stone dead! All the big masked man did for a large part of the remainder of the night was chatter on about how that poor unfortunate man now deceased, my words not his, had stolen his thunder and taken away all his "Heat!" Robbed him of his Big Finish! As a pro that had been really busy building and building the "Moment" he was perfectly correct to think that way, I would have felt exactly the same, but it wasn't in a cold hearted kind of a way, his point was the bout had, had no closure. Sadly it didn't come to an end unlike that poor unfortunate older fellows well lived life, he'd already gone to meet his maker by then!

Perhaps that was understandable given the circumstances.

Well let's face it he'd done all that work and he got a break due to my stupidity and he'd managed to grab the initiative and yet he'd had no real reward for all his ring efforts.

And you, what happened to you?

Well naturally my heart, oh god sorry slip of the tongue, went out to the deceased man and his family, poor things. It was his timely intervention that saved me from a huge thumping and I was grateful both then and now. I sent a card via the Promoter. I think it was Jack Atherton at that time he's a lovely man and a great ex Pro. If he received it he's a certainty to have made sure it got passed on. Jack retired a few years back I really miss him, his shows were great but after that night the shit really hit the fan down in

Dumfries! That's to say the era of Andy Robin the tuff wrestler turned Grappling Show Promoter got underway, and I'm sure he wouldn't object to me saying he was instrumental in turning that fantastic venue into Scotland's answer to The Bloody Alamo! [A small Christian Mission in San Antonio Texas where a brave band of around 180 people, mostly Scots and Welsh settlers fought and died trying to take that area away from Mexico] In actual fact it was bloody worse than the carnage in the Lone Star State! Davie Crockett and Jim Bowie, brave, brave men though they were would have shit themselves having to face that bunch of lunatic camp followers after that. Christ, John Wayne himself would have developed a sudden case of dysentery, called his lawyer and immediately sought some kind of compensation from his BUPA Private Medicare Healthcare Policy if he'd have been called upon to enter that vicious, now so seriously unpredictable Lion's den. I've witnessed real fear even in the faces of seasoned journeymen pros and some legendary Bill Topping Baddies as well when they got down to the bottom of the stairs and saw the venom filled punters eyes and heard animalistic baying. Some turned a sickly shade of calk white. You could taste the fear and the apprehension in the air.

I'll tell you more about the bold Mr Robin and his bear Hercules later if we can fit him in, then again maybe not? Although I will take this opportunity to at least explain the basis and the fundamentals of how to safely work a crowd properly. Shall I?

Ok spill the beans.

Now how can I put this? Let's say you've got a piece of mechanical or electrical equipment and it's not working. What do you do?

Some people might take it apart to see if they could fix it?

Of course but always remember to unplug it first, and at the end of the day you must also make sure you're not left still holding a pile of nuts, bolts, screws or wires, etc, etc after you think you've put it back together again! You need to complete the job and do everything that's required and most importantly, do it in the correct order. You get the picture? So now that you've taken it to bits and hopefully found the problem all you have to do now is fix it and put it back together again. Simple, but is it that easy? Anybody can take something apart but it's not everyone who can put it back together again exactly as it was when you started out, that takes skill and the ability to memorise a process. Some people even draw a diagram and that's always a really good idea. I do that a lot myself if it's got lots of wires or small components and things like that. Well it's exactly the same process when you **"Work the Crowd"** any crowd, but especially a big easily led excitable and potentially dangerous angry crowd like the ones you sometimes encounter at Wrestling Matches. As I said before any clown can take an audience up and have them in the emotional sense at least, hanging from the rafters, but the skill comes in when you need to take the heat out of the moment or sometimes the situation and bring them back down to earth again. Peaks and troughs, peaks and troughs that's what it's like. A bit like the weather cycle of atmospheric pressure so to speak. Do you follow so far?

And why wouldn't I? I got Higher Geography at school.

It's not a gift that everyone who works within the ring ropes or indeed on a theatre stage or even on the UK Cabaret circuit posses. In fact when you look at a lot of the younger upstarts who are getting into this business and far too easily nowadays in my opinion, all some of them seem to care about is themselves and their ego and not what's best for the show as a whole and that's really quite pathetic.

Anyway back to Andy Robin he's a good lad and man is he

strong, I'd match him against most of the top so called **"Shooters"** [In this context it refers to a persons strength and their ability in a straight contest to take on all comers in the sport and beat them soundly] in the business today for sheer strength but maybe not pure catch style technique. He was definitely not at the front of the line when the commonsense in the crowd control department was being handed out. Mostly and probably because he's so powerful he felt he didn't need to be there, he's not alone in thinking that way, and again some of the newer entrants think along the same lines. Sadly it can be so, so dangerous if a situation is allowed to get that extreme. Sometimes at Dumfries he got so wrapped up in trying to please his huge army of loyal fans, he completely forgot the key to a really safe contest is to be in total control of it, all of the time!

A perfect example was that first fateful night when it really kicked off big time and all hell really did break loose! For the life of me in my many attempts to shut the whole ugly incident out of my mind I can't bring myself to remember just who his opponent was on the night. It may even have been Kendo himself but sadly I can't say that for sure. The main thing that sticks in my memory is ending up being driven away in a National Health Service Ambulance, blue light flashing as well whilst speeding its way towards The Dumfries Infirmary with me and a couple of others on board, sporting fake injuries lying on stretchers inside it in order to safely escape the baying crowd, on a hooky Mission of Mercy. I must stress however it wasn't my idea!

That's ridiculous and especially in a Health Service Ambulance!

It was probably the only way to get out of the place alive and in one piece though? Andy had slid me in at the last minute as the referee for the night, had I been informed of that fact prior to driving down there I very much doubt I would have accepted the booking. Clearly word had gotten round the circuit and all those far better versed in that vital part of the proceedings, who regularly donned the vertical stripped refs shirt had sensibly jumped ship and as the evening unfolded it wasn't hard to see why. As his bout progressed the "Heat" was going ever higher and the pressure cooker atmosphere just grew and grew, in fact had it gone any higher the paper programmes on sale in the entrance hallway would have spontaneously combusted! He ended the contest with his now, always requested popular hold "The Power Lock" and all should have been routine. It had however been announced to the crowd at the outset of the contest that this hold was banned contractually for this contest and therefore it could not be used! This is only supposition but after looking back at the build-up in hindsight complete anarchy was inevitable! Andy was as usual "Milking" [Keeping the crowd in a state of euphoria] the adulation of the faithful and he was now refusing to break the hold, which at this point he hadn't quite completed. He did however execute it in its entirety only seconds later and even after the spine chilling screams and admissions of total defeat flowed from his opponent he then refused to break the hold again. Then equally as suddenly right out of the blue the now totally frenzied crowd's Sentinel (Who was also the promoter, remember) on a whim, whilst momentarily mentally counting the takings on a return contest, known as a **"Gee."** Then turning to me [The referee] totally off **"Script"** he instructed me to "Disqualify" him for using what in that instance (A bit of a mute point now) had been an illegal hold. So without thinking and acting like the complete idiot I had now become, I did exactly that! **.........Silly, silly Boy!**

......................And yes it really was a stupid mistake!

In a split second they were over, they under and they were through the ropes and into the ring. It would seem not only did they want to kill Mr Robin's worthy opponent, even more seriously for yours truly, now they wanted to kill me as well and quite literally that's what was about to happen!

I thank God that on at least this one occasion Andy had an Epiphany and even he could see the gathering storm! So grabbing me he pushed me to the mat and subjected me to further execution of his signature hold also, this of course left me helpless to the flailing boots and fists and the odd flying bottle and drinks can! Had the penny suddenly dropped? Had he finally learned the secret of audience control? No such bloody luck, but given the fact their hero was now in the process of administering summarily justice on whom they clearly saw as the guilty party the mob then backed off just a little. But only slightly mind you, thus allowing the mock execution to take place right there in front of their crazed and bulging, blood filled eyes!

Thankfully by this time someone in authority witnessing the riot that was unfolding and called the Emergency Services! Although somewhat inexplicably, they'd omitted to call the local constabulary at the same time, as I reiterated at the start of this conversation this was clearly a case of the main instigator not being in total control of his senses and the crowd situation. The whole episode was totally frightening but the danger was lost on the gaffer. As a consequences quite a lot of his bouts, well the ones I saw during Andy's time in charge in the Drill Hall at least usually ended up like this, or they came close to it and only because the locals had been given their head and allowed to get out of control!. This situation should never be allowed to exist anywhere at anytime. Either he just didn't care or conversely he just did not have a clue about the dangers involved. Many people including myself have tried to analyze which it was and not just regards the Dumfries venue. Other halls country wide could also get out of hand!

On these occasions if it had not been for a more on the ball, sensible referee or a good and experienced clever opponent leading both him and the audience back down to earth safely, other bouts might have ended in the same manner. What often prevailed was anarchy and near massacre! The always enigmatic commentator Mr Arthur Montford might have been heard to articulate it like this?

....**"It's a Stramash!"**

After that fateful evening a "New Risen Access" had to be erected all the way to the ringside, it stretched from the dressing rooms at the stage end of the auditorium down the centre of the hall, the surface of which was just above the heads of the paying public. This was insisted upon by both the local authority and also most of the wrestlers who appeared on bills in the Drill Hall thereafter. The most embarrassing aspect for me personally was when I had to ask the ambulance crew to please switch off their siren and their blue flashing lights and to pullover in a quiet street to allow us to get out. Getting back to our parked cars would have been a real problem had it not been for the switched on Young Starsky whom trailed us in his car with our street clothes on board. Luckily we were unobserved allowing us to get out of town unharmed by the mob! An element of personal soul searching then ensued, not entirely because I had been placed in an dangerous position, it was more the fact I had been cast, out of character yet again as a villainous pawn in a mental mind game that hurt even more and it continues to be a source a great disappointment!
I had spent years building up part of my good guy, hero persona in that top rated venue working for other more experienced promoters, helped to do so in no small way by both; Spartan Promotions and also the successful old school, time-served knowledgeable Danny Flynn and latterly by Joint's Jack Atherton in that particular town. Sadly almost all that good work and reputation disappeared on that one fateful night, almost totally destroyed in the space of just a few chaotic mental minutes. Dumfries never held the same magic ever again.

What a waste of a public service facility. You should be ashamed of yourself, and who is this Arthur Montford guy?

Ask him again ref!

Don't tell me you don't remember Arthur?

No, but I'm acquainted with Bill McLaren though, he's a lovely man, a great commentator and very down to earth.

Wrong sport we're talking good honest dirty fingernail working class people here, although Mr McLaren himself is way beyond the perceived posh school rugby image. Everybody of all classes and backgrounds likes him but we're not talking your usual University types here though. Arthur was once a popular Scottish Television Sports Commentator born in Glasgow and brought up down the coast in Greenock and by the way it's not called bloody "Grenock!" That's how some of those posh, probably rugby playing stuffed shirted BBC News Reader types pronounce it. They also get Strathaven wrong as well! [It's pronounced Straiven] Jesus you would think they'd get that right wouldn't you? After all it is the BBC for god's sake!

University types! Would it interest you to know that both my mother and my father worked on the shop floor in the Singer sewing machine factory in Clydebank? That's where they met and they've been together ever since.

In a slightly different context it's a bit like that now quite well known saying. "Who loves ya, baby?"

What is?

It's quite similar to the Grenock thing only this time in a transatlantic slang mode. It should be "Who loves you, baby?" But then again it might be just New York speak? Or just another word our American cousins can't spell?

Most people have heard of that one even me, but what's your point? Its Kojak, Telly Savalas played him in the popular detective series.

Ask him again ref!

Well spotted! You know this could go down as a seminal moment in television history.

Maybe, but then again probably not!

OK maybe you're right, so it's a bit of a rant! I get very annoyed when towns and other place names in Scotland get mispronounced it just shouldn't happen. The TV people especially should research all that before they get in front of a camera it's not as if they don't have some folks born up here working down there now is it? Bare in mind John Reith was the original Director General, it was he who almost singlehandedly built their bloody strategy and he was a Scot! They've even try to find Anglo equivalents for good old Scots words like "Dour" with the "OO" sound meaning grim or stubborn, they mispronounce it as "Dower" it's a non word in that context, the Dictionary meaning is; a widow's share of her dead husband's estate!

Yes I've heard that often in broadcasting and especially from some prominent people and a lot of M P's as well.

Singers in Clydebank eh! So you really are one of us then?

And what's one of us? I thought we were all human beings and we all have equal status in the sight of God?

Really! So we're agreed then? We're all "Jock Thamson's Bairns" then? [An old Scottish saying meaning we are all the same the world all part of a larger human family]

Yes of course we are.

If you're advocating it, that's good enough for me comrade.

Comrade! You're getting carried away my name's Jean!

Ok Jean you've convinced me well done. So there I am

well into my bout at another venue and I'm just about to execute my big finish move, where I "Drop-Kick" my opponent, usually more than once, then I pick them up off their feet and in the process spin them round up side down and then deliver them back onto the mat by means of a big strength sapping "Body-Slam" Then whilst they're recovering their senses and getting back up onto their feet I've climbed out through between the middle and the top ropes at the corner post and using the Turn-Buckles [The mechanism used to tighten the ring ropes] I've climb up onto the top rope and then I wait there patiently. When my opponent eventually gets back onto their feet, I'm now behind and above them. I've chosen that particular corner to serve that very purpose, so as they are still disorientated and as they turn to see where I might be I then dive onto them catching them across their head and their shoulders. The force of my body weight landing on top of them allied to their previous state of semiconscious exhaustion usually knocks them onto their back and onto the canvas, where I then pin them to the floor for a count of three by the ref. That particular move is a great crowd pleaser. The iconic "Crusher" Mason [Butch to his friends] and I regularly used this move as my comeback fall when we toured together in what was a memorable period for me in the mid 1970's.
Just a few short weeks after we'd introduced this particular move and during one such contest I noticed Mr Robins was watching me and on more than one occasion over that tour when I had used that finish. That's not unusual in fact it's a real compliment to have a fellow professional taking stock of your abilities, your moves and you're performances. It's usually done however from the seclusion of the stage wings, or sometimes from the side of the hall and usually in the dark. This time he was right out in the open and it was obvious he was busily trying to work out how this particular move was executed. We all do it occasionally even me but seldom if ever do we make it obvious what our real intentions are. No one should be stealing the signature holds from a fellow pro, especially their special finishes!

Can you imagine what would happen if several contemporaries of Andy's in his weight class started using "The Power-Lock" every five minutes, where would he be then? He was however clearly showing more than a passing interested in this top class finish! Cheeky bugger! One night shortly thereafter all was revealed he was appearing one bout up the bill from me in the Top Slot and I was on last. That was unusual because it meant he was on before me on that particular night, I say this only because I would normally have appeared further up in the order, probably second or sometimes third. He [Andy] was deservedly in the Top Spot and Max Crabtree the promoter; he of the all powerful presence nearly always puts on a stylish, full range of moves, real wrestling bout immediately before and again probably after the likes of the top performer. That's because in the case of before the main event it increases the expectation of what's perceived by those who've paid their cash to be coming up after the more scientific contest. The "Storm" as it were no pun intended after "The Quiet" if I can couch it in those terms. And once again after "The Big Battle" another less than frantic more semi-wrestling orientated final contest always helps to calm the crowd down, actually boring them might be a better word, whilst bringing them back to earth after the heightened frenzy of the main contest. This usually helps to send them out onto the street and eventually home in a good frame of mind happy in the knowledge their "Hero" beat the "Bad Guy" and all is well with the world. So no fear they'll be stomping around the living room angry and liable to batter the wife and the kids!

Andy has been know on occasions to be rather cruelly referred to by some top pros, all of whom would never dare to say it to his face, by the handle of "Log Head" or sometimes even as "Wooden Top" I'm very proud to say I'm not one of them. I like the man immensely and I like to think he likes me as well. So as I was saying before I went off on one of my tangents, having tight control over the mood of the crowd is a very important safety valve. If it's done properly it allows you to calm them down when on any occasion they may get overheated and therefore become potentially dangerous. Its simple psychology and yes, we do use that scientific theory in our business, actually a bloody lot of it. Anyway, let me put it this way you'll no doubt have been out having some fun with your pals at one of these Discothèque Dancing places.

Of course I have, but not every weekend. Why?

Why would you indeed, but you being young and trendy on a night out you've bound to have noticed the way everything quietens down in the last ten minutes or so and that's quite simply only because the guy on the record decks will be playing some cuddly, candyfloss slow stuff just before the night comes to a finish. Am I Correct?

Yes but that's not unusual, that's what always happens.

Yes and that's the way it should be for reasons I intend to make clearer, because lately it's been all change with some music trends and it could get out of hand and in much the same way as it sometimes does in the ring! In recent times I've been attending some of those under the "Railway Arches" music places in Manchester usually after a night drinking those hot "Blobs" in Yates's type places. I'm only in those sweaty new dancing places for a laugh you understand and I'm always with a couple of my much younger Caribbean friends. They're into all that electronic stuff they call it "Acid House" and "Techno". Their older family groupings used to frequent or sometimes even organise those "Rave" house parties in London in the 1950's and 1960's. That scene also drifted up into certain areas of Manchester and Birmingham as some of those folks followed other wider family or sometimes hopefully an employment opportunity in the north. Now it's being sent back down to "The Smoke" as a kind of "New Wave" music movement. It's almost taken over the Manchester Drugs and Dance scene in a big, big way but you'll already have heard of these kinds of places no doubt.

No not a lot really. I'm more of a Middle of the Road music person myself. Do you think it'll catch on?

I've really no idea, sadly I'm in the wrong age group, all those flashing strobe lights and lava lamp type moving pictures plastered all over the walls are not for me. My friends love it down there so you never know. Kids will usually follow a new trend and more especially if it's something their parents definitely don't want to embrace!

Sounds interesting might be another "Lifestyle" story there? I'll check it out. I might call a few Mancunian colleagues.

I would if I were you I wouldn't leave it too late if it takes off you could get left behind. It's mostly water that's consumed in these places, not alcohol something to do with the drugs or so I'm told, they sell a lot both water and a lot of drugs! I like a pint so sometimes I nip round to the Embassy Club later on. A lot of the lads congregate in there of a night time, you'll be familiar with the name Bernard Manning?

Yes I've read about him, I don't like his humour its racist!

So you'll already know he's one of the top men from "The Comedian's" TV Show. Well that's his club, he owns it and it's packed out most weekends and there's always a really good turn on more than likely one of those other comics off the television. Dale pauses. Sorry remind me where was I?

Ronnie Corbett time again I think. You were taking about what takes place as we get to the end of a night out.

Oh yes, well that slow music is not just about the DJ giving his pals an opportunity for a quick fumble and thereafter

the possibility of a wee bit of knee trembling “Nookie” around the back in the dark up against the wall, pardon the crude language. It’s much more about calming the dancers down so they don't hit the streets high on emotion and liable to be killing somebody. Well the same thing applies in wrestling only multiply that “high factor” by one hundred percent maybe even more, now do you get the picture?
So Max says to me “Go on in theer Kid and show ‘em what you’ve got. It’ll be a bit boring for ‘em but at the end of the day it’s all about what’s good of the show, it’s not about you.” He calls everybody “Kid” when as we say in the West Coast of Scotland “He's taking the Piss” and trying to sound all superior. God I’m so pass remarkable! My old mother always says “I should be nicer!” No, don't write that down you can't publish any of this stuff my days in the ring would be over pronto if you did! “Here's your hat what’s your hurry” kind of thing! That’s yet another of my old mother’s sayings, God Bless Her. I think I miss her even more as each days passes! The ultimate “Piss Take” has to be is Big Shirley knocking off all the rings Top Villains!

.....................................**What are you laughing at?**

Shirley! You’ve got to be joking. You’re having a laugh!

No I’m not that's his name it really is Shirley Crabtree! Honest. If you’ve heard anybody talking about “Big Daddy” well that’s what they’re calling him now. Some are adamant it’s not all that unusual a Christian name in the world of old Yorkshire and old Lancashire and that’s probably true! Others have told me his mother had set her heart on a girl and that’s the name she’d chosen, you take your pick. Or maybe it was for none of those reasons? Maybe it’s got more to do with that "A Boy Name Sue" kind of thing, you know the Johnny Cash song. Anyway, I’ll bet it toughened him up right quick when he went off to school!

I've no idea. I really don't know what you’re talking about.

OK so you're not a Country Music fan either. Obviously! Big Shirley had been dying on his arse for quite some time with them on the other side and no bloody wonder. There was a time however years ago when he had a good physique was in reasonable shape and had some good muscle definition. He was well into his forties when he was reincarnated so given his size now maybe it's not surprising he labours to get around the ring. That opinion is shared by a lot of his peers so we can't all be wrong!
One of them in particular who nearly always wears stripped trunks is very like minded, let's hope he uses his TV contacts to do something about it and quick. I'm really sorry about this hen it gives me no pleasure to slag off a fellow pro but it had to be said and that's the truth of the matter! The big bugger still owes me money from a show he and Norman Berry ran in The Dam Park Hall in Ayr a few years back. Something tells me I won't be collecting it anytime soon! Mark my words the situation is not sustainable, they might be getting away with it at the moment but it'll all end in tears. Even although his younger brother is now near enough the top dog and has been a cleaver manipulator even he will never be able keep him on that superstar pedestal on which they've placed him. The public are not stupid they'll wake up and in the long run it'll kill the business! As I've already said, there are a lot of top professionals some are big TV personalities who feel exactly the same way. They recon Big Belly Bumpers if allowed to take over will eventually kill grappling stone dead! Sadly most of them unlike my good self, have not expressed their opinion in public for fear of reprisals! Watch my lips; if this nonsense continues wrestling as we know it is doomed! Many of the best men are really disillusioned and some of them have already left the Joints circuit and gone over to the ever growing Independents!

....................You could say they voted with their feet!

If it's the "Blue Eye" part of grappling Max feels needs some improving, which it doesn't, then there are already a whole haul of blokes fulfilling that role. Marty Jones for instance would make a much better role model for all concerned, he's an all action mover and he works at an intensity that's not really sustainable for most of the others. The same goes for the many good rule benders now well established in the business. Kendo "Peter" Nagasaki being the main man but he too moved away from Joints years ago now but he's still around and still packing them in. Mark Rocco are great TV rule benders also; in fact the bouts between him and Marty both in the halls and on box have all been near classics! There are lots of really good men in all weight divisions still doing a grand job who can't even get near a television screen! Anyway it's folks like Big John Quinn who over the years has made those who are well over the weight-limit look good! As did other good "Villains" before him; men like Ian Campbell, Roy (Charley) Bull Davis, "Jumping" Jim Hussey, Mal Kirk, Brian Mason, The Outlaw and Gwyn Davies latterly, and the list goes on!

Anyway, back to my good pal Andy again. Sure enough having tried to work out what had to be done to get into the position to execute my, what I like to call "Crucifixion Move" he tried desperately to use it as a flash finish in his contest.

What about his Power Lock that's what they all come to see isn't it?

I am impressed. You have been taking stock, well done.

*Don't get carried away. I read about him in an old copy of **"RINGSPORT"** Magazine, one of the juniors brought it in.*

Well done anyway. Sadly Andy had only worked out half the script. He'd clearly been distracted and hadn't given proper consideration to the total build-up to the climax.

Climbing up on a chair Dale demonstrates how to execute the move properly. So imagine this is the top ropes I'm standing on, if you carry out the move correctly including the directional change of going from inside to outside through the ring ropes, then with the climb up onto the turnbuckles you should now be standing with one foot on either side of the top rope. One left and one right and you're now facing back into the ring space waiting to leap onto the other guy. But if you don't go through the ropes and you then climb up the ropes from inside the ring........!

You finished up standing up there but you'll then be looking out in completely the wrong direction!

Well spotted! You're still in the corner only now you're looking out into the audience and dare I say it; whilst you're looking down at them, they're looking up at you standing there looking down at them and at that point there's only one person looking more than a little stupid!

And that's you!

Well actually no not me, it was Mr A Robin!

Getting down off the chair Dale continues with his story. That's where Oor Andy boy finished up and all this time he was still having difficulty trying to figure out where he'd gone wrong. I've said this at least once or twice now but I'm going to say it again, I like the man immensely and I have an awful lot of respect for his abilities, both inside and outside the ring. He's a caring man in his own dear way and he's spent a lot of time and lavished a lot of love and money on his pet bear Hercules. In his own way he's a considerate and a very kind hearted man who clearly loves animals, especially his big baby the wonderfully enigmatic "Herc" as he likes to call him. Conversely don't ever make the mistake of putting your life in his hands without having a Plan B escape root stuck down the front of your Leotard. On reflection perhaps I should have started this story at the beginning, that's to say how the business of Profession

Ask him again ref!

Wrestling in Britain gained its new found legitimacy and where and when I entered my hard earned apprenticeship.

So it didn't just evolve as a natural progression of the "lets make some easy money" principle then? Or a let's take away from gullible Joe Public some of their "heard earned cash" thinking then?

The total mileage Ayr to Hawick and back: 212 Miles.
Time taken for full journey: 4 Hours 30 Minutes.

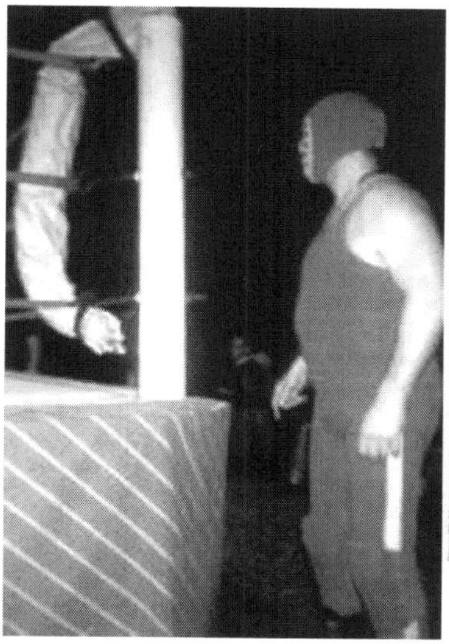

Peter's ring persona! Entrance costume! Unmasked!

"Bumpers" Disco Dragon

TV Wrestling Broadcaster

CHAPTER NINE

(A New potential young Star is born?)

Yes you do have to pay to watch Grunt and Groaners at work, that's true and yes it is a business but it's also an art form and universally accredited as such nevertheless. Professional Wrestling as we know it today was formalized by Admiral Lord Mount-Evans and the rest of the Committee he chaired. It sat in a Committee Room in the House of Commons in London around forty odd years ago now, the exact year was 1946. Up until that point the whole thing had been a bit of a mish-mash and it needed to be up dated and modernised. Most of the actual new rules were set out after some considered consultation with the very knowledgeable Mr Norman Morrell he was an ex-Olympian and the former British Amateur Featherweight Wrestling Tile Holder, he held it from 1933 to 1936. The proposed changes were debated and then formally adopted by those who were attending the assembly. He [Morrell] was also a founder member of The Joint Promotions Group [The parent company running the UK Television Wrestling Shows] Those parliamentary hearings set out the weight limits, the list of legitimate holds and perhaps far more importantly the list of the barred and the illegal holds!

Where do you fit in? How and when did you get started?

Well that's quite simple I made my UK debut in the town of Troon in Ayrshire right in the heart of the West Coast Golfing community. I had decided to roll the dice, to take a chance as it were. The local rag The Ayrshire Post [A weekly newspaper serving the South Ayrshire area] had a large Black and White quarter page advert in the always well informed Entertainment Section. **"Cape Promotions"** proudly present. **All Star Professional Wrestling!** Walker Hall, South Beach Troon. Doors open 7-15pm.

Ask him again ref!

Who was on the show that night?

I thought you might ask me that one. After a short rummage through his wrestling bag Dale produces an old **"Ringsport Magazine"** and a Flyer**.** As he lifts it out of his bag something else drops to the floor. Quickly picking it up he places it back into the bag hoping the reporter hasn't noticed. Then he hands her the publication; Here take a look for yourself I've kept it with me all these years.

Very nice, now what was it you put back in your bag?

Sorry, say again?

What was it? What fell out on to the floor?

Oh it's nothing!

It looked interesting.

No not really.

I'd like to see it. Can I take a look please?

Busily trying to avoid answering the reporter's question Dale takes the publication back, he thumbs through the pages "Cape Promotions" shows were always full of experienced top class performers listen to this for a line-up.

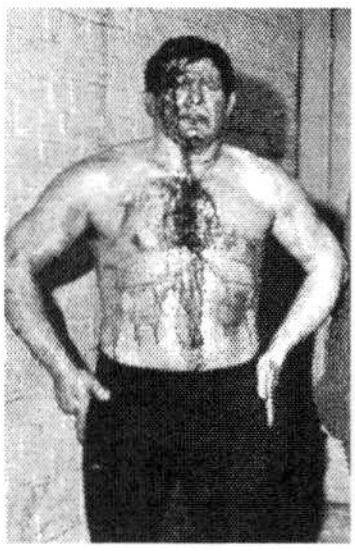

Gotch V Lion1908. **Bartelli** **Comiskey** **Karl Gotch**

(Karl Gotch shared a surname with Frank Gotch but they were not related)

Ask him again ref!

Cape Promotions
Proudly present

Wrestling

The Walker Hall Troon
Doors Open 7-15pm

....

Fred Woolley V Jumping Jim Moser

Gordon Corbett V The Zulu [Ezra Francis]

Quasimodo V Pete Lindberg

....

+ Direct from The USA New Style 4 Man Tag Team Wrestling Featuring:

Fabulous Harlequins V Les Diablos Rouges

And introducing one other Extra Supporting Contest!

Featuring Fabulous: Girls! Girls! Girls!

The Tag Contest was new at the time, well in Scotland at least having been imported from America, it was a good flash and the punters loved it. The young Harlequins lads hadn't been long started in the business but their ability stood out a mile, both teams were among the most exciting Tag Outfits around at the time. The Rouges were accomplished masked guys from the Lancashire heartland they consisted of Eddie Rose and Ian Wilson both of whom hailed from the Manchester area. Their opponents were brothers, no Twins! **"The Morgan's"** that's their pro handle they were fantastic, top fliers! They're still going strong and they're still as agile, and still almost the same weight as they were when they started out, now that's amazing. Danny Flynn wore the Quasimodo mask disguise and there was a Ladies Contest, the first ever in that part of Scotland!

As I don't see any names, am I to assume they were the Extra Supporting Contest?

Yes and that's the way it was and still is for some male or females when you're on the undercard, but still they had some headline billing elsewhere. Take a look for yourself. No don't write this bit down, for now any comments I might make about the appearance of girls on the show we'll maybe have to edit them a wee bit later? Thing is they were seen as a bit of a novelty act back then and not taken very seriously. They were mainly regarded by the punters as a bit of sexist titillation, but it was their pictures that were plastered all over the posters, no one else's. They were the only participants getting that kind of exposure on that tour. Apologies, regards you vetting my comments I'm not a lover of censorship but I don't want to be upsetting anybody. There's been a lot of water gone under the bridge since then and there are a lot of top females wrestling now.

But why no ladies names on here?

I can't answer that one I'm afraid but it could have been because generally speaking, nobody really took them seriously within the sport not even me, although I always got on well with all of the girls at that time and I'd have to admit those two ladies in particular did work well together. In fact if truth be told no real purist grappling fan takes them seriously even now, well not in the UK anyway. I'm not convinced there needed to be names on there in large print anyway. The Photos were more than enough of a flash and their handles are printed along the bottom of the headshots. Mostly folks came along for the curiosity factor.

Ask him again ref!

It was the tight fitting gear and the big breasts that put some extra male bums on the seats. No place for woman in a man's Sport! Not my words I might add, it's a view shared by practically all the directors on this side, it's not really something that's of interest to Joint Promotions. Good God we'll be having Wee Lassies refereeing Fitbaw Matches next. No, I'm only kidding, it'll never happen! Even the Palace of Westminster's formulated Wrestling Rule Book made no mention of woman taking part in the sport.

So who were these lady wrestlers then? Or has the passage of time erased then from your memory? After all it was a few years ago now.

Steady on there girl! Now you're asking let me think.

Are you playing for time here?

What? No! Hang on give me a minute it's all coming back to me now.

Dale taps on the side of his head. It's right in here somewhere. God! I think it was **"Hell Cat Haggetty"** Cowboy Jack Cassidy's daughter, No, No, I'm wrong, bloody hell, how could I forget her? The bout was **"Naughty Nancy Barton"** (Helen to her friends) **verses "Mitzi (The Blonde Bombshell) Mueller"** [Pat is Mitzi's real name] Nancy was **"Woman's World Championship Belt Holder**" at the time. Although she was not the original owner of the ring name that honour belonged to Anne Barton who by her own admission had bottled it before her first contest as the "Naughty Nymph" and was replaced by Helen. She [the stand in] was lovely and a real lady. It's been said by some she was off Romany Gypsy stock, you know travelling folks, I'm not sure if that's true though. She was quite tall with jet black wavy hair and boy was she all there? She was really well stacked but you didn't mess with Nancy she'd have broken your arm, tough as they come was that girl. She weighed in around eleven stone seven pounds but you'd have been hard pressed to have guessed it. Winking at the reporter Dale gives her a short history lesson. That's about the same weight as Marilyn Monroe was. Size 12! Get the picture?

Mitzi was the exact opposite, firstly she was blonde, very, very blonde but it came out of a bottle and unlike Nancy she liked to be among the lads. She liked to talk and she could down a pint like the rest of us. I liked them both Nancy and Pat were always very pleasant young ladies. The ring name suggests a German connection, she did in fact adopt the maiden name of an Arian grandmother or so I'm told. Her first paid venture got off the ground in1963. When she was around age fourteen she first started training under her Northern Wrestler father Joe Connolly.

Anne Barton in the meantime having regained her composure invented another handle in the form of the original Lolita Loren and was billed as such from 1964 to around1975 when she took time off to start her family. Once again the new handle was then taken over by another in the form of another of Jack Cassidy's daughters Chris Thompson. She [Anne] then made yet another come-back later on under yet another guise, this time she was called Lady Emma.

Miss Mitzi retired after a glittering career spanning well over 20 Years! Her swansong contest took place at the Royal Albert Hall London on 24th April 1987

Neither father or indeed daughter had adopted The Leader Hosen look though which would have been ok for a good **"Flash"** [Really good presentation] it was however really not an option as it gets more than a little odder effected when you've been perspiring all over the inside of it, but we don't want to go there, do we?
Yes we do! Why not?

Ask him again ref!

No we bloody don't! She liked me I could tell right from the very first time I was introduced we got on really well but only in a professional sense you understand. They both liked me! Back then I was just a naïve teenager a mere boy. I was the youngest fully working pro in Britain at the time and I was only seventeen! They were much more experienced in the ways of the world than I was, believe you me. Well girls are always far more mature both physically and more importantly mentally than boys. Don't you think and they'd been going round the circuit for the best part of a year to eighteen months before I got started. Anyway Mitzi's dad the Old Pro had a bit of a reputation and I was new to the business, I didn't need enemies. I've often wondered since if that was all a bit of a myth put in place by other close suitors to frighten off the competition?

As for Nancy or so it had been rumoured she was a bit more than just friendly with the Boss, the promoter Danny. Apparently it was the worst kept secret in wrestling at the time. Reports have said Helen moved to Germany sometime later but I've honestly got no idea what happened to her after the motorway accident. If you remind me later I'll let you into a closely guarded secret about another woman wrestler who was in fact really a man!

A Transgender wrestler that's most definitely a follow up story right there, come on why don't you tell me now?

Just hold your horses and don't be getting carried away. All will be revealed later. Anyway back to my debut. I'd gone up to Troon believe it or not on the bus.

The Bus!

Come to think of it, it was two buses, one from my village into Ayr and then another up the coast road to the small sea-side town of Troon. Well I didn't have a car and anyway I was barley old enough to drive and besides my father never ever owned a car, he simply couldn't afford to run one! So he couldn't drive me up there, could he? When I got to the hall I marched straight in the front door bold as brass right up to the box office I went, and then I asked to see the Promoter. After all I was the **"Cock of the North."** [The title of the bagpipe tune I sometimes entered the ring with much later on in my career] Well I was young and I'd done some travelling, bearing in mind I'd been round the globe. Well halfway actually and then back again and in the opposite direction. I'd been to Australia and I'd seen large parts of the rest of the world! Actually I'd visited places like Vigo [Spain] Gibraltar, Genoa and Suez, then down The Canal, not forgetting Aden and then over to Singapore. That's only because that's where the ship berthed over and I'd no choice in the matter. It broadened my mind though and all for the princely sum of ten pounds for the boat fair!

So after a few minutes this man appears, he had a dark skinned kind of a lived in face and slicked back dark hair, clearly he used a lot of the Brylcreem [A popular hair product cream of the day] It was all the rage back then.
"How can I help you?" He asks in a soft semi-lilting pseudo Irish come Salford accent. So I explained who I was and why I was there and then he asked me "So what makes you think you'd be any good then? Why would the punters want to pay good money to see you?"

And what did you say to that?

Well if I overstated my case he would probably just have laughed at me and if I'd simply gone ahead and understated my case why would he want to continue the conversation? So in a fit of youthful desperation I opened my mouth and it was out of my young and sadly at that tender age, ego driven mouth before I realized I'd said it. "I've served my time in the amateur ranks in the clubs down under in Oz and I'm very good at what I do, now that must count for something? Give me a go! You don't have to pay me just give me a go please sir" If I was being honest I think any decision he made was more about the "*You don't have to pay me!"* part rather than any ability he thought I might have. Anyway his reply was "Wait here a moment will you I'll be back shortly" He sounded a bit like that General Douglas MacArthur must have when he got flung out of The Philippines by the Japanese in 1942. "I shall return" Yankee Chancer! The General that is not the promoter! Still everyone loves a "Come-Back" [A Wrestling term for getting your own back and then going on to get the victory after you've been taking a bit of a hammering] Especially in the world of show business god this game would be nothing without them. Working a **"Gee"** is our life blood [It means setting something up for the next show hoping it will increase the advanced ticket sales] hopefully it gets more punters in, so more bums on seats and more profit! I found out later Nancy had overheard the discussion and she'd told him to give the cocky, good looking young Scots lad a go. So back he comes and I follow him backstage to the dressing room area then he opens a door. "Right get your gear on I've told the MC to announce an extra bout you're on first lad; show me and more importantly them out there what you can do. OK? Don't hold back this is your chance son. Someone will knock on the door five minutes before it's your time, be ready to go when they get there don't be holding up the proceedings now." Then turning away from me whilst I was trying to ask him about who I was on with, clearly choosing to ignore my question he walked out closing the door firmly behind him. I was left there in the silence on my own and sure enough some time later came the knock on the door. A ring second then lead me into the arena and rather disappointingly when I entered the hall there was very little response. The MC hesitated a little studying his paperwork before he made his opening announcement, then walking over to me and leaning in he asked rather quietly "What do I call you? What's your name mate?" Floundering more than little I told him my proper Christian name the one my parents had given me. Well what was I supposed to say? So he replies abruptly. "No you're ring name stupid!" I don't have one, says me, I'm not a Pro, well not yet anyway. "Well you'll need to think of one sonny and bloody quick! He'll be getting in here any second now and he really hates bad presentation, so what's it going to be?" Again it was out of me before I could think. Dale. It's Dale. He looked at me and sort of nodded! "Dale! First name or second?" First" says me. I'd had a pal in Sydney called Dale but she was a girl and she had lovely big tits! Could have been worse, a lot worse lucky for me her name wasn't Gale! Now that was bound to have solicited some audience reaction even in a posh millionaire festooned area like Troon.

Dale that's got a good edge to it sounds very American.

America! Let's not go there shall we? So the MC continues. "And the rest is" says he. Moving his hand in a circular movement as if to say speed it up. Will you? By now I don't mind admitting the whole event, the lights, the crowd whom I sensed felt something was definitely amiss were getting just a wee bit restless and in turn I was getting a little more nervous as well, in short everything about the whole occasion was now getting to me and I was at that stage and on the verge of requiring a toilet seat!. The weather on the way up had been crap, no pun intended the wind and the rain on the night had lashed on the bus windows almost constantly and now all I wanted to do was to forget the whole thing and go home, back to the safe loving arms of my wee Mammy! Devine inspiration must have taken hold, well something like that because I found myself blurting out, it's "Storm" Well what else was I going to say? It was really pissing it down outside and besides at that point let me tell you, it could have been any bloody stupid thing that got vocalised; even something like Co, Co, or Huey or Dewey or maybe even Louie? It could even have been Donald or even Mickey and once I'd said it and he'd written it down that would have been that. I was then stuck with it and the rest is history because that's been my pro-handle ever since. So after that short dithery delay the announcement rang out from the centre of the Ring.

................"And now! Introducing in the Red Corner!"

At least I was in the correct corner because Red had always been my favourite colour at school. The MC continued. "Courageously appearing in an additional contest please put your hands together and welcome local boy from Ayr making his professional debut, I give you Dale Storm!" You know I actually got a warm reception although come to think of it the crowd used to clap the Christians in the Coliseum in Rome as well and then the bloody lions ate the poor buggers! Anyway, I was now on my way! The corner second reminded me to take off my ring jacket and we got chatting and guessed what?

Don't tell me his name was Storm as well.

No, don't be daft! Where did that come from? In actual fact he was born in the same village as me and he'd married a girl from Irvine and they'd then moved into the Brassie area and as it happened, not all that far from Margaret Deans.

So who was your opponent?

Good question! I'd been so wrapped up in myself at the time I'd actually forgotten that I would have to have an opponent then in an instant all was revealed by the Master of Ceremonies to all the assembled over the microphone. "Ladies and gentleman please put you hands together and welcome into the ring in the Blue corner a gentleman whom of course requires no introduction especially here in this venue; the one, the only, the Heavy Middleweight Champion of Great Britain and the British Commonwealth the Master himself Mr. Danny Flynn!" Well the place erupted and as I turned to see who the hell this Danny Flynn fellow was my bottom jaw just dropped a mile. You're laughing at me, you are, admit it! Have you been told this story before? Has some little bird been singing?

It was the promoter and no I've not heard it previously.

Got it in one and boy was I really shitting myself now bricking it in fact and I mean big time. British and Commonwealth Champion! What the hell was I doing in there and with the likes of him.........**daft bugger or what?**

What happened then? How did it go for you?

Oh it went OK I suppose but you don't really want to know do you?

Yes please of course I do!

No you don't let's move on shall we? OK!

No come on! You can't leave it hanging like that.

Well if you insist, it was bad, I was shit, in fact I was worse than shit, lets just say there was quite a bit of **"Scurfing"** going on and I was the one on the receiving end good and proper, meaning I was being **"Ploughed"** into the canvas. [Both terms are used by seasoned mat men to describe their actions when in the ring or on the mat with new, raw, would-be pro wrestlers whilst testing their metal, their resolve and their suitability for the professional business] What's more every time I got him in a hold he just slipped out of it as easy as pie! No wonder he was the Champion he wiped the floor with me. Actually he held me up for ten full minutes of that four by three minute rounds contest before taking it easily two falls to nothing!
So back in the dressing room I'm knackered and I'm hurriedly getting dressed hoping to sneak both me and my embarrassment out the back door before anybody came in when suddenly the door swung opened and in walks the

Maestro accompanied by the lovely Nancy closely followed by Mitzi and all other wrestlers on the bill, the bloody lot of them. One by one they introduced themselves Jumping Jim Moser was first, I kept in touch with him for years after that but sadly we've lost contact now. Our paths crossed many times hear and there after that on both Joints and Indie shows. I got a kiss on the cheek from both the girls and after they all left the gaffer Mr. Flynn handed me £5. A whole bloody Fiver! It was like Christmas and my Birthday fell on the same day. "That'll get you home in one piece don't spend it all at once." Then making for the door he turned back toward me and into a short silence spoke again. "You did great lad I really liked your **"Break Fall"** technique [A means by which you endeavour where possible to get your feet or your arm down first, to try to break the impact of your fall keeping your shoulders off the mat] and your **"Neck Bridge"** [A properly trained amateur wrestler's trademark in many ways] it was really strong, well done, all good solid stuff. If you can't break-fall and you can't bridge you're not long for this business, and you're a very fit lad as well" The part about being really fit was far more important to me personally than anything else at that early stage, much better than having lots of pro skills because that had been my almost total focus in my younger years. I had a particularly bad attack of "Scarlet Fever" at an early age which had left me badly weakened and I'd struggled for a long time to get over it, even at that childlike age I began to lose confidence in myself. I would then set myself targets and goals, things like improving my running speed on a weekly basis and although I was really far too young to be doing any serious weight training I did however use a couple of old wooden Indian Clubs, the exercises helped me keep my body supple. A lot of European style "Fartlek" stamina training helped as well, a school PE teacher of mine had studied the continental theories on athletics and he introduced me to the benefits. It's a kind of walk a pole, run a pole, then walk two and run two, that's it in its simplest form but you get the picture. It improved my endurance levels no end. I would also force myself to face my other fears head on, things like searching out the highest crows nest in the wooded areas around where I lived and then I'd battle away pushing myself further up that tree, day after day, getting higher and ever higher up until I'd eventually reached my own personal summit. I couldn't swim then either but again I force myself to cross the local River Ayr barefoot. Initially where it was fairly shallow then I'd built up more and more courage or was that stupidity, who knows, forcing myself to venture out into much deeper areas where sometimes the water level would be almost up to my neck.

Danny continued this critique "And you **"Fly"** quite well." [Moves performed in the air usually above head height things like a **"Drop-Kick"** or **"Flying Head Scissors"** and other moves executed with the aid of or sometimes off the ring ropes] you'll do for me lad leave your phone number at the front desk and I'll be in touch. Dale Storm eh! I wish I'd thought of that one it sounds great. You're alright. Now off home with you, straight home mind and have a hot bath." "You'll be a bit tender in the morning but it'll clear in a couple of days" He was a lovely man I miss him a lot he started me off and he made me what I am today, I like to think if he were around today he would be proud of how I've turned out. He's been gone for quite some time now he died suddenly and his passing was unfortunate but he's not been forgotten. He was killed on the M6 Motorway in an accident during some fog, or so the papers said. He used to put himself on in last spot most nights, god love him, not that he insisted in being in the top of the bill slot far from it! It's just that he had a plan, Danny always had a plan. This meant he spent most of his time in such contests out of the ring and sometimes even under it.

Why always out of the ring?

You may well ask and this is priceless, true but at the same time priceless! He spent so much time under the ring apron during the contest because he was slowly and quietly dismantling the bolts holding the bloody thing together! Now that's got you flummoxed now, hasn't it?

That was so he could then strip-out what was left of it much quicker after the audience had left the hall, what a man. He loved that ring he built it himself I believe? It killed him in the end, it really did quite literally he was driving a Transit Van, as I remember it his was dark blue. Anyway on that fateful night as he was going home from Scotland to the Salford area he may well have had to hit the brakes rather suddenly, who really knows, it was really foggy apparently. Anyway the impact caused the ring to slide forward and it crushed him poor man, least ways that's what I was told. When I think of all the good workers he introduced into the business and to whom he gave an opening, a shot at the main chance so to speak, me included. This in turn afforded all of us the opportunity to earn a few bob and experience the wonderful sensation of the high octane adulation which could and would come your way provided you gave yourself over to fully entertaining those who paid the price of a ticket. And in so doing you fulfilled their dreams and their aspirations for you, their hero; all they asked in return was simply that you give them good value for their money! Thank you for everything Danny!

Clearly you miss your mentor.

You've really no idea just how much I miss that man!

Total mileage Ayr to Dundee and back: 266 Miles
Time taken for full journey: 5 Hours 16 Minutes

"The two men who started me off in the business"

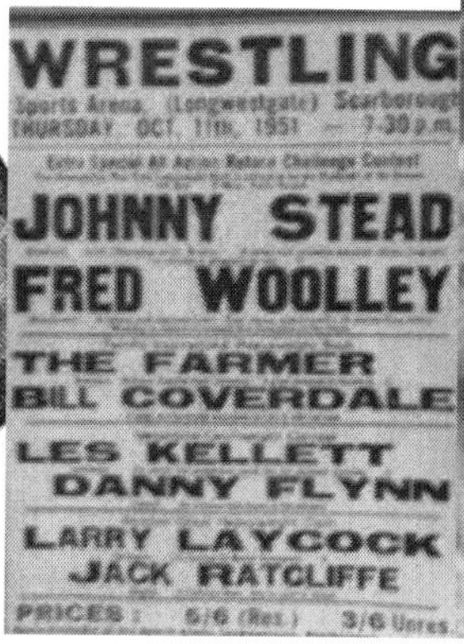

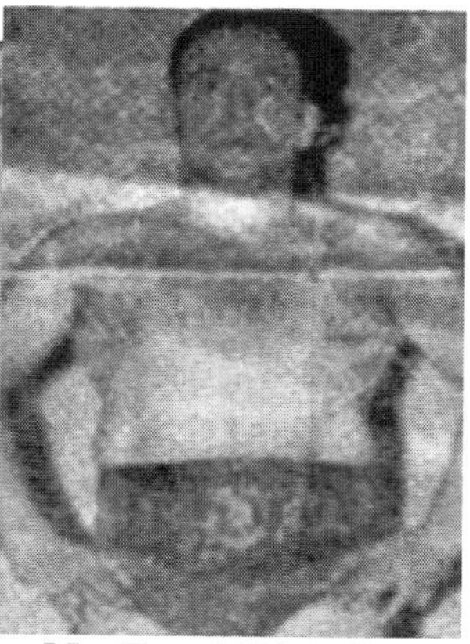

Mr Danny Flynn **Mr Fred Woolley**

An action shot from the late 1950's

Mick McMichael

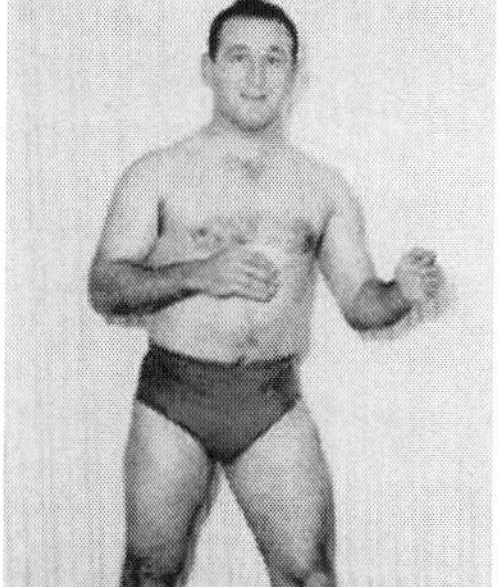

Melvin Riss

Jane St John [not related]

Ian St John

CHAPTER TEN

(Two Thirty Bloody Closing!)

Danny Flynn was one of the best. Turning his back momentarily Dale continues; sorry you'll need to excuse me for a minute seem to have something in my eye.

Are you OK?

Yes I'm fine, don't you worry about me.

So are you now going to show me what fell out onto the floor when you gave me the Magazine to read?

Well no it's really quite boring, honest.

That's ok, I'll take that chance let's have a look then?

God you're persistent! Well alright then if it'll shut you up. Taking what looked at first glance like a Tartan Tammy from his bag he holds it aloft; hanging from his outstretched hand it resembles a multi-coloured severed head. It's a Mask but it's just a work in progress, maybe the possibility of another persona. Even the likes of Clayton Thomson the clean cut Scott who is British Middleweight Champion has tried to go down another performance route, the business can get a little bit boring for some, especially if they've been at the top for so long as a hero! Although I'll have to concede and I'm fairly sure Clay would have to agree in the case of **"The Exorcist"** his masked alter ego creation hasn't really worked out for him. [Clayton Thomson left this world for hopefully a much better place in year 2010]

But I'm confident this little change of direction will work for me given time and it'll be another string to my bow, what do you think, do you like the pattern? What about the colours?

Ask him again ref!

Yes I do, very much.

Its good isn't it?

Its ok but I don't recognize the Tartan.

Why not it's The Wallace! What else would it be, remember it been adopted by my home town. He [William Wallace] was and still is Scotland's greatest Patriot! His victory against the English at Stirling Bridge in September 1297 gave us some hope for a better life a dream that Scotland might finally get its own identity back. Even your namesake Robert Burns during his lifetime wrote more than one poem which contained a reference to the Big Man now how does that go again? Standing up Dale starts to sing out a few lines from one of The Bard's more rousing songs: Scots Wa Hae Wi Wallace Bled! Scots, wham Bruce has aften led, Welcome tae yer Gory Bed, or to Victorie.

God that's truly stirring stuff! Mournful but stirring also!

Oh yes its stirring, if you say so! So what character name will you be using then?

That's easy **The Tartan Terror!** Not to be confused with the original tartan terrier description as that handle belongs to hard man Scot Chic Purvey. [Chic Purvey popped his mortal coil in November 1996] Apart from the Scottish headgear I was thinking the same in a vest and tartan tights as well. No don't laugh. So you don't like the idea?

Wearing all that check you might be in danger of looking about as cuddly as Supergran's wee daft Scottie Dug!

Point made but I think you're wrong, she didn't have a dog. Maybe I should tell you about the Rothesay Pavilion days?

Is it a Doggy story? I love them and the smaller the better.

Ask him again ref!

No! Let's save that story for later, this one isn't about one of our canine friends, although we did encounter a couple one night but all will be revealed later. Here's a better story it's Oban in the sixties, now that was an experience. Me and Sammy Taylor he's a great wee wrestler and his ring name is Jeff Bradley, we'd headed up there with a ring for a **"Spartan Promotions"** show they'd taken over from Mr Flynn and kept some of his venues going immediately after his fatal accident. Brian Dixon used to promote some stuff up that way as well at one time, he's still going strong but now his set-up is mostly in England only. He's a nice chap and a good payer but for some strange reason his move into the Scottish Halls didn't seem to last too long. Maybe I'll tell you more about the reason for that a little later on?

So we've arrive at the "Corran Hall" in the afternoon, we got the gear carried in and we got everything set up no problem. Then we're somewhat bored, I can see by the look on your face you're thinking pub, well you're wrong although that did cross our minds but it was Two Thirty Closing so sadly no booze. Then Sam spied it. Sitting in the corner of the stage was a microphone on a chrome stand. The Jeff Bradley fellow is a really good guitar player and he could sing a bit as well so we set about getting it fixed up and connected to the powered. In no time at all we were going great guns, we were half way through our third song "You'll never walk alone" when right out of the blue we start to develop an audience.

But you were bound to, were you not?

Well you may be right after all we were really good! Then the Chef and some of the kitchen staff from the Cafe', sorry the restaurant next door started to pile in, it was all part of the same complex at the time and they just appeared as if by magic. Then we got some interest from some other folks who were just walking passed they'd heard the music and wondered in out of the wet weather. It's a nice wee scenic place Oban but if it rains forget it, you're knackered.

Were they wet?

Yes just a little, why?

Soaked and obviously as bored as you were!

You're right, well spotted, that's amazing as I said not a lot to do in Oban!

Probably Liverpool supporters, up there on holiday?

Finally a woman who knows a bit about football anthems, no I'm only kidding. Yes they could have been Scousers but then again they might have been Weegees [People from the city of Glasgow] staying in the area for the "Fair Holiday" period.

Ah yes but they needed to have been Celtic supporters.

I was right you do know your anthems. So Sammy is now standing on a chair in the middle of the stage conducting them and they're all singing along, we're all having a great time, who needs the bloody Proms mate? Then, all was brought to sudden stop by a daft looking Jobs-worth in a pin stripped Montague (Monty) Burton Suit [A popular High Street Taylor back in the day] and it didn't even fit him properly, he arrives and cheeky bastard, he switches off the PA and then he orders us all out on to the street! Well everybody except the Chef and the kitchen staff they were dispatched back to preparing the High Teas in the kitchen! As for us and the tourists we were then unceremoniously frog marched out of the premises and the doors were locked behind us! So we walked the streets, round and round we went occasionally meeting up with the selfsame holidaymakers coming the other way on the opposite side of the street. One time they'd call over to us and another time we'd shout over to them and that's how we came to know, first hand that there's not a lot to do or see in Oban. Wee Sammy was well Bealing! [A Scots slang word meaning none to happy] He wasn't used to some dumpling, which in this case means a moronic jobs-worth cutting him off in mid soccer song and he's never been interested in football, anyway come to think of it he isn't even a Catholic! He was very non-religious in fact he had no interest in any kind of sport except for wrestling. He lived for far more important things like woman and maybe he'd gotten his priorities right? Who knows?

I remember taking him to see the Scotland verses Brazil game about ten or eleven years ago at Hampden Park in Glasgow the date has stayed with me all this time Saturday June 30th 1973! Well we were playing the best team in the world so you're bound to remember it, don't you think so? We left at halftime and we got beat One to Zero! A bloody own goal scored by Derek Johnston he was a Glasgow Rangers player at the time and yes you guessed it.

You were bored? Yet again!

Well mostly Sammy but still the National Football Team hasn't really changed much over the years and seldom have they been as good a squad as those guys were. So to recap, that was us out on our arses on the Oban streets with no pub to go to and now we were really, really bored.

Thank God the show went well enough later on although that too had its down side I was on with a guy called **"Murphy the Surfy"** [Brian] he had a bit of an Australian come California Beach Boy theme going on and he looked really good. He was fairly new to the business but he had the ability to go a whole lot further, he was a tough lad and definitely nobody's pushover but as George Bernard Shaw once said "Youth is wasted on the Young" in other words like a lot of the less experienced lads of that period he was impatient and impetuous. Anyway he gets himself **"Sent Out"** [Disqualified] and all before the end of the first round! Was it a misunderstanding by the referee as to the script perhaps? Well that's what I'd like to say but that wouldn't be true. God was he really **"Stiff"** on the night [A term meaning he was all over the place when taking hold. Going off script, not paying attention and not really selling it as a story] I've never really found out why he'd totally ignored most of the instructions I'd given him before we'd gone into the ring that night but he was pulled and all on my orders! We'd had a few contests prior to that night and he'd always been spot on. When next we were all due to meet up in the gym a few nights later Brian was a no show, it was then pointed out to me that maybe he had taken umbrage at something which had been said in the follow-on car in which he'd been a passenger on the trip up to Oban. Apparently only minutes after we'd set off again having stopped off to enjoy the hospitality of a small home-bake tearoom in the village of Tyndrum. [Whilst there we'd feasted on a large plate of their delicious, hot, homemade scones with both locally produced cream and some bramble jam on the side, plus the usual assortment of teas and coffees] The convoy had only travelled on but a couple of miles when Murphy made an innocent comment on seeing some traditional Highland Cattle in a field. Apparently he was viewing them live for the very first time ever "Maybe it's from those cows the shop owner got the milk for that delicious cream?" Mistakenly he'd referred to them as Highland Cows not realising and I might add it's a common mistake, that the herd were actually all Highland Bulls! This fact was then immediately seized upon by one of the others in his usual zany "Monty Python" like manner when he stated that any cream made from the fluid from their one single bovine teat wouldn't be the best thing to have spread on your scone! When he'd been asked for a more in-depth breakdown by the innocent Murphy the rather short and only answer he got was; "Ask Dale the next time you see him!" You had to be there I suppose to appreciate the moment presumably? It can get a little boring sitting travelling for mile after mile in a car and sometimes a simple game of “I Spy” doesn’t quite cut it! Some guys like to throw a spanner into the mix just to get a reaction and to break the monotony. One of the best ever “Jokers” is Mick McMichael you have to have your wits about you when he’s on form. The Surfy never mentioned the subject to me either before or indeed during our extremely short bout but his focus was clearly somewhere else that night in the ring and it was an avoidable disaster!

But surely he wouldn’t have been fixated on cream?

Well you’d like to think he’d have been focused on the show but who knows he could be more than a little sensitive. I’d worn two hats on that trip one as a wrestler and one as the promoter and if I’m honest regards the latter on the night in question I got it completely wrong. Brian like me had, had a long day and we were all stressed from the hectic travelling schedule of that whole busy week. It was the height of the summer and we’d done a few shows already and he’d had the added pressure of having to finish a work-shift in a factory before getting into the car on that particular day as well. Maybe he was having one of those nights and I just couldn’t see it, we’ve all had them and sometimes the harder you try the worse you get. Sadly he didn’t get used much on the Spartan Promotions Shows for a time thereafter. Once again that was a bad mistake on my part and it was something I should have sorted but didn’t. Brian was clearly distracted that night for whatever reason and the real cause may well have been revealed only a short time later when he announced he was leaving Scotland. It turned out he was moving to Canada and he planned to settle in the city of Toronto. The lead-up and the decision had clearly been weighing heavily on his mind in the intervening weeks, as it would mine. I’ve not heard from him since but you never know maybe he made the big time and the big money in the land of the

Maple Leaf? Maybe he hooked up with "Mr Stu Hart" or some other front line promoter I certainly hope so, although for my part in what happened that night in Argyllshire I most certainly still owe him a long overdue apology. Canada became a familiar escape root for others who hailed from both sides of Hadrian's Wall and from there some moved south into the USA. One or two made it really big in the WWF but how they ever managed that given their purely self-promotion and self-interest agenda I'll never know. Although marrying into the right family circle can definitely help boost your career prospects I suppose?

I must confess I'm disappointed, if as you've indicated you're the consummate pro you should have made sure both he and you got back in there later to finish off the a match properly. That way you've been giving the paying public a chance to get their monies worth! Why didn't you?

Obviously that's what I should have done but I didn't and in not doing so I let both myself, the punters and of course Brian down as well! It's most probably never an excuse but I'd been on the road since 6am that morning and I still had the ring to dismantle after the show and it was 10pm closing for pubs back then, what a bummer! My day didn't end till around 4am the next morning but it did teach me yet another lesson and I've never repeated that mistaken since and yes you're right it should never have happened!
Having spent summer seasons in Oban it isn't hard to see why that builder guy McCaig abandoned that big stupid posh house like monstrosity, boredom probably played its part and the non availability of a thirst quenching pint no doubt! ["McCaig's Folly" sits on the hill above the town the structure is unfinished even after all these years] My one endearing memory of Oban was travelling through the quiet streets at night whilst banks of street lights switched themselves off like a scene from a Stephen King horror movie as wee drove past, one section at a time, one after another. It's almost as if they were saying. By! By! You all

don't haste ye back and don't give us a song before ye go. Obviously like the locals they were Camanachd Cup Supporters. [Shinty's national Knock-out Competition] Not really Wrestling fans, now that's a really tough sport that Shinty all those big brawny Highland men hurtling those big heavy sticks around it's a wonder there isn't even more injuries. Good God, try saying all that with a drink in you, but not in our case because the pubs were always bloody shut! Those lights must have been on a timer or something because when we'd reached the A85 and on looking back the place was completely dark, posted missing so to speak! Obviously that must be where Hollywood got its inspiration for the "Brigadoon" film. Maybe it would have been better if Oban only appeared out of the mist every hundred years as well? Rothesay on the other hand was a completely different place we worked the Pavilion there. I remember The Manager was a chap called Dougie he was a lovely man, very helpful and a real gentleman.

Dougie! How quaint.

Well if you really think about it he lived in an Island town on the Clyde Coast so what else would he be called but Dougie [A reference to the works of the Scots writer Neil Munro who created the local Puffer Boat character of Para Handy] Dale decides to do an impression of the Para Handy character. "Well now when are we going to have any power out of this wee Puffer? Today would be good! No, no, man I didn't go upsetting McPhail our engineer intentionally by what I said, but Dougie man it can't be my fault if he took it the wrong way. The man can be a great lumbering imbecile sometimes he's even more stupid than that Sunny Jim the cabin boy, but he's got a really good excuse because he's really young and he is really quite stupid! But he's very nice with it as well." Every Wednesday we'd travel over to Bute from Wemyss Bay, we'd leave the cars in the park area there. We used the regular Caledonian Ferry boat usually in the afternoon around 4-30 and when we disembarked we'd toss a coin to see who was meeting up in Zavaroni's Café. Actually it was really into next door where we were heading into the Fish Restaurant and we couldn't all be seen to be sitting together in the same restaurant eating at the same time. It's really not professional and it creates a bad impression.

And why not, may I ask?

Quite simply because later on that night we'd be knocking seven bells out of each other! They make a really good tuck-in and it's owned by Victor and Hilda their wee lassie Lena won that TV Show "OPPORTUNITY KNOCKS" last year she was voted into first place a few times then she had that song in The Hit Parade! She's a smashing wee Chanter. "Ma He's making Eyes at me!" was a big hit for her it reached the Top Ten. [Lena was born on 4th November 1963 in Rothesay Scotland she died in September 1999 in Cardiff Wales. Whilst at stage school she developed the illness known as "anorexia nervosa" and her weight dropped to 56lbs. (4 Stone 25 kg). Some years later having enjoyed a successful show business career and after a fairly routine operation, only three weeks later she developed a serious chest infection she died from pneumonia and complications she weighed a mere 70lbs. She was aged 36 years] Dale attempts to do a Hughie Green impression. "Thank you very much, we really mean that sincerely folks." We always hoped it would rain a few hours before show start time, that would usually guarantee a good crowd and with a bit of luck a small bonus in your hand. There's nothing like the "Heavens Opening" to panic the holidaymakers into buying a wrestling show ticket!

Isn't that what the Americans call A Rain Check? Or is that when you get rained off? Just a thought!

Yes I believe the latter to be correct. If it was a sunny day that was bad news all round for us and that's when Mr.

Flynn would have us all in the back of a car, sometimes two cars! With the windows rolled down peering out like pigs looking over a Midden Dyke! [Scottish slang for a Pig Pen Wall] Whilst he leaned out of the driver's side verbally advertising the show through a big blue and white hand held Megaphone! He did all that and drove at the same time, one handed, I doubt you'd get away with doing things like that nowadays eh, and he never missed a beat. He had every trick in the book the punters had no chance when he was on a roll. Personally I found it a wee bit stupid and embarrassing most of the time but what did I know? Besides it all helped to guarantee my wages which I'm glad to say had gone up a little since that very first night down on the Ayrshire Coast. [My Guardian Angel, neighbour and good friend Wee Sammy Taylor left us in 1996. As part of his cabaret set he used to sing the Kris Kristofferson written classic "Help me make it through the night" and very good at it he always was too. So go safely through that night good buddy. RIP "My Star-man" Mr Jeff Bradley]

Total mileage Ayr and Perth and back: 222.63Miles
Time taken for the full journey: 4 Hours 8 Minutes

Mike Marino   Clayton Thomson   Wild Angus

CHAPTER ELEVEN

(I'm moving up in the World!)

I was now on six quid a night plus my "Petrol Money" and I was now driving my own wee car as well. I'd passed my test and I needed to get one to allow me to get to a lot more gigs. It was far from new and it had a lot of miles on the clock but it started first time, every time. Mainly due to the brand new battery I had to buy but it got me there and it got me back home again safely and what's more it was all mine bought and paid for and it cost me the princely sum of £25. I'd purchased an old Austin A30 from a neighbour of my older brothers it was coloured Post Office Pillar Box Red quite literally. It was a genuine one off the reason being it had been hand painted with authentic Post Box Red Paint by someone who delivered our letters! My career was on the up, all through those summer months I was making regular appearances all over the place

Monday: The Picture House Girvan

Tuesday: The Corn Exchange Haddington

Wednesday: The Pavilion Rothesay (Ferry Boat to Bute)

Thursday: The Centre Aviemore.

Friday: Town Hall Musselburgh

Later on the Musselburgh job moved to the Brunton Hall in the same East Coast town. Sometimes we went a lot further south and that usually meant going down to Stranraer, my best recollections are that shows there were staged originally in the local picture house.

For the Winter Tour we cut out Aviemore. Anyway, given the onset of Christmas and the Festive Season the local folks were only really interested in Santa and they had a real live one and he looked just like The Real McCoy. Proper long white curly hair and a long bushy white beard, he looked quite fantastic. He resembled the guy in the Coco-Cola adverts [Although as we all know he wears what's now become the traditional look of a bright Red Suit and all the White trimmings. With the passage of time we've all lost sight of the fact the original Continental Father Christmas traditionally wore a green costume]

So the sometimes very difficult place to get to the regularly snow covered Aviemore Highland Centre was replaced by Stirling's atmospheric Albert Hall. Occasionally we'd even do The Music Hall in Aberdeen, if the weather permitted. I really liked The Granite City, great crack, good company and lots of good old Malt Whisky! Although it was a long, long drive and the roads were not very good back then.

Fit Like? Aye Nay Bad! [The local Aberdeen Doric dialect meaning, hello, not bad how are you?] You'll be having a Wee Dram before you go? Many a good night was spent among the Loons and the Quines [More local dialect, meaning boys and girls] but sadly only really remembered through an alcoholic haze. Rothesay Shows apre's celebrations were more often than not exactly the same scenario.

So performance finished at the Pavilion it was off down the road to the Bute Arms. It's the Big Hotel you see straight in front of you when you first come off the Ferry. We had a pal speaking for us Big Gus and he never failed to get us served in the bar; he was a smashing guy he lived on the Island. He used to get us Special Local Privileges. It was still 10pm closing back then unless you were a resident which more often than not we were. Wink! Wink! Nudge! Nudge! No what I mean? He was one of the regular Ring Seconds and he'd done that job for years but the best bit was still to come. You'll like this so get it down on the page.

Ask him again ref!

The journey back to the mainland, remember we're on an island and there's no Caledonian Ferry's after 09-30pm.

So you all stayed over?

We'd no chance of that happening Danny was a good guy but it would have been far too expensive, he stayed over but bear in mind he had to dismantle the ring the next morning and store it away down stairs in the Pavilion's storeroom, It stayed there all year round, besides he had to make sure Nancy got a good nights sleep. Just the mention of a small boat in the dark on the busy Clyde estuary turned her a sickly shade of green.

Don't you think she could have been making all that up?

What makes you say that? Anyway she's a female and I'm a male, I'm not programmed to be able to understand how a woman's mind operates, now am I? Besides if that's what Mr Flynn wanted to do with his money then that was up to him that was his business it was no skin off my nose!

Maybe she was just taking the piss?

That's a crude way to put it and that's not the kind of language I expect to hear from the likes of your good self. Could you speak up please my hearings gone again! Anyway the rest of us needed to get back to the mainland to pick up our cars, just like me they had to get back home, remember I'd got my daytime fulltime job in the morning!

So you still had a real job as well?

Eh Hello! I was an engineer to trade, time served man me. I was a green card holder in the AUEW by that point. [The Amalgamated Union of Engineering Workers] I'm not on the tools now, I haven't been for years but back then by that point in time I had a new mortgage and a new young wife and eighteen months later a wee baby girl to support. So, a little the merrier from the good company and good ale I followed everyone else down to the Pier and there we all waited patiently for the man “Himself” to appear.

And who's this “Himself” character?

Why The Captain of course the Master of the vessel, the man who takes the letters over to the mainland in his Wee Bit Boaty faithfully in all kinds of weather almost each night.

Sounds like it was quite small, did it have a sail?

No it was a proper size Coastal Fishing Boat well a small inshore trawler to be precise and it caught real fish, you could tell that the instant you boarded her. It was the pong that gave it away. Trawler by day and it doubled up as one of the Royal Mail's finest ships of the line each night casting off just after Midnight and as far as we were concerned it was the Clyde Coast's answer to Cinderella's coach only no pumpkin and definitely no white mice!

And no glass slipper either?

No just the stale smell of the odd week old fish parts or maybe it was the crew’s Wellington Boots festooned all over the floor in the below decks living area? The only reference to something that glinted in the moon's glow in this tall tail was the cans and the bottles in our Carry-Out. I think it was the second week of the season and I’d been on with Fred Woolley, he was all go and he liked the public to get their monies worth so I was a little tired and I was aching all over, he was a good guy but he could be quite **“Strong”** when in the ring if he wanted to make his point.
It was a beautiful summers’ night and as I recall we were sitting all in a row on the ground at the quayside, a warehouse wall was acting as a welcome back support. Anyway I was just about to doze off when suddenly I was

aware of a bit of a commotion at the start of the line of off duty grapplers. Apparently some drunk had come around the corner and on encountering the array of outstretched legs in front of him, he immediately started kicking out at them but rather unfortunately for him the closest to his flying feet was Freddie. He was up and into action quick a flash catching the off guard drunk with a cracker of a right hook. Bang! Right on the chin! This sent the overly aggressive reveller flying off the harbour wall and into the water below! Shit! I thought to myself he'll drown! [Shades of the overused Taggart TV detective phrase resonated!]

.. "There's been a Murder!"

Luckily for everyone present the tide was out and he landed in around a foot of cold salty water and almost the same depth of shit and mudded harbour silt below that. He sobered up instantaneously and it really was quite funny watching him wadding through the mucky crap making his way to the far wall where a metal ladder hung fixed into the stone work, climbing the rungs a little rather unsteady eventually he got himself back up onto Terra Firma.

So the envelope the Gaffer [Danny] had given me duly handed over to the Captain we were all safely on board and off we went in the direction of the mainland. Simple! The whole process was nearly as easy most nights but it was a whole lot bloody scarier when it was fogy! All you could see then was a murky, black, nothingness and all you could hear was the sound of those bloody big ocean going ships and their big fog horns as they steamed up and down the busy sea lane with their radar in operation. Now you might be thinking that's ok with its electronics it can see everything in the dark, but remember this we're talking about a main shipping lane here and big ships can't see a wee wooden fishing boat like ours even with their technology so that was a concern to those of us in the know. Not to mention the other all too real and potential life threatening problem namely those Big Nasty Nuclear

Submarines enroot to and from the Holly Loch and the Faslane Base. Whether they were running on the surface or just below the waterline they could be very dangerous! Wee Tam Stevenson and I do mean wee! He just loved it he would stand at the pointed end pretending he was Thor the Norse worrier and whilst there he'd batter out the sound of an imaginary horn just like in the movie with Tony Curtis and Kirk Douglas! [The Vikings] You could hear him a bloody mile away doing his loud German Composer, Stuff! Da, Da, Da, Da, Da! Da, Da, Da, Da! Da, Da, Da, Da, Da! Humming along the reporter gets into the sprit.

Da, Da, Da, Da, Da! Catchy isn't it?

You get the picture now? Do I detect an air of recognition?

*It's the Ride of the Valkyries by compos*er *Richard Wagner.*

It got even louder when that other nut case Teddy Bear Taylor joined in who needs a Fog Horn!
A few weeks later The Teddy Boy buggered off to Canada as well, he's another one who's very probably making a fortune now as well, topping bills all over the place I should imagine, maybe even at The Calgary Stampede? And under some other Transatlantic name no doubt. Wee Tam is appearing here next week you should come down and see him. He's fast and really clever he may be a Lightweight but he's as tough as old boots! He's Glasgow born originally and works under the name **"Scott Thomson."** You'd be surprised whom I've travelled with on that crossing; one night we were accompanied by "The Corries Duo" (Roy Williamson and Ronny Browne) and on another trip we shared the deck with two champion greyhounds. That'll be the doggy story you asked for earlier? Perhaps I should point out at this juncture that the two lady dogs had absolutely no connection to those two talented providers of Scotland's best ever commercially successful Dirge **"**Flower of Scotland**"** The Cup winning

pooches were accompanied by their owner but he was so drunk it proved impossible to ascertain his name. Still we did get a modicum of entertainment watching him trying to keep his sea legs when we got out into what he clearly expected would be a swell. Given the fact it was a flat calm all the way I found his antics and his complete lack of any balance to be very strange during our voyage on that mirror like sea on a rather balmy summers evening. I'm honoured to say both Wee Sammy and I sat at the stern of the vessel behind the wheel house and sang a few old Scots songs with the famous totally unpretentious folk duo.

Another time we shared the crew's cabin with four very fat, actually well overweight and definitely over the hill working prostitutes. They were pig sick, nothing to do with the roll of the ship I might ad it turned out they got their day time ferries mixed up and they'd thought they were going over to Dunoon to partake of the lots of dollar bills on the Yankee Base. The Americans have had a base there for years now but instead they'd got on the wrong one and disembarked onto the island of Bute where they'd all made only very meagre earning. I'm tempted at this point to add that little episode also contained what some might have said were some more dogs but I'm for to much of a gentleman to make such an assertion! Therefore they had no chance of making up the shortfall from us lot. Anyway most of the islands population only earned a real wage in the summer so they had no spare tango and cash to invest in a ten minute frolic with the two legged equivalent of Glasgow's famous Clyde Tunnel. Life has a habit of biting you in the arse sometimes and I've no doubt they'd probably have been quite happy to sink their Wallys into your arse and most likely anything else you dared to uncover and they would probably have charged you more than a couple of pounds for the privilege. Needles to say its bit of a bitch if you get caught up with the wrong crew on the wrong boat; just ask Peter Pan, Wendy her siblings and all those little Lost Boys!

By the middle of my second season when I was promoting that venue for myself it had already become a bit of a hit or miss earner. Sadly the Clyde Coast and in fact just about everywhere else in Britain had also run out of holidaymakers by then. The punters had nearly all buggered off to Spain's "Costa Del Sol" for some Sun, Sea and Sangria! Dale treats the reporter to a few short lines from the tourist hit from 1974. “Oh this year we’re off to sunny Spain Y Viva Espana! We’re catching the Costa Brava plane Y Viva Espana!” God I was getting carried away just then it fair takes it out of you that singing lark. I think I'd better stick to my own game. No, no, don't write that down about me promoting over there on Bute. I only got away with it because it was in the middle of nowhere! As far as Joint Promotions were concerned neither the venue nor me were any real threat to their core business or their Empire Building Policies. After all was said and done unfortunately I didn't really make any real money out of it but it gave all the young lads in the gym a chance and a place to perform. The bloody Tax Man didn’t see it that way though and their local inspector clown must have spent a good few bob trying to get blood out of a stone. My blood! He gave up eventually. I’d like to say I’d enjoyed the thrill of the chase but I didn’t as their policy is always to estimate what you owe them and they set a figure way higher than anything you could have made realistically, then the onus is on you to disprove his crazy total! I could have taken the easy way out and dobbed in all the lads I’d paid but that’s not the way I do things! So I bit the bullet and sent the Inland Revenue a Cheque. The Nasty Wee Buggers!

One night coming back over from Bute it was a bit rough and the boat was really heaving a lot, so when we got over to Wemyss Bay side getting off it and on to the wooden pier was proving difficult, and getting hold of and then managing to climb up what was left of the rusty old metal ladder on the side of the wooded jetty was quite frankly a nightmare. Anyway first up was “Johnny Powers” when he got to top he shouted down he'd have a look for something to attach onto the other bags eventually he came back with a length of old rope but we were not to know at that point it was rotten inside, a consequence of all that sea salt over the years. The first few bags attached included my own, they got about eight feet up in the air and the rope gave way. Splash! The bags went tumbling down on top of us and one went into the cold salty brine! Yes it was mine! To this day I've still no idea why I shouted out that there was £100 quid in because it was most certainly not true, even the bag itself although it gave the outward appearance of being made from a good quality leather in fact it had been purchased from a Bum Boat [A term used in the 50's 60's and 70's to describe the small boats full of local inferior quality goods made for sale to the tourists] in the Suez Canal era. So it was more likely to be made of Camel or goat hide and not very well cured. The content consisted of my ring gown, two towels, two pairs of trunks, one pair used in the ring that night and a spray can of cheap "Smelly." [Personal deodorant] an essential part of ring equipment, my spare ring socks, some odds and sods and my Lonsdale of London purchased, black lace-up leather wrestling boots!

....**Definitely no money!**

Truth is I'd lost money that night in fact I'd "Done my Bollocks" and it had been an unusually "Big Loss Night!" I'd made some excuse to the lads that I'd been paid by cheque so I'd need to pay them out in the morning. The next thing I know Mr Powers dives headlong into the sea off the Pier! A perfect bloody 10 Pointer! Then he swims over and grabs the bag and then to his dismay he then realizes he can't use the ladder again as it's far too short and the sea is now getting even rougher. There's the boats propeller to worry about as well plus he's getting just a whole lot colder. If you're not on the boat you can't get the height to grab the ladder and he was obviously not on the boat and therefore he couldn't get to the ladder! Stupidly and I can fully understand his anxiety he then tried to climb up one of the wooden supports and immediately his lower legs are ripped to bits on the spiky crustaceans which had attached themselves there over the intervening years. Best "Claret Job" I've ever seen, blood and lots of it everywhere! Eventually we all got off the boat and semi sorted! I took a detour and stopped off further down the road to take him to a Casualty Department in Irvine's "Ayrshire Central Hospital" I'm glad to say he made a full recovery but my "Sea Water" drenched gear was quite another matter. It took me two days of immersing it in clean fresh water, then another week to dry it out properly especially the multi stitched leather sole grappling boots. The only good thing to come out from all of that is the Tax Man's been quiet ever since! So fingers crossed!

Why did you bother with all the hassle and no real profit?

Well it was one of my mentor's favourite venues in Scotland and I didn't want someone who didn't share his love for the Island coming in and taking over, that would have been a great disappointment to me if anything like that had happened. A really big disappointment! There's another story right there and if I get the chance I'll fill you in on that one later but then again I've gathered a lot more than just a few stories in the intervening years there was one good thing though Miss Selina Scott! You know that rather good-looking reporter girl off the box, she does the top celebrity interviews and stuff like that.

Who Selina Scott the Journalist?

Yes her! Tall slim, long legs, great figure the "Hot Lips Hooleghan" of the small screen news programmes. Well she worked for "The Rothesay Tourist Association" in the wee office on the Pier that's whom I arranged to hire the Pavilion from, so I suppose you could say technically she worked for me in a manner of speaking. Not bad for a miner's son Aye! Actually it was mostly her direct boss I dealt with he was a lovely character called Mr John Dougid he was well into his sixties when I approached him about taking over and without his help and his contacts well things might never have gotten off the drawing board for me and that's where the Woman who really wasn't a proper Woman comes in.

As I said before that could be an attention grabbing headline, something the Sunday's would probably die for!

Even if they'd offered me a fortune there's no way that's going to happen I love this business far too much, besides it's been really good to me over the years in the main, but I will tell you and only you mind, all about one particular aspect of a series of bouts I arranged and promoted for a few years and I think you may find it very, very interesting.

The mileage Ayr to Dunoon and back: + Ferry 98 Miles
Time taken including Ferry Journey: 4 Hours approx

(Courtesy of Mr Jim Lee)

Billy "Bull" Wilson applies a backbreaker
(I was recently informed Billy may have died some years back?)

CHAPTER TWELVE

(The Woman who never was a Female!)

Back in the day it was all about saving money for some promoters and things were no different on the circuits I was regularly associated with and in which I promoted as well. However one basic difference was always apparent; by keeping their expenses, wages and petrol money payouts etc down to a minimum those operators I'm referring too maximised their profits and that was their only concern. At least that seemed to be the Zeitgeist with some of my Gaffers. That disbelieving look you got from the odd tight-arse when you stated your genuine out of pocket fuel costs could be really hurtful, a bit of an insult to your intelligence really and an obvious question-mark against your honesty. Some of my contemporaries may have been guilty on occasion of trying it on but I wasn't one of them. Unlike me when they [Those particular promoters] put a show together their thought process was seldom if ever about, if I can fill a car and save on fuel then think how much more I could have to then pay out a little extra on the performers wages? That was always my priority and my philosophy and in return my lads always gave me their all, every time!

Female wrestlers were initially used extensively as just another tool to maximise bums on seats but over the years they'd taken off and now everyone was using them. Well on the Indie side they are, but it's still a definite no, no, on Joints shows regards them working in the ring at least. It may have been the tight bums and bouncy tits attraction with some but that was never the primary motivator on Danny's Flynn's Shows. Some including me would argue he was always well ahead of the next big thing, he was truly a trendsetter, a showman and as such he was always well ahead and in fact he helped create the next fad in many instances. He could see both the business opportunity and also the breakthrough that could be achieve for woman in the sport in general and in most cases long before they themselves took up that challenge. I made up my mind early on that this type of ethos was always, investment permitting, going to be the driving force with anything I produced and not just where the ladies were concerned. In Scotland wrestling ladies who were both native and based here in Scotia were like hens teeth. In other words they were almost non existent at that time!

So what did you do?

As a stop gap I enlisted the help of a wonderful lady who from this moment on we'll only be referring to by her ring name. Her billing was **"Miss Diamond Lil."** What started out as a stopgap and an afterthought was actually a bit of a revelation in the end, an Epiphany if you will. She was brilliant and let me tell you given the fact she learned her trade in my gym working with the men she could "Shoot" with the best of them. Her father had served his time as a Blacksmith and like him she too stood around Five Foot Two inches tall in her stocking feet, and again just like him she was as strong as an Ox. You wouldn't have wanted to be falling out with her especially when she was younger. She was all power and she had a right hook like Sonny Liston. [He was the most feared boxer in the world at one time but "Cassius Clay" as he was named originally finally ended his reign of terror] In fact she still has! Her father could lift a solid steal Anvil off the ground with one arm.

Anyway, now I had one and a very good one at that, but I needed another one to make up a sellable bout and that's where my good old pal "Romeo" Joe Critchley and his expertise came in very handy. As well as working on my shows Joe and his wife Helen used to come up to holiday with me and my folks. So over a cup of tea one day he didn't drink alcohol by then, and in a quiet moment he leans over and says in a really thick Wigan Lancashire accent. "If you can't find another girl I'll fill in for you for while if you like" and he did just that. He donned a wig and we were off, He was so good at it nobody sussed. Even although I thought Danny always had all the angles covered. I'd have to concede Joe was equally resourceful but then again he too came from the same working class background and like all my family he had at one point worked down the Coal Mines for a period. He'd also had a stint as a Chip Shop owner on Gidlow Lane Wigan if my memory serves me correctly? There was nothing he didn't know about the secret and the art of the real, properly prepared, perfectly fried, potato slice. Many a café or chip shop owner got short shift when we stopped off during a long and tiring journey to sample their pommes frites. Many were less than pleased when he could tell them the cheap and nasty shortcuts they'd all employed in their lack of a preparation process just to maximise their profits.

I've already said several times now I wouldn't be here if it wasn't for Danny Flynn and also his faithful side kick Mr Fred Woolley and that's most certainly true but after Danny left us only a few short years later when we first met up the chemistry between Joe and yours truly was very similar.

As it was a given Joe would have to return home to Lancashire at sometime the "Houston we have a problem!" syndrome was now ongoing but again before he left he had it all figured out and he had it all sorted. Taking me aside again he availed me of his simple but at the same time quite masterful plan of action. We had both been attending a training night at the village gym when he hatched a really cunning plot. Indicating to me to study what was going on in the ring he retorted. "That young blonde headed lad there, the athletic one, him in the blue trunks" he asked. What young Harry says I? "Harry yes he'll be fine" he replied. "Put him in an all-in-one add a padded bra but not too much stuffing mind, plus a decorative "Thermos Flask" and advertise him, sorry her as some Masked Female European Villain!" And that's exactly what I did and young

Mr H. began appearing regularly as not only his Drop Kidding, High Flying lightweight male self but he also worked regularly and successfully as a nasty European rule bending female for a number of years after that as well, and once again nobody sussed! Strangely he was equally at home and equally brilliant in both guises and in both genders. He was one of the best Scots Lightweights.

As for Mr "Nice Guy" Joe Critchley; did you know he once went into the ring to fill time when a second car of performers had been delayed getting to the venue. So undaunted he climbed in through the ropes on his own to appease a very unruly crowd who were getting more and more annoyed at the delay in starting the show. His wrestling opponent was of all people; now wait for it because you'll never guess not in a month of Sundays.

.................................It was "The Invisible Man!"

In other words the character of Peter Brady [He was the main character in the black and white TV series based on the famous H. G. Wells book] It was announced as an eight round two falls, two submissions or a knockout contest! He needed to fill time until the other car eventually got there and that turned out to be a lot of time to fill! Luckily the crowd warmed to his efforts and he deservedly he got a standing ovation at the end, oh and guess what? Remember Peter Brady the opponent the audience couldn't see well he beat Joe! The only guy who was actually in there lost by two falls to nothing vanquished by an opponent who was never there! That has to have been a truly memorable performance from a top class professional. What a Showman! [Joe Critchley my good friend left this world a far, far poorer place in 1992]

* This story was previously featured having been expertly penned by the former wrestler turned author Mr Eddie Rose in his excellently crafted e-book/paperback publication entitled **"Send in the Clowns"** If you've not yet

read it I wholeheartedly recommend you do. It's a great read and is undoubtedly one of the best books ever written about the inner workings of the British Professional Wrestling Scene. Joe was also as much of a good friend of Eddie's as he was a mentor to me. He [Joe] recounted this story to me round by round, blow by blow and fall by fall and given all the help and advice he gave me over the years I knew him, I felt it inappropriate not to mention it again in memory of a very dear friend.*

And Diamond Lil! What happened to her?

No sorry, you don't really need to know that do you?

Yes I do! Might be another story in there somewhere?

I think not she'd never be up for that not in a million years.

And why not may I ask?

Oh it's really not important.

It is to me! I'm afraid I must insist.

OK but this is definitely not for publication! She's going to murder me if she finds out! She accepted my proposal of marriage and she left the business and I'm forever grateful. She retired and we have two wonderful children together none of whom will be following us into the ring! Good god is that the time I'd better be getting a move on!

No hold on a minute. Tell me more about some of the other girls you've worked with!

There are a lot of them in the business now but as I've already said only the odd one or two when I became a travelling pugilist, so some I've only heard of by name or reputation. Over the piece I've only really seen work done first hand by the more established and the more experienced ones. But over the intervening years Britain has become outwardly more and more promiscuous and sex sells it's as simple as that. Now are you sure you want to go there?

Yes of course. Why not?

Are you really, really sure?

Why not? Germaine Greer's slant on all his has really stirred things up so let's hear what you've got to say! More skeletons in the cupboard, is it?

No not at all. I've always treated woman with the greatest of respect after all my dear mother is one and I've got a wife whom I love very much and a daughter as well so you could say I'm somewhat surrounded!

Total mileage Ayr to Troon and back: 16.4 Miles
Total time taken to complete the journey: 50Minutes

(Courtesy of Mr Jim Lee)

Ben "Thunderbird" Michael O'Hagan Barry Potter

CHAPTER TWELVE + 1

(Real Ladies)

Really "Good Workers" among the ladies mainly due to more interest and the introduction of better coaches now number quite a few who appear regularly on the circuit. Many have very quickly become part of the mainstream fabric of the business and almost all have now earned their rightful place in its colourful and continuing history. In other chapters I've already talked at some length about the established First Wave Stars [For the purpose of this book that period includes the decade of the 1960's and the early 1970's] who ably represented British Woman's Wrestling in that era and who have now been joined by those from the Second Wave, although some of the originals are still to the fore like Mitzi [Pat] Mueller/Dixon but eldest Cassidy sibling and "The Naughty One" although formally Mitzi's nemesis Nancy Barton seems to have fallen off the radar completely as has both The Hell Cat of the Haggerty persuasion and also Anne Barton not to be confused with namesake Nancy. None of these have been seen in Scotland regularly for a while now! The Newer Kids on the Block who have entered the fray since then are headed up by the likes of Klondike Kate Mark 2, this persona first saw the light of day when it was adopted originally by Big Kath Cassidy who like all of her era have brought great credit to the female side of the business. Potential greatness adorned Kate [Jayne] when she first set out on her personal career journey and she's gone from strength to strength. She alone must be considered by most to be the present day top draw and only second top billing to Mitzi when she was in her prime. If you don't mind I'll fill you in on a lot more detail about her later. Not that far behind comes the likes of Paula Valdez, Lolita Loren [again Mark 2] Susan Sexton, Blackfoot [Linda] Sioux and of course my now favourite girl the classy buxom siren Diamond Lil! Although these were and are the top ground pullers others have also helped to swell the numbers appearing in halls on the UK mainland. There are of course others currently both teaching and working over the water in the North of The Emerald Isle as well, folks like 1980's late developer **"Miss Jackie McCann"** who combines both her good looks and her gutsy determination with a sharp intellect and her informed working knowledge of many traditional "Catch" moves. These skills combined with her more than a passing interest in the wider early history of the sport from its origins through to the one time very popular travelling fairground booths etc. Make her somewhat unique and had it not been for an advert seen by wrestling siblings Peter and Vic Stewart in Manchester's Evening News stating someone was looking for lady wrestlers, she may never have gotten started. The instigator of the advert turned out to be Harold Weller and she started training in his gym almost immediately under the banner of "Action Promotions" Her speciality move is the "Victory Roll!" Like a lot of moves of its type it can be a very dangerous to execute but she never puts a foot wrong. Going back to the 1960's Cowboy Jack Cassidy introduced his girl siblings into the business back then they're names in no particular order of character are; **"Patty McGoohan"** played by little Kath. **"Klondyke Kate"** [Mark 1] and **"Miss Hell Cat Haggetty"** played by big Katherine and Chris who wore the mantle of **"Miss Lolita Loren"** [A persona inherited from its original owner and regularly performed by Anne Barton before she took time-out to start a family. There can't be many wrestlers either male or female who've invented and then given up two successful personas like she did] There was another girl sibling in the Cassidy fold who dabbled but she didn't seem to fancy it much so her career was short lived. They were all smashing girls as far as I was concerned I first met "The Hell Cat" in the town of Haddington its not that far from here just along the A1 through Musselburgh heading for Dunbar but coming from around here you'll already know that I'm sure. It was during the autumn months of 1964 the venue was the "Corn

Exchange" she too was working for Danny Flynn at the time and I think her dad was on the same bill as well. In fact it's probably the case she got started in the business around the same time I did give or take a few months. Mitzi Muller due to her new found status and her early success was moving between shows for a few of the Indie organisations at the time, these included Danny's **"Cape Promotions"** and Jack Cassidy's own organisation in particular. She had a lot of pulling power and therefore I assume she could then negotiate more money from the highest bidder. Those gaps she vacated meant there was a ready made opportunity for the likes of Cowboy Jack's girls to grab a chance of a leg up so to speak. It also gave "The Hell Cat" and her other siblings the chance to develop further and learn a lot more from working with the likes of Mitzi's main nemesis the formidable and equally talented Miss Nancy. Barton

At that same time the former Jim Breaks Fan Club secretary who only a few short years later was to become the New Kid Block Powerhouse Indie Promoter "Mr Brian Dickson" was busily serving his time; Firstly as a ring second and later he turned his hand to refereeing and from there it was only one final short step to taking up the roll of silver tongued Master of Ceremonies. Brian's first show promoting under his own steam and his own banner was in October 1970. Reportedly it took place in Marple near Stockport in Cheshire. History has a way of bringing people together in a matrimonial sense in all walks of life and so it proved with these two youngsters also. They married just a few short years after she [Pat] first met up with Brian. Although I was not aware of any romance at the time and I suspect neither did most of the others who were working with them on a regular basis. Maybe she had designs on him all long? Before they got spliced they could be seen on the road together quite regularly. Maybe that's why she decided to work quite a lot of the time for Orig Williams, Brian had a tie-up there early on but it didn't seem to last.

They do however make a lovely couple. Brian as I've hinted at before was obviously on a mission and he certainly achieved his goal and correctly so unlike others who were not quite as successful he worked very hard at building up a network of contacts, eventually bringing over to his side of the fence some of the biggest stars in the business from Joints. Over to what they all at one time or another regarded as the "Dark Side" but it's important to bare in mind he had learned more and more about the business with every small step he took along the way from the bottom up whilst working for and with other established industry operators. There's nothing not to like about the man and even now he still maintains his little boy lost look and his undoubted charm. On a personal level perhaps my biggest regret regards Brian is that as he got bigger I got left behind somewhat but that was entirely my own choice. I had a young family at the time, a wee girl and a bouncing baby boy born in that order and as well as having those parental responsibilities I was also becoming more and more involved in the day to day running of my gym. I was also engaged in some promoting activities of my own but on a much smaller scale than this fast blossoming entrepreneur. Besides I was also trying to hold down a forty hour a week, fulltime day job as well. Not only was I in love with my healthy, young and beautiful wife I was in love with life itself. So I had no wish to be flying about up and down the English Motorway system stopping off when given instruction to do so at places like the "Tickled Trout Services" on the M6 and once there to wait around for passengers who would undoubtedly always turn up late again and again! This gave the opportunity to other Scots born guys to benefit from my absence and I'd be lying to myself if I didn't make the point their misdirected egos were far more developed than any real wresting ability they thought they had but sadly that was not entirely their fault!

Anyway as well as The Diamond Scotland was now producing the likes of **"Rusty Blair"** although she didn't come into this business through my now busy stable, she hails from the quaint rural hamlet of leafy Blairgowrie in the heartland of Perthshire. She's a buxom, red haired solidly built individual but I've never really gotten to know her very well, she's ok when it comes to a performance but only up to a point and at that time a bit limited in content depth when she first started wrestling sometime around the mid 1970's although I'm sure that was more the fault of whoever had her in tow originally. I've not seen her perform much since then but as that old saying goes "Practice makes perfect" so like a good whisky she's hopefully improved over time. The bottom line for the guy who runs the stable she was with originally is he's really only interested in the financial gains to be made from the "Big Tits" aspect on his shows nothing more nothing less.

"Lolita Loren" is another girl in the new groupings who's clearly going to be a star. When she first stated Chris was really quite small and lot lighter than big sister Kath but over the intervening years she like many others including my good self I might add, have bulked up somewhat. Clearly that's just a posh way of saying too much good living and far too many pints of Guinness, if like me that's your favoured tipple and again in my particular case far too many breakfasts from the frying pan also. She [Lolita] is a feisty wee girl and like the rest of her family she's all heart and tough as old boots but she's also got a nice gentle womanly side to her personality. Many a long and interesting chat I've had with her in our down-time after a show over a pint. It's really fascinating watching her rolling herself a hand made fag and all from scratch. She's had seasons touring in England under all the top Indie guys, folks like Brian Dickson predominately, I think. She's also worked in Scotland on tours on the Orig Williams circuit and she's sometimes been associated with the likes of Andy Robin and his wife Maggie on their shows but a bit more about that outfit and the lovely Margaret later maybe?

"Miss Klondike Kate" [Jayne to her friends] as I indicated earlier is for many now the top dog and she really sticks out for me also. Kate 2 started out in the later 1970's having been mentored by Bobby Barron [Dave Shillitoe] in and around Blackpool where he ran shows in places like The Pleasure Beach back then. She has most certainly clocked up the miles travelling up and down the length and breadth of the country but that's all part of what you have to do to hone your ring craft. She's developed at a phenomenal rate and she can work a crowd masterfully now. The TV people in Europe are keen to get her over there so that should be a huge boost to her earning power. There's also a lot of talk she may well be going further afield, maybe even Japan and the USA? That's got to be testament to her ability and her professional pulling power. She's also been back in Scotland working quite regularly for Andy and Maggie Robin since both made the decision to se up their own Independent circuit.

"Steve Peacock" [Les to his friends] also has a connection with both Dave and Jayne. He's another Scots lad whom I worked with a lot when he first came into the business, again in the latter part of the 70's and I like to think I helped him with his development in some small way back then. I really liked Steve when he was younger. [Later on he took up the handle "Gaylord"] He always gave of his best and was a particular favourite in the white hot atmosphere of places like the Liverpool Stadium. [Pun intended] I'm told he too was instrumental in showing the young Kate some of the holds back in Blackpool whilst helping her to perfect some of her moves early on in her career. Some I've spoken to recently however have indicated to me that he's become, rather sadly quite unreliable and erratic. I can't confirm that personally as that's not based on my own experience, although our paths have not crossed for a few years now.

Apparently initially Jayne had been at a show as a punter

and had got herself involved in an incident which resulted in some damage to her clothing. She then demanded the gaffer [Dave Shillitoe] pay for a replacement item. Apparently he was so impressed with her feisty persona he talked her into giving wrestling a go instead. Good move on his part but then again **"Mr Bobby Barron"** knew the game inside out and he was nobody's fool. [Very, very sadly Bobby passed away on 19th May 1994 at 4pm in the afternoon] Most probably yet another of the influences on the overall persona of the new Kate character would also have been Dave's wife, the lovely Rita, more about her later. Young Steve [Gaylord Peacock] also worked very successfully for other Indie promoters but apparently if it had not been for a chance encounter with **"Mr Peter Thompson"** who's another really good guy [Pro name Steve Fury] in a café in the land of the "Autumn Electric Multi-Colour Illuminations" some months before hand things may well have turned out differently. Peacock who had a job in a Bingo Arcade had noticed Peter handing over a copy of a Wrestling Magazine to a friend in a local cafe and expressed an enthusiastic interest. If that conversation hadn't facilitated a friendly recommendation from Peter that he should talk to Bobby at his gym about becoming a grappler then the main chance might well have passed the young Scot by. Later on having fully adopted a "Villain" persona Gaylord as he'd now become teamed up with Adrian Street for Tag Contests after brother Street decided to leave Joints. [Sadly Steve "Gaylord" Peacock passed away in February 2006, he is sadly missed by all his fans. RIP Young Sir] He was brave and he had the heart of a lion, a memorable Scottish Lion]

"Busty Keegan" is another of the names down south but I've never actually met her so I know next to nothing about her except to say she's married another Scots lad. His name is Robert Thomson and he came from Wishaw in Lanarkshire originally. I first met him when he was doing the odd job, sadly very badly back then for Orig Williams.

He was trained in Martial Arts and he found our way of working difficult to comprehend at first. Many a cup of tea I had at his house late at night over a chat when he first came into the grappling. I liked him a lot and I like to think he liked me as well back then, but as time went by Orig's influence on him tended rather sadly to drift us apart. I'll never understand the need for the back biting, untrue stories some in this industry continue to employ and nobody I might add was as good and as devious as the Welch-man when it came to bill-shit invention! Robert worked early on under the handle of "The Dragon" later taking up the more westernised name of "Sandy Scott" Although that has been a wee bit confusing for a lot of folks because there have been a lot of characters named Sandy Scott in the wrestling fraternity over the years.

"Chris Thompson" [Lolita Loren] came north of the border to work regularly in the late 1970's early 80's doing shows in particular for Andy Robin. The Manchester based mat man **"Mickey Gold"** had been the contact who put them both in touch he'd been asked by "The Bear Man" himself if he could sound her out about headlining in the female slot for him on a whole lot of shows he was lining up. Mickey's another former Joints man and another really good worker. [Mickey left us for a better place on April 1st 2010 he liked a laugh so would have enjoyed the irony of the date of his earthly departure] Lolita and Diamond Lil as a ring pairing were always interesting to watch mainly because early on at least they always tried to include an array of real wrestling moves rather than an over emphasis on big belly bumps and the obligatory play ground favourites, like the unladylike hair pulling routines. Although the full stomach bit would always have been a bit more difficult for them at that point in time as both sported rather shapelier, cuddly and curvaceous womanly figures back then. Most of their bouts were near wrestling classics and they have been acknowledged us such. Some Scots punters and pros alike still talk about there action packed encounters. [Chris passed away after a long illness in January 2012 RIP]

Miss Linda "Blackfoot Sioux" Adrian Street's lovely lady wife is a stunningly attractive lady with her slim shapely figure and long dark hair. She came into the business later than most of those I worked along side but she was always pretty street savvy even then. [Again pun intended] Which was quite unusual for most of the newer participants but given she learned all her tricks from someone who is undoubtedly one of the best ever on both the presentation side and also the art of controlling an audience, so it's perhaps a little unfair to compare her with anyone else. On a personal level I always found her to be friendly, considerate and very intelligent. She was undoubtedly and clearly continues to be a steadying influence on Adrian, they are clearly deeply in love and I like to think I can call them both good and treasured friends. Linda used to be matched fairly regularly early on in her career up against an equally stunning girl entitled **"Miss Susan Sexton"** although she has blondish hair colouring and a slightly lighter skin tone. She's also fairly tall and very, vey voluptuous, she's a much more powerfully built Australian "Sheila" need I say more? If you can imagine a Miss Dawn Fraser the former Australian Olympic swimming champion look-a-like in a leopard pattern leotard and tights then you've cracked it.

Dawn Fraser. Never heard of her!

Sorry obviously the wrong generation, as I said, she's a former Olympic swimming sensation from OZ a stunning looking, big solidly built girl. Susan when inside the ring ropes often displays the same dogged and fearsome fighting qualities that made the "ANZAC" soldiers feared by their foes in every theatre of war but she sometimes struggles against the free thinking and very clever Linda. There were lots of Aussies in the Vietnam War but if you take a closer look at a lot of the tosh that comes out of

Hollywood's Dream Factory, which is mostly Right Wing politicised nonsense, a whole lot of it by folks like Republican supporter actor John Wayne, the Aussie troops seldom get a mention. Sadly I lost some really good mates in Indo-China as it used to be known back in the day when the French were in charge. In fact if I'd still been a resident Down Under I too would have been called upon to do my bit for the flag that bares the emblem of the Southern Cross and I'd have gone albeit more than a little reluctantly! I not a lover of Capitalism led wars! God bless Australia mate! Luckily for me my perceptive father was clearly up on the politics of the time so he got me out of there back to Scotland before the uniform arrived!

"Miss Princess Paula" [Paula Valdez] was a standout when she first came on the scene and for much the same reasons as Linda. They are of a similar height and hair colour, Paula being just slightly heavier. She usually enters the arena in a full American native Inuit Head-Dress, white boots and a really tight fitting fringed white squaw type costume. It's just stunning and when bathed in the limelight glow of the overhead ring light she looks extremely alluring. Nevertheless this girl has no airs and graces about her, she's very down to earth and always finds time to talk whenever she has the opportunity. Sadly some of the older more established lads continue to give little credence to these new and most of the time definitely much better looking ring entrants. When it comes to having a good working knowledge of a range of moves Paula has a lot more than a good grip of the basics and as I said she looks great. Most importantly she always gives of her best she's a great show woman and a great professional!

I should perhaps mention at this point that although some of the top villains of this genre also posses a varying knowledge of a wide range of moves most are unlike many of their male counterparts handcuffed somewhat, in as much as they are usually not required to showcase or indeed use those real wrestling skills as most of the largely male dominated audience sitting there, mouths wide open, are simply just there nursing the expectation of an alluring Mammary Gland popping out to say hello! I got involved a couple of times in a film project for video release in the USA and Europe both Miss Valdez and I took part in a short Scottish tour as Tag Team Partners. We were up against The Viking and Lolita Loren in the other corner. Most of the film run went ok but I was never fully convinced and I suspect neither was Paula as to the real wrestling merits of the content. To put it mildly the performance values and these bouts were not really up to scratch, they were not all they could have been and indeed should have been. No disrespect intended to all or indeed any of the other three contestants but we didn't exactly set the heather on fire on any of the tour dates. I've also got to hold my hands up and admit that I too was equally off colour. The mix we had simply didn't gel; the usual magic quite simply wasn't there. If truth be told being of the old school and a well built man, muscularly that is, mixed gender bouts never have and never will do it for me personally. There's no way its ever going to be believable unless it's performed in a comedy vane, that's to say a woman opponent would never ever normally get the chance or indeed ever have the strength to put on a particular hold and be able to keep it there on most males. The restraining of a fully grown, full bodied male adversary by most of the fairer sex falls down completely on the first rule of what makes our sport successful; "it's just not wholly believable!" As a consequence our good business image suffers badly! Keeping the genders well apart in the ring makes far more sense although as I've previously demonstrated a few people, one being good old Joe Critchley could and did pull it off regularly the fact Joe was a slightly smaller built, wiry man may have helped but don't ever make the mistake of under estimating his strength and his catch ability, or perhaps his habit of turning out in his pink ballet shoes etc because this was only undertaken to enable him to blend into that zeitgeist more easily. His undoubted comic genius was always used to good effect and it regularly shone through and carried the day. If he'd appeared in those filmed Tag Team Contest it would have been a nightly Oscar winning "Hollywood" performance! Paula has now teamed up in an everyway sense of the word with young Dave "Fit" Finlay and let me say they make a handsome couple. She's a strong willed lady and she's managed or so I hear to perhaps be generating for herself some wider exposure by getting herself featured on the classic Saturday afternoon World of Sport programmes as his manager. Only time will tell if Max gives that ground breaking move the nod of approval. I personally hope she makes it because she deserves it, let's hope it happens. Thank god for glorious colour television screens black and white broadcasting would never have been able show her off to perfection but the new technology undoubtedly will. Personally I can't wait but given the conservative structure of some of those in power at ITV and also within the New Joints structure I'll be keeping my fingers crossed. Dave's done well in Germany and he's was also talking about trying his luck over the pond in America, as are many of the other young bucks. On a personal level I wish him all the very best. [Dave got his wish and finished up in the USA but he was not accompanied on his odyssey by Miss Valdez. [Very sadly Paula left this world behind on Thursday 5th December 2013. RIP you're are not forgotten]

"The Cherokee Princess" [Gloria] another capable performer looks fantastic. She too has that jet black hair look with white boots and a light blue costume and those long, long shapely legs, she looks really dreamy. She started out in 1975. Coming from Borehamwood originally she then moved to Rhyl around 1976 where she worked primarily for Orig Williams and occasionally for Brian Dixon. She toured South Africa and the Middle East and was one of the first females to work in Dubai and Abu Dhabi. She maintains her toughest opponents were Klondike Kate and the Manchester siblings, the Cassidy girls. She moved back to Hertfordshire some years later and worked almost exclusively for Jackie Pallo's and Jack Junior's promotions on the South Coast. [She retired in 1985 after a successful tour of India and now follows a different career path]

"**Rita Shillitoe"** Bobby Barron's good looking misses is another who has dawned the feathered headdress under the guise of **"Apache Princess"** she was trained by her husband around the same time as he was putting Klondike Kate through her paces in 1978. [Rita hung up her boots in 1992 two years before husband Bob died. Although she still refereed the ladies bouts and carried out MC duties on many shows, as well as handling the day to day running of World Wide Promotions for many years after that sad day]

"Tina Starr" I'm told she has a large following. Sadly I've never met the lady so I'm unable to make any considered comments as to her various attributes and her abilities.

"The Black Widow" has been played by more than one lady over the years, in this instance I'm referring to Claire Mathews' version. She's another lady who's breaking through on many levels although she seems to prefer to keep a much lower personal profile than some. She's an exceptionally good looking lady and really nice with it. She's also been doing a bit of promoting but like a lot of the smaller operators she tells me she finds it hard a lot of the time to get those she's booked well in advance of her show dates to turn up on the night. It would seem their commitment to fulfilling their entered into verbal contracts are questionable. Most of the time these situations come about after they've been leaned on by one or more of the bigger promoters who continue to threaten them with being put on a Black List for appearing for anyone else. This type of action is of course totally illegal but there's never been a truly effective and lasting Trade Union in the grappling business, as Equity the Actors Union won't recognise wrestlers it's a practice that's used to good effect even by Joints Promotions. That's another of the reasons why a lot of the lads moved over to the Indies in the first place but that old adage still rings true:

.......The grass is not always greener on the other side!

It's really sad to see this deplorable action happening but it's only being done by one or two and they came into the business through the back door so they've never displayed any sense of loyalty to the integrity of wrestling as a whole. They are of course Cowboys in every sense of the word!
Some of the other girls are: Miss Tina Martin, Miss Melanie Barker and Miss Nickie Monroe. I can't resist and yes I know it's corny but that's a lot of Misses but then you've got to ask yourself will any of them ever have big Hits? Boom! Boom! Three single girls by all accounts as their title seems to suggest maybe they could start a new craze and form a Three Girl Tag Team? They could have a novelty entrance theme where they could even sing a wee song before the evening performance gets underway, maybe even a dance routine? A good musical idea might be a rehash of the "The Beverley Sisters" [A three sister act in the 1950's and 1960's] signature tune appropriately entitled "Sisters" One of many hits for this popular London born sibling trio. No on second thoughts maybe not Gingham Dresses and White High Heels with Beehive Hairstyles wouldn't be a big enough **"Flash"** for the audiences we get now? Maybe the day will be saved by some lucky chap asking for one's hand in marriage then they'd only be two maidens left in the mix so a conventional Tag Team would then make the perfect fall-back position. Then we could forget the song? Which is a pity as it's a catchy wee tune.

No list of Grappling Gals would be complete without mentioning the ground breaking star born in Pudsey West Yorkshire **"Ms Sue Brittain"** a feisty lady willing to take on all comers, sometimes even bolshie local authorities.
Finally regards the ladies and their undoubted contribution

over the intervening years, let me finish with this brief tribute to all the lassies and their flashy female form which has done this business proud by mentioning one lady in particular and simply saying this; although they've been many female stars inside the ring ropes she is still the undisputed queen of them all and strangely she does not ply her trade between those tape covered restraints or on any canvas anywhere in the UK or indeed anywhere else for that matter because she is not a ring performer. Nevertheless her knowledge of wrestling is in no way diminished by that fact because she is the wife of perhaps the greatest post war anti-hero and self publicist wrestling has ever produced Mr Jackie Pallo! I am of course referring to the wonderfully enigmatic lady by the name of **"Mrs Georgina (Trixie) Pallo"** she has undoubtedly done her bit on many different levels including television to help build and promote the modern, thrill filled world we are all proud to call this Wresting Business! Well done "Trixie" we the Gladiators who perform and who do our very best to keep traditions alive at every level gratefully salute you! [Very sadly Mrs Georgina "Trixie" Pallo [nee Wilson] passed away in February 2013 RIP God bless and keep her]

What about everyone else involved in putting a show together? Where do they appear in the pecking order?

Are we talking about the M C and the likes here? Is that where you're going with this?

Yes, and why not?

Why not indeed but you'll need to bare in mind that just like those who at one time preferred to wear the standard oversized knitted trunks as opposed to the multi-coloured Lycra wearing younger generation who have now taken over and moved things onto a totally different level, for good or for bad. Those on the margins of the fights without whom we would never ever be able to complete any performance are a bit of a mixed bag some are really good and some rather sadly are not! Others have become rather inexplicably shadows of the highest of standards which were always regularly presented nightly in previous years.

Mileage Ayr to Rothesay and back+ a Ferry: 117 Miles
Time taken for full journey (+Ferry time): 2.5 Hours

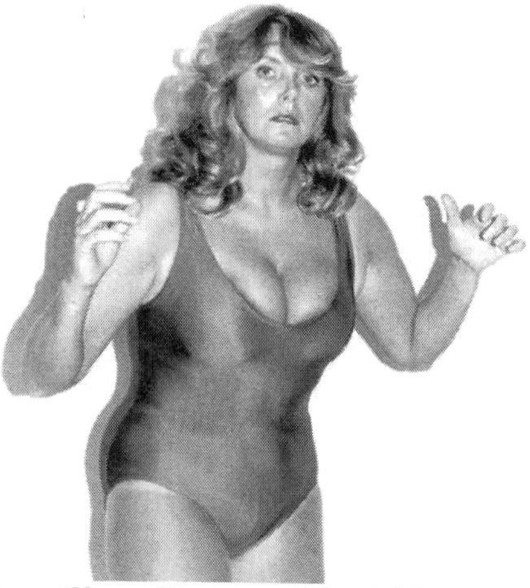

Lovely Paula Valdez & Wrestling Doyen Mitzi Mueller

Jack "Cowboy" Cassidy and his wrestling daughters

CHAPTER FOURTEEN

(The Gangs all here)

The Masters of Ceremony, Referees, Timekeepers not forgetting the Ring Seconds are all part of the team and without every one of the collective components there is simply no show! Within these ranks just like in life there have been some crackpots but then again there have been some wonderful performers as well. Especially among those who've donned the Dinner Jacket and the Bow-Tie and quite frankly the cornerstone of any show is undoubtedly a really good MC. The overall performance would be all the poorer, believe you me without this basic element but let's leave them till the end just like the top of the bill slot. We'll begin instead by taking a closer look at the best and the rest in the refereeing department.

"Mr Ernie Baldwin" is perhaps the best known former Wrestler turned Referee having had a long and glittering career whilst wearing the boots and trunks in the Heavyweight Division before making the transition into the obligatory black trousers and white shirt uniform to uphold the rules. It's rather sad that his long and respected odyssey should have been somewhat blighted by at the very least the hint of some allegation of wrong doing. The suspicion or so some have been heard to repeat is that he in association with others was responsible for an exposé that appeared in certain quarters of the national press supposedly giving away all the inner secrets of the British Grappling Business. Personally I like old Ernie and I totally respect his undoubted contribution to the business and the longevity of his personal professional involvement, as well as the considerable achievements of those whom he trained over the years. Among these was my mate Peter Preston. Therefore I prefer not to make any derogatory comments that might besmirch his good name, well deserved and well won in the ring. Except to say if he was responsible for some of those articles and therefore those accusations are true, presumably he was paid for his services and therefore he must have felt he'd earned the right to do so. Some did go to the press and they collected blood money! I find it very hard to believe Ernie was one.

Luckily as far as the public turning up at live shows is concerned, none of these exposés articles printed over the years seems to have affected the numbers of punters paying their entrance fee. Well not thus far at least. [Ernie left this world in 2000. Rest well good and faithful servant] If TV wresting as we now know it today is suffering and it truly is, it's got a lot more to do with the poor quality of some of the so called superstar performers and not press innuendo. Sadly most of their focus and interest seems to lie only with their own ego and maybe that was in some small way in Ernie's thinking if he really did do the dirty on the sport that continued to serve him well over many years.

Other ex-ring performers now refereeing include **"Peter Szakcas"** welterweight brother of the famous Hungarian Heavyweight Tibor has also had a long career but it's I think fair to say he lived in the shadow of his taller and more enigmatic brother during most of his time in the mat men ranks. [Tibor Szakacs passed away in 1981] As a man in the white shirt Peter is clinical and always attempts to make sure contests he's officiating over totally adhere to and upholds long established rules and UK traditions.

Brian Crabtree on the other hand prefers to try and re-write these traditions and the excepted standards with his own over the top dress-sense and his over inflated ego which is always reflected accordingly. He's unorthodox you could say. [Using the language of the boxing ring] Personally I feel the word "Twat" probably best describes this little "Popinjay" of a man although he is undoubtedly a good basic ref who totally understands the business and the way it should work within the ropes. bearing in mind he was at one time a ring Pro himself. I've really no experience of his wrestling abilities myself but the old adage which states "Those who can do, and those who can't teach!" I feel probably correctly sums up his mat abilities? He can be and regularly is on almost every performance level a total pain in the arse! As soon as he steps inside the plastic tape wrapped restraints he's already doing his very best to steal not only your show, also your space and your heat as well. Even when you're in the dressing room you still can't get a minute to yourself, in short if it wasn't for the fact he's the sibling of Max the Gaffer he would most definitely have been on the receiving end of a good hard punch in the mouth far more often than on the odd isolated occasion.

Yorkshire and Lancashire wrestlers are the salt of the earth and rightly demand the respect they undoubtedly deserve the younger Crabtree on the other hand although a son of the White Rose does not typify the down to earth top qualities normally associated with those who are Tetley's, Theakston's or Boddington's beer drinkers.

Moving further south London with the involvement of Dale Martin's gave us men like 60's superstar and former Royal Air Force serviceman **"Tony Mancelli"** perhaps better know to us now slightly older guys under his grappler name of "The Blackfriars Thunderbolt" due in no small part to his rugged all action bustling ring style. He's a real gent and was a top performer in his day and he's become one of the best referees to emerge out of the southern part of Britain.

"Mr Raymond Plunkett" is another of the better liked and well respected of those whose responsibility it was to try and keep the other two trunked protagonists grappling moves well within the Rule Book. He is also a dedicated devotee of wrestling, its origins and its history collecting not only old posters but perhaps much more importantly Facts, Figures and Statistics of both the British and also most of the European fixtures as well. Some results stretch back many years. In short he's an irreplaceable goldmine of information that will prove invaluable when we've all thrown off our mortal coil and flown off to stand in line to enter the ring at the ultimate tournament of tournaments in the sky and shake hands once again with the Great and the Good.

"Mr Brian Dixon" although he's been promoting for many years now excelled as a ref and he was never afraid to mix it with the guys if that's what the instruction was from the man paying the wages. I'm glad to say his particular ethos regards the business has never changed over the years it's a very simple but a very effective set of principals the main one of which has never altered and it remains. "Always send the Punters Home Happy!"

"Mr Barry Potter" is better known to all his many friends in wrestling rather endearingly as "The Badger" he's the man promoter boxer/wrestler Gordon Corbett likes to use on his World Wide Promotions Shows and having worked with him a lot back then it isn't hard to see why! He's a lovely man and not only does he know exactly what he's doing, much more importantly he also knows exactly what you're doing! Patrolling the rope perimeter is what's made him so special. He [Barry] always gives you a lot of space in which to work and as a consequence the bout is much faster and it has a much smoother edge to it. In other words it flows and it tells a story and the public then got a chance to see what good presentation is all about. He for his part only appears in your face, so to speak down on the canvas when he was required to count a fall or at your shoulder when he is required to make sure you allow your opponent space to get back into the ring when he'd either fallen out himself or gotten thrown out by you.

"Bobby Palmer" is another of the better known former pugilists turned referee, who's even turning his hand to the grand art of the Master of Ceremonies at which he's a natural. He hails from the Bow area of London so he could rightly call himself a true cockney lad. He started out as a thin lightweight way back before the war years and he too like many others served in the R.A.F and before that he worked as a Steward on ocean going passenger vessels. Coming from the "Smoke" he was employed almost exclusively under the banner of Dale Martin Promotions. [Bobby Palmer died in 1999]

"Don Branch" was a top man in the same mould and yes you guessed it he too had been in the RAF so he too had been an "ex Brylcreem boy". He worked almost entirely under the Morrell and Beresford banner and like most he too had been a one time ring performer in his own right but a knee injury eventually ended his successful mat career. Sadly latterly even he or so it's been alleged by some also let the cat out of the bag by telling all about our business to the press. If it can be proved beyond doubt that he in fact did it then that's all the sadder as it was this business and Ted Beresford in particular who had given him the means of earning a steady living following a succession of bad and painful ring injuries.

Wryton Promotions can boast the versatile **"Martin Conroy"** who not only proved to be a very popular referee among all the lads mainly I suspect because he too had a proven pedigree as a performer. He was also considered by his peers to be a really good an honest person. He could also double up as a really good MC also, now that's not bad for a rough and ready boy who some have alleged came to these shores supposedly somewhat ambiguously from Down Under in Australia.

"Joe D'Orazio" always adorned in his usual dark coloured T-shirt top was another popular ex-pro turned fall counter but under his own Italian family wrestling name of **"Bob Scala"** he was much more than that, he was in fact one of two people who put together the biblical: **"The Who's Who of Wrestling"** the other contributor being Pam Edwards.

Those who have chosen to go down the path of doing MC only, are in the main an altogether different animal from those who've had a mat career previously because without that they are clearly sometimes at a bit of a disadvantage and may struggle to understand how complex a bout can become and how it's constructed can be sadly lost on some of them. Nevertheless they are the first point of contact with the paying public and as such their skills are invaluable and most are treated with total respect by everyone else on the show. Orig Williams inherited a top man who had been well established for some years with Joints and who finished up working as effectively the industries very first real "Freelance." He was continually being pressured by the Joints camp to stay loyal and exclusive to them but luckily he held his nerve and stayed strong maintaining a foothold in both camps. After all he was then getting far more bookings from the Indie side in a calendar month than had ever been allocated to him in blocks by the other lot. His name is **"Mr Peter G. Baines."** It was initially a bit of a surprise to see him under the Welshman's banner as I'd been acquainted with his style and his classy performance skills from the work he did on George deRelwyskow, Norman Morrell/Ted Beresford and Peter Keenan's shows for a good few years previously. He's a lovely man and I can honestly say I liked him instantly from the moment we were first introduced. His daytime employment was at that time as a Senior Government Driving Test Examiner I've no idea if he's still doing that now or indeed if he's still living in the Paisley area either. He's always very well dressed and apart from a dark dinner suit he could be quite often seen in a dapper, Green Tartan Jacket. He stands out even more when decked out in his White Dinner Jacket which he only wore for Title Bouts! He's English born coming originally from down Essex way and his diction was and still is just about as perfect as it was possible to get. I'm also quite certain by the way he carries himself he's probably an ex-navy man. Someone told me he's added yet another string to his bow and he can now be seen doing his Red Tail Coated Toastmaster bit at some really posh celebrity functions the length and breadth of the UK. That alone indicates the true calibre of the man as that's a very hard usually closed shop nut to crack. He can also be seen with the microphone in hand on regular Saturday Wrestling TV shows as well.

"Mr Colin Brown" is another of the Scottish contingent. He lives in Old Kilpatrick near the Erskine Bridge over the River Clyde and his daytime occupation is running a Bus Company. He's a really nice guy and can do almost anything, and everything he does he always does it well. He's a good referee and if required can also fill in as an MC of the highest calibre. Should your car breaks down or you miss your last train home perhaps, you can always be assured for a small fee [only kidding] Colin is very happy to drop you at your door. Well he's got to make a living.

"Mr Jimmy Hughes" is another familiar name on this side of the border he's a Glasgow east-ender coming from the Easterhouse area of the city along with his younger brother Brian they run a really good stable of hard working, fully committed dedicated semi-pros, every one of whom are keen to make the step-up and the breakthrough into the ranks of full time professionalism. Without these two siblings people like Big Jimmy Wilson, Ian McKay, Billy Robertson and Bill "Bull" Wilson may never have seen the light of day and as a consequence our domestic circuit would have been all the poorer. Jimmy is not only a good MC he can also on occasion if required officiate at the highest level as a stand-in referee. Brian on the other hand is primarily a lightweight go at it wrestler and a good one at that, like his older brother he too can also double up he's comfortable when decked out in white shirt and black tie.

"Wee Tam Stevenson" would regularly pull out all the stops to help me through any minor crisis, so much so he became known as Spartan Promotion's Mr Versatility. He would turn his hand to anything at the drop of a hat without a word of complaint when required to do so. He would patrol around the often not so white coloured mat [Blood jobs, although few and far between in British rings, will invariably lead to dark stains on the ring canvas] and although a very kind and sociable person, nevertheless he was and still is in some ways a really shy and private wee man, he most even quieter when we first met! But a few months in the company of the lads changed all that and now he's not backward at coming forward. Personally I admire that in a person and I like to think I helped to foster that attitude in him. Now if he feels really passionate about anything and it needs to be said he's happy to voice it. Being brought up in what had been at one time the Second City of the Empire in the gritty working class streets of Glasgow in the ship building area of Govan made him a lot tougher than his slightly built persona suggests. He is very resourceful and can turn his hand to almost anything, even lending his considerable expertise if there's any small electrical or maybe even a time consuming mechanical equipment hitch along the way. Mankind over the centuries has undoubtedly benefited greatly from individuals with his same selfless, true humanitarian qualities. Wee Tam is undoubtedly the most loyal person I've ever encountered.

Gerry Carroll" was the very first Spartan Referee and the most pedantically dedicated person I ever encountered. He always carried his wooden clipboard around with him in a small imitation leather cardboard construction brown case. When he did his pre kick-off paperwork his preparation was meticulous, he would spend ages writing out the full bill in his excellent longhand, details included each and every detail for each and every contest, which wrestlers were appearing and in which order, which colour corner they'd been allocated, their weight, the colour of trunks they'd said they'd be wearing and god-help anyone if they'd changed their mind and hadn't informed him of any last minute alterations before they entered the arena. He would even have had a quiet discussion with some of the less switched on to the "real strength" as to whom and in which round they considered one of the protagonist would be **"Going Over!"** [A wrestling term used to inform you and your opponent as to whom would be the winner on any occasion and in which round they'd be getting the winning falls etc] He was however a young man who liked a bet and being a sharp cookie and University educated he could work out all the odds and all the permutations on all the horses and the dogs etc. He was a rum guy and if not **"Sussed**" [Another pro term meaning found out] he was happy to take any bet on any aspect of the show and the performers on it. For years he got away with the fact that as referee he was already in the know and therefore if it all went wrong, which of course seldom if ever actually happened, he was best placed and could and would then influence the course of a contest if it suited his purpose and his pocket to do so. I'm just amazed that more folks never woke up to that scam and strangled him for running his rather cheeky wee, beer money dodge. These schemes were of course only successful when visited by him on those with a much lesser knowledge [i.e. the locally hired seconds the odd gullible punter, groupie or their friends or hangers-on] he'd never have attempted to fleece the grunt and groan gladiators themselves as self preservation dictated that root be avoided at all costs. It was always only for a few pence anyway and I was nearly always able to make up the small shortfall to the unlucky losers if I'd been made aware at the time, usually by adding it into their fee without any of them knowing something was afoot. So at the end of the day all had, had some fun and everyone was happy meaning everything and everybody usually ended up on an even keel all round. On the odd occasions when we'd all hit the pub I'd usually order the first round and then inform "The Bookie" that he was paying for it! Strangely I never once heard him complain and I'm quite convinced he only did that kind of thing in the first place for the sporting buzz or to relieve his monotony. Sadly I've absolutely no idea what happened to him as the years rolled by. He's probably a multi-millionaire by now having got in on the ground floor in computers or maybe the Internet Betting Industry or something like that? Perhaps even the Stock Exchange or perhaps he's working in the ultimate place to make real dishonest money the Corporate Banking world?

"Mr George Dougan" is a native of the metropolis of Greenock and he'd already spent half his life running a small boxing club in the town when I first met up with him. As well as being a really decent person and one of life's caring Christian souls he'd also been a handy wee man with the gloves himself, mostly in his younger days and even then you would not have wanted to take the Mick! Back then he was also a very gifted wrestling referee and his knowledge of what can happen on the "Blindside" away from the referees view was second to none. He knew exactly when to go in and break it up and more importantly when to stay out of things. He has a wonderfully strutting wee walk and a multi-tooth laden friendly smile. For a long time he held down that post of Danny Flynn's main man with a Bow-Tie in Scotland and since Danny's demise I've done my best, where I could to keep him in some pocket money. People with George's love, drive, belief and determination are few and far between and if I learned anything from him it was this; "If you work hard enough and believe enough in your own abilities then anything in this life really is possible!" I thank you for that advice George and I hope and pray life continues to be good to you and the sun always shines righteously on you and yours buddy.

"Mr John Harris" has for most folks always been regarded as one of the best MC's of all time. He developed his smooth skills firstly under the Ken Joyce, Paul Lincoln/Devereux Promotions setup in places like the Wimbledon Palais, then when Paul sold up John went on to become perhaps Dale Martin's top Master of Ceremonies." He later moved over to top Indie outfit All

Star Wrestling Promotions. There is no doubting his abilities with a microphone as well as his friendly manner and his natural charm. His final appearance on our TV screens took place on 15th October 1988 at the Civic Hall Bedworth in the Midlands. John spent his retirement years in Spain. ["The Captain" left us to take up a position officiating in the Biggest Tournament of them on 25th May 2007. He is sadly missed. RIP Captain John]

"Mr Gordon Pryor" is another of the Bow-Tie brigade whose abilities are never in question he cuts a memorable figure of a man given his height and is build. [Gordon Pryor was the very last MC to make any announcements regards anything on ITV's British Television Wrestling as he was the man in the Dinner Suit appointed to officiate at the very last televised show. It was broadcast in December 1988]

Timekeepers can be a strange lot and in most cases they're a law unto themselves, sadly on a few occasions they have to be brought back to earth and sometimes with a bit of a bang. There have been occasions when I and many others have quite literally had to throw ourselves out of the ring and onto their table just to give them a hard slap on the side of the head to get them to pay more attention to the clock! Of course as far as the paying public is concerned it's all good fun from an entertainment perspective, they just love to see anybody getting a slap. Luckily they're clearly unaware that the blow to the ear did in fact hurt and it was bloody supposed to! The guy I used to "Dunt" [A Scots word usually meaning to push] on the side of the head, quite regularly in fact on almost all of my shows is and was even back then, a bit of a punter himself. He would get carried away when it came to keeping an eye on the timing of proceedings. He was always a real character and he was lovely with it, he was a real gent and smashing company when we'd settle down for a pint or two, especially for a Sunday morning session when we'd made the trip to the likes of the mining village of

Dalmellington, a distance of some 12/15 miles away from Ayr to listen to one of only a very few Colliery Silver Bands in the Ayrshire portion of The Scottish Coalfields. Or to break bread in a manner of speaking upstairs in "Peggy's Pub" with the older retired miners who would enlighten all the company as to the realities of the hard times they'd had to endure and the trials and tribulations that had gone before. Some would even draw from past experience of the devious tricks and underhanded ways of management when making their considered predictions for the future of the industry. Some of which were frightening at the time but given where we are now with all these draconian ongoing attacks on miners and their jobs, the old miner's prophecies are coming to fruition. He, the Timekeeper in question getting carried away with all that's unfolding in front of his eyes has been known to glaze over with a punter like admiration for the wrestlers in the ring. Before you or your opponent know it you're liable to be well into a third or forth minute overrun of a six by three minute rounds contest. You could if you were of a mind to do so witness this happening right in front of your eyes from the sanctuary of the ring canvas where you could take a few unscheduled seconds for a breather pretending to be working out how to escape from a tough and maybe rather painful looking hold being applied by a now equally out of breath ring advisory. His eyes would be totally transfixed and he would go into raptures, at that point he became in fact the ultimate and most dedicated, number one, non-paying, totally orgasmic punter and a real grappling fan. Only there in lies the rub, I suppose both I and all the others he worked with should see his star struck interest as a genuine unbridled compliment as from his point of view it undoubtedly was, but when you're covered in sweat and fast running out of breath it can be more than a little difficult not to resist leaning through the ropes to give him at least a verbal wake up call, which on many occasions was a lot less than complimentary. Mine would more than likely be along the lines of "For God sake Davie wake up man, I'm fucking knackered in here!" Or maybe on a good night it might have been along the lines of. "Will you please wake up and ring the bloody bell you dozy fucker!" His name was **"Mr David Simpson"** [Timekeeper, Ring Second and sometimes stand-in Referee] He too had been a miner and he'd been invalided out and he was quite simply the salt of the earth! Sadly he's no longer around and we who knew him really miss him, even although more often than not he was just not clued into actually keeping the time. He left us some years back but he will always be remembered especially when a bell of any sort sounds off and just like in the best traditions of the movies that chime for me at least suggests that not only did he get his wings, he'll also be hard at work making sure all the others around him won't be dipping out on a pair either. That's just the kind of guy he was, I really hope I share his company again some day. His twin sons, their older sibling Hugh and their younger brother Alex were all the great love of his life as was Madge his hard working, totally devoted wee wife. Undoubtedly he was a good father and one of the best when it comes to being an honest, a true person and a good and a faithful friend. He could sing a bit as well and I loved to hear his melodic unaccompanied version of "Robert Burns" classic song: "Flow Gently Sweet Afton" His middle two sons are better known as "The Fabulous Harlequins" [Jim and David Morgan] and he was rightly proud of what all of his offspring continue to achieve, both inside and outside the ring.

"Mr Willie Boath" was the name of the regular man on the clock at the Pavilion Rothesay when both [no pun intended] Danny and Freddie ran there and I was more than happy to use him again in that capacity when I resurrected the venue when Danny passed on. I even promoted him to the higher earning position of MC much to his great delight! He too was quite a loveable wee man and a great character. He was a Wee Free Church member [A very strict protestant religious order based in Scotland] and very straight laced. He was a shopkeeper from the nearby village of Port Bannatyne but when Wednesday's show time came around he would change completely and then metamorphosis into a fun loving jolly little man with a great sense of theatre and a gifted comedic persona. I liked him a lot, God only knows how he got through the long cold, wet winters on the island of Bute without going stir crazy whilst waiting for the summer months to come round again. So he could once again escape from his oppressive religious prison and pursue, if only for a few brief hours once a week, his other free spirited impish inner passions. One night in particular we were having a Scottish tile contest as the top of the bill slot it was scheduled to be first on after the interval. A title match was very special occasion anywhere and back then Champions were deservedly looked upon with some reverence. As I was giving him his instruction regards the proceedings during the halftime interval, he asked rather strangely "And what does the winner get?" to which I replied the Belt! So take it out with you when you go and make sure you give it a really big build-up, sell it well over the microphone because it's not every week the good folks in Rothesay get to see a real champion contest. Only a few short minutes later as I watched from the side of the stage I couldn't believe what I was hearing. After introducing both the contenders he then proceeded to lean through the ropes and on taking hold of the Time Keepers Bell Willie then proceeded to tell the crowd about the history of this wonderful object! This very special ships bell and all the history surrounding it and the fact the winner would be collecting it in recognition of his achievements tonight. As he continued to wax lyrical I felt a hand touch my shoulder, as I turned I was greeted by one of the other wrestlers who had his arm extended in my direction and in it dangling forlornly was the Scottish Championship Belt. All that was said as he thrust it into my hand was "Your MC left it in the dressing room." Needless to say comrade Boath got a dressing down for the faux pas although that had to be done without giving any indication that I'd already given him ten out of ten for the excellent improvised skills displayed in his audience grabbing build-up and the totally captivating bull-shit story he'd created!

Over the years, I, like all my sporting contemporaries have also had a succession of nameless Ring Seconds and in most cases that's how they've remained. The only two that spring to mind whose handles I recall are cousins from Prestwick. One was **"Mr Joe Carol"** and the other **Mr John "Jockey" Alexander.** [Joe is still with us and I still bump into him occasionally, sadly Jockey passed away some years back after a short and unexpected illness] There was also a father and two son's team from Ayr who worked for years for the onetime regular promoter at the Dam Park Hall, the Family name was "Hendry" and they consisted of the moustache wearing father who was the regular timekeeper his name was "Robert" senior, he was ably assisted by his two sons "Jackie and Robert Junior" and very good they were too. The guy who paid there wages and who promoted the bills there originally was an individual who really stood out in a crowd, a man by the name of Norman Berry. He was a very tall chap with a strong military bearing and he always wore a thick, wool based dark tweed, wide belted very long coat. He had a slightly reseeding hairline and he sported a rather large slightly handlebar moustache and he had at one time been an army officer. He seems to have fallen completely off my radar nowadays, his onetime business partner was a smaller rather ordinary man who walked with a prominent leg impediment unfortunately I can't remember his name.

Back on the island of Bute there is another individual the Head Second in actual fact, a title he gave to himself but it suited me to indulge his fantasy back then as even if I wanted to ignore him he would never allow me to do so! Thus it would be totally inappropriate to deny him a wee historical mention. His name was Gus, remember I talked about him earlier, he was our passport into the after hours drink in the Bute Arms. He himself was a hard drinking, hard working family man with a heart of gold! His craggy face was full of big yellow teeth which lit up when he smiled and he smiled a lot. If you are familiar with the phrase: "He would have given you his last" that sums him up perfectly. He worked in the building trade and he was a giant of a man and his straight to the point line of patter whilst towelling you down between rounds was on occasion nothing short bloody brilliant. Things like, "What's keeping you man the pub closes in half an hour stop pissing about stick the fucking head on him and let's get ourselves down there in time for last orders. So finger out! OK?" Another phrase he oft times liked to use was: "He's too young and too fast for you man but that's nothing that a hard boot in the stones won't cure. Just throw him over here and I'll crush them with my size fourteen steel toe-caps that'll slow the wee bastard down!" I must confess even now it took a lot of professional willpower not to do just that to the odd opponent as the big man could be pretty convincing and pretty persuasive, especially if you'd been taking a bit of a breathless beating for a few rounds and all in the name of giving the paying public value for money! My life so far has been greatly enriched by spending time with everyone of these wonderful characters I only hope I've given them the same level of comradeship and amusement.

That's very commendable but why don't you tell me about some other situations that have given you a laugh over the years. Or maybe a bit more about some of the more interesting people you've met when you've been doing the rounds. Some who are maybe not from the world of wrestling then you can give me a lowdown on your gym after that. What do you say is it a deal?

Total mileage Ayr and Oban and back: 252.8 Miles
Time taken for the full journey: 5 Hours 14 Minutes

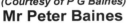

(Courtesy of P G Baines)

Mr Peter Baines

John Cortez

Mr Brian Dixon

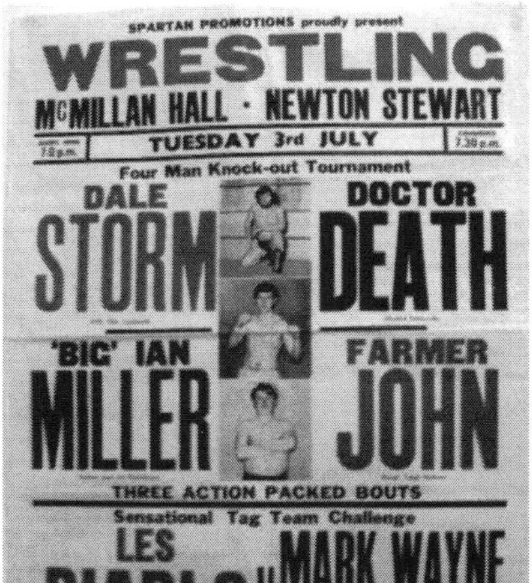

(Courtesy of Spartan Promotions)

Spartan Promotions Poster!

A Bogus Invitation Poster often used by dishonest promoters clearly a highly questionable ploy!

CHAPTER FIFTEEN

(Fun, some frolics and some maybe famous Folks)

There have been a few quite famous personalities I've been fortunate to meet over the years most I've liked and some I've even admired.

Whom might you think deserve just small a mention then?

How about the former British Heavyweight and Commonwealth Boxing Champion Henry Cooper, but let's start by going right back to basics and begin the journey back up to the A List Status at a much lower level.

Nights out with the all lads from the Gym were only possible when we were not all on the road at the same time. They were always a really good laugh and usually full of minor good humoured incident. One such get-together took place at the New Toll Bar on the boundary between the towns of Prestwick and Ayr. It's just a ten minute bus ride from the local International Airport which is on the Monkton Village side of Prestwick. We'd usually try to end up in there when there was a live band playing. One of the better groups around at that time were a bunch of seasoned local semi-pros who were collectively known under several different names but at that time they were recognised all over Ayrshire and beyond as the Rock Band "Southbound" You'll have to go a long way to hear a percussionist batter drum skins any louder or harder whilst still maintaining the bands tight rhythm and his personal rating as a top back line exponent than Girvan Town's own Mr Ronny "China" Mills. He played originally on a Premier Kit but later on due to the emergence of the Beatles and Ringo Star's influence he changed to a set of Ludwig's but they were not to last Ronny simply battered them to bits. He's also a sound technicians dream as he never needs to be fully rigged up with microphones. A Bass Drum hook-up is almost all he ever requires complimented by maybe two more microphones, one above and between the symbols and another on the High Hats. On a completely different tact Monty McGill's daytime employment as a self employed hairdresser, over the years helped him to maintain his supple finger dexterity when caressing the keyboards, add to that the attributes of rhythm syncopation plus baking harmonies and a great vocal lead when required from rhythm guitar aficionado Brian James "Spike" Milligan and it all starts to come together. He arrived in Ayrshire as a thin very shy fifteen years old from Stornoway in the Western Isles. The backline Bass section was completed by the addition of the seldom if ever sober but always extremely sociable Campbell Morrison. He in particular continues to be popular with the ladies, well those who had the capability to accommodate his rather large manhood that is. You'll be hard pushed to find a better threesome assortment of accomplished musical journeymen anywhere in the UK. The other two member's names and attributes I'll mention a little later.

If our social outings coincided with a training night that was all the better, so suitably sprayed from head to crotch with deodorant to mask the sweaty odder from our exertions in the ring and on the weights etc, there were no showers in the gym, we then headed off to savour the joys of a long cool refreshing pint. The younger single lads would usually be out "On the Pull" and us married very jealous older guys would sometimes just stand there with our tongues hanging out as sick as jealous Parrots! Whilst queuing at the bar trying to lift our shoes out of the beer sodden carpet our main focus quickly shifted from a cool drink as our eyes now straining out of their sockets feasted on the well stacked young blonde in the tight white jeans who was strutting her shapely backside on the dance floor to our left. The second things that caught our attention wobbled proudly whilst straining to break out of her totally inappropriate modern design undergarment. It goes without saying these were her more than ample perfectly formed mound tipped boobs, as they wobbled proud almost freely whilst all the time threatening to jump out and escape from the warmth and safety of her frilly lace edge black half cup under-wired bra. Only moments thereafter and just for a fleeting moment we were treated to just a glimpse of the top part of her now fully aroused dark brown tinted right areola. So duly challenged by some of the others to show some Manish leadership skills it was then left to me to ask her for a dance. Mocking laughter from my comrades followed closely after a rather rude onslaught of words not normally associated with good looking, educated dainty young ladies was the main thrust of her terse and blunt rebuff. Honesty dictates that I must admit this was a bit of a brain numbing blow and the hilarious reaction from all the others was almost as hurtful. Didn't she realise she was in the company of an almost and maybe nearly famous athlete? After all and you being a feminist you'll hate this next bit, but of all the people in the room that night, I ask you who was doing who a favour? I was clearly the closest thing to a near celebrity she was going to encounter.

Life can be a cruel learning curve and some lessons can be hard earned, hindsight can be a great and very uncompromising leveller when sound reasoning has not being applied but sadly on some occasions by the time common sense eventually kicks in it's already far too late to repent. Because a fool is still a fool whether at that particular moment or indeed some hours later after some quiet, personal and honest reflection time, there is still no fool like one clearly out of his time and out of his depth.

As the tight all round sound from the band continued to fill the room mainly due to the exquisite lead guitar playing from my long time good pal Mr Ian "Beef" Seaton, his all knowing cheeky smile which was now beaming out at me from the stage finally caught my eye my face now became even redder than the polished finish on his classic Fender

Stratocaster. "Beefo" worked in the same garage as me in Kilmarnock and I broadened my knowledge of music by talking to him almost daily. He'd played guitar from a very early age having studied it originally at a classical level, my cousin Margaret Dunlop who worked for his parents, Ian's father had at one time been the owner of the very first Renault franchise in the south west of Scotland, she told me it had been almost impossible sometimes to use the toilet in the house as Ian considered it to be his personal rehearsal space and he would regularly sit in there for hours at a stretch. Even the soulful sound of Billy Bryant the lead singer's rendition of "Listen to the Music" one of the "Doobie Brother's" many hits failed to fully resonate with me but in many ways all of this was already irrelevant as my focus had move on somewhere else and I was now busily engaged hatching my plan of blatant revenge!

On reflection it was probably Ian's all knowing smirk which really set me off, so duly accompanied by a chuckling Teddy Bear Taylor [no relation to Wee Sammy] and at his impish insistence we headed for the "Durex" brand name Condon machine in the gents. Moments later back at the crowded bar we were busily queue jumping trying desperately to grab the busy barman's attention, with utter disappointment clearly written all over our faces. The reason being the non availability of the man made rubber necessaries from a clearly "Out of Order!" vending unit.

Strangely the only uplifting moment in the whole infantile saga thus far came unexpectedly but it was nevertheless gratefully received when Bobby the pint pourer having opened the till handed us both a couple of fifty pence pieces. I can only surmise with all that was going at the busy bar, he'd wrongly assumed we were tying to tell him we'd fed cash into the white clinical looking wall mounted beast and no return had been forthcoming. So once again but this time two quid to the good we set off out the front door and across the busy main road to the slightly more upmarket Carlton Hotel where we were hell bent on raiding their machine. We returned a few minutes later laden down with lots of lovely multi-coloured prophylactic playthings. Once again we headed for the toilet area; small things will always amuse small alcohol blurred minds! Having filled one of the population explosion stopping balloons with copious amounts of cold water, we then rather over exited and giggling only just narrowly avoided bumping into the other revellers as we continued on our trek weaving our way through the now even busier hostelry. By this time our intended target was sitting next to a new goggle eyed victim and had once again managed to coax this witless male into buying her yet another free drink! No doubt with empty promises of a cunningly overstated delusional short fumbled feel of her ample orbs in the dark car park later!

Again armed with our now rhythmically bouncing bundle which totally dwarfed even her large pointed toped mountains we continued our assault to the more sedate tones of another great song, a ballad written by the band entitled “Diana” which at that time had been highly sought after by several record companies but the leading lights in the band wanted to get signed to a major record label and refused to contemplate their song being recorded by another pop outfit. Luckily we managed to position our charge just above her head and all without her noticing our attempt at some Mack Sennett type comedy cappers. Once there we proceeded to bounce it up and down in perfect harmony with the in demand melody and as expected just a few short seconds later it burst showering its cold contents all over the dodgy damsel! Our perverted amusement was complete when we were enthusiastically applauded by more than a few of the other halfwits standing at the bar. Needless to say that incident brought an abrupt halt to our night out, well in that bar at least. Brenda the under-manager’s face said it all as she entered the room through the sliding plastic door which lead to the Public Bar! So having pushed a few notes into the hand of a now strangely silent and socking wet freeloader by way of a thank you for a job well done and a really good laugh provided, we downed our pints and left. What we got up to that night was of course well out of order and it did my personal reputation and standing in the wider community among many local woman, wives and mothers no good whatsoever, in fact some have never ever forgiven me!

................Yet another hard lesson learned hopefully?

Not too many years down the track that well stacked young lady and her stunning body became one of the best Miss Scotland contest winners ever carrying out her duties in an exemplary fashion wherever she went. I like to think perhaps that minor drowning was a bit of a lesson in humility but who knows? She also ended up proudly plastered all over a Famous Scottish Drinks Can. [Tennent's Lager] Just maybe I too learned a little something more about myself and my attitude to life on that fateful night as well but and this really is sad, the memory of that night still brings a rye smile to all our stupid faces when it's been recalled on other nights out since. Now I ask you how sad is that? As the night rolled on we then moved further on into the town of Prestwick proper eventually taking refuge in "Bumpers Night Club and Discothèque!" So called because it had become quite famous for exhibiting a sculpture of large, chromed steel Chinese Dragon which had found the perfect home situated at the side of the walkway area which lead to the seductively lit dance floor. It had been fashioned from a collection of old car bumpers by "George Wyllie" MBE widely regarded as an expert in his field and onetime Gourock based artist, having been commissioned by the then lease holders of the building Mr David Cummings and brother in law Josef the proprietor of "The Josef" hair dressing studio chain. I had worked there occasionally on "The Door" early on when times were tough for me financially. I saved money on hair cuts as young Tom Speirs one of the really nice local shop Manager Harry

Ask him again ref!

Downie's apprentices did it for me at home. Tom later married local beauty Carol, John Cheshire ABA regular turned professional boxers' tempestuous sister.

Working the Door so you were a Bouncer? Did you wear black leather gloves and bash people up? Throw them out onto the pavement and kick them when they were down?

Good God no! What do you take me for a thug? **"Bumpers"** was a classy place OK occasionally we had to deal with trouble but that was usually at the front door it never got passed us. Once the local Nut Jobs knew they were Persona Non Grata they seldom if ever showed up again. Michael Calder the manager a New Cumnock man was innovatively clever, building in later years a Glasgow Club Empire, retiring to Marbella Spain a multi-millionaire!

Come off it! You must've had to get violent with somebody.

Yes there were times like that, usually on the Sunday Night after the original owners of the building who by this time had recognised an already thriving business opportunity and reclaimed the lease. Arthur the oldest son who's only real claim to fame was his ability to be good at absolutely nothing was allegedly the proud possessor of the equally well deserved title of being the biggest "useless arsehole" in the local area! To give you an example; the first thing he did when he took over the day to day running of the complex was cut the wage bill, stupidly that meant pruning the bow tied personnel levels, thankfully initially only on The Lords Day in particular. Clearly he was under the misapprehension that thieves, gangsters, hoodlums, drug dealers and other assorted bother causers were far less likely to be out of order or become especially violent on the Sabbath. Obviously he too was wired to the moon and sadly he just wouldn't be told by those who clearly knew a whole lot better. He couldn't or wouldn't take on board the fact we the Frontline Troops had, had months of hassle after we'd taken on the job under the new name above the door when Big David and Josef had first opened up. In truth we'd worked our arses off clearing out the shit element. Apparently they the local dregs had all been gifted almost unlimited access by the security staff who had been employed to keep the peace at the previous venue, predictably given the introduction of this "Alamo" element the place used to blow up nightly! The flashing neon sign shinning out into the dark night above the front door at that time said it all! **It read: "The Bow and Arrow"**

The fresh far more sensible approach that had existed before the Feriole Family moved back into the premises had allowed the new regime, proper Night Club format to attract a more discerning music loving, trendy dresser element to attend who travelled from miles around to spend lots of their money relaxing unhindered by the previous rough element who would have see them as an easy target for both ambush and violence! The fact they had a few quid in their wallet and the three weekend nights in which to have some fun also assured us the hard working Doormen ongoing and gainful employment!
Around the witching hour of mid-night on the first shift after the staff cuts, which surprisingly was quite appropriate given the lateness of the hour a "Ghoulish" figure descended on us unannounced. For my part I was standing near the cash register in the foyer somewhat fatigued as it had been a long and a busy weekend and I had worked every night. I was dreaming slightly head hanging just a little when suddenly the front door was flung wide open by a Garth of a man as he stumbled in nearly falling in the process! Bloody hell he was a Monster all that was missing was the stitched high forehead, big heavy boots and the Neck Bolt!

Standing easily 6Foot 6inches tall and weighing at least twenty odd stone he cut an imposing figure given the size of his whisky barrel type chest. His thighs and arms would have looked good on the likes of Arnold Schwarzenegger! Luckily for me he was pissed or it could have been drugs? Who knows? Who cares? If you're that big you do what you want! Anyway the ambience from the low purple coloured neon lights in the long rather narrow entrance corridor must have fazed him just a little, as he stood there motionless like "The Terminator" glazed red eyes looking around the place rather menacingly. His head turned to the left then to the right, his eyes went up to the ceiling and then his eyes down to the carpet! It was as if he was being controlled by some kind of inner computer feeding him environmental information allowing him to size up everybody and everything in his path before making his move! His trancelike state was only broken by the loud high pitched scream being emitted hysterically by the young girl at the entrance hall till point. Rather insultingly perhaps it became patently obvious that on realising it was all down to me to turn this "Volcano" around and run it out the door she'd clearly decided I wasn't up to the job and just maybe she could frighten it into instant submission by going into Girly Scream Mode! Big mistake as it only added to the problem; for a start it seemed to wake him from his standing slumbers. Due to the afore mentioned staff cuts the Dinner Suited Brigade that particular night consisted in its entirety of yours truly and only one other, he being one Mr Andrew Campbell who's "Daytime Job" was that of a local building supplies companies' top lorry driver and delivery man. Brother Campbell was one of the nicest people I've ever met and I learned everything I needed to know about bouncing first hand and straight from the horse's mouth. The riggers and the perils of putting your wellbeing on the line when standing at a doorway entrance can be taxing especially the telling those too drunk part or that they are inappropriately dressed and they could not at this time gain an entrance can set some folks off! ....

"Sorry mate not tonight you've already had a bit too much to drink" "Please come back another night when

you're sober. Oh and don't forget a change of footwear, the management does not allow trainers!".....

It should have been child's play but it was seldom if ever as simple as that. Andy Campbell was kind, well spoken and he had a touch of working class charm about him, standing around six foot tall with hands like Number 10 Shovels, he was thinning just a little on top and was aged around 45. He had a lovely fatherly smile and I'm very glad to say on this occasion as on every other occasion his timing was as fortuitous as it was immaculate! No sooner had "The Ogre" taken a couple of shoe size sixteen steps towards yours truly, which was clearly for me at least fast becoming a seminal moment perhaps best remembered and summed up in the words of the Batman cartoon characters sidekick Robin when he utters those now famous words like; "Holy Cow Batman!" Or sometimes a simple Cartoon punctuated Eee..k! Or maybe a Kapow! So I thought to myself what are my options here? Given his large frame maybe a swift hopefully well aimed boot in his clearly over-large bull like nuts? That might well be in order or it might be more direct, safer and equally painful and a bit more permanent perhaps if a strong downward movement side-kick was executed to the leg joint area, thus taking out his knee cap! Hopefully that would bring his rather large "Loud and Mouthy" head crashing earthbound down to my level just like the Giant in Jack and the Beanstalk! Things were now definitely beginning to warm up and naturally I was concentrating some of my efforts in trying to work out how best I was going to impress this rather attractive looking, although momentarily just a little unhinged overly hysterical young lady! Thankfully all that potential nasty rough stuff was instantly avoided, somehow having heard the scream or maybe it had been the telepathic prayer for help I'd been busy transmitting through my thought process that instigated his appearance, we may never know? Just like a true Knight in Shinning Armour he entered the fray calmly emerging through the swing doors at the function suit end of the corridor then having gently moved me to one side Andy wasted no time in meeting his advisory head-on. I almost found myself feeling sorry for that big lump of super testosterone filled very dangerous Man Meat! The Nutter had absolutely no chance of coming out on top against this highly experienced “Hard as Nails” worldly wise Sage. I must admit I was really looking forward to learning a whole lot more from whatever martial arts technique my confederate was now going to employ, given all this action was about to take place right in front of my eyes. Without Brother Campbell ever having to break his long and always measured stride pattern he continued to close down the space between himself and the enemy without any fear!

When did the Ambulance arrive, how many broken bones?

What Ambulance? Who’s broken bones, Andy’s?

No the Big Silly Guy!

Actually nobody got any broken bones and rather unexpectedly I did not learn a new self defence technique, quite the opposite in fact. It was more of a lesson on the observance of your surroundings and using to best effect what might be available to you at the time. An ego did get badly shattered but that’s life and after all the Man Mountain got everything he deserved! Placing one hand on the beast’s chest, Andy just continued to push the intruder back down the hallway towards the entrance doorway. Even although the big guy did try several times to get a word in, my pal the lorry driver just carried on regardless. “Sorry son you’ll have to leave!” Was almost the only conversation they had, there were other words but they were brief. “You’ve had far too much to drink! Go home and sober up, come back next week! No hard feelings and we’ll see you then! OK? Good night to you. Have a safe journey home!” Everything was going to plan when suddenly from out of nowhere the Big Man swung his huge right hand! It seemed destined to smash into Andy's face, but some timely rather fancy evasive footwork meant it missed his chin by millimetres. Both men were now only a foot away from the front door, so grabbing hold rather tightly of the front of the Arran Wool knitted cardigan being sported by the now helplessly off balance intruder with his right hand and then in the blink of an eye pushing one side of the front door open with his left hand, thus allowing his advisory to fall though, Andy then quickly pulled the entrance door shut tight again, thus he dispatched the problem in one masterly stroke with no blood being spilt! This potentially nasty situation had with one clever piece of genius now been averted and a complete fate accompli had been visited with pure comedic effrontery on the Giant. He was now back outside the Club on the pavement with his face squeezed up tight against the thick wooded front door and with most of his very nicely home knitted cardigan still inside meaning he was now helpless and hopelessly trapped. My fellow Steward then pulled the garment even tighter whilst instructing me to fetch a Claw Hammer and one 6 inch nail from a tool box some workmen had left under the till shelf at the rear of the makeshift Box Office. So one large 6 inch nail having been dispatched into said front door through the knitted cardigan and thereafter two large stainless steel slip bolts having been located into position across the door by my good self, making it impossible for anyone then to enter into or indeed leave the Club! Andrew then none too quietly hammered the remainder of the nail bending it against the door, then he quietly instructed the now quite calm young lady in charge of finance to call the Police to take charge of the now impaled intruder. Having handed her the hammer he further informed her that he and I would now be taking our leave of the situation through to the restaurant to enjoy a well earned cup of tea on the house. I couldn't help but laugh into myself as we set off at the now rather quiet wimpy words that were coming rather more politely now from the other side of the entrance door, and all from a now much less aggressive Big Bad Guy! It went something like this: “Come on boys I’m really sorry. I won’t do it again, honest. Just let go of my cardigan and I’ll just be on my way home to my bed.” They were not quite the follow-up words I expected to hear coming only a few short minutes after the outburst of the previously overly aggressive “I might kill you if you don’t let go of my cardigan! My Mammy knitted it you Poofy, bow-tie wearing bastard!” Big Andrew Campbell said nothing as he quietly dipped a digestive biscuit into his mug of steaming hot tea he didn’t have to say anything his calm ability said it all to everyone. His prompt and decisive action and the look of quiet contentment he always displayed said it all. He was quite simply the best at his trade in the sometimes very dangerous world of being employed as a Club Doorman!

You Poofy bow-tie wearing bastard! That’s quite funny! Not very PC but funny nevertheless! God I’ll be wetting my pants in a minute!

Strange you should say that! Helen the young till operator had to slip into hers, she kept a spare pair in her handbag. She availed us as to that fact when we arrived back at the crime scene about fifteen minutes later to remove the nail and allow the local Bobby’s the opportunity to take our intruder into custody, clearly the stimulus for that action was entirely different from yours though! Shall I carry on with my original story now!

Yes of course please do.

As we approached the Discothèque still in raptures about the incident in The Toll Bar our attention was immediately drawn to the pastel coloured Rolls Royce car which was proudly taking up both the parking spaces outside the front door. Joy of joys were forthcoming as we entered the small candle lit VIP eating area and all because who should be sitting their enjoying a cool refreshing bottle of Lager.

You're never going to believe this but it is true, on my life none other than almost all of The Kings of the Draped Jacket and Velvet Collared Stage Show, the now legendary British Show Band**...........“Showaddywaddy!”**

They were seated all together in the largest corner booth having just taken charge of a bottle of Bacardi dutifully served by the youngest of the new bar staff, yet another result of more of Arthur's economies! Young Ricky Munro! His older sisters May and Christine also worked the bar but they were off duty that particular evening, boy were they a couple of stunners! I had a lot of time for Ricky and his girl siblings back then and I still do. Ricky's face light up like a Christmas tree decoration when told by Dave to keep the change after he'd handed the lad a crisp new Twenty Pound note. The youngster got hardly that amount for a full two nights work plus tips. Great merriment ensued as I'd met the lads quite sometime back when they played regularly at “The Fosse Way Pub” in Leicester in two different bands before they achieved their fame by winning “New Faces.” Some of the wrestlers from that local area I'd gotten to know when on the road in and around the Midlands would drop in for a pint if they were on a bill somewhere close. That's how I was first introduced to Dave Bartrum (Lead singer) Malcolm Allured (one of two drummers) Bill “Bubby” Gask also lead vocals) Russ Field (guitar) they were all present when we first got there. Romeo Challenger (the other excellent percussionist) arrived after us although I must confess that did strike me as being a bit strange at the time as the flash car outside belonged to him, he always showed good taste. The rest of the lads were posted missing apparently they'd stayed in Kilmarnock the band had been performing at The Grand Hall earlier that evening. Only a few short weeks earlier as I mentioned previously, I'd had the pleasure of being formally introduced to one of my sporting hero's at a Water Rats Charity Function for a Sunshine Coach launch in Glasgow where at long last I shook the hand of a great and a true gentleman Mr Henry Cooper, he's a lovely man and very down to earth and really quite light for a Heavyweight.

Sadly the proceedings were almost spoilt by the antics of a couple of tables of what could never under any circumstances be remotely described in anyway as gentlemen. They were amusing themselves by throwing large and very dangerous hard ice cubes into the ring much to the dismay and disappointment of the two hard working occupants, both good friends of mine who were doing their very best to entertain this lot of charlatans in dinner suits and bowties. Needless to say yours truly was less than impressed so with the metaphorical sword of justice in one hand, I stepped forward determined to rip their school boy like perverted sense of amusement from their grasp. The fact I was ambushed and immediately surrounded by a posse of minders who came right out of nowhere stopped me in my Do-Gooding tracks! One of them who was surprisingly articulate for his station in life then took the time to announce that the cigar smoking, clearly bored older guys busily launching the hard water at my buddies were if fact a bunch of the most feared of the Glasgow's Gangster Godfathers! Needless to say by that time it was already far too late to back down so "Brassing My Case" [A Glasgow expression meaning to face up even if it's really a squeaky bum moment] my immediate retort was short but to the point! Well am a member of the street fighter clan pal and I will be only too happy to take everyone of your lot outside and kick fuck out of you, one by one should this shit continue. I must have been off my bloody head at the time and if I was being really honest immediately thereafter and wishing I'd kept me big mouth firmly shut, I was somewhat over the moon when their self appointed spokesman, having been summoned to appear at the side of the Head Honcho by means of the merest of head nods. Thereafter on returning to my side just a few short seconds later assured me that it would now stop, albeit temporally, but the boring crap that was happening in the ring would need to improve greatly as they had paid a great deal of their not so hard earned cash to be there at this good cause fund raiser. Four tables of ten in total, God me and my big mouth, and shit I was on the bill next! Talk about digging a hole for yourself. I'd only come down into the hall to gauge the crowd size and to grab a soft drink. I can honestly say from the moment the opening bell rang out I've never worked harder, but would my supreme effort be good enough? Would they be impressed? The next twenty five minutes or thereabouts would answer that question. I gave it my best shot and I'm really glad to say no more ice was thrown, everyone, and perhaps more so the four tables filled with scar faced revilers seemed at least to enjoy my wholehearted, lung busting efforts and of course that of my opponent "Young Mr Starsky" who in not being in possession of all the facts was naturally more than a little confused with both the speed and also the added entertainment content of our contest. Strange to say later on that night the short walk through the damp and dimly light underground car par to the relative safety of my car seemed to take a lot less time than it did when we'd arrived earlier in the day! Although it is more than a bit Mario Puzo and completely over the top, I did nevertheless find myself taking a quick glance under my car on the pretext of tying up a loose shoe lace. So my Ford Cortina GT closely scrutinised for any sign of hanging wires, finger prints in the dust or cylindrical bundles which at the time seemed to me to be totally sensible and somewhat obligatory, we then drove off at a much faster rate than when we arrived!

To this day Adrian Street and company are still not fully aware as to why I insisted on stepping on the gas as we left the building! Perhaps I should have told him, Linda and the other young lady wrestler who accompanied her but why go raising their blood pressure for something that thankfully never transpired.

Why would you do that? Looking under the car and stuff?

Ask him again ref!

Well it's just like this; paramilitary organisations not too many miles away over the water were being readily supplied with hand guns, ammunition and also explosives by the likes of these unscrupulous chaps and their associates and sometimes visa versa, if a relatively difficult to trace gun was required for a job anywhere in the UK it was delivered. Some who lived on The Emerald were also busily employed blowing up places like Belfast's world famous Europa Hotel and on more than one occasion! And here I mean no disrespect to those who lost family and friends both on the Emerald Island itself and also on the English mainland, thankfully things like that were not commonplace in Scotland in fact they never ever happened! Maybe if I hadn't been so careful that night we might well have become the first ever Scots casualties?

That's a bit paranoid don't you think, a car blown up in Glasgow just because you upset a Godfather gangster. A razor slashing or a stabbing well maybe, but explosions in hotel car parks are you sure you didn't take a hard blow to the head during your bout and imagined the whole thing?

Well I don't think it's that over-the-top so there, as far as I'm concerned questions have never really been asked by Scots national newspapers as to why Auld Scotia was immune from the "Troubles" unlike the rest of the British mainland. Shortly after that night I sold my beloved GT Super Car! Well it was customised and it had been re-painted to my own specifications, that livery made it blend in more than a little but when I opened the throttle "Boom!" In other words it stood out a mile then and there was no hiding place after that and It was well known in Ayrshire and beyond. Maybe on reflection yet another of life's sharp and lasting lessons learned**?................I'd like to think so?** Just to prove my point about not being too careful let me tell you about a strong rumour that circulated around the Scottish Wrestling circuit in the 1970's. It supposedly concerned a grappling native to Northern Ireland whose identity was thankfully never disclosed to me. Allegedly on hearing about some unwanted advances being experienced by his girlfriend, whom at that time was still in the province, took a Friday late night ferry ride "Over the Water" dealt with the problem and returned to the mainland on the following the Sunday night. Apparently like similar incidents that were occurring regularly in the North at that time it was later reported in the Ulster press as just another ordinary everyday, sectarian, doorstep execution! That's what I heard I've no idea if it's true or not thank God!

The financial differential between the rich and the poor, the haves and the have not's in the UK has never been greater and it continues to grow. My next story kind of sums that up, well for me at least, it's a classic case of how the Super Rich spend or don't spend their cash. I'd been working for Andy Robin and I'd made a few trips up to his pub The Sheriffmuir Inn just north of Dunblane. It sits just off the A9 to the right as you're heading for Perth, along a fairly short tree lined B road. On one such visit I was invited to share a ring with **"Hercules the Bear"** naturally I politely declined. Actually if I were honest I think my real reply went something like "You've got to be fucking joking mate! Big Softy or not you've no chance of getting me in there!" [In 2014 a statue was erected commemorating the time when the bear swam off, disappearing for three weeks in late 1980 whilst filming an advert for Andrex toilet paper in the Outer Hebrides on the island of Benbecula. Langass Woodland Trust arranged the unveiling. According to a reliable source Andy suffered a debilitating illness attack in 2013 but he seems to be well on the mend now] Anyway Andy and Margaret his wife had another visitor that particular day in the early part of 1980 and I was formally introduced. Shaking the hand of a Multi-Millionaire was not an everyday occurrence for one such as I but this chap was no ordinary high born man with lots of money, he was perhaps Scotland's best known retailer at that time Sir Hugh Fraser. The connection to my host Andy was of

course through his wife the wonderful Margaret, maiden name Nimmo her social circle and the world she'd competed in previously had meant she'd held at one time the Ladies Scottish Show Jumping Championship and he moved in high born circles. Andy would refer to her as Maggie and she was and I'm sure still is the love of his life. Although she had a strong rival for his affections after the bear entered into the family circle. "Call me Hugh" he insisted when she introduced us on that first day in the Robin's kitchen and he repeated himself in exactly the same manner only a few short weeks later when we met for a second time at a headline wrestling tournament held in the 2,500 plus seated Perth Ice Rink.
It had been another successful show but for me another incident filled night, on the way back home we all travelled through the picturesque village of Auchterarder. [A community boasting the longest main street in Scotland] Andy had lived there at one time so we stopped off at what was back then one of the best Chip Shops in the land. The dark blue pin stripe suited Lord entered first and we his camp followers followed on behind, all perhaps anticipating the possibility of a feast fit for a King or maybe just a Lord? Rather sadly that was not to be because disappointingly the landed gentry ordered one bag of chips for himself and having paid for them in cash, he then applied a liberal helping of the free salt and then some free vinegar before leaving the premises. There he stood outside on the pavement munching away merrily. My order was two dressed fish suppers which required a short wait as they were considered to be a separate special order and a Haggis Pudding Super. I think that one was devoured by Big Ian Miller and thereafter the first part of the order was then not so daintily downed by both Young [Jim] Strasky and myself. Well we were hungry hard working boys!
Having finished his chips almost before we'd even gotten started Hugh having first asked if it was OK, then proceeded to drink down the first swig out of a large glass bottle of Barr's world famous Irn Bru I'd also purchased in

the café whilst we waited. It was a wee treat for all the lads and it was a fitting end to a truly memorable night.
Big Stadiums is where it really happens and Ice Rinks of which Britain and Scotland in particular has many are the ideal Show Case Venues. I had never been in the company of anyone with as much financial back-up before that period and I've never been in that same situation again since. I can honestly say being a boy from the working class area that the bold Lord Hugh was always a really very nice guy and he displayed absolutely no signs of any hang-ups about being surrounded by those whom many others in his class might well have felt in some way superior to. He was clearly as comfortable talking to us the plebs as he'd have been closing multi-million pound deals around a large well polished oak table in the boardroom. And we were equally at home with him around, I for one really enjoyed the time we spent together he was good company. He may have had money to burn but he was not pretentious or snobbish in any way in fact he went out of his way to make sure we didn't feel excluded whenever we were in his company. It is however ironic that whilst I was busy purchasing food for almost everyone else, he on the other hand was more than content to buy only his own. Nevertheless I would never dream of holding that against him after all he's a huge wrestling fan although sometimes I still find myself thinking; god he could have a least bought the Ginger! In short he was a gent and the kind of man the Aussies might well refer to as being a Fair Dinkum Bloke.

Oh and I nearly forgot here's something else that might be of interest? Some years back I knocked Dennis Wilson the drummer and sometimes singer with the Beach Boys on his arse in the middle of a rain soaked busy Glasgow Street. Do you think that deserve a wee mention?

Why did you do that? He's a singer and a musician not a wrestler! Whatever possessed you to go throwing your weight around like that?

Ask him again ref!

You're really not listening are you? Does he get a mention?

Definitely! He was a member of one of the most iconic bands of the last twenty years! Please explained how that happened and why?

You're of course correct about them being a great act not many before or since have had such close harmonies but I thought he might have been a bit tougher than that. After all I'm sure I read somewhere he'd let Charles Manson [The Californian hippy commune leader who's "Family" was responsible for Sharon Tate's murder in the 1960's] share his house in the LA hills for a few months. Anyway keep your hair on I didn't jump all over him or anything like that. I like their music a lot as you are about to discover and believe it or not both my future wife and I were actually heading to the Odeon Cinema, the front door of which stands on the corner of Renfield Street and West Regent Street. It's an impressive Art Deco Style building and it takes up a whole city block going all the way back to West Nile Street. [The building still stands on that same corner, it was originally set for demolition but over the years several plans have been put forward to restore it to its former glory. Glasgow back then could rightly boast two of the biggest seating capacity picture houses and sometime concert venues in the UK. The Odeon being one with approx 2,750 seats and The Green's Playhouse being the other. When The Playhouse was originally erected it held the European record as the number of seats available was 4,200 but by the time the late 1960's came around movie audiences had dwindled somewhat, a consequence of which meant its capacity was then reduced to approx. 3,500. The Green's as it was know locally stood further up the street at the intersection of Renfrew Street and the top of Renfield Street at number 126. The Greens had effectively stopped operating as a cinema as in the late 1960's. That's when Unicorn Leisure, Billy Connolly's management company at the time took over a lease and operated a popular city

Discothèque in the top half of the building called "Clouds" in 1973. The building was closed again in the September of that same year. Unicorn again arranged a new lease only this time taking over the whole building. Turning it into what was to became one of the worlds most famous and iconic Rock Concert Venues known as "The Apollo." All of the top international groups played there to rapturous applause from some of the best and most appreciative audiences in the world. These artists included top rockers AC/DC, Ozzy Osbourne, Black Sabbath, The Clash, The Sensational Alex Harvey Band, Meat Loaf, Queen, The Average White Band and Simple Minds. Others of differing music genres included Abba and Phil Collins and the International star who opened the venue with two concerts on 5th and 6th September 1973 was "The man in Black" Johnny Cash. Another American band Dr Hook featured in the second last concert before it closed in 1985 and the last band to appear on its famous high stage were the Style Council. It's perhaps a pity they never ran Wrestling Shows in the space as there's a strong possibility it might have become to some extent as famous as Glasgow Empire as a real "Love you!" "Hate you!" venue! It was later demolished making way for a new high-tech Multi-Plex Cinema which opened in1987] The list of stars appearing on the Bill that night at the Odeon was also very impressive for the period. It included people like Barry Ryan, Bruce Channel of "Hey Baby" fame and Miss Susan Maughan. The show was headlined by himself [Dennis] his brother Carl Wilson his cousin Mike Love on lead vocals, boyhood friend Al Jardine on lead guitar and on back-up vocals and keyboards was former session artist Bruce Johnston. He had effectively taken the place of shortly to become a Country Music sensation Glen Campbell [He'd played backing guitar for them for a time] when he left to further his own solo career. Over the years others have come and gone from the California based originally Candy Striped Shirt wearing Surf Sound band. Brian Wilson the oldest brother and the driving force behind the writing of almost all their big hits had suffered a breakdown in the mid 60's, some say due to drug abuse and depression related problems and had stopped touring almost immediately. [Dennis Wilson was drowned in 1983, he was the only true surfer in the group and it's perhaps fitting the sea took him as one of its own. His brother Carl the bands Base Player passed away in 1998 of a cancer related illness. RIP]

It was a pretty scabby night in late autumn as my fiancé and I hurried along the busy street. It was cold and it was raining and he like me had his head down trying to avoid the cold biting wind that almost ripped your face off! It reminded me a lot of the wind that comes off the Hudson in New York City in January time as opposed too surfing in a balmy hot wind and the thrill of Waimea Bay or The Banzai Pipeline both of course in sunny Hawaii! Jeffrey's Bay South Africa, Bells Beach in Victoria near Melbourne Australia or even San Diego USA in the balmy July breeze!

God you make that sound terrific, like you know what you're talking about when it comes to waves and stuff!

Really! You've obviously never seen me "Hanging Five" or maybe even "Ten?" Or Shooting the Curl and the likes!

Sorry! You got me there!

Yes I probably did but that'll give you something to research later, anyway, back to Dennis and his wet back-side! He'd just come running out of a Department Store, Woolworth I think or maybe even Marks and Spencer? It was all such a long time ago now, he was weighed down with an assortment of tartan travel rugs. He must have had about six or seven so it was just about as difficult for him to see me as it was for me to notice him in the middle of a chilling rain shower! Anyway the street was mobbed with lots of people milling around, most just trying to get home for the night to a warm fire, it was still the tail end of rush hour! So bang! Down he went in a heap in a rain filled puddle! He just lay there like a sack of spuds that had spilled out onto the pavement from a delivery van!

And what did you do then?

I jumped all over him and stole all of his shopping!

You didn't, did you?

Only joking! I picked up a couple of the rugs or it could have been three or perhaps four. I threw them on top of him and then walked off into the wet autumn sunset with one under each arm as a memento!

Now you're just taking the proverbial!

OK! So I'm having a laugh don't get you knickers in a twist! What do you take me for? Like a true Scot I helped him to his feet rearranged his jacket etc, both of us assisted him further by picking up his scattered shopping, wished him all the best and walked on. Then only a few seconds later it hit me, clearly the accent gave it away as he said "Thank You Man!" and turning to Lilian I uttered these now forever immortal words; "Shit! That was Dennis Wilson!"

Some of the strangest wrestling shows ever cobbled together in the last twenty years have taken full advantage of the euphoria being created by the loudly trumpeted "60's Sound" nostalgia movement. These being the amalgam of one hit wonder Pop Bands now on the Cabaret Circuit and Wrestling Stars! This idea however did not go down too well at first with the purists, especially on the grappling side, but they did have their place in the broader show business sense and they were eventually very well supported by all sections of the public. One show in particular was staged in of all places Dunoon and it featured a stunningly delectable big draw headliner!

Although I can't help but think, the close proximity of the local naval base packed full of Dollar wielding, over sexed American sailors loomed large in the minds of those putting it together a whole lot more than the thought of bringing some culture to the local Scots based Islanders. The star in question not only had a wonderful voice she had the stunning body to match it! Having a "Hit Single" always helps to put bums on seats and the vivacious Miss Kathy Kirby whose powerful revamped version of the old Doris Day hit "Secret Love" had done just that, flying high in the Chart for a period of four weeks, pretty good going for a top song back in those days. She's a really nice young lady coming originally from Essex, Ilford I think she said and stardom according to those who really knew her did not change her one little bit. Her stunningly strong vocals are supported by her huge lung capacity, a legacy perhaps from her Convent School Choir days which in turn resulted in the formation of two of the biggest sources of libidinous thinking at that time in Britain. Her huge bosoms were amongst the most talked about in UK show business circles and were seldom out of the Sunday newspapers. Over an all too brief cuppa she told me of some of her hopes and her ambitions, first and foremost she wanted to conquer the USA something two of her contemporaries Dusty Springfield and Petula Clark had already done.

From the moment of curtain up she had the audience eating out of her hand and all the men in the front row, including me standing in the wings were also drooling heavily! When the Cabaret ended it was all hands to the pumps setting up the ring as close to the stage as was possible and then it was our turn. When we finished and showered we made our way out of the building in search of a meal, both she and the paying public had long since disappeared but once again I got lucky when I encountered an equally well endowed young lady who was working in one of the larger upmarket hotels for the summer. Rather strangely though or so she led me to believe she was heavily into the very versatile vegetable “The Cucumber!”

What’s wrong with that? Vegetarians have been around since the beginning of history in more sophisticated cultures! Just look at Egypt the Greeks and the Romans.

The Greeks! I can’t argue with them, democracy and all that, great stuff! I’ve read somewhere that Cleopatra had a lot of kinky skills when she finally got her head up and under Mark Anthony’s Togo but I think we can safely say this girl was more into the Romans! Full-on orgies would not have been a problem for her she’d have definitely enjoyed them and hopefully some freshly washed salad for afters as well as during! I sometimes find myself in a quiet moment reflecting on that all too brief encounter with Miss Kirby, most notably when I hear that tune again and yes I freely admit it, before you ask, I did buy the record I still have it somewhere in my vast and varied vinyl collection.

Glasgow’s famous Ashfield Club is another of the successful duel Wrestling/Cabaret Show venues. On one occasion when I was there Mr Glasgow himself, singer Glen Daly not only compared the show he also topped the bill and as his title suggests he had the place heaving! I’d like to say most of the crowd were there to see me and all the other wrestlers but I’d be lying. I’m sure you’ve already surmised they were all there to see and hear their hero, the legendary Glen. Not one empty seat to be had and what a night that was, it was very, very late when I got home and I’ll have to honestly declare I’ve got almost no recollection of the drive down the A77 back home! The headliner was one of the nicest people it’s ever been my pleasure to be introduced to, he was as you might expect very sociable hence the usual alcohol led indiscretions! With his red tartan jacket he cut a fine figure of a man as he worked the room effortlessly giving the audience his renditions of all the songs they’d come to hear and fully expected to get! His latest LP has done very well again, it’s aptly entitled

"It's Glen Again Live at the Ashfield Glasgow" he's sold a good few copies since its release, you should nip out and buy yourself a copy you'll love it! He made me a present of one on that very night and autographed it for me as well! I've taped it and I play it in the car, it always gets the blood flowing and it's got a great selection of Scottish favourites and a lot of the more popular modern songs as well. He's got loads of charisma and a huge following. Let's hope he never takes up the grappling as he'd steal the show.

Regards TV and the Movies local lad made good Freddie Boardley is another treasured acquaintance of mine and yes we have shared a few drinks over the years, me on the Malt Whisky and him on the Vodka and Perrier Water. He may not be the greatest actor Scotland's ever produced but he's very capable nevertheless and he's been in almost everything on TV both north and south of the border and he's very down to earth with it! That persona was probably formed whilst working as a youngster for his father Ivan in the family fish business based in the harbour area in Ayr. I don't think I'm letting the cat out of the bag when I say father was not all that keen on his boy taking up a career in a profession of which he and others of the time might have said real men should never be seen to venture! Young Freddie over the years has proved both his dad and also the other doubters wrong you've only got to take a look at his long list of credits and achievements to see that! There are not many around who's CV could boast leading rolls over half a lifetime in some of the most popular TV series of all time, things like: Coronation Street, Taggart, Brookside, Monarch of the Glen, Rab C. Nessbit, Heartbeat, Bad Boys, High Road, Casualty, The Professionals and many, many more. During a glittering career he has also featured in some of the classics from the Play for Today series; many written by the controversial play-write "Peter McDougal" in which he worked with such greats as Billy Connolly, the Rock Singer Frankie Miller [Freddie's a decent singer and an accomplished guitarist himself] and other Scots acting stalwarts like craggy John Murtagh. I met John one time back stage after a theatre performance of my own in a production of Animal Farm. I had played the cruel farm owner Mr Jones but rather sadly I doubt he'd remember that night or indeed me or my performance. Freddie also toured Europe with the English National Theatre and was at one time part of the cast of the world's most famous television "Street" where he played Elsie Tanner's lodger. With all that ground breaking black underwear on show live on the screen before 9pm. Fantastic! Sexy Pat Phoenix not my friend Freddie of course! We only appeared in one production together, he had a cameo in one episode in "The Sword and the Cross." for the BBC, I was lucky enough to have several personas.

Moving on again I've kind of left the best to last in a sporting sense well to some extent and especially from a Scottish perspective. He's another boxer who like Brother Cooper had a very good Domestic, European and Commonwealth career record, but even he'd have to admit to having a far lesser British profile. Sadly he was never afforded the opportunity of taking any real financial advantage from such memorable events in the ring as the now infamous "Cooper–Clay" incident during a non title bout at Wembley Stadium in 1963 and the controversy which ensued thereafter where for the most part the American contingent were stunned into silence when surprise, surprise their Golden Boy's backside landed on the canvas in the dying seconds of round four as he became a victim of the famous left hand known as "Enry's Ammer." In fragrant violation of British Boxing Board rules smelling salts were used in the corner to revive a semi-conscious, soon to change his name, rather groggy Cassius Clay. He later recovered and went on to win the contest after Cooper sustained a badly cut eye. As Muhammad Ali he went on to conquer the world and more than once. Cooper's "Splash in on Henry" a very popular TV Commercial of its day served him well financially I'm sure but more importantly it gave him another career opportunity which did every bit as much as boxing to endear him to everyone in these islands. An unexpected Lloyds collapse meant his investment as a "Name" proved a little shaky! [Henry Cooper died May 1st 2011 aged 76]

You may have guessed by now my next afore mention candidate is also a boxer although a lot lighter and a lot smaller than the former the former Heavyweight. He has an equally big heart and was as brave as a bull! Standing only a few inches above 5foot he too had a very powerful punch, especially with his left hand and he was well loved in Scotland where he successfully bridged even the religion driven sectarian divide. Peter Keenan and Henry share a common thread both coming from working class inner city deprived areas. The Scot came from Partick in Glasgow and Ernie from the Lambeth area of London, both hold Lonsdale Belts outright! You need to successfully defend your title three times to be awarded a belt and it's not something all title holders over the years can claim to possess. Peter was in fact the proud possessor of two such belts. Fellow Scott Flyweight and former World Champion Walter McGowan is another. Whilst attending a popular gym in my home town at Tam's Brig I'd encountered one of McGowan's sparring partners a chap called Jim McDonald, he was as fit as a fly and sported an almost perfectly formed array of muscles which he developed whilst serving at sea in the British Merchant Service. I took an instant liking to this gentleman pugilist and would often seek his help and assistance in future years. I even attended some of his training nights and I'm proud to say we've remained good friends ever since.

I also used a gym in Glasgow which had a close association to the "Wee Man" Mr Keenan for quite sometime after I returned home from Australia. He would flit in and out but always tried to give the impression he had to real interest in the wrestler on the weights surrounded by sweaty boxers of all shapes and sizes. I was however kept well informed by the old guy who looked after the place, strange to say his name was Peter as well. He would tell me that the Gaffer had repeatedly instructed him to keep an eye on the youngster's progress and had insisted he make sure I got safely to my bus every evening after my workout. It dropped me off at Central Station and from there an hour long train journey got to Ayr and then another bus ride got me home to Mossblown. He'd apparently told the caretaker the city could be a dark and very dangerous place for a lad from the county side. "So for God sake keep an eye on him!" Perhaps a guarded reference to what I eluded to earlier about religion and the violence that stalked the dark city streets, where neighbourhood strangers regularly fall victim to sectarian violence! [Peter died on 27th July 2000 he was aged 71] The caretaker told me a story about his Dad who was in the Second World War, when he'd come home on leave the first thing he did was head for the bar in the Central Station and whilst there he'd sink a quick pint, which some kind gent usually paid for after feasting his eyes on the highly polished cap badge he was wearing. Then he'd purchase two large dark green coloured McEwen's screw top beer bottles. Once out in the street he'd then push a bottle up into each of his greatcoat sleeves before heading off home. If he was unlucky enough to be stopped and challenged on his way through the dark city streets, after the first two strangers had been taken out by means of a dropped down into a hand bottle being smashed into their face anyone else present, on seeing the blood streaming from their friends heads generally lost heart pretty quickly and turned and ran. Incidents like this happen all too often back in those days in Glasgow so it was far better to prepared for the unexpected rather than have to make an unscheduled visit to the local Infirmary to have your face stitched up! The caretaker also enlightened me rather ironically regards his uncle the bookies collector. He was proud of the fact he was famous for slicing his victims buttocks with an open razor and not there faces. Standing at the bar with your back to the door could be a bad thing if you were late with your repayments! On a non ego trip level I hope you'll forgive me just one short reference to something which happened to me on my journey back to Scotland from Australia in the early 1960's. The ship in which I was travelling had called in at Colombo Sri Lanka's [It was called Ceylon at the time] capital city on the west coast of the island. I had been ashore a few times during our two day stop-over and I really enjoyed all that I had experienced and everything I'd seen, except for the open sewers and the hoards of badly crippled beggars that is. With only an hour left before the ship was due to sail I was handed a short message from one of the white suited Italian Officers employed by the "SITMAR LINE" the vessel's owners the ship was named "Fair Sea" and at that time all their fleet were based in Naples. So not knowing a thing about what was going on I made my way to the main passenger lounge area, there I was greeted by the chief reporter and the staff photographer from The Daily News. It transpired it was the countries biggest selling newspaper and I believe it still is, the situation was this. Apparently I had been observed during a couple of my visits on shore and reports had been picked up by the local press about a white, long haired "Englishman." I have no idea why I or my looks should have caused such a stir inspiring the editor of such a prestigious national newspaper to feel it necessary to send both a head reporter and a photographer just to talk to lowly me! Not only did they want my story, much more importantly they wanted my picture also. Apparently the phenomenon of "Beatlemania" and the "Liverpool Sound" knew no musical boundaries clearly it had also reached the lower part of the Indian Sub-Continent and beyond and all this was happening well before John, Paul, George and Ringo had ventured forth on their path of spiritual enlightenment. So following the old showbiz adage that any publicity is good publicity naturally I was very happy to oblige with both my life story thus far, and the all important photograph. I might add I've no idea if either the copy or the snap ever appeared in print!

What no Footballers?

If its footballers you want then footballers you shall have! I've known quite a few over the years most of whom played at one time or another for my local team Ayr United. Some then moved on to bigger clubs and International recognition. "The Honest Men" as they are known [A reference to a Robert Burns poem] earned the right to be included in the original mix when Scotland formulated the original Premier League concept, sadly they only lasted a couple of seasons in the top level. Their fortunes have taken a bit of a downward spiral ever since although some truly great players have come and gone over the years. Many of whom it's been my great pleasure to have known personally. Jackie Ferguson (Inside Forward) a local lad who came from the Maybole village area was a good player and very good company. He'd transferred back from England where his career was faltering slightly. Billy Walker and Tommy Reynolds both (Inside Forward/Wing Half) players they are two really nice guys and although small in stature made up for that with their footballer brain. David Stewart (Goal Keeper) was snapped up by Leeds. Big George McLean (Centre Forward) was ex St Mirren, Glasgow Rangers then Dundee, Dunfermline, Ayr United and finally Hamilton Athletic. He used to come into Bumpers in Prestwick occasionally, always a trendily dresser hence the nickname of "Dandy." Quinton "Cutty" Young (Right Wing) moved on to Glasgow Rangers eventually he was a short term Scottish Internationalist as well. He's another local lad who came from the village of Drongan yet another strong Ayrshire coal mining community. He his pal Jinky Kean and I have shared a few pints on occasion where the convivial company sometimes included another local worthy, and a really nice guy known as "Billy the Kid." Hugh Sproat (Goal Keeper) was yet another great guy, always full of impish fun he too came from one of the other local villages he would wind up the Rangers supporter by wearing a green top, changing to a blue jersey had the same affect on the Celtic contingent. Big Alex McAnespie is another in the roll of twin (Centre Half) regularly lining up along side Club Captain Stan Quinn, Stan wasn't the tallest guy on the park but boy could he jump, he was also noted for being tough and uncompromising in the tackle. Joe Fillipi (Wing Half) came back to United from Coventry City eventually moving on to a Celtic team in transition. Jock Stein the Celtic coach and the Ayr manager were close friends. I still see Joe regularly around the town. Lastly Johnny Doyle (Left/Right Wing) he established himself after "Cutty" left for Ibrox then he too moved on to Glasgow to sign on at Celtic Park, better known as "Paradise." to their huge fan-base. I had a memorable fall out with him over a parking space outside the main entrance to Somerset Park. (Ayr's Stadium) Going down the street the Main Stand is on the right and to the left was a long block of Sand Stone Tenement Flats. I lived in No 3 down stairs on the right hand side. One night after my training in the Mossblown Gym on returning home I couldn't get my car parked in the street never mind outside my house. It was also a football training night. Young Mr Doyle's car was abandoned over two spaces, one of which was mine! Naturally I had to speak to him about it! He wasn't very pleased. Arrogant Bugger!

Was he really? Footballers can be like that, so I'm told.

No not him, me! What an arse hole I was being he didn't deserve that, we made up a couple of weeks later. [John Doyle died in a tragic accident at his home in Kilmarnock in October 1981 he was only 31 years of age] He was born in Uddingston in Lanarkshire on the south east side of Glasgow. The world famous Celtic right winger Jimmy "Jinky" Johnston voted the clubs best ever player came from that same area. Ayr's manager signed John as a youth in 1970 from the "Viewpark Juveniles" team. "Jinky Johnston" was born and lived in Viewpark and when he married he moved to Tannochside. Young John had a sadly short lived Scotland international career but he's still revered by Celtic supporters the world over as is his hero "Wee Jimmy." Rather strangely Ayr at that time had supplied both right wingers to the Old Firm at almost the same time. I can't remember any other team doing that, their (Centre Forward) at that time was Alex "Dixie" Ingram he had that gift of being able to hang in the air. He moved south for a time under the tutelage of Brian Clough at Nottingham Forrest in 1970 and whilst there they tried to change him into a mid-field player, within eighteen months he was back at Ayr. He was sold to them for the princely sum of £40.000 and for a club like Ayr that was a whole lot of money back then. Ayr bought him back for £15.000 the transfer market was of course not all one way. Over the years Ricky Fleming and Eric Morris arrived from Rangers (albeit a few years apart) and in the teams heyday Johnny Graham came from Hibernian, former Celtic players Johnny Gibson and Brian McLaughlin also graced Somerset Parks originally imported Irish Turf and a few years before that Fullback Dick Malone had gone to Sunderland and played in the team who beat Don Revie's star studded Leeds 1-0 in the FA Cup in 1973. The last player to leave for big money was Stevie Nicol from Troon. He hit the dizzy heights of stardom with both Liverpool FC and Scotland. For me personally living in the street where the football park was situated also had its advantages especially if like me you were both a football supporter and also a person who likes to talk at length to others. I was often very privileged to have been in Somerset Park sometimes just about as often I was in my own house and the smashing Wee Woman who did the teas and sandwiches for the players lived only a couple of houses further down. So I got my tea as well and more often than not an extra chocolate biscuit! I also got the chance on a regular basis to discuss football with the Ayr, Aberdeen and later on Scotland manager Mr Ally McLeod. He could charm the birds out of the trees that man, it's really sad the way the World Cup failure in Argentina almost destroyed him, he didn't deserve to be pilloried like that. He would send those impressionable young lads who'd pulled on Ayr's Black and White shirt out onto the field thinking they could beat anybody, and back then more often than not they did! They outplayed Glasgow Rangers all too often and Hibernian and Hearts almost at will and even the first British Club to win the European Cup Celtic FC on several occasions as well! Regularly English opposition during the then cross border Texaco Cup Competitions lost to Utd as well! Even the Mighty Black and White Striped Newcastle when they brought their big guns up for a game that opened the new Somerset Park Floodlights, they too lost two goals to one. [Ally McLeod left us on 1st February 2004 and Big Jock Stein passed away on September 10th 1985]

You've been acquainted with a good mix of people. Some of note as well! Who's your favourite out of the lot of them?

On the football front probably Big Billy McNeil, in another entertainment capacity I met him at a big posh wedding do and we spent a few minutes discussing the merits of his move south to manage Man City, sadly by then the top team Malcolm Allison had produced in the mid to late 1960's had broken up. The job by then had become a bit of a poisoned chalice and "Cesar" [The Celtic fans name for the big man] like many others before and since failed to bring any new and lasting success to the City's Blue half.

So your main man is a footballer?

Actually no it's not but you me and everyone else has surely got to recognise the fact McNeil as a Scot held aloft the most sought after trophy in football. Sadly that fact is not always acknowledged enough elsewhere, more so in England. I still haven't mentioned my top man for two reasons, one he does not pull on a sporting shirt in fact he's been known to take his off to perform and the other is simply because I didn't want to be accused of "bumming my chat" as we say in Ayrshire.

Oh come off it! Don't be like that! Anyway deep down you're dying to tell me, aren't you? Who is it? It's got to be someone quite famous but someone who might be described as a little controversial. Isn't it?

Dale smiles a little enthralled by the reporter's assessment.

I knew it, I'm correct aren't I? I can see it in your eyes.

Ok you're correct, obviously reporter's intuition well done.

Right! Do tell!

It's "Ollie Reed" Happy now?

Oliver Reed! Fantastic! Was he drunk at the time?

A definitive no! He's a real professional and a real trooper to boot, yes he likes a drink and yes he comes across to some on TV Chat Shows as pain in the backside but he turns up on the set every morning ready to do a professional job no matter how long the days shoot lasts and what's more he's usually word perfect!

So how did you come across him then?

He was doing a film for Cromwell in the Scottish Borders, it was a Scottish history period piece entitled "The Bruce" Obviously about the guy who came out on top at the Battle of Bannockburn in 1314 Robert the Bruce! He's not my favourite person I might add, he was an opportunist, only really interested in furthering his own Norman ancestry family's personal fortune. An early thirteenth century self-centred wanker some might say. Give me "The Wallace" every time. William Wallace defeated the English at the Battle of Stirling Bridge in 1297, like Bruce he too was an

Ayrshire born man although some might deny that fact! Oliver was playing the influential Scottish Bishop of the period Glasgow's Robert Wishart. Anyway he used to drink in a pub in the main street in Peebles and in the corner of the bar stood a tired and battered old armchair. As you might imagine he liked to hold court, a bit like King Lear a classic part which rather sadly he himself never got around to playing, well not the official Shakespearian version anyway and like Lear his later life was full of pitfalls. The difficulty was it was a very popular bar and even more so when he was in it! Why is that I hear you say, perhaps because of his personally status or maybe for another reason entirely, although I choose not to view it from a narrow minded free-loader, hanger-on, buy me a drink perspective because he is a very generous man and of that fact there is no doubt, drunk or sober! He has always been equally generous to his fellow actors. He could've fitted right into many of the situations highlighted in lots of Robert Burns' famous bawdy poems "The Cotter's Saturday Night" being perhaps the best one! Anyway Ollie was not always first to sit his now broadening arse on the chair and if it was already occupied he could and often would get a little annoyed, but when and if said occupant went to relieve himself on returning he'd find it moved slightly and occupied! On one particular occasion when words were exchanged with a disgruntled punter Ollie asked the owner straight out! "How much do you think this old chair is worth landlord?" When he was informed the figure was probably in the region of £25, he immediately placed that amount on the bar in cash and then jumping up onto an adjacent bar stool he proudly proclaimed to everyone present. "Oliver Reed from this day forth is the new and proud owner of this here chair!" From that day to this the chair still sits proudly nestled between the bar area and the rather steep and narrow wooden staircase leading down to the back lounge. Sadly nowadays it remains largely unoccupied still patiently waiting for the great man to once again rest his weary posterior on its lovely new green upholstery with no danger of injury from the now fully restored new springs! On the downside for some strange reason there's no polished brass plaque on the wall commemorating this truly talented man. [Oliver Reed died 2nd May 1999 age 61 in Valletta Malta. Rest in peace free at last from all your earthly trials, tribulations and cowardly backstabbing insults]

You're remarkably well informed. How do you know this?

Simple, I was there and I was witness almost all of it!

So you're a pal of Oliver Reed's then?

Sadly in all honesty no I'm not and I've never claimed to be. Another good friend of mine Big Chick Allan has worked with him though. [Charley Alan is an Edinburgh man who formed the "Clanranald" charitable group. The organisation has been busily raising funds to build the Duncarron project, this replica medieval wooden fort is primarily an educational aid built near the Carron Valley Reservoir. Over the years he's developed a close friendship with actor Russell Crowe, if you've watched the movie "Robin Hood" or maybe "Gladiator" you'll have seen Chic holding up the severed head of a Roman soldier at the start of that picture playing a Northern Tribes leader who's mocking the Roman Legends just before Crowe playing the General "Unleashes hell" on the usurpers]
Anyway, he and the rest of "Clanranald" were in the borders doing the action shots and I just tagged on through an Extras Agency, well it was an earner and it helped get me through quiet times. Not a huge payer but the après filming pub nights made up for the lack of big cheque. I did however have the great pleasure to be back in Peebles a few years later, by then I'd spent some of the intervening time training as an actor and through a friend Al Anderson I'd landed the roll of the daft henchman in the pilot episode for a possible series slot on US television. In the production I'd been tasked with the capture of "Merlin the Wizard." The

Ask him again ref!

Lead Role [Merlin] was being played by Mr Jason Connery. Roger Moore's daughter Deborah was playing the female lead; she's a really lovely girl with classic Italian looks just like her mother. Like Jason she too has no pretension and presumption of star status she had been in the original Scottish Widows Advert and she looks stunning! Big "Gareth Thomas" who played Blake in "Blake Seven" one of my favourite TV Shows also had a leading roll as did the really versatile Scots born actor Mr Graham McTavish. He played Regal the Black Wizard who was desperately trying to kill the young Merlin. Graham has now gone on to receive some Hollywood recognition. The storyline was loosely based on the King Arthur although his character never appeared. I used my Equity name in that production.

That's great what a lovely wee story.

Anyway, we were all based in the same hotel "The Tontine" in the High Street in Peebles. It's the same one that was used before for the other movie starring Mr Reed although not by me at that time. There was no way I was going to pay those prices off the pittance I was receiving first time around. It was a little different on my second visit to the town as Cromwell picked up the bill, although I'd still nip over to the bar in the Crown across the road for a cheaper pint sometimes, I decanted over there to stay a couple of times as well when the Tontine was fully booked after returning to the borders from a shooting break. I was quite happy to make myself at home there; it was really quite comfortable in an old worldly kind of a way. The Crown Hotel is situated at 54 High Street Peebles. On my first day back in the area I held my breath as I crossed the front door threshold and sure enough there it was in all its splendour, still sitting proudly, although it had been move around the corner slightly. That once old and well worn faded brown liveried chair was now proudly decked out in its new green coloured tweed finish material covering its high backed, wing sided frame, Ollie's Chair! It seemed to

be saying to me and me alone "Hello how have you been? Sit your arse down here and make yourself at home!"
A short time before that I got really lucky when I got a few days work in roughly the same area of the borders on a film starring Mr Billy Connolly, Ms Judie Dench and a very young far less experienced Gerard Butler. The film directed by John Madden was about a controversial period during the reign of Queen Victoria. It had the working title of "Her Majesty Mrs Brown" later shortened to a feature film length by Miramax when they bought it from Scotia/BBC. The release title then became "Mrs Brown" and deservedly it was a really big hit. It was made originally with a Sunday Night TV slot in mind and was destined to go out as a Three-Part-Drama. When it was edited down most of my stuff, which I must confess was not huge finished up on the cutting room floor along with a whole lot from far more gifted performers. Connolly was great to be around and occasionally I got to spend some time with him, he's really funny all the time and he's always very approachable when he's not as he says "At his work man!" He's clearly well read and can talk on almost any subject although I don't know the man all that well, it's really hard not to like him, well most of the time that is! But I do get very annoyed sometimes when he prattles on about Scotland knocking the Tartan, Golf, the Bad Pipes, Short Bread and our national drink, please not our lovely malt whisky man! Maybe that's why some years earlier in yet another life, I'd pissed on his multi-coloured Bell Bottomed Strides or maybe it was the fancy Cowboy Boots that annoyed me who knows? Or maybe I'd just had an epiphany or something and seen the future and maybe I'd got a sneak preview of coming events of what he would be saying about his fellow native Scots. Things like blatantly denying on shows like Parkinson that his humour was the stuff of Pubs and Shipyards and the Football Terraces of Glasgow and the West of Scotland. Or maybe I and the rest of the nation were just jealous of his success? We Scots can be like that sometimes! We just love to down the successful.

Ask him again ref!

You urinated on the Big Yin! And he didn't say a word?

Yes he said several words but none of them are suitable for your young ears and I was very drunk and he was very sober at the time, I was three sheets to the wind! I thank God he was rushing to get on to the stage on time. He's a big fellow you know with a neck like a Bull. The venue was the Folk Club in the Caledonian Hotel Ayr I was there to see my brother-in-law performing he played guitar and sang. He used to be quite good, his name's Jimmy.

That's a great clue to his real identity. There aren't many folk in Scotland called Jimmy. So he'll be fairly easy to track down for some corroboration before I go to print then.

Yes, yes very funny Jimmy's his name and that's all you're getting as it's not for printing! Anyway, Connolly got his own back fifty times over and he didn't even have to work for it, he was still playing a lot of Banjo back then and singing as well. We two nut jobs were sitting in the centre of the front row right at his feet and we were even more out of our faces by then and yes we were talking gibberish. Going on and on at him continually, shouting up at and him to play "Dueling Banjos" which was really rather stupid given its the tune was featured in the 1972 John Boorman directed movie entitled "Deliverance" Talk about back-woods folks inbreeding, at that point we two wouldn't have looked out of place in the Tennessee Mountains! It's a classic film and if you've seen it you'll remember there was a tall guitar playing character named Drew and a squinty eyed, strange looking young kid called Lonnie, he had very little hair and the really nice innocent little smile. He's was sitting on his front porch repeating everything the other fellow was playing on his guitar, only he had a Banjo. Now bearing in mind we were not bald, my hair was down my back and we were more pie-eyed than squinty eyed, remembering "The Big Yin" had only his Banjo in hand and was on stage himself, now need I say more? Jimmy having been on stage earlier whilst I was at the bar had finally managed to catch up and like me he was now well pissed! In actual fact it had been all Jimmy's fault I decorated the fancy boots and Billy's trousers in the first place! I'd been standing minding my own business at the urinal taking up the usual position when you're overly inebriated; head resting on the wall for some balance as you do. Jimmy was standing to my right, the door opens and I'm only vaguely aware after the bang as it closes shut that someone must have entered. Next thing I know Jim's nudging me trying to point out that its Connolly who's taken up the only remaining egg shaped Piss Pot. So as I'm already in mid stream, on getting the nod I turn to my left "with my Willie still in my hand" and the rest as they say is now history!

God I wish I'd been there that must have been hilarious!

You in a Men's Cludge! Totally unthinkable! With Connolly, Jimmy and yours truly and all three cocks unbridled and two of us groaning with utter relief, the relief only a man can utter! No, No, I don't think so! I can think of one or two of the wrong kind of girls who worked locally who might have been very happy to have joined in but once again that may be another story for yet another time. Besides one Gerry Helmet didn't have the time to stay for any party even if it had the inclination, it and the guy it was attached to were now well overdue for a different type of performance but this time holstered and on a totally different stage. Keep your Forum frolics to yourself thanks!

...........Forum! Once again are we talking Rome here?

If that's how you see it, then that's just fine with me. Now can we please change the subject whilst we're both still in a slightly jocular mood.

If you wish, carry on.

So let me enlighten you and perhaps amuse you further.

Whilst in Oz in the 1960's I occasionally went along to watch some Pro wrestling friends and in some cases boyhood heroes of mine who worked regularly on Shows at the Sydney Stadium and afterwards we used to frequent a small Basement Music Club at the top end of Elizabeth Street called at that time "Beatle Village." Actually that's not quite true, they would turn up and get paid for working on the door and I would pay, go downstairs enjoy the music have a drink or two and chase a few of the good looking local girls. The place was obviously dedicated to the Merseyside Mop Tops, anyway, the Fab Four: John, Paul, George and on this occasion not Ringo were coming to Australia, the drummer was having some throat problems and was having a tonsillectomy back in the UK! His stand-in for some of the Aussie Tour Dates was Jimmy Nicol. Mr Starr arrived in Oz sometime later he [Jimmy] like the all others were making their very first visit to Australia and were arriving at Kingsford Smith Airport around 6am on Thursday 11th June 1964. Those Down Under have always been a hardy nation so not to be put off by the earliness of the hour it was decided by most of the regulars and the staff etc, we'd walk en mass from the city centre club out to the Mascot area to greet the new arrivals when the Club closed at 2am.Through the dark hours we tramped singing the songs of our musical heroes as we went. Rather unusually it pissed it down in torrents almost continually and we were bloody soaked before we'd gone a hundred yards, but we were not about to be put off or get disheartened, our resolve was far too strong for that. On the walkabout across the city I inherited an old wooden dinning room chair from a pile of rubbish at the roadside. Someone was having a clearout and had also slung some old carpets, a kitchen cabinet and a broken mirror. Maybe I should have viewed the broken mirror as a sign of things to come but doom and gloom were the furthest things from my mind that joyful morning. I carried that chair all the way to Mascot much to the amusement of everyone else but I had a cunning plan or so I thought. Almost on 6am the

Boeing 707 BOAC [British Overseas Aircraft Corporation] liveried plane landed and taxied over to where we, the devoted but by this time almost drowned fans had been marshalled. As the three mop tops + one exited the plane appearing on a motorised portable staircase the whole Airport erupted in a crescendo of noise, everyone went bloody crazy! The Beatles were immediately ushered under large black umbrellas and led away, most were sporting shoulder bags, trendy black corduroy caps and posh dark fully tailored suits. They were then assisted onto the back of a make-shift, wholly inadequate obviously hurriedly prepared converted service truck and thereafter they were paraded now equally as wet and windswept as the bloody rest of us passed the rows of twenty, thirty, forty and fifty deep devoted fans. This part was quite reminiscent of watching the Queen on TV inspecting her Troops on Horse Guards Parade during the trouping of the colour, only that's in June in London's summer months and it usually doesn't rain. Apart from the incessant heavenly fallout everything was going along just great, until I decided to execute my cunning afore mentioned, master plan.

...Silly Boy! Again!

The timing of which unfortunately for me came just as a clearly distraught young mother broke free from the police cordon, running out on to the soaking wet, puddle covered tarmac, her eyes tear filled she proceeded to throw her handicapped infant child into the air in the direction of her hero, her own personal St Paul! He distracted and unsighted was standing quite still trying desperately to take what shelter he could get under his now relentlessly windswept black umbrella. As the lorry platform approached clearly overcome by heightened emotion she just stood there rooted to the spot watching her little bundle flying through the air! This incident unfortunately for me then became the catalysed for not only the destruction of my cunning, utterly brilliant plan it also resulted in the total match stick mashing, wipe-out of my now short lived new best pal. My Faithful Chair! At the very moment those Scouse lads approached the area in which I was standing I was up and onto my wooded platform in a flash, waving wildly chest out and proud on my now far less closely guarded mini-grandstand. Only to have my antipodeans visit highpoint cruelly taken away from under me by what seemed like hundreds of drug crazed invaders, all of whom were equally anxious to witness what was going to happen to the forlorn, helpless infant who was still flying through the vapour soaked sky in the general direction of the Beatles makeshift transporter. Thanks are due to God for shaking St Paul out of this trance and for giving him the ability to catch the innocent baby but at what cost to my poor wee chair? If Bill Shankly the then Liverpool Football Club Manager had heard about the save Paul made he'd probably have signed him up the very next day. Tommy Lawrence eat your heart out might have been the headline in the Liverpool Echo. Lawrence was the Liverpool goal keeper at the time. Incidentally he too was a fellow Scot and a fellow Ayrshire man as well, an ex-coal miner from the village of Daily, it's not all that far from the previously mentioned hamlet of Maybole. Daily's a place I know quite well my beloved former soldier grandfather was born there.

.........And your faithful chair what happened after that?

As I said Firewood! Nothing left but bloody Firewood! It was a longer and far lonelier walk back home to the "Matraville Suburbs" without my faithful wooden hearted companion its remains had been left abandoned on the wet tarmac as a small makeshift but proud memorial. Left lying on a rain soaked battlefield where he/she had fallen and given his/her all in the service of Australian musical history! [RIP! Good and faithful but sadly not made of strong "Norwegian Wood" servant!] Sadly the previously mention broken mirror had, had an influence on what happened later, but circumstances were about to get even worse!
Months before I'd been lucky enough to get hold of one of the hottest tickets in town to see the Beatles in their one

night only show at the Sydney Stadium, but disaster had struck a couple of weeks before the due date. My two year old niece, unknown to me had been rummaging through my room and on finding said ticket, lodged for safe keeping inside a book, had damaged it beyond repair. She had in fact chewed it and what she didn't swallow now bore no resemblance to the original format. These facts were known to both my mother and also my sister-in-law, her mother but none could bring themselves to break the bad news to me. Had they done so I may well have been able to rescue the situation? Billy Box who came originally from Kilmarnock had a ticket for the seat next to mine but he'd been struck down by the love bug and he never turned up on the big night. He's obviously been heavily influenced by as we say in Scotland "The Lure of the Toosh!" So on the night I'd got all dressed up and was about to leave to go to the concert, so having popped my head in the Living Room door to say I was off before retrieving my precious ticket, then and only then was I finally given the bad news. Bugger! Much as I tried, and I did try and really, really hard throughout that whole evening outside the Sydney Stadium venue, but I just couldn't get anyone in charge at the concert to believe me when I'd enlightened them as too my tale of woe. Stupid uncaring disinterested Bastards! Why oh why hadn't anybody told me earlier about the accident that had befallen my ticket? I even tried to enlist the help of an on duty member of the 21 Squad. A Special Riot Squad Division of the Federal Police who were all well over 6foot 2inches tall! He turned out to have a Scots dad, but as before, all was too no avail! Even he carried no real weight! Maybe that's why I've hated the police ever since?

Maybe that's just a Freudian thing?

The Mop-Tops were staying at the Sydney Sheraton at least the policeman could tell that but going down there would have been more than a bit girly. So sadly I never got to see them live at either venue

Ask him again ref!

Never ever, that's a real shame.

There was one other thing Alan Bennett the actor/play-write almost killed me as he careered down off the Charring Cross Road near the National Portrait Gallery in London He's a tall man and a bit of a beast on a bike!

And whose fault was that?

Mine, I was standing in the roadway day dreaming.

Didn't he say anything?

He'd no time but he didn't half draw me an anguished look.

So you got the message, did you?

You could say that, he's a lot bigger in the flesh than on TV, sadly that run-in all but put a hex on my theatre career!

[Around the summer of 2004 I was in the village of Alloway where Robert Burns was born, they were having their annual art exhibition. A good friend who worked there had recommended I see the exhibits, they were both fascinating and at the same time quite haunting but I was captivated. Some years before I'd represented my school in an art competition in Glasgow sadly I didn't win but I gave it my best shot so I've always had a passionate interest in new and contemporary works. Anyway I'm busy studying this particular canvas, it looked great and this really tall guy appears out of nowhere at my shoulder and we get to talking and he asked if I like the composition. I reply, yes very much and he says "that's nice, glad you've not had a wasted journey." All this time I'm thinking to myself I've met this chap before somewhere and knowing me it was probably in a pub. Then he introduces himself holding out a huge right hand. "My name is Peter, Peter Howson it's my exhibition I'm the artist." Apart from the big hands he was very tall, well over six foot and what really stood out for me was the size his feet, they were hue I'd say about a size 14 maybe and they were encased in brown, well polished leather shoes Then it struck me I had met him before in the Red Lion pub in Prestwick although that had been the second time our paths had crossed in an alehouse because Ian Seaton the guitarist with the band Southbound had first introduced us one night in his regular watering hole the St Nicholas Hotel on the Ayr road in Prestwick. A few years had passed since that first night when over a pint or two he'd talked about trying to get into The Glasgow School of Art. Now getting back to the Red Lion encounter that being the second time we'd met, he'd then informed me he'd eventually got himself enrolled in 1975 and he went on to tell me he'd been born in London but he'd been schooled in Ayrshire at Prestwick Academy. A lot of my friends were educated at that school as well one went on some years later to become a pro wrestler working under the Viking guise. He and others had commented about the artistic talent Peter had displayed even them and how it had been a constant source of amusement to them the way he would caricature some of his teachers, not that the tutors were amused far from it apparently. So back in the gallery we continue having a look at some of his other stuff and then he asks me what I'm doing at the minute. Not wishing to spill the beans completely regarding my former Wrestling career I told him I was kind of dabbling in short film and was working on a wee documentary about the coal industry, given it had been about twenty years since the Strike I'd wanted to do something to mark the passage of time. All of which was perfectly true only I'd been engaged in the process for months. That's where my father worked for 40 odd years I told Peter. He was fascinated and asked if he could have a look, so I sent him the project. The very next day after he received it he called me saying how much he'd liked it and could he use it as it had given some fresh ideas and inspiration regards some work he was thinking of revisiting on "Miners." Most of the exhibition paintings portrayed them deep in the bowels of the earth! Naturally I said yes and again some time later I got another call from him, telling me he'd now finished the paintings, well some of them at least, he also said he'd called his agent in London and if I'd give him my email address he'd get someone there to email copies of his work to me and if I wanted to use the images on anything I was working on in future then I had his permission to do so. He's a really nice man and a very talented painter I only wish I could afford to own some of his work I've long since pictured a large crucifixion canvas hanging on the wall in the Dinning Room in my long forgotten Boarding House by the sea]

Total mileage Ayr to Forfar and back: 260.2 Miles
Total time taken for the full journey: 5Hours 40minutes

(Courtesy of Mr B Robertson)

Lolita Loren **Bill Robertson** **Apache Princess**

The top men in the Joint Promotions Organisation

Dale, Morrell, de Relwyskow, Beresford, Best & Green

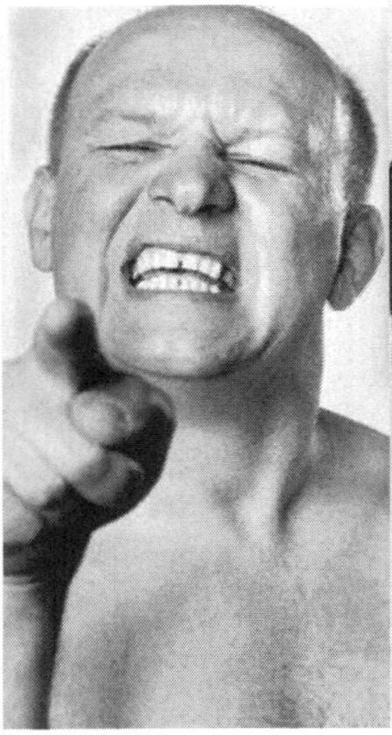

Leon Arras **Dr Death** **Eddie Hamill**

(Courtesy of Andrew Brodie-Frew)

Bill (rear) with Tag Partner Ron Clarke.

Ex-Celtic and Man City Manager Billy McNeil, Willie Henderson ex Glasgow Rangers & Me, glowing!

CHAPTER SIXTEEN

(The Old Mossblown Village Gym)

The Gym set-up used by us was born out of a very forthright and helpful suggestion made by the Headmaster of the local village school Annbank Junior Secondary which rather strange to say is not situated in the village of Annbank, it was in fact a further two miles away approximately in the neighbouring hamlet called Mossblown in Ayrshire in South West Scotland. His name was Mr George Nesbit sadly our benefactor has now passed on but he's fondly remembered by all the lads. When I'd returned from Down Under in the 1960's I'd struggled to continue with my amateur career mainly because there were no clubs in Ayrshire and not all that many in the nearest city of Glasgow and it was forty miles away. Incidentally almost at the same time as I was coming home to Scotland the Young Family from the Cranhill area of Glasgow were contemplating their arrival. They settled on the North side of the Famous Sydney Harbour Bridge in a Migrant Hostel called Villawood. I had been resident at one time in Matraville on the opposite side of the harbour in a hostel complex named Bunnerong. Two of the family's sons went on to form my favourite Rhythm and Blues/Rock Band AC/DC. I've since paid to see them several times.
So having initially spent some time travelling backwards and forwards to the "Dear Green Place" the old and historical name for the city of Glasgow my older brother and myself managed to talk the committee of the local Health and Strength Club "TAM McKEAN'S," in the Tam's Brig area of the town of Ayr into allowing us to use the mat in their very well equipped Martial Arts Judo Dojo. That turned out to be quite a feet some might say, no pun intended as normally no one is allowed onto such a sacred surface wearing footwear of any kind. Mathew Paton coincidentally he later became Hughie Sproat the Ayr Utd's Goal-Keeper's father–in-law was the leading light and he

was right behind our ideas, maybe he saw a further potential revenue earner for the club's coffers but we didn't care we were in and we were very grateful. **"Wee Jimmy Moffat"** was the main exponent of the noble art of Judo there and regularly I'd use his excellent knowledge of throwing techniques to further perfect my essential "Break-Fall" skills. We'd only been there a few weeks when my local village opened a newly refurnished, multi-purpose community centre revamped from what had been an old grey rough cast façade of a building, framed at the corners in old red sandstone. Originally it had been called the Roger Memorial Hall and it had been gifted to the community by some rich benefactor long before I was born, so once again we approached that committee. Initially their enthusiastic response seemed quite favourable but sadly that situation didn't last very long, to this day I've no real idea why there initial baking waned. Personality clash maybe, who knows? A former neighbour of ours Robbie McCurdy was the Chairman of the newly formed committee and he seemed to have some axe to grind, who knows why? After the Headmaster's very helpful intervention we were sorted, he too was on the community centre committee at that time, clearly he was far more aware of what was really going on than I was so he arranged through the local authority Education Department for us to take over and use a old and disused prefabricated building standing empty within the existing school premises and for that I shall always be eternally grateful. Because quite simply without his timely intervention we might never have had a gym in the first instance and all the lads who built part-time careers in the Scottish and to a much lesser extent in the British grappling scene would probably never have gotten started and that may well have included me. Over the years the total numbers attending regularly on the four days we were open, namely Sunday (Afternoon), Mondays, Wednesdays and Fridays for evening training sessions, must have totalled around 35/40 and most appeared faithfully night after night, week after week. We only closed on Christmas Day and the New Year period and as their personal wrestling popularity grew so did the reputation of the Wrestling Club, So much so we also began to develop a regular stable of around 6 young rather good looking very fit, lady performers. When we first started we had no ring only some old mats donated by the school but when the regular promoter deserted the local "Dam Park Hall" the ring which had originally belonged to him was confiscated as collateral for rental money owing to the council and it seemed to have been almost totally forgotten by everyone else except me. So I put in an offer to buy it and it was accepted. Yippee! Now we were on our way, now we had a ring and now if we were good enough and had enough capable personnel we could run our own shows. Later on we built a slightly smaller, lighter, more easily transported ring. Big Lil's [The Diamond] clever blacksmith father used all his welding skills and his clever engineering knowhow to put together a brilliantly simple piece of cantilever metalwork. A structure which served us well for the best part of 25 years before it was passed on to Brian Dixon. The whole thing was completed in a weekend mainly because all the lads attending the gym turned up to help with the building process. The space had no shower facilities and no central heating so it could get very cold in the winter months, but hard working young men with their future grappling careers uppermost in their minds didn't need fancy tile clad washrooms or warm radiators. It did however have plenty of wall mirrors and a varied selection of gym weights. Some bought by my brother and myself and the rest very kindly donated by Michael O'Hagan. Every facility in the gym was totally free of any charge to those who turned up. Neither I nor anyone else for that matter made a penny piece from any membership fees etc from the day it opened until the day it closed. It wasn't **"Wigan's Snake Pit Gym"** and it sadly didn't have a Billy Riley but it had some parallels and it did build a reputation and a history of its own. [Billy Riley was a one off, a legend. He passed away in 1977 there will never be another like him] The only stipulation to getting over the threshold of the gym was by way of a word of mouth recommendation and the last word lay with my judgement and my decision in all things! Well someone had to be the sole arbitrator and I'm very glad to say we must have been doing something right as over the years I only had to eject two lads in all that time. The membership consisted of lads and lassies who in the main came from the local area and also from the town of Ayr, the villages of Cumnock and Coylton as well as the other Ayrshire towns like Prestwick, Kilmarnock, Irvine and of course the local villages of Mossblown and also Annbank. Wee Sammy [Jeff Bradley] even brought his young family along on special nights laid aside especially by me for them alone. Young Sammy, Martin, Cameron and youngest Steven, he was always the jaunty one and he loved to sing all were among the regular sibling attendees and of course not forgetting their only wee sister Michelle. Stevie Blachard and Billy Baird who developed really good definition were two of our regular bodybuilders and on the Taylor family nights Big Stevie was more than happy to be the fall guy for this bunch of mini-worriers. During this time both he and young Steven Taylor would line up facing each other singing the Eddie Grant hit "I Don't Wanna Dance!" However it quickly became rather obvious the building was becoming more than a little overcrowded on a Wednesday night especially, it having been set aside as Ladies training. Most of the older married guys never showed they kept to the own well established training regime, whilst most of the younger guys turned up in droves and just sat around the ring side area ogling. An executive decision was required and it was taken by yours truly. The girls were moved to a Thursday and the space was off limits to all accept the instructors. Eddie Rose, Mark Wayne, Ezra Francis, Adrian Street and his lovely wife Linda, Joe Critchley, Jackie Pallo, and many more all paid both me and my lads the great honour and the kind compliment of visiting our Gym and I shall always be grateful to them for taking the time to do so.

Ask him again ref!

So it was mostly used by wrestlers?

Yes mostly but no not entirely, we had those lads who only used it as part of their weight training programme. Of the two I mentioned earlier Steve Blanchard was the taller and originally the much better built, it was later on my cousin Debbie's husband Billy joined. They were also into marathon running and both were good, strong consistent athletes. Another chap who in many ways mentored and encouraged the younger kids was the ex-pro boxer "Evan Armstrong" he was the former British and Commonwealth Featherweight Champion. Evan was originally an Ayr boy who after marrying moved to the village of Tarbolton about ten miles away. He would come down regularly to our local shows, the ones that mostly involved the young lads who were just starting out. He seldom missed one and he always had an encouraging word and some helpful advice. He had the heart of a lion and although he was a small built man he'd face up to anything and anybody. He too just like Big Ian Miller, Jim Farrell occasionally brother Bob The Viking and I could be seen regularly in the Somerset Park Enclosure every second week watching our beloved Ayr United FC play their First Team home fixtures.

That's a fascinating insight into the workings of your gym. Thank you very much but was it typical of most of them?

Yes I believe so, maybe not the female member part though but in style everything else would be very similar. As I said earlier it was definitely was not "The Snake Pit" there can only be one of them but we produced an awful lot of good hard working honest pros in our time, probably as many as any gym in Britain and probably more than most. Bobby Baron's set-up in Blackpool can rightly claim to have produced some top performers also as can Charley Glover's, Ernie Riley's and a myriad of others establishments UK wide especially in Lancashire and Yorkshire.

Why don't you tell me *about the people who've influenced, for good or for bad the Wrestling Business in the UK!*

It's only my opinion mind but if you're asking me whom I'd pay money to go and see I'd have to say basically everybody in wrestling world! We all deserve an audience and a following, some are of course better exponents of our art than others but without all the lads and now the lassies to fill all the bill slots we simply don't have a show. My personal favourites are people like Adrian Street and I've probably already covered all the reasons why, the same can be said about Old Jackie Pallo and that also includes and for all the same presentation and performance skills reasons, the other Top TV bad guy Mick McManus! Although regards the company of the last two mentioned outside the ring, I preferred the company of Old Jackie. Anyway I've only had a limited experience of Mick over the years. I also admired and I still do the good honest, hard working type of pros like Mr Peter Preston but me being a purist apart from those three what really appeals to me is what I like to term the Real Wrestlers. George Kidd that's the man for me, incidentally some of the best crowd pleasing bouts I've ever witnessed have been when Kidd took on all these afore mentioned ring villains and they all put on truly great bouts! My pal Adrian or so I'm told had some issues with George but you take as you find I feel and I'm sure none of those two will be losing any sleep over such matters. George in my pinion thoroughly deserves the title of Mr and all the respect that should always go with it as well. On the mat, in the ring and on the street he's not only the greatest ever thinking Lightweight the world has ever seen, he's also proved himself outside in the business world. His successful TV Chat Show on Grampian Television is a testament to that ethos and he also runs some popular licensed premises and he has a finger hold in other ventures mostly in Scotland's North East but not exclusively. I've never been in the ring against him and don't forget I started out as a

Lightweight myself but he was a big star even then so no chance of lowly me getting a crack at his World Championship Belt! I did however work for him quite regularly in Dundee and I always found him to be at all times an absolute gentleman! No tracksuit and trainers for him, a nice dress suit, a shirt, a tie and a pair of nicely polished shoes were his preferred get-up. Irrespective of the way this bent business is run at times with win results handed out sometimes to those far less deserving than the men who've had to carry and assisted his victor helping to push them even higher up the ladder to further ring glory. I still tend to think that George could have, would have and indeed did tie almost all of his opponents up in tidy little knots fairly easily. He had done a bit of boxing as a youth but his small; nine and a half stone frame did him no favours, so he quickly turned his hand to the study of Ju-Jitsu and Self Defence. After joining the Royal Navy he took up wrestling whilst serving his country, a spell in the Fleet Air Arm followed and whilst there he learned to be an Aircraft Mechanic. Some time later determined to expand his wrestling knowledge he moved to Bradford where he sought the help of Norman Morrell, after a brief pull round Norman sufficiently impressed by George's fitness and dogged determination took the Scot under his wing and the rest has now become wrestling folklore. Although he personally never lost sight of the fact it takes two to put together a crowd pleasing, totally believable contest sadly a number of other singularly blinkered, fame seeking Scottish based wrestlers seem to believe in their particular case their wins have been achieved through their superior skills, although this delusional notion is not exclusive just to one side of the Roman Wall. They choose to forget completely all could never have been achieved without the other guy who was also in there with them and who usually helped to make them look good, more about these fellows later perhaps? Whether he [Kidd] had the reserves of physical strength and endurance and could have sustained his level of speed allied to his gift for quick thinking on the mat in a “Shoot Contest” against others of a similar weight who trained elsewhere and not in Wigan is anybodies guess. some are correctly of the opinion that George also trained in Wigan under Mr Riley at one point. Some better known pros than me have also stated that they had been given tips by George on several ways to really hurt an opponent and again several ways to avoid being hurt yourself, should you make a mistake and step in too close. I tend to think that with some northern opposition he’d possibly have been found wanting on the mat but that’s not the business both he and we were in. We’re all in the entertainment game but this important point did however get lost on some in the business. As the man says: “If it’s not funny its not comedy” The same type of adage applies to wrestling also: “If its not show business and if it’s not good enough to entertaining the punters, then you’re in the wrong sport son! Why don’t you go away and work in Tesco’s? That’s not to take anything away from the memories I have of watching my hero work as he was always far too intelligent and to astute to put himself in such a position where he could be caught out in the first place. Although the question still remains in the minds of many as to who really was the best ever Lightweight! My ideal lighter weight wrestler, real fighting machine would have to be a combination of Glasgow’s **“Mr Jimmy McKenzie”** tough amateur trained, hard uncompromising approach on the mat, incorporating both his wealth of experience plus his reserves of strength and power, now if you allied that to Dundee’s George Kidd’s physical strength, agility and speed of thought and limb, that combination would have to have been seen to have been believed and it would have been quite simply unbeatable! [George Kidd “The Master Craftsman” died age 72 years on 5th day of January 1998] **“Mr Melvyn Riss”** some might argue was every bit as good as George and you’ve got to take into consideration that he was the Lightweight Belt Holder in the original Joints set-up. If you take all of his Flying Skills into consideration and then add his tough

Wigan style training, learned the hard way on the mat in Riley's Gym where to survive you really needed to know how to look after yourself in every way, then after adding in his natural athleticism as well, it would probably be hard to argue the point as it would have been well made. My old buddy Mr Joe Critchley an almost life long friend to "Little Mel" [This phrase was often used by others when going to the toilet to relive their bladder, more rhyming slang as in "Riss.] Always maintained he was always the better man and I seldom met anyone who was a better judge of a top mat man than Joe. There are others who could correctly argue George's case by pointing out he had trained for some years under ex-Olympic master Morrell as well as maintaining first class levels of fitness and stamina, he also studied other self-defence theories such as martial arts techniques. He also used his engineering background and applied it as only he could, in his clever leveraged approach to some of his well worked speciality holds he so regularly applied to opponents' bodies "The Surf-Board" being a perfect example. Joe himself was always slow to admit that he himself was also a truly masterful worker, he too had all the mat skills needed to survive and he'd also served his time in the travelling Boxing/Wrestling booths over the years and like Melvin he too was well capable having been Snake-Pit taught as well, he could be Wigan tough when he needed to be. On the other hand he was a true gent and a wonderful human being, I really miss him.

"Mr Johnny Saint" as far as Joints is concerned at least has more than filled George's well travelled boots since they presented him with their version of the World Lightweight Crown in 1976 and let me say personally he's always carried that accolade very well. Actually both he and I share an almost parallel past and I'm sure he like me will be forever grateful for the gift and the life changing opportunity given to him and which started him off in the grappling business. Johnny earned his boots so to speak back in the late 1950's just a few years short before I did. Like me he too was under the wing and the tutelage in the

professional style by one really tough little man in the form of “Mr Freddie Woolley” Under the patronage of Fred’s onetime Salford based wrestling business partner “Mr Danny Flynn” whom I still like to refer too as the Governor! My fortunes blossomed also and John’s and my career paths crossed a lot back then although I always found it hard to workout why he [Johnny] back then, was nearly always building the ring on his visits to Scotland. Whilst I was working between the ropes! I always felt then and I still do now that I could have moved on in the basic skills department a whole lot quicker had we two been “Taking Hold” and having a “Pull Round” on the mat a lot more often over that early period. Although a real wrestling bout one for the purists so to speak, was not the kind of encounter our two Lancastrian mentors liked to publicise on one of their shows. So why argue with their expertise?.
Lastly but by no means the least important comes one of the best ever Heavyweight workers of all time in the history of the British pro game **“Mr Kendo Nagasaki”** he is in my opinion as far as presentation is concerned right up there with all the other top class Hall of Famers. His use and his understanding of good professional skills are first class. Maybe some might say it’s an art form learned from Crew’s **“Geoff (Count Bartelli) Conliffe”** but then again are we really sure that’s where his close influences lie? Big Peter [Nagasaki] has taken the masked man genre to a whole new level and although quite tall and fairly well built he is by no means huge in the grand scale of things. He was however and clearly still is, very strong and very, very tough! His well thought out and clever use of gimmicks and rouses were strangely never even considered by any other top drawer villains before he appeared on the scene and have now been to some extent both adopted and adapted by a couple of good doppelgangers, whilst he himself has now become the stuff of wrestling legend. The Red Eyes, the Eastern Style Pig Tail, the Head Tattoo, the Stripes on his masks, the Red bonnet one night and the Black one the next night, and then the Blue! All which matched the vest

and tights. Even the salt throwing and the missing finger part on his left hand have all added to the mystery and the mystic. That digit injury may well have been nothing more exotic than a simple everyday working on the tools Motor Trade Accident at Jenkinson's Coachworks? Given my own engineering training background and workshop experience I can empathise with that episode if that's how it happened? God I bet it was painful at the time, I once witness a similar accident with a Massey Ferguson tractor flywheel. The use of Manager Gorgeous George is however most definitely not my favourite ploy, I first came across that particular gentleman when rather strangely right out of the blue he turned up on some of Orig William's Scottish shows in the second half of the 1970's. Although at that time it proved to be impossible to work out exactly what he was actually doing there as he contributed nothing to the nightly proceedings, some months later in hindsight and in his defence given Kendo's eventual move to the top Independent Brian Dixon, could it have been The Taffy promoter was trying to negotiate with George a shift away from Joints for Big Peter and had invited him along to have a look at the full extent of his nationwide venues set-up? You just never know, do you? Anyway, getting back to my original point The Manager being his mouthpiece introducing Peter into the ring etc was ok but for him to then have the audacity to try and perform on the canvas in tights, boots, make-up and everything else was for many journeymen, a truly insulting pretence. He was not trained and had no background in the business and he was a crap mat-man, therefore legitimate proper wrestlers quite rightly saw him as a bit of a joke, although not many ever addressed that fact directly to his masked charge. Many still wonder if the fact George was then not really seen in a wrestling capacity too many times after these less than credible TV ring performances, could have been the catalyst which eventually lead to the Big Man making the decision to move to the Independent banner? Or could it simply have been the "Mindless Match Making" of the God

like character Kendo [A reference to a clearly very fit, fully dedicated man with a strong ring preference and a love of all things Eastern] being fairly regularly matched particularly on the box as a “Knock Off” opponent for the Fat Bellied less than believable Big Daddy? In my humble opinion these farcical contests had already started to slowly diminish his almost perfect persona of complete and utter career invincibility! Having him “Die” for Shirley whilst at the same time having to continually carry him, in the performance sense for round after round was for me and for many others, simply stupid and at the same time from a watching brief totally without credibility! Quite frankly it was overly insulting to the best traditions of the business as it proved to be later and a sad reminder and a pointer to the direction in which things were already headed**................!**
Another of those I really admire and I don’t use that word lightly is **“Mr Tony Charles.”** Now working as a light to mid-heavyweight but still having total command over all his previous speed and agility he possessed as a much lighter man. He can work with anybody, folks lighter and crucially many who are a lot heavier as well, whilst still giving a great all round performance. He’s always been very popular both inside and outside the ropes and his moving to America’s was undoubtedly their gain every bit as much as it was the UK’s loss. His gleaming smile was and still is a joy to behold and it says everything about him. If I could have worked regularly with a man like that and learned from him with I wee bit of luck and a lot of hard work I might have become even half the star he is on both sides of the Atlantic. God an awful lot of the muscle bound posers across the pond must have cringed when they first saw their name up in lights alongside his. Tony represented Wales in 1958 as an amateur in the Empire Games, yet another reason to like him for me at least, is the fact he hails originally from Treorchy in the heart of the Rhondda Valley another really strong mining community! I’ve waxed lyrical on a couple of occasions about his fellow Taffy Mr Adrian Street and how I admire him also so it

goes without saying Tony too would be on my special list.
"Mr "Butch" Crusher Mason" is another in the Heavyweight Division whom I'd like to give a mention to, his persona always gave the impression he was well capable of pulling your head from your shoulders and then pushing it up your backside! In actual fact both outside and inside the ring especially if you were fortunate enough to be matched with him he was a true gentleman and as meek as a lamb. It was he who schooled me in the proper way to execute the truly spectacular usually contest winning fall by launching myself through the air from the top of the Corner Post, leaping spread-eagled across his shoulders as he struggled to get back onto his feet, having been double drop-kicked, followed by a body slam from yours truly It's a great move but it was he who set it up and it was him who had to sell it properly and in so doing he made me look really good in the process. Without his immaculate timing and his gift for showmanship it would have looked pretty ordinary. [Rather sadly Butch "Mighty Chan" Mason passed away in 2000. He was an honest man, a great worker and a good person I liked him a lot]
Lastly my number one main man is none other than..........
"**Mr Billy Robinson"** there isn't anything I could say about this man that hasn't been said before and by far more articulate men than me. He is for many purists without equal as the best "catch" wrestler of his generation. He like the previously listed Tony Charles is blindingly fast for a big man, he's clever, he's as tough as the come and he's "Shoot Proof." Having served his time in the amateur ranks in Riley's Gym in Wigan he went on to win the British Light Heavyweight Catch Title before moving to the USA in 1970 to further pursue a pro career where he was an immediate success. You will perhaps by now have gathered I'm not a huge fan of the Yanks or their wrestling style but I do however take my hat off to such men as: The great Verne Gagne, Lou Thesz, Buddy Rogers, Karl Gotch, Bruno Sammartino and particularly the Family Dynasties' of the "Funks" and the "Harts" because to a grappling fan

everyone of these exceptional pros, as well as having great "Catch" ability have had only good things to say about Big Billy Robbo and you don't have to ask them why. [Lou Thesz another grappling legend passed over in 2002]

You alluded earlier to some shortcomings in some Scots wrestlers would you care to be a bit more specific?

For you and for this one time only I will honestly and truthfully try to analyse what some of these people thought they were achieving although that might prove to be quite difficult. I rather sadly have to point out that their misguided almost constant ego tripping was fuelled in some of them by a strange belief that our business, the one that paid their wages was not in fact fixed and was therefore real! Plus they also suffered from another rather obvious flaw in that they clearly believed everything ever written about themselves on posters, in programmes and in the odd magazine article and that's both worrying on one level and also quite frankly truly laughable on any other. Sadly in most of those I came across personally the fact was their tinny minds had been filled with a load of shit by two rather glaringly dodgy promoters in particular. One on the Indie side and the other a Joints top dog! Ultimately it has to be said about the Indie promoter is the fact he got into our business in the same way as some of the wrestlers and that was through the "Back Door" which quite frankly was simply far too bloody easily done! Subsequently he in particular showed very little respect for the standards, the ideals or the culture of the long established British Wrestling business, let alone display any regard for those who paid their hard earned cash to support it. The contempt and over-the-top profiteering displayed during the Yuppie 1980's Thatcher era had in many ways already been articulated by him in particular back in 1970's. Orig Williams was at one time notorious for **"Pulling Strokes"** by putting the names of top draw Joints lads on his bills knowing full well there was no chance of them turning up!

Names like; Adrian Street, Les Kellett and even Mick McManus would appear in "Knock-Out Contest" set-ups usually displayed in large print on poster for shows in towns UK wide. On reading the small print it would actually say only that ***"they'd all been invited to appear"*** This was apparently the barely legal get-out-of-jail card played by the less than honest Welshman. I can't swear to the others but I'm sure Adrian threatened him with legal action on more than one occasion if he continued to ruin his considerable reputation by what the public perceived as his cowardly non-appearance on these totally bogus shows.

That's a rather broad and sweeping statement to make.

It is? Well you did ask so there it is and there it stays! What really annoys me about the whole thing is the way we north of the border were pigeon holed by some workers in the south purely on the strength of the attitude being displayed by these Scots grapplers. In the Joints ranks in particular native Scots were occasionally viewed by some as being greedy and self-serving in the ring, some even thought of us as "Tight" and "Stiff!" What was even more annoying for me was the added perception of us being seen as more interested in promoting ourselves and not the best interests of the business. Sadly most of that rather blinkered opinion is nevertheless hard to argue against because to some extent it was true, of a few, in Old Scotia's ranks!

But we were not all like that, those of us taught in the right way from day one by those who really cared about protecting the sports good name and preserving its ideals, its traditions and its integrity would have dragged us all over the mat and buried us in the canvas and rightly so, had we shown the same levels of contempt for opponents often displayed by this band of no-gooders. Then they would have thrown us out of the gym, again correctly, never to be allowed to show our egos ever again. In short we would never

have gotten into the Pro business in the first place!

Then again the same can also be said regards misguided perceptions held by some of our contemporaries in England about such so called "Gods of the Ring" although most of these are second and third generation entrants delusional about folks like Dave Boy Green and the Dynamite Kid, there were others but these are the two most prominent names. I myself have often reflected over the intervening years that perhaps I should have taken for myself a far bigger and fully deserved share of the glory and the limelight. Although blowing my own trumpet has never been my style but that's not to say however I did not have every faith in my own all round abilities to do so, had I really wished to press my case. I much preferred to coach and nurture my pupils in the gym, hopefully improving their chances of going further in the right manner with both good ability and the correct attitude as to what really matters within the sport. Some individuals, particularly on the Joints side may well have seen this as a weakness in me but none can ever say both myself Dale Storm a native born Scot and anyone who came out of my Mossblown Gym, again all Scots born lads and lassies did not do their very best to make all their opponents look very good for the paying public at all times, because that's the way they were taught to act. As for naming names that's not my style but I will mention just a few and I honestly feel they'd have to concede they were never suited to working in our professional ranks and they should never have been allowed an entry root into pro wrestling the first place. One was an Edinburgh based ex-army chap by name of Andy Bremner had been originally introduced by another capital born citizen, a man who came back to it by way of England's sunny south coast. Andy was a nice guy outside the ropes and I actually liked him a lot but he was very dangerous inside them, rather sadly he was oblivious to that fact never having been trained properly. Another area of concern which was far more important was he the fact just wouldn't die for you! Losing, selling it or conceding ground of any kind was clearly not something he understood! During a Tag Contest "The Hillbilly" as he was sometimes known was tied into the ropes at the corner post by myself; so sitting nicely on the middle two ropes with one leg right and another placed left, both suitably entangled he was helpless and totally defenceless as far as the baying public were aware. Given the fact I was always billed a "Blue Eye" I wouldn't normally have executed such an underhanded dirty move but I had little or no choice in the matter, as prior to this moment I had died all over the place for him even throwing myself out the ring at least twice. When it came to my comeback, as I said earlier he just would not sell anything for me and he definitely would not die an inch! Must have been an Army thing? So in frustration I aimed a perfectly timed flying boot into his now fully exposed "Ball Bag!" I might add it didn't even come close to touching him although the punters would never have noticed that fact. Appealing to his better nature with a rather anxious look on my face and my fingers crossed, I was thinking to myself surely now he must recognise the fact that even he, Superman's wee brother must at least sell this one for me! No! Not a bloody chance! Still no bloody dying!

...What to do next! Dah?

Yet he was still being used blindly and continually by Orig Williams god knows why? Perhaps he was cheap or perhaps Andy just liked the glory and he didn't get paid anything at all? I can honestly say I never ever left a ring even half satisfied I'd given the punters the bout they deserved and usually got at all times, except when I as on with The Hillbilly. His mentor Mr X [Name withheld] was a different stick. I respected him a lot except for the fact every time I bought him a Single Malt Whisky he would insist in pouring a full bottle of Coke into the same tall glass

....................I can only describe that act as sacrilegious!

Ask him again ref!

Anyway I had been told to meet him in Perth, I planned to leave my car in the city and we'd then travel up the A9 together to a job in Elgin. Having been picked up at the prearranged time I settled down to read my newspaper. The warm spring sun was shinning brightly and there was a nice hum off the exhaust and both made me feel quite contented, in fact in no time at all I'd drifted off to sleep but nothing lasts forever and I was quickly brought back from the "Land of Nod" by the sound of his voice asking me to retrieve his fags from the glove compartment. So half asleep I did as I was asked and got the fright of my life!

Oh don't tell me it was a spider! I really hate spiders!

No it was a lot worse than that!

Even worse than a spider, what could be worse than that?

A bloody Snub Nosed Smith and Weston .38 Revolver!

A gun! Oh my God! What did you do?

Panicked, what else! Then I asked him what it was doing in there to which he just laughed it off saying "He had to leave "The English Riviera Area" in a bit of a hurry!" Apparently he'd upset a couple of people, he went on to say "The Gun was his insurance policy it guaranteed him some longevity!" I might add I travelled back to Perth with someone else! Another in a similar vane to Andy was a real Bampot calling himself Brian McInally, apparently he used to teach amateur style at the Argyll Youth Club in Stirling, although I did wonder more than once what real experience he'd had and what qualifications he'd achieved to allow him to take the mat with keen and overly impressionable youngsters in a tutoring capacity. He was only a boy himself but once again rather sadly he was full of his own importance. Some might even have described him as "a punter" who really knew very little about the pro wrestling business, he was clearly just "star-truck" and guess what, he too had no intention of selling anything either. In other words he thought he already knew everything so what more was there for him to learn and from whom? Short answer bloody everything mate! Being quite a bit lighter than me I usually managed to avoid him but given the erratic manner the promoter had of doing things back then, it was perhaps only a matter of time until I'd be shoved in there with him and that night arrived in a small out of the way venue in the Highlands. No disrespect intended to one of my favourite areas but at least the damage to my reputation was perhaps minimal? Anyway a familiar pattern then arose, yes you guessed it, the little shit didn't die either and even more disturbing was the fact he also lacked any skill factor when it came to selling anything whatsoever, it was quite simply not in his radar! Great if you're going onto the mat in a Freestyle amateur contest that's the way it should be, willingly concede nothing whatsoever to your opponent! But this was the pro business and he was being a "Useless Wee Shit!" I could have and some might say should have taken his knee out but in so doing I would have been taking advantage of a considerably younger inexperienced and more importantly much lighter guy although he did in fact deserve that fate. Maybe in hindsight a **"Grovit"** would have sorted him out but that was just not my way of doing things, as you can probably guess it was not my finest hour bearing in mind the fact I had 17 years of hard won reputation under my belt and even more importantly, some of my long standing earning power to lose. As for him well he was still being a wee shit and with that attitude he will probably always remain so. There was at least one other individual I could mention but I won't be soiling these pages with his totally unworthy overblown ego name!

These chaps were all on the Independent side were they?
Yes at that point there was one and he did appear on the reconstructed version of the TV side of the business later

on. He's the one guy I haven't yet named.

What about the others you eluded too? Who used them?

Joint Promotions and strange to say most of then were attired in predominately white gear and nearly always to enhance their permanent tan. Although in at least one case his skin colour was a whole lot better than his performance skills, generally speaking. That doesn't include my former employer Andy Robin, he of course was seen in white often these guys were a whole lot lighter than him although the size of their self belief dwarfed everything else in sight.

But you've not mentioned any names.

Correct and I won't!

And why not can I ask?

Simply because they don't deserve a mention inside these pages, it would be a total disservice to all the others featured in this opus to mention then at the same time. I've met the heavier of them only a few times over the years and having watched him in the ring, both live and on TV I thought he was very limited and quite frankly very pedantic, in fact at times really quite boring. The other one was less so and at least he could do a bit of flying about when it suited him, that part was commendable for a guy who was mostly self-taught. Given that fact alone I suppose he could be forgiven for some of this attitude. He was a lot busier as a worker than the other guy but frankly that would not have been difficult, but both focused on only selling themselves at all costs. What really annoyed me about these two in particular was simply this, in all those years of sitting together in dressing rooms and with one of them in particular in the ring on more than one occasion, apart from a short nod of acknowledgement to the promoters instruction as to what he wanted to happen in the ring there

was never any friendly banter, although his ego was always well soothed because he "Went Over" every time. In all that time over all those years none of them ever said as much as a "Hello" or a friendly word to me at anytime, so why would I bother to give them a mention by name? Others on the Joint side were better at least at communicating the odd handshake or maybe a guarded hello and again I'm convinced Max Crabtree in particular would wind up the more gullible Scots in some way before they left the dressing room, he seemed to think in his perverted logic this act would in turn produce a far better contest due to his quite, perverted but gifted shit stirring.
"Lenny Ironside" was always much more forthcoming but he too I feel could also be influenced, but thankfully to a much lesser extent by Max and his refereeing smaller brother, the "Jack-in-the-Box" called Brian. Bill Turner another east-coaster, whom I grew to like an awful lot over the years, was manipulated repeatedly, early on by the "Brothers Grim." Then again he unlike me had to some extent accepted their offer of tutelage in Yorkshire when he first got started as a youth and at that tender age we were all impressionable. Things might well have been different for me had I also taken them up on their original offer but that's all water under the bridge now. In the ring Bill never showed any over stated ego tendencies and for that I give him every credit, originally he'd had to "Sell" himself and his abilities to the Crabtree brothers in the first instance by way of asking permission for him and a friend to use the Edinburgh ring in the late afternoons before the punters arrived. So initially largely self-taught he finally, just like I did finally earned his chance to shine in Leith at the Eldorado Stadium but luckily for him not in a bazaar Tag Tournament Contest! Personally I have no axe to grind with Lenny either, he did his own thing and I did mine and our paths never really crossed all that often. Latterly he too made the changeover by joining the Indies after taking up the offer of work from Andy Robin around the early 1980's. McInally followed suit round the same time as the Scottish

map was then changing fast on the promoter front. The one saving grace was due to my severe injury problems I was excused the sight of the twat from Stirling appearing on a show at the hallowed Paisley Ice Rink. Many who'd performed there with aplomb and who'd by that time passed over to the other side must have been turning summersaults in their wooden boxes at such an affront! Furthermore I get the impression that he might well have been led there by the hand with Len assistance? If so that would be yet another disappointment to me, I'm however sure if he really did he must have thought he was doing the right thing but sadly he wasn't. I by this time was now out of Andy Robin's organisation and out of the Scottish scene permanently so perhaps to be fair the Bear Man was then left with little choice as to whom he used after that point? The lads in my gym were also off his card, I'm both disappointed for them but grateful also they had almost to a man decided if the old team couldn't continue in its entirety then they did not wish to continue without me in the fold. Invariably that meant the public on the larger circuits could no longer get the chance to continue to enjoy their exquisite talents but that was a decision made entirely on their own I took no active part. I can only add this, I was always loyal to my lads and in the end they stayed loyal to me, should it have been any and indeed all had wished to carry on and perhaps try their luck with the likes of the now crumbling Joints Organisation on a more permanent basis, I would have been happy to have used any influence I still had to make sure they got a leg up on that career ladder.

"Big Ian Miller" by that time had married Big George McDonald of Elgin town's daughter Elaine and as her big Highlander father was now promoting more and more shows for himself Ian worked away for his father-in-law for a few years. He also trained some rather raw recruits in the Morayshire area teaching them the basics of the grunt and groan business. All I might add with both the blessing and best wishes of all the other lads in our fraternity. He'd been in training since he was around the age of twelve and when he was sixteen he joined the police force as a cadet. One night at Prestwick Airport a real desperado who was between flights was causing havoc in the departure area. He was kicking lumps out of a row of mini TV's. He'd been delayed because his transatlantic flight had been held up somewhere else due to fog and being so far out of his face on something or other, he failed to realise you needed to place some money into the slot on the side in order to get a picture. Security weren't able to calm him down so they had to call in the local police and he was duly arrested.

But why are you telling me this?

I thought you might find it interesting. Anyway you haven't as yet asked me who the desperado might be.

Ok I'll play along. Who was it!

Who? Indeed?

Come on who is it?

Almost there he was a member of the rock band The Who.

No, not in Prestwick!

Yes and he spent the night in a cell in the Prestwick Cop Shop! It was their rather eccentric drummer Keith Moon.

So Big Ian is now the proud owner of his autograph?

No that's the worst part of this whole story, he didn't get it.

A lost opportunity maybe, worth a lot good nowadays!

Eighteen months had passed since my spinal surgery and I'd used that period of convalescence to allow for some muscle building rehabilitation. George McDonald

suggested a "Come-Back" bout and having thought long and hard I decided to give it a go. It had now been almost two and a half years since my initial injury and I needed some questions answered. "Big Mr Miller" was my opponent on that memorable night. The Elgin Town Hall crowd's support will always hold fond memories for me and hopefully they also have fond memories of me. I eventually "Went-Over" winning the contest with a two to one wining score in the 7th round. In what I hope looked for all intensive purpose like a hard fought, hard won contest. I'd have to admit the occasion was for me personally much more about the marked improvement in the performance of my opponent and I don't mind admitting he carried me through most of the rounds and he did his very best to at least make me look even just a little like my old self on that memorable and very emotional night in the Scottish Highlands. Sadly the one thing to emerge from that night was the reality of my lack of confidence in both the reliability and the sustainability of my spinal skeleton. That contest highlighted the weakness caused by the original damage and it had clearly been made all the weaker by the surgery. I just couldn't bring myself to put both my very supportive wife and my young family through all the stress again, should I injure myself further. Apparently unknown to me at the time because of some side effects of the painkilling medication I had been taking, I had been subjecting them to months of frustration and some very angry words! This had been at the height of what was for me, by far the worst extremes of pain imaginable. I had been on at any one time, eight different pills including "Diconal" and I have no lasting knowledge of anything which took place during most of the first twelve month period after I came out of hospital. It was only many months later when I was on the mend slightly that during a frank discussion with my wife Lilian, at which time I complained to her about the lack of visits from

my long standing friends, she rather abruptly enlightened me they had visited faithfully, some at least once a week! She then went on to tell me my two young children when returning home from school were in the habit, almost daily of slowly opening the front door to apprehensively enquiring as to what my mood was before they felt it safe to enter into their own home! Can imagine how devastated, that made me feel? I was truly shattered! So having stepped out through the ropes teary eyed and whilst making my way back to the dressing room drinking in all the love, affection and applause which was still buzzing in my ears. I needed no one else to tell me that it was now all over! The curtain had descended for the last time and my long career had now finished! I'm very glad to say however my association with all things athletic took on a different life form after that when I joined the local Harriers club "Ayr Seaforth" My daughter was at that time one of their budding talents. Long distance endurance running seemed to suit both my ongoing back problem and my temperament so I entered a period of Marathon Running and having built up my mileage, my stamina and my experience over a long period, running in towns and cities like: Glasgow, Motherwell, Edinburgh and the Galloway Hills Race, with the Scottish Cross Country Championships thrown in for good measure, I soldiered on and finally I was accepted for the Big One! The most popular event on the planet: "The Mars London Marathon" Because of the faster times I'd achieved in both Glasgow and in Edinburgh, I'd been allocated a slot in the elite fast start section of the event. I really enjoyed my time running on the roads, your mind is free from everyday problems and in many ways it's a God send! The Galloway run was made all the more enjoyable because both my good friend Eddie Rose and his lovely wife Marie also competed. Eddie also ran in my second Glasgow that same year. On my first outing

Ask him again ref!

over the full distance I'd broken the magic three hour mark, my times continued to improve and on my last outing I completed the 26 Miles 265 Yards in what for me was an astonishing time of 2 Hours 38 minutes. Subsequent knee trouble and a hip problem sadly forced yet another sporting retirement!

What was Lenny Ironside like as wrestler then?

Most importantly he was always safe! He was never "**Stiff**" or indeed "**Strong**" when involved with me, his amateur background however meant he liked to keep things tighter and closer and sometimes we'd be down on the mat or locked in certain holds for long periods as opposed to more **"flying**" which I usually preferred. That meant my natural style was restricted somewhat but what the hell I liked him as a person and we did our best. We put on a show, nobody died and we got paid our due. Hopefully my experience and background meant I got more money than he did but we'll never know. Will we? He was as far as I'm concerned always more of a mechanical and a pedantic style wrestler but always a good solid journeyman professional with it. Never over flash at anytime in fact quite ordinary some might say? He's had a turn more than once on the TV and he's acquitted himself well but they did him no favours by giving him very little room for manoeuvre in the self promotion department given whom they put him in with.

All good things must come to an end and the Gym died a death killed off by another Head Teacher who can only be best described as being an arsehole called Andrew Niven! We turned up as usual and it was boarded up. They raised it to the ground weeks later!

What was a mining community like when you were a child?

The total mileage Ayr to Leeds and back: 439.6
Total time taken for the journey: 8 Hours 52 Minutes

CHAPTER SEVENTEEN

(The Long Row)

The place of my birth and my formative years was no different from most of that time. The years immediately following the Second World War were tough for everyone in Britain, although those whose families fortunate enough to live in rural areas were at least able to walk out into the county-side and help themselves to a boiling of potatoes growing in the fields or a turnip or two. Technically this was stealing but local farmers were a different animal back then and they understood only to well that they would get that goodwill back 200% and more over the long term from a grateful, basically honest local community. Life was hectic at all times in 1940's and 50's in Britain, food rationing was still to the fore and the little luxuries especially important to children, things like sweets etc were not that plentiful. Rationing stamps were required for everything so we had to make do with a cone shaped brown paper container filled with sugar into which we dipped a stick of freshly cut summer rhubarb. Occasionally we enjoyed the fizzy drink "Creamola Foam" from a small silver tin was my favourite treat or some home made "Boston Cream." Local recipes were very closely guarded secrets. The seasons determined what vegetables were available and exotic fruits of the day were Jaffa Oranges, Tangerines, Pineapples and Bananas but again these were only available at certain times of the year and only if you could afford to pay for them. Usually they were out of my mother's price range, established favourites were British home grown apples but we seldom if ever did we get these regularly. Coconuts were not purchased in shops they were usually only won, if you were a good enough shot with a lead pellet air gun at the local Fair Ground. These only appeared in our local area once a year in late summer, just in time for the Ayr Gold Cup Weekend Race Meeting at the start of the long weekend holiday in the third week in September. My miner grandfather's only day out every year was his visit to Hamden Park Glasgow to see the Scottish Cup Final in late May. It didn't matter to him who was playing that was of little importance more importantly it was a day out. In order to get the train to Glasgow he had to walk into Ayr a distance of five miles.

Number 44 The Long Row in the Baird of Dalmellington Company owned miners houses was my home and it was pronounced "The Long Raw" by those who lived in the village. Each section of long terraced blocks of around (12) twelve units ran the length of the roughly finished black tarmac covered street with access spaces at either end allowing the occupants access to the joint facilities in the grassy area beyond. This row of houses ran for almost half a mile and they had a flag stone pavement on only one side, there was another row of houses half its length running at right angles which joined it at the bottom of the hill. The other one was known as the Pole Row, it was a tribute to those from the county of Poland who'd come over to the UK, not only to join the British Armed Forces some of them actually worked in the local pits as well. There was another equally long row of miner's cottages on the other side of a central railway track which cut through the community, it stood directly in front of the street where I was born. They were separated by two large wooded railway sleeper fences placed on either side of a deep gully along the top of an embankment on which we used to like to play games where we pretended to be Cowboys and Indians or Soldiers in the long summer months. One of the stars of the period was Billy Saunders, he finished up a highly qualified Judo instructor, another was Jim Lee who became in later life an unsung quiet intellectual The front row had another street of small manager's cottages situated in front of it but it was a lot shorter, only about twenty houses in total, being they Gaffers cottages they were slightly larger. The main Stranraer to Carlyle railway ran through the cutting. It was quite a sight once a week or so to witness all the "Ladies of the Houses" each armed with a stiff bristled long handled wooden brush standing in a long processional line at predetermined intervals scrubbing away, sending any rubbish which may have collected on its way down the natural incline. Given the fact each community had an open sewer running down its length, measuring approximately twelve inches across and approximately five inches deep all this hard work meant it didn't take long for the rubble and the dirt to be sluiced away down the incline and into the slow flowing burn at the bottom of the street. Helped of course in no small measure by the force of the water cascading out from the mouths of the ornate cast iron Lion's Head shaped communal water fonts or "Pumps" as they were known to us back then. There were around six communal water taps running the length of the street from which all our domestic water had to be drawn every day in life and filled into large white enamel pales, every household had one! The thick wooden door on which the house number had been hand painted led to a small square hallway, to your right was the entrance leading into what doubled as the Dinning Room, the Sitting Room a Bedroom and sometimes even a House of Prayer. Once inside to your left was the Set-In Double bed, this was my parents sleeping quarters. The fireplace directly across was a coal burning open fronted shinny "Black Lead" coloured cast metal unit. Which as well as providing the only form of heat in the place it also doubled up as the stove on which all our food was cooked. My mother like all before her took great pride in keeping the fireplace immaculately clean at all times. My granny was an equally studious cleaner but her task was made all the more difficult by the lung curdling coal dust spit my grandfather used to summon up from his boot straps and then try to deposit onto the flames. Occasionally in a fit of uncontrollable coughing his aim was a little off and the blackish green speckled phlegm slithered down the grate front staining the shinny black lead. The wooden floor was covered in cheap dark brown coloured linoleum; there was a small well worn rug in front of the fireplace and a slightly larger one across the front of the set-in bed. Avoiding treading on the colder parts of the floor was a necessity during the long snow filled, icy winter months. Cold feet were a constant discomfort from November to March and warm slippers were generally the domain of the middle classes. The back bedroom where I shared another set-in bed with my older brother was very sparsely furnished with only a large old fashioned wooded wardrobe, linoleum on the floor and no carpet. Positioned between both rooms, was a very small narrow kitchenette, consisting of a Belfast Sink and a small wooded work surface, all hot water had to be boiled up on the open fire. The weekly full body wash was taken in a portable Tin Bath which hung on a wooden peg on the wall in the entrance hallway. The whole family excluding father would take it in turns to use the same water, youngest first. After the formation of the National Coal Board one of the first improvements in the miner's working conditions was the building of communal washing facilities at the Pit Head generally referred to as "The Baths." We had no inside toilet only a second white enamel pale under the sink for night-time pee emergencies. It was of course vitally important not to get the two liquid containers confused. Number two's required a walk down the street in the dark and around the corner to the communal outhouses. I was usually accompanied by mother, battery operated small torch in hand. Locked family units stood in a square pattern, they consisted of your own coalhouse and of course the toilet. They were all built around a communal Cast Iron Wash Tub and a fixed Mangle type clothes ringer. The Tub sat embedded in a brick built plinth, below it was a grated base into which you built a fire to heat the water. The surrounding grassy field doubled up as your clothes drying area, each woman of the house would be allocated one half day per week. That's the only time you could officially use the boiler to do your washing. No washing and no other work was allowed on a Sunday! Life was simple and life was good back then and we didn't know any better. The one thing I personally hated was the weekly finger nail cutting and the manicure and even more so, the tight toothed Bone Comb being dragged through your newly washed hair in search of the dreaded head lice. They seemed to be an obsession among mothers and grannies back then. I'm very glad to say I don't recall ever having any. A visit to your house by the "Nit Nurse" and the application of the dreaded "Gentian Violet" onto your scalp for the whole world to see and to gossip about was a black-mark on your families standing in the community? The Lords Day meant church in the morning and Sunday school classes in the afternoons and all in your only set of so called bespoke "Good Clothes." We were also destined to be visiting my Grannies, both of them in turn, one in the late afternoon around teatime, usually my Dad's mother and in the early evening it would be my mother's mother, where we'd get something to eat. The welcome that greeted us at our first port of call was usually rather sadly "You'll have had your tea?" My Dad's mother was a stern lady who loved us in her own way although I could never figure out how she could be continually buying soggy Smiths Crisps! The living room furniture in our cosy wee hoose consisted of two wing sided armchairs, one on either side of the fireplace a dinning table four chairs and a sideboard with a wooded surround clock ticking away on it. Every household had an "Art Deco Radio" or the "Wireless" as it was referred to by my mother, it sat on a small stand in a corner of the room. On which we listened to such classics as The Goons, Dan Dare Monday to Friday at 7-15 for fifteen minutes each night, an episode lasted five days. My second favourite "Dick Barton Special Agent" on the BBC with the voice of Noel Johnston, it started on July 2nd 1951 and lasted five years. My older brother was allowed, but only on School Holidays to stay up to listen to the Top Twenty on Radio Luxemburg 208 on the Medium Wave and on1440KHz with Barry Alldis and also Pete Murray. After that on a Sunday night at 12midnight you had "Top of the Shop." We would sometimes have a sneak listen in on an old Crystal Set under the blankets! It featured the voice of the man who was destined to become the main commentator and occasionally the face of the Saturday afternoon 4pm Wrestling Mr Kent Walton. He introduced all the top songs featured in the chart which were on the Pye Records Label but as I mentioned earlier all this musical excitement, heaven forbid, could mean you got caught short during the night but there was always the White Enamel Pee Pale hidden behind a small curtain under the sink, a must for any working class family without the luxury of a warm internal wooden seat toilet on which to place your bum should you require it. Of course it did have to be emptied each morning. [Some present day prisoners seem to think they have it rough. Get a life mate!] Amusement consisted of games in the street all of which involved running and exercise, no overweight, sedentary kids in these days. "Fire Cans" made from empty Lyle's Golden Syrup containers were a favourite, we used a nail and a hammer to knock holes in the sides and the bottom, we then added a handle, a wire one was preferable then we added wood and other flammable material. Then hurling it in an arc around our head having lit some paper we'd stuffed in it, with a bit of luck we were away! They made a great sight as it got darker spinning away in the low light of a cold winters evening. "Kick the Can" was another running game where you hid whilst someone counted to one hundred. They'd then attempt to find you and if spotted and they could get back and touch the "Can" sitting in full view in the open roadway before you did, then you were captured and thereafter out of the game. But if somebody who was seen and therefore technically caught was then able to out-run their capture get to kick the can away, all who had been captured previously were immediately set free again and so the game continued until you got called in for your tea or on a really long night your bedtime. Summer school holiday breaks were about nine weeks long and the sun seemed to shine everyday! The winters were cold and it always snowed but we coped and we still played outside making long ice slides by pouring water onto pavements. We also built Snowmen and happily played away belting it and then each other with cold icy Snow Balls. If we got really bored we'd sometimes use a clothes line to tie two doors together, then we'd knock on both of them at the same time and stand back pissing ourselves at the antics of both households trying to get their door open, only to have it pulled from their hands as the other victims over the way tried to open their door at the same time! Simple things amuse simple minds but we did no harm to anybody and at the end of the day nobody got hurt. Children were far fitter back them and no old ladies were hurt of mugged in the process. Equally importantly no one went hungry, if your mother was busy any neighbour, if asked would provide you with a tasty "Jeelly Piece." Life was good, we were happy and we didn't know anything else. One of my fondest memories as a wee boy was walking every three months a distance of around two miles to the local church hall which lay between Mossblown and Annbank to stand in a long winding queue waiting to hand over the note my mother had given me. I'd kept it wrapped tightly in my hand, then after being handed the remuneration by the official behind the long wooden table, wrapped again in the original note. Hand closed tightly once again I was off and running all the way home with my Mammy's Co-op Dividend. The total amount was always less than one pound but it was needed and to see the smile on her face as she patted me on the head was priceless. Happy Days!

Total mileage Ayr to St Andrews and back: 220Miles
Total time taken for the journey: 4Hours 30minutes

(Courtesy of Ms J McCann)
Jackie McCann

(Courtesy of Ms A Barton)
Anne Barton

Susan Sexton

Klondike Kate

Ms Sue Brittain

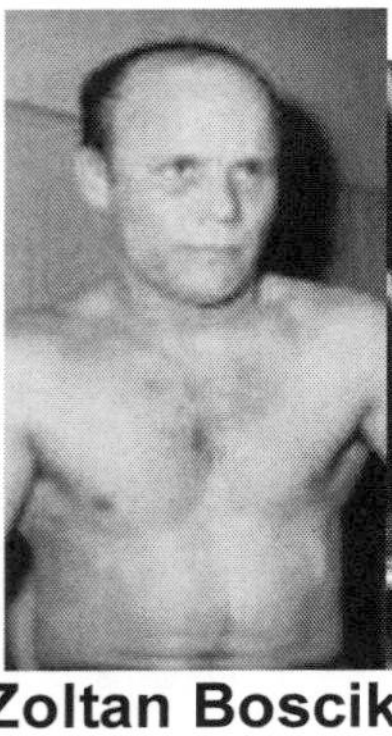
Zoltan Boscik

The Eagles

The Royals

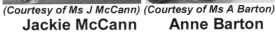

Al Marshall

CHAPTER EIGHTEEN

(Sorry Boys I've lost my Specs)

Other laughs not involving so called Celebrities, TV Personalities, Millionaires or Pop Stars were usually an unbelievable Hoot! Most occurred closer to home and among individuals whom I've always felt more comfortable with and most empathy towards. Here's a couple that spring to mind; The first took place on Ayr's long sandy beach following an evening show in Ardrossan, we'd been working at the Civic Centre and due to building works the hot water was off so no shower afterwards. It's not good when you can't get a hot wash that's when muscle pulls and strains etc tend not to settle. So afterward we're on our merry way back to Joe Cassidy's Coffee Stall down in Ayr Harbour. He had been an ex-semi-pro footballer and he was no relation of Bronco Jack Cassidy, his was always a very popular meeting place for performers and band members in the South West of Scotland. As we approached the Glasgow Gailes Golf Course on the beach side of the original A737 running from Brassie to Irvine. The summer's night warm breeze that had been filling our nostrils with the familiar scent of salt and seaweed suddenly changed and the odour of death filled the air. Rounding a bend into the low glow of a lingering sun silhouetted in front of us we could see the familiar shape of a Land Rover half blocking the road but something else lay on the blood stained tarmac barely covered by a tarpaulin. After stopping we left the car and walked the short distance ahead to find out what was causing the hold-up, as we rounded the muddy farm vehicle in the middle of the carriageway what greeted us was the sorry sight of a dead horse and the Triumph Herald sports car which had hit it embedded halfway through the hedge about thirty yards further along. Apparently the horse had jumped the fence giving the poor driver no chance of stopping. The putrid smell of spilled entrails ripped from the stricken animal made it even more imperative we left the scene immediately. So a quick three point turn headed us back towards the roundabout just as an ambulance arrived on the scene to deal with the driver. Now on the duel carriageway A78 we continued on our journey into Ayr. Somebody in the car I can't exactly remember who had a bit of a brainwave, apart from the lack of a sweat cleaning shower the odour of the poor unfortunate equine now clung to our clothing like a dark mist. “Let’s have a dip in the sea wash off the dirt and grime and now this awful smell!” Yes please was the unanimous decision so having arrived on Ayr Beach, there we were running down the sand full pelt! The time was now around the10-20 pm mark and nearing the end of a long, warm summer's evening. “Last into the water is a sissy!” Having been blurted out just moments before everyone’s clothes were being tossed around everywhere, the result of which was of course lots of naked bodies and no cosies but what the hell! The tide had gone out about a quarter of a mile but eventually we're in. Splish, Slosh, Splash! Cool soothing salty water, it cleans out all the pores so no chance of any nasty black heads now. Then we hear his cry for help transcending the peaceful tranquillity of the summer half-light. Mr Ronald "Moon" Isdale one of our drivers and a sibling to the wrestling brothers Jim and Bob suddenly shouts out. "I've lost my specs boys” I forgot to take then off before I dived in!”

....**Oh Shit!**

It took us almost half a bloody hour to locate them and by that time it was almost dark so we were getting cold and the tide was coming in really fast! Still the tomato sauce filled hamburgers tasted extra special that particular evening, mostly perhaps because Moon paid! We all insisted, well it was only fair don’t you think? He was another good lad but sadly he's not with us anymore either. Whist moving flats he had a horrific accident involving a really heavy old solid wood wardrobe on a concrete staircase which unfortunately proved fatal. [Ronald is very sadly missed he died in October 1984] Another reasonably regular event that verges both on the ridiculous and on the sublime was when Jeff Bradley and I were doing the Batman and Robin Tag Team thing. The late 60's TV series was very popular and it had all those daft Americanism cartoon slang words flashing onto the screen! Things like Kapow! Eek! Wow! and my personal favourite "Holly Cow Bat Man!" but there were many, many more besides! Anyways in that TV series when the Cape Crusader ran he did it in a slow motion kind of a way! Yes you've guessed it we had to perfect that technique as well.

No you didn't! Did you? I'd love to have seen that. Funny!

Stop laughing! It's not funny! Have you tried to running slow motion?

That must have looked a bit mental!

Got it in one, it was effective but at the same time stupid! In fact it was bloody stupid and just plain crazy but that's what the kids and the punters wanted some gritty cartoon realism and that's what they got! It was in many ways a really good gig for me personally in as much as how little the script required from Batman. Quite simply it consisted of me letting the opposition, the bad and the nasty villains bash Robin to bits, then me jumping in at the appropriate time meant I then rescued my comrade in arms and I'd take all the glory lavished on me by an adoring audience. It just doesn't come any easier! What more could you ask? Masked Super Stardom status assured for at least one more week! Tag Team Contests have always been popular. I recall the time Adrian Street had put together a run of shows in conjunction with an Edinburgh entrepreneur, his company had been especially created I suspect, for just this very occasion and was entitled "FAME" *(Female Aggression Movie Enterprises)* Thank Christ the bouts were mostly performed in privately owned clubs, that at least meant no outside advertising and little or no chance of Max the Gaffer finding out. The Edinburgh guy's name was Hamish McGregor his family were in the agricultural feed transportation business in a big way. He was a musician by night and up to that point he'd formed a couple of very successful bands. He played the trumpet I think or it could have been the clarinet, maybe both? I remember he drove a light green coloured 7.2 litre 440ci two door-four seat Jensen Interceptor Coupe a popular playboy sports car in its day. When you lifted the bonnet you had to wonder how they ever got that V8 Chrysler engine unit into such a tight space. Anyway, he wanted to film the bouts and sell the footage to America and probably Europe as well, least ways that was the plan. Once we'd signed over the rights we had no control over what happened to your performances after that and sadly there was no buy out clause and no repeat fees either. Equity the "Actors Union's" recognition refusal regards Pro Wrestlers meant we had no Full-time Official representing us at any stage. Hamish was particularly interested in the Tag Contest portion of the bill although during this one particular show during the run no filming actually took place. So Adrian was teamed up with Linda his misses and Princess Paula was in the other corner with me. The ring was lit up in more ways than one on that particular night because of the presence of The Master of Wrestling Glam decked out in all his finery and his make-up. Princess Paula in the other corner adorned in her multi-coloured full feathered American Indian Headdress; was also quite a sight to see. So the contest starts and Paula's in with Linda and then I take over. I've just about got her in a headlock when Adrian grabs my hair and pulls me onto the ropes then Linda throws me with a head-mare and she finishes up with me in a head scissors hold on the deck in the centre of the ring. Into a momentary silence as I was planning my escape she [Linda] makes an honest observation and shares it with the audience. "You've forgotten to shave!" She calls out at the top of her voice in a neutral London accent. The audience respond with lots of loud laughter, so as quick as a flash I come back with a counter retort.

And what was your reply to a comment like that then?

Given I'm in a "Head Scissors" and just about as close to paradise you can get without actually dying.

Come on spit it out! What did you say?

What do you think I said? "Well from what I'm now seeing, it's quite obvious you haven't shaved either. Did you?"

And what was the audience response to that?

They erupted even more! They were convulsed with laughter! It almost brought the dammed roof down!

Sounds like fun! Tell me more about your other friends.

Total mileage Ayr to Bridlington and back: 527.8
Total time for the completed journey 11 Hours

Bill Turner

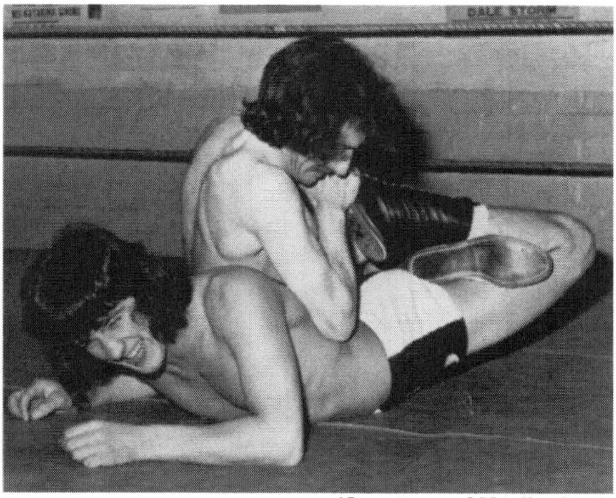

(Courtesy of Mr Jim Lee)

Scott Thomson applies a figure 4

CHAPTER NINETEEN

(Good Friends Fondly Remembered)

Good friends and fond memories. There's been one or two of them over the years on both counts one in particular was a road trip when we were in Manchester, we'd gone down to see City play Wolverhampton Wonderers. The trip had been arranged by Mark Wayne and Eddie Rose and we met up with another good friend Ezra Francis outside "Main Road" stadium. On one of his early visits to Scotland Eddie had very kindly brought my young daughter a present, it was a Man City football top. She slept in it that night and thereafter we had a great deal of difficulty getting it back off her! Just to be able to put it in a washing machine now and again proved almost impossible, she's been a devout supporter of the Blue side of the city ever since. Naturally City won and in some style so for us, all was well with the world. After the game we headed over to the London Road near to the Piccadilly Station area of the city to a pub called The Robin Hood for a wee celebration drink. Ezra was a regular there as were many other wrestlers from around the city. Over the years it had, had a long history of Landlords who'd had some connections in the grappling world. Folks like Arthur "Terrance" Ricardo [Big Tough Lad] one of the three Belshaw brothers; as in Cliff Belshaw [Very Acrobatic Welterweight] and Jack Beaumont [Heavyweight] Arthur if the memory of good and trusted Mancunian friend is spot on and it always is was credited with a private gym win over Billy Joyce in a shoot money-match. They were Wigan lads as well, but they were not from Billy Riley's Gym they trained with Pop Charnock. Another of the men behind the bar for a time was Carl Dane he worked a "Masked" job fairly regularly for Mr Jack Atherton and others as a very good version of "The Outlaw." He was a Charley Glover Barnsley trained lad who'd been befriended by other equally tough men for the same gym people such as Mr Jack Land and Mr Sam

Betts, on other nights Carl carried out his more regular refereeing duties for various promoters. So we're half way down our first pint of rich and creamy Boddingtons Ale when Scott Thomson and Ezra get busy debating the relative merits of whether the rather curious apparition at the end of the bar in the Red High Heels with the Red Handbag was maybe not one thing and maybe more of something completely deferent so to speak. I must confess even with all that was going on inside that vibrant and very busy bar, my focus was now being slowly drawn in that general direction also and mostly because of the complete lack of any real dress sense allied to a complete lack of any discernible colour or costume coordination, the net fronted dark blue hat was the give-a-way! By this time almost to a man we'd now all joined in on the conundrum debating feverishly as to whether in fact it was truly a male or a female! To prove a point Ezra tossed him/her a heavy glass ashtray which he/she caught rather effortlessly on the full with one hand! For that clearly accomplished act of athleticism he/she was given a standing ovation from all who were joylessly assembled led of course by Ezra, daft bugger! Something no doubt to do with the game of Cricket given that my good pal Mr. Francis hailed from good Saint Catherine, Jamaican blood stock originally. Cricket a game I have almost totally failed to comprehend completely was another sport he liked to watch. Sadly we never really got to the bottom of the cross-dressing conundrum before it was time to drink up and move on! The debate did continued however as Ezra drove us in his Austin 11000 to another very popular Reggae Club whose patron's were normally and exclusively only of the music loving, hip gyrating West Indian persuasion. He was strongly of the opinion that if the vision of doubt had been a woman he/she would have caught the ashtray on his/her lap. So I think we settled on an agreement that he [the vision] was therefore most likely to be a male but with a large degree of confusion ragging between his gold ring filled, rather large ears! What he had between his legs was quite another matter and none of us was brave enough to volunteer find out. That however was not the case only a few short days later when another West Indian born, good friend of mine took a completely different point of view. Convinced the enigma of the he/she was in fact all female, red bag matching shoes and all, in the back alley later on after an ice breaking noisy gobbling sexual encounter which by all accounts had been most enjoyable for my very athletic buddy, all was still going well in the kissing and cuddling department but it all came to an abrupt end immediately after the man with the muscles finally got his hand down inside the rather flimsy but very expensive knickers the he/she was wearing, only to discover a full set of the proverbial "Three Piece Suite!" Naturally this disgusting discovery stopped him in his tracks as his ardour rather quickly waned. I have no wish to embarrass my good friend further by naming both himself and his short time girl friend so I've decided to leave it at that. I can however disclose he became the laughing stock talking point of almost the whole grappling fraternity for a long time after that. He had at that time and he still has my deepest sympathy because under a completely different set of alcohol filled circumstances any one of us might have succumbed and in so doing become just another of that predatory local club owner B - - - - / - - - - - unsuspecting young bitches.

A similar situation happened to another good pal of mine in Sydney Oz years earlier when we were on a night out in a club in the Kings Cross area called "The Jewel Box." It was always a popular place for all kinds of genders maybe because the floor show was usually performed by a bunch of Lady Boy Dancers from Thailand and stunningly beautiful they were too. After a few beers we got fixed up with a couple of tarts and decided to take in a late-night movie at a local art-house theatre. All was going well in the back row although the movie was no classic when all of a sudden all hell broke loose! It would seem my mate Adrian

[Not the wrestler but he did originate from London] had just discovered a similar set to his tackle only much smaller consisting of two Balls and a small Penis! He went absolutely Bananas, later giving the usurper a good slapping after dragging he/she outside into a darkened alleyway. I'm very glad to say my babe was female in every sense of the word and she had a smashing pair of tits as well! I must confess I was more than a little peeved when I had to abandon her and comfort my now totally distraught mate over a few more beers. However it struck me only a few days later that just maybe mine had, had the razor blade treatment! God what a totally terrible thought but we'll not be going there, alright? Thereafter as the Manchester night out progressed both Scott Thomson's interest in the whole debate faded very quickly as did our own when we finally entered the club and witnessed the gloriously well built, real female ladies who adorned the small intimate dance floor. Although getting to this point in the evening's proceedings had proved to be more than a little difficult as two huge doormen had firstly barred our entrance! Obviously being strangers to the area and we being Caucasian guys with mostly Scottish accents, all this was proving to be a bit of a problem. I might stress at this juncture from their point of view they were perfectly correct and they were obviously working to instruction, we had no right to be seeking entry under what we'll just call for the sake of argument, normal circumstances but this was not a set of normal circumstances because as far as our host and good friend Ezra was concerned, we were in his city and in his part of town and we were his guests. We were his friends in the exactly same way as he had been when he had been in visits in Scotland, staying in my house and enjoying my family's hospitality. So he took the view that where he went freely we too as his guests would go freely also and we did eventually, after the briefest of huddles in the doorway and a few quiet and well directed words from our chaperone, we were in! The fact that although these two guys were big didn't matter because Ezra was even bigger, he was built like Garth. This clearly influenced their decision making process to a large extent. The music was wonderful although at the time I was only marginally aware of the Reggae genre. Given that one of my hobbies was a love of music I had been exploring it for a couple of years but I was really only scratching the surface although I was then and still am one of a growing number of Caucasian fans. I had however never heard these songs or indeed these artists before. The room itself was very dark lit only by a few Ultra Violet strip-light bulbs which were strategically placed on the walls and on the ceiling. This of course was engineered to accentuated the white underclothes of the sexy full bodied ladies as they danced away totally oblivious as to their real purpose. This also created one of the strangest effects I've ever witnessed. It reminded me just a little of a cartoon like backdrops used by “The Pink Floyd” on their tours. All we could see were rows and rows of white eyes and equally white teeth shinning out at us from the blue darkness. The effect was doubly enhanced as almost all of the tables were overflowing with glasses and bottles filled with a very popular drink of the day, they too were milky white as well! The drink was not only popular in musically enlightened Manchester it was liked and enjoyed UK wide. It was called a "Snowball" Well given that rather theatrical build-up what else could it possibly have been? It was our host who first drew our attention to the bazaar sceptical of the glowing white molars and it was Ezra who laughed the loudest. Boy did he laugh and the more we enjoyed ourselves the better he liked it. A really good night having passed so quickly saw us some hours later back out on the street and most of us by this time were very drunk. “Take me to “Harvey Gardens” driver please!” was the garbled sound that flowed from Scott Thomson’s lips after he’d flagged down a passing Black Hackney Taxi!

..Silly, silly, Boy!

He was in fact blurting out his home address back over the

border in Scotland but a combination of the drink and the Scots accent made him almost totally incoherent to the bemused driver. An English fiver in hand and an explanation from Eddie Rose in his Manchurian patois sent the driver happily on his way allowing us to resume our “A Night to Remember” odyssey. Thankfully some of the troops had not totally forgotten we had still to pick up Ezra's Austin from where he had abandoned it some hours earlier. A brief search successfully concluded and the vehicle duly located we proceeded one by one to pour ourselves into the light coloured British built motorcar. The street had been quiet when we parked earlier but now it was mobbed and nose to bloody tail with little or no real room for manoeuvre. Eddie being University educated told me later on, the next day in fact that Ezra on seeing the chaos had clearly decided to apply a working example of Sir Isaac Newton’s Second Law which he expounded thus; “For every action there is an equal and opposite reaction" Applied in its simplest form by our chauffeur it had then been further reduced by his actions into some rather basic steps and then immediately executed like this.

Gear Stick forward into “FIRST GEAR” now bash your way forwards! Shunting car in front forward about six inches! Next! Gear Stick into REVERSE GEAR” and bash your way backwards shunting the car behind backwards approximately the same distance! Then repeat these actions as often as was required to facilitate enough free space to allow all on board the opportunity of proceeding happily too the next watering hole. Simple don’t you think?

The scientific lesson is then interrupted by an announcement from the Tannoy Speaker on the wall. “This next lot are now half way through their contest Dale. Oh sorry its Mr Storm isn’t it! The Gaffer has told them to cut it a bit, looks like he wants a shorter show tonight it's his daughter's birthday party so he wants to get away home sharpish later.”

Ask him again ref!

Dale looks momentarily confused, then turning to the reporter all is revealed. That's a bit strange because he's only got boys unless I've gotten that totally wrong for all these years? Another Tannoy announcement: "Please remember the Top of the Bill contest has now been switched to last spot and don't forget he wants that early finish! And be ready to go!" Dale shouts at the Tannoy on the wall. Stuck up little shit! I'll be ready when I'm ready! Somebody needs to throw him in the river out the back!

Given some of your opinions and some of your attitudes you've displayed up to now, you wear the mantle of a political animal rather proudly?

Why not I'm an engineer! I've always worked with my hands. I've seen at first hand a lot of the shit these multi-national companies get up too these days! All things being equal I see nothing around me that makes me want to change my opinions either!

Ceterus Parabus!

And what does that mean?

All things being equal!

Really! That's handy to know.

The Ancients had phrases to fit almost every occasion.

History is fascinating but we don't always learn from it!

And the disappointment you eluded to earlier? What was it, something with a political connection perhaps?

No not at all but it is something almost as worthy of note.

***This chapter is dedicated to the memory of a good pal, dearly loved and sadly missed. The funny, the gracious, the flamboyant "Mr Ezra Francis" very, very sadly he passed away in 2008. RIP my good friend ***

Total mileage Ayr to Morecambe and back: 346.4
Time taken for the return journey: 6 Hours 44 Minutes

Gordon "Klondyke" Lythe

(Courtesy of Mrs Rita Shillitoe)
Bobby Barron

Rusty Blair

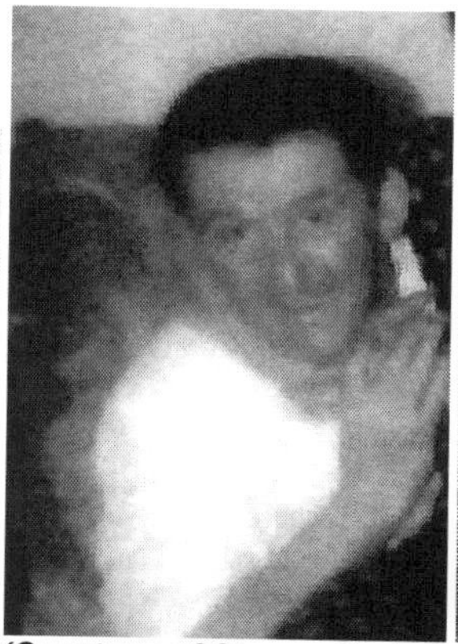

(Courtesy of Steven Taylor)
Jeff Bradley

(Courtesy of B McClung)
Murphy the Surfy

CHAPTER TWENTY

(Is Blood really thicker than Water?)

Yes I do carry the burden of a real disappointment, a family disappointment and believe me when I say it really did hurt a lot at the time and it still hurts almost as much today. It was a real kick in the Nuts! Would you say I was a bad person? Difficult question I know.

I can't say for sure we've only just met but given reports given to me by others and my own gut feeling; are you a bad person, I'd have to say probably not.

Thank you you're a star, anyway there's a guy I know, another wrestler although unlike most of us he's quite independently wealthy. So he's on this charity committee and he asks me if I'd be willing to put together a show to raise funds for the Rotary. So naturally I say yes. I decided to work on it myself and I incorporated a slot for him as well, why not? His name was Bill Robertson he's a good worker in his own right, others who helped out and they all did a grand job were as follows: Young Starsky, Bruce Welch, Big Ian Miller, The Harlequins, Scott Thomson, Jeff Bradley, Michael O'Hagan, The Masked Viking and Harry Parks from Edinburgh. I even throw in my Ring for free! It was for a good cause and it was what's known in the business as a "Bill Money Job!" Meaning it was a full package paid for by themselves which meant I didn't need to bother about advertising and ticket sales, hall rent, etc] Sadly they picked The Albert Hall in Stirling, it wouldn't have been my choice but what the hell and they "Did their Bollocks!" Meaning they lost money! Evidently their patrons were not really the typical wrestling type so even although it was for a good cause they still don't turn up in strong enough numbers! Nevertheless we got paid, although we'd all taken less than normal to try and minimise the loss. Rather sadly shortly thereafter the shit really hit the fan big style! Orig Williams a Welshman and a promoter who ran regular shows in the same venue wasn't at all pleased, can't think why it's a free county and the standard of the participants on the bill was high, in fact most had appeared for him over the piece so his reputation didn't suffer. Maybe that was the problem? Anyway we Scots are not down there in Wales working in his patch are we now? It would seem he blamed me! Only me and although he had me billed on other up and coming shows and I'd worked for him faithfully for years he decided to replace me! On the first of these bills an afternoon show he was complicit in a complete lie when he instructed the MC to announce to the punters over the microphone a totally "Bullshit" reason as to why I hadn't turned up which in turn totally tarnished my reputation! I had never failed to turn up for a show in my life not even once in twenty years but I'm now out in the cold! Rum Doo especially as all the others were still ok, just me, I'm the only one out on his ear! So I try to reason with him on the phone with no luck, I even travel to a show in Motherwell at the Civic Centre another one where I was originally billed to appear my thinking was to have a word face to face and make my peace, but still I'm out! To be fair Young Starsky came alone as well and that act of solidarity sunk him as well. So here I was a man who had as much if not more service time in the business under my belt than he had and I was now being ostracised and placed in a career threatening situation by a guy from the other end of Britain, a fellow Celt and all for no good reason. Strangely he was stupid enough to think I was going to just dry up and disappear without a word! No such luck arsehole! After all I'm a bloody Scot and remember this fact, I've been training and supplying lads for him as well as working for him myself for years and years long before all of his shit! I had even acted as his trusted representative at some Ticket Outlets and whilst there I collected all the cash money etc when he did not have enough time to get there personally before they closed for the night. I had always been totally honest and above board with him right down the line and my actions in supplying local wrestlers meant he continually made savings on travelling expenses, wages, meals and accommodation costs! And still I'm the one being shut out and the only one who's being fucked over! All the others on that fateful Charity Bill job had been forgiven but forgiven and for what you might ask? Earning a living, who the hell did he think he was bloody God?

Very righteous I'm sure clearly he did think he was a God.

I'll leave that for you to judge.

Well what other conclusion can I draw from his actions?

Young Starsky, The Harlequins, in this situation the wrestling entrepreneur guy Bill Robertson didn't count because by that time he didn't work the circuit anyway. Michael O'Hagan, Scott Thomson, Jeff Bradley who as usual had been the first to volunteer to help me build the ring, Big Ian Miller and the Viking all support me and refused to work for the El Bandito again until some fairness and applied commonsense on his part prevailed. Sadly Mr Parks did not give me his support he continue to work on but he was going through a messy divorce and he probably needed the money so no hard feelings Harry boy. Disappointingly the biggest kick in the nuts came from one of my own siblings, my older brother who despite me asking for his full support, not only as a sibling but also as another of those who like me had appeared on the show and who like me had also accepted the wages on the night! Sadly he refused to support me and he too continued to work for Orig the Ogre. That meant without his full support there was now no hope and no way back for me. It left deep scars; we've had more family disagreements since!

So plans were laid out to now get back out there again promoting my own shows once more, just like I'd done years before; I talked it over with all the lads at a meeting in the gym a week before and thankfully they were all up for it. Thankfully sometimes in life as one door closes another one opens and as luck would have it Andy Robin who'd also been working for the Taff decided and correctly I think, as it was his name on the Top of the Bill and his name that was putting most of the bums on seats every night he'd decided to take what for me was a very fortunate decision. He proceeded to promote shows in Scotland for himself and indirectly in so doing he squeezed Williams out of Auld Scotia and back over the border, back down into his native Wales. I shall always be eternally grateful to those lads who supported me, God love them all and I shall always be equally grateful to Andy and his wife Margaret for their most timely intervention! Sometimes I find myself thinking and wondering if Maggie had, had a hand in the whole episode. She is clearly nobody's fool and apart from recognizing a good solid business opportunity I just wonder if just maybe she somehow decided to help me out of my predicament and come to my rescue! We'll never really know will we? Anyway I like to think she and Andy did?

A classic case of woman's intuition I would have said and the intelligent application of it.

Could be? But Maggie is not one of those men hating mental, so called Woman's Libbers! She's a well educated free thinking lady with a good and a true heart!

Let's just leave it there for the moment shall we? We don't want to be having a falling out over feminist issues now do we? Tell me about some of the others and include some more masked guys as well! Are most of you married men? Oh and the woman also for that matter do they all have kids that need looking after and stuff like that?

Total mileage Ayr to Lockerbie and back: 156 Miles
Total time taken to complete journey: 3Hours 26Mins

(Courtesy of Mr Jim Lee)

Big Ian Miller

Ezra "The Zulu" Francis

One of the World of Sports top men Mr Johnny Saint!

CHAPTER TWENTYONE

(A Villain or just a devote family man?)

Wrestling undoubtedly has its arse-holes and misfits but the good will out as they say just like in every other walk of life. Grappling is no different from any other sport in that regard many of my contemporaries work away tirelessly in the background raising money for children's charities but you'll seldom hear about it and most certainly not from them. Those who are married and that's probably much more than half love both their wives and their off-spring in equal measure but all are very passionate about the business! You may look upon that as strange, you'd need to be a grappler to fully understand where I'm coming from but ultimately most wrestlers are very, very special people.
"Mr Jimmy Wilson" is a perfect example, he's a big lad very strong and very athletic as well but he's also very quiet, very polite and very unassuming when not wearing his trademark black tights! He's a former Professional Football Player; a Goal Keeper and if my memory serves me well and he played for Clydebank FC or it could have been Dumbarton maybe? Next time I see him he's going to give me a very loud rollicking for not getting that one correct believe you me! He's a good pal of Alex Miller the former Glasgow Rangers defender! So one Sunday morning religiously as always he's out for a morning drive with his lovely wife and their kids. He's quietly minding his own business negotiating his way along The Boulevard. [A local nick-name for the Duel Carriageway which runs more or less from the Glasgow's West End at Anniseland Cross out to areas like Clydebank and Bonhill. The latter being a small hamlet quite close to Alexandria on the Loch Lomond road. Ian McKay Jimmy's best buddy on the Scottish grappling circuit lives in Bonhill he's a very athletic lightweight, somewhat self-taught but a very good and a totally believable worker nevertheless. All of a sudden a young wiz-kid boy racer cuts Jimmy up and then drives on

having given the family the fingers as he disappears down the road. The significance of the fact it was a Sunday morning will also become apparent later so please bear that in mind! Unluckily for the guy in the other car with the Go-Faster-Stripes on the side was the fact that the next set of lights were at red and even more significantly they were slow changers! So having drawn up along side the youngster Jimmy then proceeds to climb out of his VW Beetle Car. A look of total disbelief crossed the face of other driver as he watched this Giant of a man and the metamorphosis he was going through as he slowly emerged from this quite small, green coloured motor vehicle. The whole episode must have put an awful strain on his bowels and this episode could probably be the origins of the phrase: “A sticky bum moment?” Having arrived at the other driver’s door a huge fist then opened it very slowly and very gently! The other driver was now somewhat sheepishly apoplectic but then a rather strange thing happened which seems to have been an epiphany moment. What influenced the whole proceedings thereafter was the sound of a lone church bell as it started ringing out solemnly someway off in the distance!

You’ve just added that bit for maximum effect haven’t you? Go on admit it you did, didn’t you?

I had a feeling you weren’t paying attention earlier when I mentioned Sunday morning and religion were you? The Big Man was like a whole lot of other people including me, he too was an ex-Boys Brigade member. Those young boys wore a brown leather waist belt, a “Sam Brown Belt” style white coloured sash with a fake ammunition box on the end and pillbox headgear. Always a far more popular pastime when I was a lad than the Scouts! Clearly the whole family were on their way to the local church! Got it now? Meanwhile as the offender cringed in fear holding his arms above his head and face he was heard to shout out. “Oh ***please*** mister I’m really ***sorry*** don’t hit me will you!”

Ask him again ref!

Luckily for the motoring moron those were the two words Jimmy really wanted to hear. “Please” and more especially “Sorry” and because of those interventions he at least gave the impression to his family that he had no real intention of ever landing a painful blow on the cultrate! Unexpectedly the cheeky boy-racer had gotten very, very lucky, although there was no logical reason for Jimmy’s air of a cool head, giving the explosive venom I’d witnessed first hand pumping through the big man’s veins on a show just a few nights before when he’d been unexpectedly noised up by an irate punter. But for the sake of this story let’s just settle on this simple reasoning that he did not want his wife or his kids to be further upset by the sight of spilt blood even although it would most certainly not have been his! So the driver having been summoned from his flashy red car to wholeheartedly apologise to Jimmy’s wife and young family, which he willingly did, the offender was then escorted back and then sat once again back into his black and red imitation, fake leather copies of proper Recaro seating. Then leaning in close so he could not be overheard by anyone in the VW our intrepid anti-hero spoke only a few short words to the driver: “You are the luckiest little shit alive just at this moment pal” Again bear in mind the significance of the word alive. Ok? Jimmy then continued! “You’re only saving graces are these; it’s Sunday and I am travelling with the wife and kids! Oh and you were also saved by the sound of the church bell which could be a call from God to you to change your ways and I’d think about that one for a few minutes if I were you”

Was the Big Man really that religious?

Who knows but apparently the fact the young driver had said ***please*** and ***sorry*** and didn’t swear in front of his wife and young family helped Jimmy to help the driver to keep all his teeth still planted firmly in his entirely empty head!

Very slowly and deliberately the young man clearly relieved

began to speak. *"Is it ok if I go now please, the traffic lights have changed to green?"*

"Sorry" Says the big man "I'm afraid that's not possible!"

Stuttering the driver asks again *"Why is that then?"*

"Simply because of this!" says the giant, Jimmy then turned his engine off and removed the keys from the steering column! Then leaning in again he continued to speak. "I'm going to keep these keys safe for you ok, oh and you have a really good day now!" With that Jimmy got into his own wee car and drove off with his family to enjoy morning services leaving the cocky youngster totally stranded!

....**Now that's Priceless!**

The self same man was doing a show for me a few miles south of Paisley about a week before, when the assistance of a strangely low slung balcony allowed a smart arse clown to lean over, whilst being held tightly by two drunken mates thus affording him the opportunity to get close enough to grab hold of and remove the Thermos Flask the big ex-goalie was wearing as a disguise! Big Mistake! That's when the balloon went up and Jimmy jumped onto the corner post and then launched himself in a Tarzan like leap onto the balcony, clearing the front row as he went! The culprit was only momentarily frozen to the spot as my wrestling buddy attempted to catch up with him! His other two mates having run off meant the offender was now left to face the music all on his lonesome! Given no real choice and no real chance of outrunning his pursuer he then decided the prospect of a possible broken ankle was far more preferable to being set upon by the now getting ever closer unmasked assassin! He did however throw the stolen head gear at the now very angry performer but this of course proved to be a pretty futile gesture indeed. I might add however Jimmy never broke his stride as he caught it in mid-air with one hand and being the true professional he undoubtedly is, he stopped but only momentarily to then pull it back over his head and all in one seamless movement. With only milliseconds to avoid a battering the now regretting every moment of his rather stupid action the overly enthusiastic punter opted to jump down into the ring. If I could have caught up with him I'd have signed him up right away because believe me when I say it was a really brave decision and no mean feat from where he was standing at the time! You've got to ask yourself did he really have to take that crazy leap, short answer oh yes he feckin well did! Jimmy showed remarkable restraint by not chasing after him down the rain socked street after that and I'm very grateful indeed for that rage restraint. I shudder to think what might have happened to the silly culprit if he hadn't jumped! It goes without saying however Jimmy pursued him to the end as he too descended back into the ring as well, only his was more of an Olympic style Swan Dive which I've no doubt would have gained him no less than a series of 9.9's topped only by the odd perfect 10.0! It was truly that good but bare in mind he'd been a Goal Keeper so what else was he going to do. Although even the good shot-stoppers are always going to be prone to do some rather stupid things on the odd occasion if it's in their make-up! Albeit who was going to remind Jimmy of that fact, certainly not I mate! I might add he had a really good bout thereafter putting on a great show and like his quick impromptu costume change earlier his performance after the resumption of normal service was also seamless, a real work of art! So there you have it Hero or Villain you decide!

Hero! Definitely! No question he had been anything else.

Good call Jimmy Wilson is undoubtedly one of the good guys. He is a gentleman and a real pro in everything he does in life, he cares about everything and everybody around him, people, animals and lasting friendships as well. He continues to do his very best not only for himself but for all others. Another example of such actions happened not so very long ago when a team representing Scotland were on their way down to Manchester for a big charity show, the opposition was of course another bunch of lads in England's colours! Sadly it never went ahead due to a serious road accident at the junction between the A75 and the A74 (M) before it joins the M6 Motorway. The journey had been dogged with incidents from the off; the lads had willingly come to the aid and assistance of others involved in two separate shunts as we journeyed south! The first one was just north of Cumnock on the A70 and there were bodies; both male and female strewn all over the road and also on the surrounding grassy verges, luckily they all missed hitting the surrounding trees! None I might add were seriously injured in any significant way but all were very drunk and that included the driver! So having rounded them up and made sure they were safe we called for an ambulance to attend and then we carried on going south. Another incident occurred further down the track involving a similar story and again there were no fatalities thank God. The fact it was a Friday night might explain the bad driving and the alcohol but this pattern of incidents was perhaps an omen, a sign of what might be about to happen later on but who could have known that then, certainly not anyone of the happy bunch of real friends who were looking forward to representing their country. We were merrily travelling on board the brand new, first time out on the road Ford Transit mini-bus and to a man we never ever felt the least bit uneasy about continuing with the Odyssey, even after it started to snow and rather heavily at that. With no sign of the bad weather abating a quick verbal vote was taken and the positive result with no dissenters meant we continued to travel! The driving was being shared by Scott Thomson and I and that was only determined by the fact it was us two who picked up the vehicle from the car higher firm of "GODFERRY DAVIS" on the Prestwick Road Ayr that afternoon! So we two licence in hand had then signed on the dotted line and took charge of our transport. As it turned out some months later in a small country courtroom in Annan Dumfriesshire that isolated and totally innocent act taken in good faith on behalf of the group by two good friends almost cost me my sanity and my totally innocent wife and my very young family their future happiness! I truly shudder to think what might have ensued had the first spell at the wheel been allocated to someone else? Luckily the true and endearing close friendship of one of the very best people I've ever had the pleasure to call my good pal, latterly saved me from what at the time would have been further mental turmoil and almost certainly economic disaster! The intervening years have however taken their toll, a head full of greying hairs being the only real outward and visible sign of the painful inner turmoil and constant regretful soul searching. That good and faithful friend was sent flying, shunted forward into the solid dashboard after we hit the large articulated vehicle which was travelling north up the main carriageway minding its own business. He [Scott Thomson] was very badly hurt smashing both hip joints in the process which required months and months of painful hospitalisation, on top of that he and therefore his family had no wages coming in. The other main casualty was my cousin's young son Ronny a lightweight lad I particularly liked a lot at the time and in fact I still do! He was one of identical twins and both were very good wrestling pupils and great fun to be with but rather sadly the possibility of a large Accident Insurance payout loomed large in the minds of some

**** The extra level of insurance had not actually been taken out by us at the time of the original hire, purely because it had been an optional extra and an additional extra cost to the group as a whole and it was not compulsorily. We had however diligently taken out all the other insurance cover required by law ****

The level of insurance cover seemed to evoke more than a passing interest from Ron's parents in particular and was clearly far more important to them at that particular moment than almost anything else. Clearly their concentration should have been centred on their badly injured son and his worried sibling twin. Inexplicably during the passing of Ronny's long months of convalescence they took more time to devote to their dream of large pounds note signs and these clearly had some precedence over any wider family considerations! This meant my dear mother's older sister's daughter and her pseudo middle class husband were clearly hell bent on screwing me and mine into the ground for cash, with no consideration given to where I was at that time mentally or where my personal physical wellbeing might take me in the future! I had been the driver at the time and I could not turn the clock back, I only wish I could. Please believe me when I tell you I've had to live with that fact ever since and at times even yet, it has proved to be a very heavy load to carry! You can I'm sure imagine the larger family fallout which ensued after all this came to see the light of day, especially the impending lawsuit etc. I bare no ill will to anybody who was in that vehicle that night and I never will and I'm also deeply and truly sorry for all that happened. Strangely the fact Jeff Bradley [Wee Sammy Taylor] was not there perched as usual behind me in attendance in his usual guardian angel mode, keeping me safe still haunts my mind at times. Although they had sustained very painful injuries both Bruce Welch and Big Jimmy Wilson took charge at the scene of the carnage and I shall always be grateful to them for all their help and kind words at the time. Bruce in particular had sustained a badly dislocated shoulder, another of my confederates and a very close friend, whom I still see regularly, suffered a badly broken wrist which meant months being added to his engineering apprenticeship period and once again there were no wages being earned in the interim for his family either. Others had what are normally referred to in the press as the usual assortment of cuts, bruises and sprains normally associated with such a dangerous and sometimes fatal collision! The full extent of my hero Mr J Wilson's ailments have for some strange reason completely escaped my memory banks but I'm sure they were also varied! The only one who walked away completely physically unhurt was in fact yours truly. I have no idea why although my good lady wife some weeks later enlightened me to the fact she had fallen pregnant with child for the second time only days before we set off and she'd kept it as a future good news surprise! Maybe that was why the gods had been good to me in particular but we'll never really know will we? The statement issued by the police months later during the court case hearing praising my quickness of thought and my life saving evasive action, pointing out that had I not applied myself in the manner in which I did then fatalities would undoubtedly have occurred. However all that seemed quite hollow at the time because for me it didn't change the fact that people in my care had been badly hurt and I had been the driver at the time!

That must have been a particularly difficult time for you?

It was but these things happen or so they say. The subsequent proposed Legal Action did however fall apart due to the helpful police statements, that and Scott Thomson's total refusal to back stab me when encouraged to do so by Bert and Marie young Ronny's parents. That blew their case right out of the water. Scott [Wee Tam] had been continually pressed and cajoled to support their argument with promises of a fat cheque but still he refused to get himself dragged into any legal compensation case. That gesture of total friendship towards me was all the more commendable given the fact as I mentioned earlier he too had no earnings coming in for many more months!

The fact family were involved was clearly devastating?

Yes it was but that's what you get when there are a lot of people involved including greedy, sneaky, money grabbing lawyers. Friends or even some, so called close family in circumstances like this one matter not a jot, as you just never know which way they're going to jump. Even in our sport we have some seedier individuals who are a lot less than nice and sometime a few come along who are only driven by the thought of some easily gotten financial gain!

Really! Go on, do tell!

Total mileage Ayr and Fort William and back: 282Miles
Total time to completer the journey: 6Hours 30Minutes

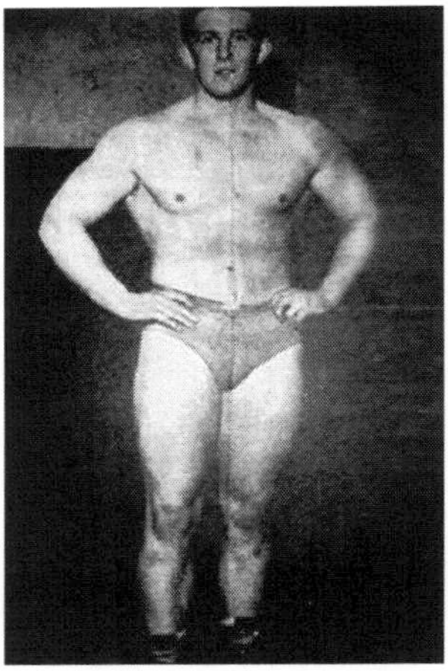

Bob Sweeney

Malcolm Kirk

Judd Harris

"Farmer" John Allan

CHAPTER TWENTYTWO

(The Nice and the not so Nice)

Some people in public life are not as nice or as innocent as they outwardly appear one promoter in particular, who shall remain nameless was known for being consistently sneaky and impishly infant like in the way he approached some situations. He was also rather cheeky with it but normally not in a bad way, he harboured an unexplainable passion for opening doors on which the word "PRIVATE" was boldly displayed totally unannounced and knowing full well what he was about. He just loved to prowl hotel corridors etc, usually alone and usually in the evenings! Quiet boarding houses and small family run units seemed to be his favourite, quite what he ever hoped to find on the other side of these barriers is anybodies guess. On a personal level I like him a lot but those types of actions and those types of hang-ups have never sat well with me at anytime!

Other colleagues have been know to drill holes in dressing room walls and I'm not just talking about taking a peep at just the fairer female form exclusively either! On that particular subject most of the Heterosexual performers were not always aware for obvious reasons given the law at the time that occasionally they were working very closely and intimately and coming into sweaty bodily contact with some men [Only a few] who were in their sexual element when touching other males! In making this observation I must emphasise I'm not coming down on any one side or the other of the same-sex debate I merely mention it as a point of information. Some straight workers after finding out the score and having later on analysed the contest content, blow by blow were more than dismayed as to where hands and other body parts had been placed during the ring time! Some have even been known to cringe and squirm rather uncomfortably and at other times some dressing room post match debriefings have been known to become more than a little strained! On the really seedier side occasionally there have been one or two rather suspect owners of some small hotels and boarding houses in some of the larger cities UK wide where grapplers were regularly billeted who were known to indulge frequently in a frenzied helping of perverted excitement, whilst sitting watching their normally sex starved slutty wife's kinky action and antics with others. Frequently strangers were invited to watch or even join in as these females indulged their particular sexual hang-ups with some over zealous young wrestlers. Things have been known to get little out of hand regularly when the bar closed for a night and the other guest, that's those not in the know, had long since dropped off to the land of nod! Some energetic grapplers [And again only a few] employed some really strange ways to pass away their down time when they were on a tour, this practice was usually more the preference of the younger "Star-Struck" element and always after they'd been let loose away from some parental control for the first time. This meant they would regularly end up falling into the clutches of some over the hill, black stocking clad, overweight, large arsed femme fatale who was clearly one of the long term bored, married, large saggy breasted old tarts! Whose sexually inadequate perverted hubby's preference was wielding a video camera whilst she worked her way through the well thumbed pages of the "Kama Sutra" with a virile young man with lots to prove and the excess energy to get the job done! Even if it took him all night! Other performing misfits have been know to take up a position in a cubical in the "Ladies" Toilettes and whilst there they'd peer down over the partition walls whilst innocent and unsuspecting ladies went about their everyday bodily functions.

...Dirty, Sick Buggers!

Most promoters, particularly those on the Independent side would pay for basic Hotel rooms or Boarding House Bed and Breakfast stopovers but that start to the day fried breakfast meal usually had to go along way, because once again in a lot of cases full subsistence levels which you would always, as a matter of course get on the likes of a theatre tour etc were seldom if ever totally forthcoming in the way they would have and should have been if we'd all been part of a nationally recognised entertainment industry Trade Union! That meant for most there nightly wage, such as it was had sometimes to feed you as well! This could invariably prove particularly embarrassing if you were then travelling in a car with others, as it more often than not facilitated the adult version of a game of "Hide and Seek." At break times grown men made up silly infantile excuses to lose each other so as to avoid the embarrassment of having to admit they couldn't afford to buy a colleague a cup of tea! Comradeship however always stayed strong among the lads and these obstacles were usually overcome amicably although the feeling among some was always that they were being exploited to the full regards subsistence. Others might disagree and they might be correct when they say they were in fact exploitation all of the time! Bearing in mind the established Promoters were making good and regular money which afforded most of them a handsome residence and a decent standard of living, considering the fact our industry trades largely in cash it could well have been the case box office returns were not fully declared and therefore not fully subjected to full scrutiny for the purpose of Income Tax payments here in the UK! This view has been regularly been articulated over many years now and probably with some justification?

On a completely different level other wrestlers have sometimes covertly enjoyed the trappings of other people's fame from time to time; some look-a-like physiognomies sometimes gave rise to cases of mistaken identity on the part of the all too gullible "Joe Public" or in these particular cases the more demure but equally blinded "Josephine Public." These situations have been quite literally grabbed with two hands so to speak and again quite literally been enjoyed to the full. One friend of mine in particular who had been a professional cyclist back in the Caribbean before entering the realms of trunks and leather boots, regularly dined out in and around Manchester and sometimes in other cites and towns solely on the fact he bore an uncanny resemblance to the song writer and lead singer/ front man with the successful 70's band "Hot Chocolate" We're are of course talking about the legendary "Earl Brown." Strong rumour has it that more than once Earl's doppelganger scored regularly with the ladies so let's hope he has been extra careful as a proper calling card was probably never produced by way of provable identification! Ironically I've also heard it alleged that the self same popular front man singer has claimed when the occasion warranted it, to actually being the other fellow! Now that's what I call making a statement of intent! The grappling world just like life in general can be a bit of a lunatic environment at times, a weird place where greed and the pursuit of a pound note can turn ordinary, usually reasonably decent men into cunning back stabbing individuals, who given the right set of circumstances will take on the role of the slimy "Gollum" of "The Lord of the Rings" fame and in so doing instantly show the seedier side of their personalities. These cruel spectres are not a pretty sight and they leave a really bad and sometimes bitter taste in the mouths of their unsuspecting victims! Because innocent others and this has happened to more than a few over the years, have been royally hoodwinked and robbed by their peers when they've enthusiastically and rather naively entered honestly into the odd joint business venture partnered with fellow pugilists in promoting a one-off Professional Wrestling Show! Invariably the more astute of these business partners on realising almost immediately the night was clearly shaping up to be a **"Bad House"** with no real chance of a profit to be made, would then set about hatching a plot to trick the younger usually less inherently dishonest and perhaps a little street wise! Although for all their lack of savvy they were nevertheless unlike the other robbing bastards always entirely honourable people. Sadly their naivety usually meant them falling for the old and well tested chestnut of going on in the last spot on he bill, only to discover on getting back to the dressing room sweated and out of breath that the others had scarpered with what was left of the meagre takings! [This really low life action was known in the business as "**Getting the Knock**"] Leaving the now sadly drastically enlightened victim to pick up the things like the hall rent bill, staff wages etc! One such venture after I had been recruited and encouraged by a larger heavyweight, in his leaner career years before he became an appointed superstar [Who incidentally still owes me my money for this particular failed venture] had duly disappeared out the back door with all the takings! What a cowardly bastard! I am likewise still waiting to be compensated by an Indian born fellow professional who regularly earns his living under the guise of being a non-domesticated, untamed, native of a certain so called exotic island in Malaysia. He too dishonestly disappeared into the dark of the cold and wet night in Ardrossan town after Bruce Welch and I had entered into a short term business venture with him on a handshake. He of course was supposed to be the Top of the Bill, Big Name! Big Draw! The more astute and discerning of those who usually pay at the door were obviously way ahead of the game as they failed to turn up in sufficient numbers rather obviously totally unimpressed with what was on offer as a package. As I and the third partner slugged it out in the ring in The Civic Centre once again stupidly filling in on the last spot, on getting back to the dressing room my heart sank I just couldn't believe we'd fallen for that same rouse again! This guy was a so called top draw with Joint Promotions not some fly-by-night upstart from the less glamorous Indie Circuit ranks and still he too turned out to be just another charlatan arsehole. Bloody hell I'd got "The Knock" for a second time! I'm clearly far to trusting but if there is a heaven and it is exclusively for nice honest people, then thankfully there is clearly no way I'll be sharing my little cloud with the likes of these two totally crooked, gutless backstabbers. Others or so its been alleged have been known to steal from the coat pockets of their peers in dressing rooms, although I'd have to admit I've personally never been a victim of this totally unsavoury practice! I have however had a very valuable gift from a dear friend taken out of my bag whilst I was out of the room and barefaced denials were the order of the day thereafter, from all my lying contemporaries on that same bill when I confronted them. I even pleaded with them as to where it might be found in order to save my embarrassment at losing such a precious memento. Other jealous performers clearly wishing to gain some favour and thereafter more work have been known to lie and carry back totally made up, untrue stories to promoters and the likes in the hope they'd be getting their reward for their cowardly back stabbing act of treachery in the form of the other paid dates you had been originally allocated. Others but thankfully not that many, have also been know to try to Bludge [Australian slang meaning to freeload] a free and a totally non contributory daily car ride on a week long tour never ever offering even one penny piece for some petrol money or any cash gift by way of any thanks for the ride!

That's disgusting, what a bunch of tight fisted arseholes!

Thanks for that, now you're getting into the spirit of things.

Has anything ever happened that's really shocked you?

Well there was this one time and this story is probably the strangest thing that's happen to me on the road. I'd been appearing in Fife and a good pal of mine and his very attractive lady wife both Cabaret Entertainers were living in Kirkcaldy at the time, so they'd suggested I drop in for a visit on my way home. As I was travelling with Young Starsky and in his car we both obliged. They were out working that night but they had left a message with the babysitter, the wife's rather frail mother to make us up a sandwich or something and to entertain us until their return, as it was we didn't get there till around 10-30 pm. Our meal was waiting for us, rabbit stew lovely! I hadn't had rabbit for years and even at that late hour it tasted just great, so after thanking our elderly host for a great tuck-in we settled down with a cool beer and some polite chat with our pleasant but just a little bit wandered host. Gregory and Isabel arrive home around 12-15 pm and a few more drinks were consumed. Oh I should perhaps have pointed this out before, Starsky the driver was on Coca-Cola. Eventually it was time to set off back to the west coast so on saying our good-buys we headed for the car, just as we reached the end of the pathway Isabel popped her head out of the front door to enquire from Gregory if he'd noticed the cat when they'd come home earlier, he replied in the negative. The mother-in-law had by this time gone to her bed as she'd started to act even more strangely. Gregory tried to explain how she'd been in a local psychiatric ward off and on for most of the previous eighteen months and according to the doctors she was now on the mend. So during a handshake and a manly embrace our host enlightened us to the fact he'd have to locate Isobel's new kitten before retiring as without it on her pillow to cuddle, his pet loving wife would never drop off to sleep. As we drove and my head drifted through a haze of tiredness and euphoria into what seemed like a long silence, Starsky commented on the rabbit stew and the fact he'd never had anything like that before. Then suddenly it all fell into place, God do I really want to be going here I thought to myself. No she couldn't have! Or could she? Surely not that poor defenceless wee kitten!

....**Oh shit!**

No you don't mean?

Yes sadly I do mean! The mental babysitter had killed the kitten stewed it and then fed it to us. Clearly she was off her bloody head! I pretended to drift off to sleep after that busily trying not to throw-up all over my mate's car. I've never mentioned anything about that night to him since. So unlike me he is thankfully, hopefully blissfully unaware of the real contents of the casserole dish. What's even stranger however is the fact neither Gregory nor indeed Isabel have ever mentioned that fateful night either or that poor wee cuddly creature ever since!

The mileage Ayr to Birmingham and back: 592 Miles
Total time for return journey: 10 Hours 18minutes

Gordon Corbett

Ace Sports Bill

Marty Jones

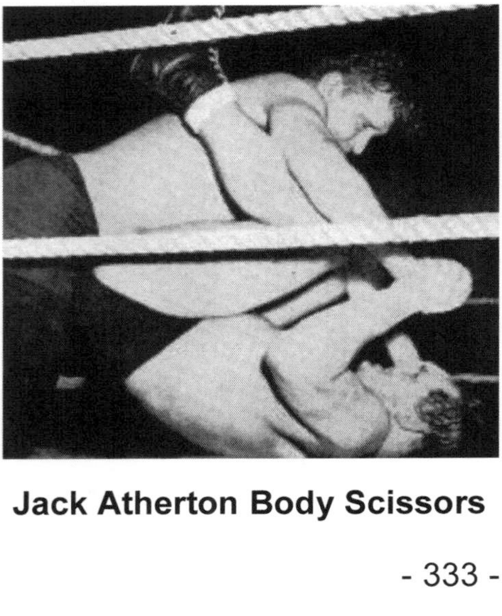

Jack Atherton Body Scissors

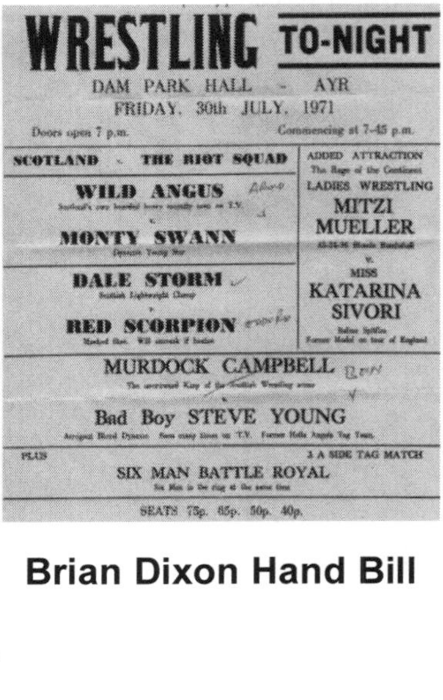

Brian Dixon Hand Bill

CHAPTER TWENTYTHREE

(The "Heat" of the Moment)

The Anglo lads almost to a man rave about the **"Heat"** [A slang term for a good atmosphere being generated] in some of the halls in the North of England, The Midlands and also in the South of the country. You get it at its very best or so they say in places like: Belle Vue Manchester, The Stadium Liverpool, The Fairfield Hall in Croydon, Digbeth Birmingham, The Assembly Rooms Derby, The St James's Hall Newcastle, The Nottingham Ice Rink, and of course the pesto résistance namely London's Albert Hall. I've worked some of these halls and I've been in many others besides, and I've enjoyed them all, and yes they're not wrong audiences there have been great! But I' haven't so far at least been billed on the Big London one but hopefully there's still plenty of time left? As far as I'm concerned and I'm not alone when I say this the Drill Hall Dumfries on an "Alamo Night" [A reference to the mission in San Antonio Texas where around 180 men, mostly Scots and Welsh souls died when it was overrun by General Santa Anna's Mexican troops] is mental! A couple of others that come close would have to be the Ice Rinks in Paisley and Ayr but right here in The Eldorado Leith is definitely the tops for many. The vibe is quite simply unbeatable! This venue has been going since the 1930's now isn't that's amazing, it can be an uncompromising and unforgiving place though! I had my first Joint Promotions bout here in a Tag Team Tournament along with the likes of **"Mr Bill Clarke"** and his younger brother Ron. Strangely it was also my sibling although he's the elder who was my tag partner on that memorable occasion! The Clarke lads went on to form the tag team "The Boston Poachers" and on that particular night they were on just before us. They got a very rough ride indeed, most of it self induced given their roughhouse tactics. To his credit on this occasion Max Crabtree had been taking notes from the wings and he made a beeline for the dressing rooms to tell my brother and myself we should remove the Thermos disguises we had been instructed to wear originally. We were then further instructed to go easy with the villainy as we could and probably would be lynched if we went too **"Strong"** [Meaning far too much Rule Bending] because the crowd were now in one of their infamous mental moods! As we entered the ring having negotiated the steep wooden staircase down into the Cockpit! We were then introduced to cries of: “We’re gonna kill them! Throw them out here to us we’ll deal with them, we’ll kick their heads in!” and so on and so forth. The Clarke's had really noised them up big time the heat was off the scale! I'm grateful to Max for having the foresight to calm the situation down a least a little which resulted in the safe preservation of most of my body parts! Our opponents on the night were none other than Ian Gilmour and Wee Jimmy McKenzie two very popular lads and especially so in Leith. [Both being members of the Eldorado All Stars Team] Jimmy hails from Glasgow and Ian Gilmour although based in Yorkshire and communicating in a broad Yorkshire accent was in fact born north of the border in Dumfries! He's even represented Scotland in the cross border “All Star Team Events” on FA Cup Final Saturday afternoons in recent years. Needles to say we had no chance and we got slaughtered, both when outside and even more so inside the ropes! The Storming of the Paris Bastille was tame compared to the “Heat” and the “Hate” in the air that night! You will I'm sure, have noted that I was forced into playing the villain on that occasion purely because we were trying to get ourselves a foot in the door at Joints! Everybody had to play by their rules and follow their instructions to the letter and that could and in most cases would mean a dismantling of personas you'd spent time introducing previously whilst on the Independent circuit. Although had you accumulated a big enough following already then they were usually perfectly happy to get the extra support in cash terms from the extra bums on seats you could then bring to their table! Both yours truly and my brother had been busily building careers outside Joints on the Indi Circuit since I had been taken under the wing of Mr Danny Flynn some years earlier and we'd been busily concentrating on building a larger and still growing good grounding of holds and moves in the pro style. This was always more important to me at least than any ego driven, would be, super-star nonsense! Although in hindsight I think it may have been at that point I decided somebody else should take the thumping from the irate over hyped fans and I immediately jumped ship to be resurrected once more as a clean cut, crowd pleasing Blue Eyed Boy Hero! Besides I was and in fact still am far, far too good looking to be a Villain or a Heal. I still take regular anti-inflammatory pills to ease the almost constant pain from a very badly strained almost dislocated right shoulder joint injury, which I had sustained that fateful evening courtesy of the baying for blood audience who've always inhabited this wonderful old stadium. If truth be told the events of that night are still to this day a rather bizarre blur in as much as we the two New Scots Boys on the chopping block were almost totally ignored by everyone else in the dressing room area, everyone except for the Clarke boys and I thank them for that compliment and the comradeship they displayed at that time. As the time grew nearer for our particular personal "Showtime" still we'd not been given our full instructions as to what was going to be the script! Perhaps it was possible Max having been concerned and maybe distracted by what had been going on in the audience during the preceding rather volatile contest, had genuinely been fazed but we'll never really know now, will we? Some in this business do like to stand in the wings looking forward to a good laugh, sadly and usually at the expense of the unwitting and the unsuspecting. On reflection I'm now fully convinced this had become one of those moments as it soon become clear we were being used as cannon fodder to further the careers of others, we were expendable. Some wrestlers and in Scotland in particular clearly feared for their work share and others were clearly more concerned with the preservation of their considerable egos. As we finally entered the fray my sibling and I were still almost completely in the dark, although that fact held no fear for us as we had every confidence in our ability to perform and we were of course happy in the knowledge that communication within the ring ropes was commonplace among us grapplers, so we fully expected during the course of the proceedings we would be informed as to when they, our more experienced opponents would be **"Going Over"** and in what manner it was to happen but it never came! One fall or one submission was all it would take to progress to the final, Ian Gilmour when he first took hold was not stiff in anyway and for a time we three went through the motions, the crowd were not particularly pleased but what the hell we the brothers were following to the letter what little instruction we had been given, slowly, slowly catch a monkey. Things changed however when Jim McKenzie stepped on to the canvas he was in some ways a lot stiffer although in fairness, in later years when we became good and lasting friends he always exhibited a tighter grip with not only me but everyone else he encountered. Obviously he could never fully forget his amateur days, he did however convey to me much later on in my career when we worked more regularly together that in his opinion all four of us had been hoodwinked to some extent that night and we had all been victims in one way and another. He reckoned he was only looking after his own body and his professional reputation, plus his earning power when he almost tore my arm off. I didn't have back then and I still don't have even now, any problem with that position taken by Jim but when I reluctantly recall the god awful pain I endured in my right shoulder socket when he applied an unexpected amateur submission hold and in so doing he had taking full advantage of the fact I had given my arm to him freely, fully expecting him to look after it in exactly the same way I was looking after his. I can't help but feel more than a little anger at the way he took liberties!

Liberties that might well have finished my career! That was a long time ago now and he's been a good friend ever since, he has also apologised for this lapse of professionalism more than once over the intervening years.

A slightly similarly place but a lot more modern and not quite as dark or dingy a structure as the former engine shed is Elgin's very atmospheric Town Hall! Big George McDonald is one of the Promoters up there in what for many including me is considered to be God's Country. Morayshire is beautiful and the people are so nice and so friendly, George and I hit it off right away the very first time I met and we've shared a lot of good times and a lot of drink ever since. I've seldom if ever seen anybody consume whisky like him and to top that, he's a very highly rated Bag Pipe player as well, having learned his stuff in the Army in The Black Watch regiment. Getting back to the Wrestling there's a whole family of season ticket holders from the Indian Sub-Continent who regularly occupy almost the entire front row on the stage every week. There must be about seven or eight of them and they love it, can't get enough, they are all true fans! I can't remember exactly who it was but it was one of the top villains and he was shouting his mouth off. Come to think of it, it could have been Butch Mason? He's a truly great worker or maybe it was Danny Lynch they look so alike! Anyway no sooner had the contest got underway when those on the stage had been spied so there he is hanging over the ropes badgering the whole family! It went something like this: "A family outing is it well that's nice! Did you lot shut the shop early tonight it's only just gone 8-00pm! What happens if somebody wants a bottle of milk, a loaf or even a packet of Condoms they won't get any of them and why, quite simply because you're now closed." He was of course only having a laugh, no racism was intended and no offence was taken either because everybody else including those being sniped at took it all in good part. You could do things like that back then but not now, since that PC nonsense has taken over! The social equilibrium was fully restored however later on when the mother in the group got her own back during a fourth round flurry. She broke the spine of her fancy umbrella over his head and boy was he in pain and didn't she get a standing ovation from the rest of the crowd, it was all great theatre! We stayed at the Grove Hotel when we were up in that area, a bit more about that later perhaps? A few of the local bars were also home to my piping pal and me, we would strut around like sixteen year olds playing pool and generally talking shit and the more we drank the more shit we talked! I remember a particular day long session with some relish, although due to the fact I was posted missing from the hotel I was therefore unaware that because of an injury to another wrestler due to arrive that night, the running order had been changed for the rest of the week. I had now been re-scheduled to meet Big Bill Clarke, our paths were now crossing once again, he like me had made a temporary switch back to the Indies having been offered a chance of some extra work! As a true Pro the big man was far from impressed with me being somewhat unsteady on my feet, in fact he was appalled at my general condition. The strong scent of alcohol when I finally entered the dressing room was a giveaway and on top of that I had got there a little late. The look he gave me said it all and he was of course correct. For that unforgivable lapse he battered me all over the mat that night, it was all I could do just to stop myself from filling the ring seconds pale with the dregs of a six hour Amber Nectar session I'd been enjoying earlier in the day. I felt so guilty and so bloody ashamed! I've have never forgotten that night and what preceded it and I'm as humbled even now thinking about it as I was then. My opponent got the full and unreserved grovelling apology he deserved and he was gracious enough to say that probably most of the paying punters hadn't really noticed my complete lack of respect for them. I might add I've never repeated that lapse into alcohol and apathy, he taught me a hard lesson and I thank you for that Bill. Another reference to that fateful day out on the tiles was uttered by The McDonald some weeks later; again it went something like this: "Did that song about you ever get to number one slot? Remember the one that used your name in the title?" Song about me George what are you on about? "That song you kept playing on the Juke Box the one you said you liked a lot, the one about you!" It turned out to be a late 70's double A Side of a Wings number one release which I been playing over and over on that particular day. The Beatles had been my favourite group although I lost interest for a time after John Lennon got mixed up with Yoko. The song was "Girls School" and how you get Dale Storm from those two words is way beyond me. Although it became rather obvious he'd remembered a lot more than I had about that day's events. It's fair to say pop music was never the Big Man's forte, now Jimmy Shand the world famous accordion player that's a whole different story! I must admit though my ego was flattered more than a little at his mistaken recollection of a song supposedly written about me, no bloody chance. A few Wrestlers have actually had songs released, one was Adrian Street and that disc was an original recording and it was really quite good. It had a Double A. Side "Breaking Bones" and the flip side track was "A Mighty Big Girl!" Another release was by Jackie Pallo's and his lad JJ; a family photo adorned the front cover consisting of Old Jack, Jackie Junior and Trixie, Jacks lovely wife. I never bought that one but to the best of my knowledge it had a sing-a-long format of all the old London pub favourites. Then there was Andy Robin he released a version of the Johnny Preston 1960 hit "Running Bear" just after Herc his bear decided to take a closer look at the Outer Hebrides on his own taking himself of into the sea he swam away and disappeared into the woods on the next island. Andy of course was devastated. He was located safe and sound a few weeks later!

The total mileage Ayr to Berwick and back: 278Miles
Total time taken for the journey: 5 Hours 12Minutes

CHAPTER TWENTYFOUR

(The Scottish Highlands in January!)

Mr and Mrs Hosie of Elgin Town are truly wonderful people and a great credit to reputation of Highland hospitality.

So was it another of these big drinking sessions, then?

Well we had our fair share, when I say we I'm talking about The Viking and I. He's usually all dressed up in a lot of fur and wielding a big double sided axe as well, oh and he grunts a lot, to some it can be totally frightening! The owners of the Grove Hotel had sent us both invitations for their Burns Night Celebration so how could we refuse? He was in his civvies so no one knew who he was on the night. Sobriety passed us by for days after that 25th of January. Jim Hosie himself does a really good version of "Holly Willie's Prayer" one of Robert Burn's better know poems about the hypocrisy in the Church of Scotland in his time. So Night Shirt adorned and old Candle Stick in hand the lights were dimed and we were off, he was terrific, word perfect in fact! On the journey up we stopped off at a hotel in the picturesque Highland village of Blair Athol and yes you guessed it, we were on the drink again, what else? I might add my congenial confederate behaved himself a lot more than I did but he'd always been far more sensible than me. There were a lot of Aussie tourists frequenting the bar so I was in good form and they loved it. Thank God!

But you were driving a car!

Sorry, what was that?

Driving, in charge of a car remember.

Yes I was but at that time it was acceptable. Everybody was doing it! It didn't make it right but everybody did it!

Ask him again ref!

Well I don't drink and drive!

Good Girl, well done you! No vices then? How boring! So having entertained the Lunchtime Foreign Visitor Patrons with some stories and a song or two it was time to get underway again! We'd had a really good time and I must confess I was in what could only be best described as a bit of an Impish mood! Somewhere along the road I took a wrong turning and in order to get back on track I stopped to ask directions from a local worthy. He was a tall kilted highlander in his late sixties adorned in the Harris Tweed jacket and a Tammy bonnet. He proceeded to instruct us thus: Pointing to the top of a long steep hill stretched out in front of us he stated "You go up the hill here and at the top you go left!" More than a little confused I asked him to repeat the detailed instruction and once again he blurted out "You go to the top of the hill and then you turn left!" The problem was he was pointing to the right and saying we were to go to the left! So I repeated his instruction as he had done and I too then pointed to the right just as he had indicated, I also added the verbal; then turn left just as he had done! "That's correct" says he. "Top of the hill then you turn left" and once again he was using his arm to indicate we should turn right! My passenger looked at me, looked at the local man then back to me before shaking his head! I thanked our benefactor and slipping into first gear I got ready to move off, but just before I did I made one more enquiry as to his gift of local knowledge! Again it went something like this; “Just one more thing old pal can you tell me how far it might be to our destination do you think?” He stared at me rather strangely then looking up at the horizon and then back to me he replied. "Well it must be the best part of quite a distance!" So further confused we then drove off.

And what did you do at the top?

We did exactly as the local had instructed and turned right!

Ask him again ref!

But your hand was pointing left just like you said he did!

That's correct! Well spotted! That's what he said and he repeated it more than once so that's exactly what we did! He's pointed left and we actually turned to the right!

Did you reach your destination by turning left, sorry right?

Yes we did his directions were spot on obviously he was very familiar with the terrain but again clearly he didn't know his right from his left! Sadly we got stuck on The Daviot Moor coming home again between the villages of Forres and Aviemore. They can get a lot of snow up there in late January! We ran straight into a ten foot tall wall of the white fluffy stuff, a bloody "White Out" now that was very surreal as we simply couldn't see it! So we had to stay on for another couple of days what a shame, even more lovely alcohol! We'd given some of Tam's pals a lift up to Aviemore, they were going to do some hill walking we'd shared a few laughs in the back of the Land Rover. One giggle in particular I recall was at my expense, bugger! I'd had to hang my White Dinner Jacket up in the back of the vehicle and I made the fatal error of saying that there was something in the carrier that made me look like a bit like James Bond! No sooner had those foolish words escaped my lips when quick as a flash back came wee Jack Elliot's retort "Well it must be a False Face!" Really funny man!

Wee Lenny Ironside as well as being a local performer from up in Aberdeen is also a leading councillor on the Granite City Administration. He's a very conscientious campaigner for the Left being a Labour Party member. Still that's no bad thing given this Tory Bloody Government we have at present, the quicker they're out the better! It's a beautiful City Aberdeen with all that gleaming stone. The Music Hall is a really good space to work in and there's always an appreciative audience but it's got a really high stage! I nearly came a cropper up there one night, we'd had a day off and we were travelling up to Wick a day later, so me and two of the other lads went out for a pint or two.

You don't say!

I think you're ahead of me here.

You went overboard again didn't you?

Yes just a wee bit, I couldn't even bite my finger later on that night! Anyway, we were driving back to the hotel, no not me this time but come to think of it none of us should have been anywhere near a steering wheel! So I'm told we were negotiating a busy junction near Union Street when I opened the window and launched an almost full can of Lager! It had a photo of that good looking lassie on it. Remember that other Miss Scotland, it's really funny how I can remember that part! You know the one that married the Scotland Goalkeeper Alan Rough, you'll remember him Eh? He was famous for losing goals from both Holland and World Cup no hopers Peru. No hopers my arse they murdered us and both scored from about forty yards! Michelle, that's her name she comes from Ayr as well, it's quite amazing the amount of really famous people who've come for my home town. Not me of course I'll never make the grade and that small aluminium lager holding tube is probably a collectable by now. Over the years Ayrshire and Ayr has boasted being at one time or another the home of such greats of the musical world as: Singer guitarist John Martyn, Mike Scott of "The Water Boys" Lloyd Cole of "The Commotions" actually that was Troon but its close enough! Then you've got the world famous Jazz guitarist Martin Taylor. Stacia Blake whose rather large breasts really did front top Rock Band Hawkwind, well she moved into the general area and she's living in the Maidens near Girvan now. [Eddie Reader of "Fairground Attraction" fame has an Irvine association and the former mining community Cumnock boasts a female singer Deacon Blue connection]

Ask him again ref!

Some of these I can relate too but who's this famous Michelle girl?

No she's not famous it's the metal can with her photo on it that's of some note! Apparently there's a whole set to collect in glorious colour. The little bugger had slipped out of my hand and it was rolling around among my feet. Dale laughs out loud. Again I still can't figure out how I can remember that bit! Anyway how was I supposed to know there was a great lumbering Policeman directing the traffic! Luckily it missed him but only just! Thank Christ for the rush hour traffic because by the time he got himself back together again we were long gone! Lucky me I'd say!

Let's change the subject shall we who'd you say have been the best opponents in the colourful sense you've been up against. The ones you're happy to talk about that is, apart from Jackie Pallo and your flashy friend Adrian Street!

Total mileage Ayr to Falkirk and back: 122Miles
The time to complete the journey: 2Hours 34Minutes

(Courtesy of Robin Christie)

The Fabulous Harlequins

CHAPTER TWENTYFIVE

(A Motley Crew!)

My most colourful opponents! God that's quite difficult they've been a lot of very gregarious performers over the years, after all that's the name of the game! I'll stick to some of the ones I liked personally if that's OK? There's been Lord "Bertie" Topham, Bobby Barron [Dave Shillitoe] "Cowboy" Jack Cassidy, Billy Two Rivers, he's reputed to have been a genuine Canadian Mohawk Indian from the Quebec area or so I'm told and he's done a lot for all the tribes on a political level. He's also quite a deep thinking man but he does have a smashing and at times very wicked sense of humour. In our sport just as in life there are a lot of imitators and one such guy who shall remain nameless decided he would cash in on the interest in the commonwealth born native Inuit which was rightly being generated because of his top class performances during periodic visits to our shores! He was on the same show as Billy and I one night and continued to get in Mr Two River's face about a good name to use to promote himself in the guise of an American Plains Indian. He made it blatantly obvious he fully intended to change his persona and pursue a similar vane to that being ably demonstrated by the big man, when Billy eventually went back home to Canada! The nuisance failed completely to comprehend that only the red man's ring antics and performance were an act every other part of him was in fact the real thing. So into a very brief silence and right out of the blue the Canadian made this suggested whilst nonchalantly leaning on a dressing room bench lacing up his moccasin type wrestling boots! Looking over his shoulder at the chatterbox he uttered three short words in his broad colonial accent "Eagle Who Walks" The other guys face light up like two hundred Christmas Tree Lights, he was quite clearly impressed, in fact he was over the moon! It was all I could do to stop him going into a mock war dance right there and then such was the level of his ecstasy! Later on I congratulated the likeable Billy on how nice he'd been in very trying and very awkward circumstances. He looked at me and a rye smile washed over his face as he took me into his confidence, putting his arm around my shoulder he leaned in close as he spoke. "Back home Eagles are very sacred birds we worship and we respect them partly because they are so majestic when they soar and the hover on the winds way up in the sky!"

So why give him the benefit of a wonderful name like that I asked?

"Quite simply for one reason and one reason only and its this! You will never ever see an Eagle walking and if you did like that fellow who just left, it's probably because it's so full of shit it won't be able get off the ground!"

That's just priceless I remember thinking to myself at the time and I still laugh to myself every time I've thought about it over the years! In fact I'm laughing into myself right now.

Les Kellett is another good guy most of the time, although away from the ring he's not always the most popular chap on the circuit. I can guess why but I don't really care, I like the man and he seems to like me as well so I'll settle for that. Then you've got others like: Buddy Ward, Butch "Crusher" Mason, Masambula, The Undertaker (real wooden coffin in toe). Klondyke Bill [Gordon Lythe] and his one time Tag Partner Klondyke Jake dear old Barry Hawkins and of course Jumping Jim Moser, also Mr Ezra "The Zulu" Francis he's a smashing lad! In fact he's one of the best, when he's not performing in the ring or watching City at Main Road or out socializing with the lads. Quite often he's been known to mill over in his head what's really going wrong with the world and in his own way he's quite a philosopher. He's got young lads of his own and they keep him busy with what they get up to at times. Having met both my daughter L—she prefers me not to give out her full name to anyone, she's quite reserved unlike her father, Ezra had also been introduced to young Lorraine-Lynn, Mr Scott Thomson's cute and bubbly offspring, so one night over a pint he came away with a cracking statement. It went something like this; "You know lads I have sons and you Dale you have a son as well man but like Scott here you also have a young daughter! That means I have only one maybe two cocks at a time to look out for as my sons grow up and you too with your one young lad will be exactly the same as me brother Storm!" But there is also a growing and potentially difficult problem brewing here namely both you guys have daughters so you'll both be very busy because you'll then have lots of cocks to look out for! So God help you man!" That may seem like a quite simplistic observation to some, but to others like me it's quite a prolific statement for one who preferred to give the impression of being a bit of a simpleton and to some extent a lesser uneducated man than his peers when it suited his purpose to do so. Eddie Rose in all his guises, qualifications and trades will do for me and every time! He too is every inch an honest gentleman and he's always been a good friend to me, as has the blonde "Poacher" from Lincolnshire Big Bill Clarke masked or not! Also Mr Mark "Handsome Boy" Wayne he too has been a good pal over the years and he always looks great in his all white ring gear, unlike some who insist on wearing the same colour north of Hadrian's Wall. Mr Big Bill Turner has been known on occasion to let his alter ego run wild in the form of "King Kong" a totally hilarious big rubber suited Gorilla disguise and apart from Jim McKenzie and the lads in my own gym circle he's perhaps the only other wrestlers based in Scotland I've grown to know reasonably well over the years. I've worked on a few shows off and on with Bill for other promoters and I've sometimes assisted him on his own shows in Summer Season at Port Seton, a small holiday resort to the east of Edinburgh. The big bugger frightened the shit out of me one night when he sneaked up behind my car as I was heading for the main Edinburgh bypass home, he had turned the lights off on his vehicle then all of a sudden he switches on a revolving Blue Lamp! Boy did I get a wake-up call naturally I thought it was the bloody Police! Needles to say it was a real squeaky bum moment! Then there was the time in Aberdeen at the Music Hall when like a fool I gave him a huge assists to get me up, full length head to toe above his head. It looked really spectacular but suddenly he started to lose his balance, he then went into a bit of a speed wobble and coggled to one side. Doubly worrying because he moved very close to the ropes at that pint, so I had to get myself down out of there and quick before I fell headlong the almost twenty feet to the hard wooden floor beneath! As I tumbled ground ward I only just managed to get my legs straighten up as I crumpled into the floor boards like a sack of useless spuds! I think I mentioned earlier that due to the very high stage in the “Music Hall” the drop-off on every other three side [not counting the stage side] was unusual and it’s frighteningly steep! Get the picture? Oh and we mustn't forget my top man Mr Peter Preston he's perhaps better known by those who really know the history of British Wrestling for that bout with Mick McManus live on TV in January 1967! Someday we'll all get to the bottom of what really happened although I will now, on pain of death give you and only you a wee taster but it’s definitely not for any form of publication because as yet it’s only my interpretation of what might have been and it’s not as yet a verifiable fact. It’s based entirely on the odd hint I’ve picked up over the years and pieced together from very little the great man and some others very close to him have perhaps hinted at over the period. Firstly there was no upfront money, no “Golden Back Stab” pot of Gold, no collective master plan to get one over on the main man McManus as such, well certainly not on Peter’s part and again there was most definitely not a plan to hurt him physically in any way! You have to appreciate at that time he was decidedly not very well liked by a great number of his peers, especially those north of the Watford Gap in particular! He was however undoubtedly one of the most popular performers as far as the vast majority of the TV audience on a Saturday was concerned! Although in truth they loved to hate him and most wanted to see him soundly beaten and defeated! Whether the manner and the circumstances, in which this whole incident was played out, live on prime time television was the correct way to settle alleged old scores manifesting themselves at the top among some directors was the best course of action is up for debate. Bearing in mind the victim had for a few years been perceived by the British public as the epitome of the Unbeatable TV Arch Villain. Because of his unique and privileged position within the organisation that employed him, many of the other wrestlers had for sometime resented his perceived power. Given the fact he worked in the Brixton offices of the top London promoter Dale/Martin some argued he was ideally placed to keep himself in the position of the most high profile wrestler on British television screens. It was regularly alleged he used that power to hold back the careers of others! He was however both loved and hated in equal measure by most grappling fans and although Max was unlike Mick in total charge of the whole shooting match latterly within the total Grunt and Groan fraternity as it reached its end, the Crabtree's and not McManus have to a large extent to take the lion's share of the blame for what in years later brought about wrestling's sad demise. Mick himself has to take some blame for the way he personally manipulated certain "Billing Orders" and for the personnel who both appeared and more importantly didn't appear, but if this situation actually did happened it took place long, long before Max took over. These allegations seem to have been the main reason for the peer mistrust and the growing resentment of the south Londoner. Again I repeat all this is only an allegation made by some and based on that allegation these are my honest considered conclusions. I never worked for Dales directly or indeed for anyone else based south of Birmingham, so I have no first hand knowledge of any potential improprieties but many unimpeachable colleagues assure me it is in fact true and I have no reason to doubt those who informed me in good faith. His hands on position would undoubtedly have helped to place him at an advantage eclipsing even the standing of the now very popular other London based bad boy, top dog villain Mr Jackie Pallo. As it turned out regards the lead-up events to that day in 1967 it was a one in a million chance that just came right out of the blue due to a call off from the Lime Grove Baths Show. Mike Eagers was originally booked as Niggly's opponent for that day but due to some genuine injury problem he was unable to meet the original commitment. This meant Norman Morrell the promoter needed to appoint a stand-in, it was he who gave Peter the gig, all Brother Preston would add and I might say very reluctantly was he was then told this was his big chance to make a name for himself, to put him on the grappling map so to speak and to get himself further up the ladder of wrestling success! With Peter one fall up it was becoming worryingly obvious to everyone and that included the Londoner that he might now have to take the next two falls by force if he was to get the much needed and totally expected win and avoid losing his mantle of supposed invincibility. The only outcome that suited him and his status would have to be achieved without any of the usual assistance being afforded him from his doggedly tough, amateur trained northern opponent! If it came down to the Shooter Stakes Mick was no match for Peter Preston. Never coming close to having the ability to just take what he wanted he was stuffed and in a bind so to speak and this whole scenario was being played out live on Saturday afternoon prime time television. Panic quickly set in and his only form of escape from total humiliation was to try and get himself disqualified and that's exactly what he did! Even the referee Don Branch had no idea what was going on as he naturally assumed that just like always Mick was "Going Over" Two to One! McManus seldom if ever suffered a defeat and definitely not on television, he always made sure he never looked vulnerable especially on a "World of Sport" broadcast. Boy did that iconic episode cause rubbings and big, big problems. Don Branch said as much to Peter during the course of the mêlée. So there you have it that's as much as I have pieced together so far, it's only my opinion but that's what I think happened. Although as you're now sworn to secrecy actually you don't really know anything, now do you? Peter has always been one of the good guys and a real credit to his mentors among whom, as I mentioned previously was Ernie Baldwin. He's always had a very high regard for those who've given the business proper respect. One story he tells included a TV Show when he was on with Tom Dowie in Bathgate. Tea and Digestive Biscuits had been served in the dressing rooms prior to things getting underway. The incident when he removed the meat from the Pork Pies and placed the pastry back together again is another! I've no wish to steal Peter's thunder as hopefully he too will publish his own long awaited memoir soon, so I'll only say this; the pep-talk hand shake in the ring left Big Tom holding a little surprise!

I'm going to add **"Mr Eric Taylor"** to my favoured list simply because he's a really nice man and great to work with. [Eric passed on in 2000] Incidentally he was another of the men who helped train Peter and it's no great secret he too is nobodies fool on or off the mat! I've worked with him a lot and he's always been very generous to me. He too had problems with Joints when as British Middleweight Champion he had that wonderfully made [It was one of a classic looking matching set one for each of the Championship weights] belt round his waist for a long time. Something or somebody within that organisation upset him I've no idea whom or what so he decided to tell them to stuff it and of course they wanted their belt back. The story goes Eric told them if they were big enough and tough enough to come to his house to take it from him they were welcome to it! So far I'm told he's still the proud possessor.

Ask him again ref!

So that special set of belts you referred to made to represent the full weight rage of all the Joint Champions still has one missing has it!

It most certainly does.

Anyone else you want to mention whilst we're here?

Yes indeed I'm very proud to give a mention to Scotia's own Wee Jimmy McKenzie from Glasgow and for all the same reasons as with Eric Taylor. He is not only a fantastic worker and a former lightweight Champion he's an equally nice human being. Jim tells me he's been thinking along the same lines as me when he retires only he's setting his sights at a slightly higher level, he wants to buy a small hotel maybe in Aberdour in Fife? Oh and by the way you've yet to ask me about gimmicks and the likes this business is quite clearly full of them!

Oh go on then fill me in!

Total mileage Ayr to Kirkcaldy and back: 194 Miles
Total time to complete the journey: 3Hours 50Min

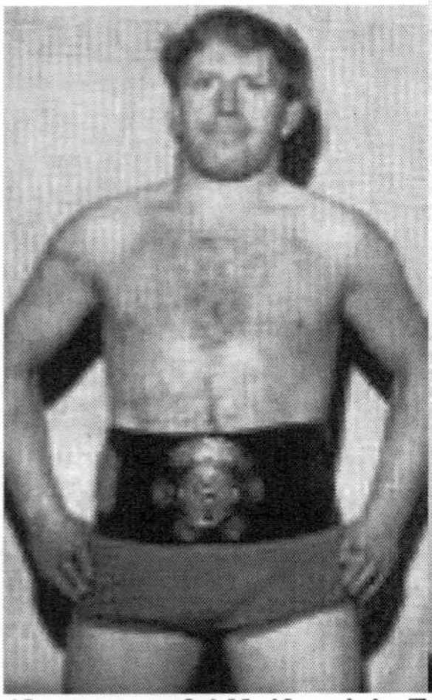
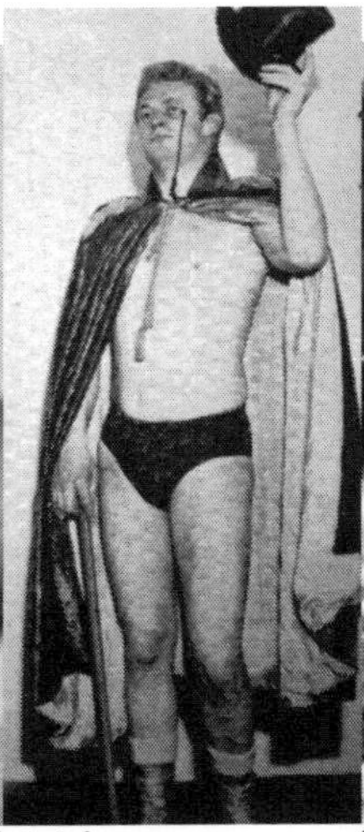

(Courtesy of J McKenzie's Estate) ***(Courtesy of Mr Len Ironside)***

Jim McKenzie Lord Topham Len Ironside

CHAPTER TWENTYSIX

(All Show and some Blow)

There have been lots of gimmicks used over the years but all of them are purely for the good of the Show! Something different always keeps everything fresh and interesting but they're really only to get the punters attention then hopefully word of mouth gets your message across to others who may turn up at the next show at the next venue in the next town to see a different persona? Any Television exposure helps tremendously but it's not always available and at the end of the day it's all about numbers of bums on seats that's what pays all our wages! One guy in particular **"Mr Pete Lindberg"** has one of the best gimmicks of all time and no one else has the physical ability to replicate it!

So what is it and how is it so different?

He blows up Hot Water Bottles!

No, you're winding me up.

No I'm not and he just keeps filling them up with air until they burst. They literally blow up in his face!

Good God. That must play havoc with his ears?

Well I don't know about his ears, but I worked with him a few times especially in the early years and it certainly made my ears ring and a few old grannies have I'm sure had to pull on a spare pair of pants stashed away in their handbag at the interval on more than one occasion after being subjected to the sound of an exploding rubber bed warmer! On a completely different tact the business has got some really strong muscle bound guys like **"Mr Andy Robin"** for instance! He's been known to bring a feckin great big Wagon Wheel into the ring!

Ask him again ref!

What in a Tupperware dish like the school children do for their play piece?

Now you're being just plain stupid, I'm trying to give you some story options hear and you're taking the piss.

OK, I'm listening now!

It's a big lorry wheel, happy now?

Those in the Midlands and further south towards London don't use the term Lorry. They call it a Truck or even a Wagon, are we sorted now?

Yes I've got all that carry on.

Andy lifts it above his head and pumps it up in the air. Please believe me when I tell you it's not exactly easy in fact it's very difficult and very heavy and I should know I was in the motor trade. When it comes to repairing a puncture on one of those or fitting a new tyre on a big metal rim like that, it's a specialised job and it can be very dangerous if it's not done properly! Quite simply if one of those metal retaining rings springs out it could and it probably would take your head off! The man from Perthshire has got huge biceps and triceps and a hugely powerful set of thighs as well! Like that Superman guy in the Marvel comics very few are stronger! Rather stupidly a young friend of mine accepted an invitation from him to take the big bugger, a reference to the wheel of course out of the ring and back to the dressing room after he'd done his party piece! Big mistake! He's also a big lad but he really struggled to get it up off the deck after the TV star had thrown it down following his stunt! The bouncy ring boards caused it to be launched out onto the concrete floor, luckily no one was hurt! He got it back to the dressing room door eventually but he was well burned out by then. He had to wheel it upright like a small child would do with a

Hula Hoop! Occasionally the seconds will be instructed to carry a table and two chairs into the ring. This is **Clive "Iron Fist" Myers** new party piece. I've never seen him lose an arm wrestling contest. Many of his opponents, all villains sometimes refuse to sit down opposite him or on the odd occasion they just up-end the table in anger. Some have even tried to hit him with a chair! Again Big mistake!

"Mr Jackie TV Pallo" has his sequenced gown, a ribbon in his hair, his golden boots and of course his I'll just cut the audience to the bone silver tongue! Need I say more?

"Catweazel" aka (Garry Cooper) has his stupid bowl cut blondish hair, a long goatee beard and an old fashioned Edwardian style striped swimsuit costume and of course his small green rubber frog for a friend which sits on the corner post. The kids love him to bits and most of the time he's really quite funny, I fought him a couple of times for Joints. I liked him a lot as a person but my style and his were not really compatible so they were not the most enjoyable shows I ever had. Both were in Scotland so not a lot for my fans to crow about, one in the Hamilton Town Hall, the better and more memorable bout was staged at one of my favourite venues the Civic Centre in Perth. [Gary came originally from the Doncaster area he died in 1993]

"Mr Jack "Bronco" Cassidy has his Ten Gallon Texan Hat and his Shinny Chrome Six Guns and boy do they go off with a bang when he pulls the triggers! You wouldn't want to be on the same bill with him and Pete with his water bottles every night. You'd tend to look a bit stupid wearing a full set of Ear Protectors reminding everybody of the "Star Wars" movie Princess Leia look. You'd probably have had to pay for them yourself because just like the ongoing debate regards personal insurance cover promoters don't much care about these so called side issues. [Jack Cassidy died in 2006, he was a good person and he was respected by almost everyone. RIP buddy]

"Mr Ricky Starr" is an American gentleman who prefers to wear ballet shoes and tights, usually coloured pink. He loves to ponce about on the ropes for a long time, doing his stretches and stuff before he gets started. That always gets his over anxious opponents at it! After a couple of Plies' he'll suddenly jump forward then he goes into his face slapping routine, later and fully warmed up he's then ready to dropkick them all over the place. [When British wrestling lost its profile and started to go down hill, Ricky who I think I'm correct in saying still lives in the UK decided he'd had enough and ever since he's continually refused to speak of it to anyone not in his close group of friends and relations]

"Mr Kendo Nagasaki" [Big Peter] has his ritual of salt throwing over the guy in the opposite corner before he gets stuck in. The waving of his now unsheathed Samurai Sword in front of himself then up over his head and eventually up above yours is also a top notch Flash! To me it's just about one the best opening flurries ever.

"The Viking" [Big Tam] the Scottish version that is, on the other hand does a similar thing whilst being introduced only he wields a Large Two Sided Axe! The fur leggings and the Cow Horns on the side of his Metal Helmet also add to the mystique of this Northern European marauding character.

Then there's lovely **"Les Kellett"** who's pretending to be injured and in pain and then a little unsteady on his feet continues to fool many an opponent into a totally false sense of security by almost falling through the ring ropes before bouncing back in again and of course he's very funny with it!

"The Black Diamonds Tag Team" originally consisted of Abe Ginsburg and John Foley. [After John moved to the USA in the early1970's] Thereafter Eric Cutler, and sometimes occasionally my old buddy Mr Versatility Eddie Rose stepped in. They like to wear black leather headgear, black tights and black leotards and they're regarded by most as one of the best villain Tag Team in the business, no matter what line-up they use. The crowd always bays for blood, theirs of course and from the minute they enter the auditorium. Abe in particular sets great personal store in always giving as good as he gets whether he's in or indeed out of the ring at the time. [Abe Ginsberg died of a heart attack in November 2001]

"Mr Leon Arras" aka [Brian Glover] is forever talking and sometimes even before the bout gets underway, thereafter you'll never be able keep him quiet! He's also a really good actor and a former Grammar School teacher tutoring in both English and French at Longcar Central School Barnsley. Before appearing on screen where he was a standout in the film about the young boy with the pet Hawk called "Kes" after initially being recommended for the part by the writer Barry Hines he stole the show. "Ken Loach" the Director is noted for getting masterful performances out of new or even inexperienced performers in front of the camera. No doubt he'll be looking to be doing a lot more of that Thespian type stuff now. Then he'll be rolling it, money wise that is compared to the pittance he and the rest of us end up with after doing our very best to look as if we're really bashing each other to bits. Clearly we're all in the really badly paid branch of the arts! [Brian Glover aka Leon Areas left us for hopefully a better place in 1997]

And then there's **Mr Adrian Street** there's not a lot more I can say about him that hasn't already been articulated or written about the man already. He is in my humble opinion quite simply the ultimate, he's got the lot, looks, style, star quality, muscles and all that fabulous gear as well. He's just the tops and a really nice person into the bargain.

"Mr Billy Two Rivers" is for me one of the biggest and nicest imported showstoppers ever to visit the UK having first come over to Britain in1960. When he enters the arena wearing that colourful full feathered headdress the crowd usually stand up and clap warmly giving him all the reverence a worker of his undoubted quality fully deserves. When he takes it off his Mohawk Chief Hairstyle looks even more fantastic! He hails from Quebec in Canada and his speciality Tomahawk Chop can and will lay you out flat, if you sell it well in a manner of speaking. With all that colourful build-up he still gets down to the business in hand without much of a delay when he hears the first bell.

Londoner **Bobby "Bad Boy" Barnes** is intentionally the exact opposite in as much as when he gets into the ring he just slows everything right down and that deliberate act gets the exact effect he's looking for, pure unadulterated hate from the baying, paying punters. It takes him an age to take his cloak off, eventually removing it in its entirety only when he's good and ready! Then after taking another age to steady himself he takes even more time to fold it up! Then there's even more time used preening and posing, especially his curly hair and by that time the crowd wants to lynch him! All that anger being show to him is now one hundred times worse than before and still there's not struck a blow! When the bell eventually does sounds he dives in immediately fouling his unsuspecting foe who is now lying in a heap on the canvas in some discomfort from a painful low blow and all this time many more wasted minutes have elapsed! A Job really well done says the happy promoter.

"Oddjob" Real name [Toshiyuki "Harold" Sakata] who sometimes uses the alias "Great Togo" caused a sensation when he first appeared in the James Bond movie "Goldfinger" Oh and by the way that steel rimmed bowler hat really does have a deadly edge! He was born in Hawaii but he has family connections which originated further afield in the Pacific in Japan. He won a Silver medal in weightlifting for the USA in London's Olympics in 1948 and became a full-time pro wrestler a few years later. He's a big draw wherever he appears! He also takes an inordinate time to get down to his trunks; nothing is ever rushed even when he's going for a big finish! Must be the Japanese side of the family tree coming out in him? They have this quiet time relaxation calm culture thing going on constantly.

Another Polynesian performer who's having a huge influence on the changing, modernising style that's slowly been developing in the UK movement, thankfully in a really good way is the "American Samoan Islands" Heavyweight performer **"Mr Peter Fanene Maivia"** [Peter's son also entered the business back in the USA some years later and his grandson became not only one of the most successful WWE Stars, he's gone on to pursue a very lucrative movie career and he' still to the fore. His very successful wrestling persona was as "The Rock"] Peter was simply sensational and so cool and so laid back, his use of the middle ropes as a type of between rounds hammock where he took up a prone totally relaxed position across the ring corner. Just like he was lying supported between two Palm Trees on a beach under a sunny blue sky waiting for a ripe coconut to fall into his lap. Its quite novel to witness and it's just so different and so refreshing. He has however on at least one occasion shown how he can really lose his temper! It's been alleged he left his teeth marks on Bill Robinson's rear shoulder during a dressing room disagreement. The flower garland hanging around his neck, the Polynesian design multi-coloured trunks and the brightly coloured ceremonial wraparound as well as the bare feet set him well apart from all the rest. The long dark oily hair helps as well! He's just so colourful and very clever with it! [Sadly Peter passed away in 1982 but his legacy lives on in his famous wrestling family]

The top masked man over the last twenty five plus years has to be without question: "Doctor Death" He's the Australian born ring man **"Mr Paul Lincoln"** and he's every bit as tough a performer in the ring as he is a hard nosed businessman outside it! Both he and his business partner Ray Hunter who's also an Aussie and absolutely huge and full of muscles! They've built up a really good and a varied portfolio. Paul's ring record commands some respect and he gets it! As an entertainer he's definitely one of the best and he influx of the better oversees stars has largely been due to him, especially those he brought over from the USA and beyond. He's doesn't run his own shows anymore having sold off his ring interests around 1966, but he still continues to build on his other business interests.

When it came to the introduction of the Kilt and the Full Highland regalia into the wrestling ring, thus broadening public awareness of the Scots as a Nation, that honour has to go to the man from the town of Stornoway in The Outer Hebrides Scot's Strongman Heavyweight **"Mr. Bill McDonald."** After the war he settled in Manchester and he was definitely one of rings top men during the 1950's and into the mid 1960's. His CV is full of first class opponents and his win to loss stats are a stand out, they rank highly set against most of his contemporaries. If you're an "Only Fools and Horses" fan you may be interested to know his son Mike played the barman. [Sadly Bill died in 1964]

The tall thinly built very colourful African born performer **"Masambula"** with his Leopard Skin Headdress costume strikes a pose when the ring lights reflect off his shinny dark skin. He's a really nice guy and his style is different enough to allow him to stand out, even among those of a similar culture, heritage and birth! I love the animal skin trunks as well! Looking good Masa! You don't want to be on the receiving end of his specialist Head Butts! Ouch!

....................................Very, very painful! He! He!

And who's really the most colourful then? You must have an opinion as to who the top man really is!

Total mileage Ayr to Elgin and back: 450 Miles
Total travelling time for the journey: 9Hours 36Minutes

CHAPTER TWENTYSEVEN

(My Old Mate the Real Showman)

My Top Man would have to be Adrian, without a doubt it's definitely my old mate **"Mr Adrian Street" h**e's a real showman and a real master of his trade,. He was born in South Wales but he still buys his round in the pub. Actually it's a bit of a myth about the Welsh not putting their hand in their pocket and we Scots aren't really tight either that's just another lie. Not that he's much of a drinker, he's not his body is a temple well most of the time. He settled in London when still quite young having moved there from Brynmawr in the Principality, probably, like me he wasn't too keen on going down the pit. Whilst there he trained in places like the YMCA in the middle of the Capital's West End on the Amateur Mats, later moving on after a tip-off to the famous "Foresters" Wrestling, Boxing and Bodybuilding Club in North Kensington. He also worked dammed hard in a Travelling Boxing Booth for a time and finally got his pro break working for the cities Independents. His first bout proved to be a bit of a physical disaster but not for him. [The full story of his first paid wrestling show against Geoff "Gentleman" Moran can be found in the really well written book entitled "I Only Laugh When It Hurts" The second of Adrian's autobiographies] Eventually word got round and he was then invited to join the ranks of London's Joint Promotions representative, he then worked almost exclusively for a time out of the Dale Martin's stable. "Kid Tarzan Jonathan" was on his way! Eventually he went back to his given name but that was a long time ago now. He spends a lot of time working on his immaculate appearance. His "Barnett" is always in good order! [A rhyming reference to Lady Isabelle Barnett the Scots born Doctor of Medicine's immaculate hair doo's of the period. She being of the "What's My Line" TV Programme panel!" A very popular Sunday Night BBC1 posh quiz show of the time hosted by the then very popular Irish presenter

Eamonn Andrews in the 1950/1960's] Adrian tagged originally with another southerner I've already mentioned him earlier Bobby "Bad Boy" Barnes! They were really good together but now he's moved over to the present day Independents again he's been teemed up a lot, especially in the south with a very good young Scot name of Steve "Gaylord" Peacock. Outside the ring Adrian is a gentleman and we get on very well socially he's a really good pal. He paid me the great compliment of coming up to my gym to give my young lads some tips, he stopped off when he was travelling back from the Highlands one time. My dear old Auntie Ina treated him and Linda to some tea and some home made scones. My uncle Joe was the janitor at the local junior school they lived in the school cottage next door to my Gym, my mother's sister still raves about meeting them both even now. At the moment he's in front on the head to head count of ring encounters. He's as strong as an ox and he's getting stronger all the time, he's clever and he's really tricky to beat! Have you seen those costumes he wears and the blonde hair and then there's all that make-up and what about the big eye shadow, not to mention the bright red lipstick! Usually he likes to kiss you when you first come into the "Take Hold" position leaving it smudged all over your face! He's so flash you've got to laugh, he's just great! He continually works on his presentation and he's always on the go sorting out new costumes. Always thinking up new angles he is, he's a real entertainer. The girls just can't get enough of him what a personality. He'll do really well in Canada or maybe even America he's over there now building a good following luckily they're not all heavyweights over there but then again he'd be far too clever for most on that side of the Atlantic at any weight. A wee bit like me really! No! No! I'm just winding you up. I'm only kidding! He's much, much better than I'll ever be!

So is he's better at everything or just at certain things?

Ask him again ref!

Naughty, naughty Girl!

Will he be coming back to the UK?

I doubt it, would you? Especially with all this industrial turmoil! The first time I fought him when he arrived back on the indie side was in Glasgow. I think it was The Albany Hotel at a Variety Club Charity Show in the City Centre, his original opponent had gotten injured a couple of days before hand and as I was one of the established guys working in this area they called me. Naturally I was happy to step in. it was always a great pleasure raising cash for good causes! My instructions were to meet up with Adrian and the others in Hamilton Lanarkshire.

Why Hamilton?

I've no idea our paths had only crossed briefly before that! Maybe he'd suggested me as the stand-in and the time and place were his idea? Anyway I was grateful for the booking and the chance to try out my skills against him once again. I'd faced him on three occasions previously and I'd lost the first and the last. The second meeting of that trio was a close fought encounter as well. Meet them in the car park at the side of the Town Hall at 4pm was about the sum total the message. I had another two really spectacular contests in my home town against him later on after that, both were title bouts. At the end of the first one I'd “gone over” taking it two to nothing and it raised the roof. Of course that's when the Gee was introduced and this ensured an even larger crowd the next time around. I've always been thankful to all the local punters who turned out for the re-match, you just couldn't get a ticket it was standing room only and guess what? I lost! It turned out to be a bit of a waste of time and good old Davie Simpson had even surprised me with the gift of a Piper to play me into and out of the ring. For that reason alone I should have done better. Then some months later we both got another call to appear at another Big Charity Doo once again in Glasgow and again the hook-up was the car park in Hamilton. It was clearly convenient for Adrian as all he had to do was swing off the M74. Only this time I was parking my car there and travelling into the city centre with him. Just as well because the starter motor on my car had packed up the night before and it was lying in bits on my workbench in my garage, the brushes had burned out. I just "Bumped Started" my car on the slope on the street at the side of my house, who needs a starter motor when you know what you're doing. When I got to the meeting point I parked the car on a long gradient, it's a big long car park. Hoping of course no idiot would parked their car in front of me as that would have presented potential problem later on that night. Adrian and the others couldn't believe I'd driven all that way there without any means of getting me started again if I'd stalled the engine at any time. It's really easy but if you don't know what you're doing don't try it at home folks. I've even driven cars and some heavier vehicles for miles and miles with no clutch, but that's an art you've really got to learn. Things went like clockwork when they dropped me off later that night, the ignition cycle did not let me down! Our chauffeur was Adrian's gorgeous misses Linda, she's a smashing lassie and she'd even offered to give me a push to get me started and underway, she was a little lost for words in fact all three were when I assured them everything would be kosher. I would not require their help! I of course had every faith in my mechanical abilities and driving skills anyway they had a lot further to go than me so I ushered them on their way, well it's a long way to London from Lanarkshire and it had been a long enough day also as the time was now well after 10pm. So having left me they headed off towards the A74(M). You should have seen the look on there faces when only a few minutes later I manoeuvred myself up along side them, I think I woke Linda up she was in the back seat by this time trying to get some well earned kip. Adrian was driving. The other passenger was the really good looking Aussie girl grappler called Susan Sexton, a sexy full busted very attractive Sheila! As I came up along side I'd given them a loud blast from my American Style Air Horns. De, De, De, De, De, De, De, De, De, De, De, De! Just like the Dukes of Hazard, god they were loud! Then having given them a wave of thanks I dropped a gear and left them for dead! I had a 1966 GT Cortina at the time and Warp Speed had been engaged! Although the original motor was powerful enough I'd fitted an accident right-off Lotus Twin Cam unit in under the bonnet! Which I'd completely striped and rebuilt beforehand. New Pistons, even Bigger Valves it had been gas flowed and the con-rods had been shaved and balanced, brand new Lumpy Twin High Lift Cams fitted, up rated SU Carburettors, two Oil Coolers, bigger Racing Style Clutch, a Limited Slip Differential and Racing Spec Air Flowed Disc Brakes and Pads! A Classic Rear Spoiler and a Chrome, Specially Designed Air Intake on the strapped down Mat Black Bonnet! I'd had a lot of horsepower previously but now it had even more! Boy was it powerful, it was quick beyond belief in fact it was a Beast! The livery was a very neutral dark coloured paint job almost black. Insignificant would be the best way to describe its look and it ticked over like a bag of chisels but it didn't half sort out the Young Turks when they tried to gun me at the lights when you got into the Power Band the G-Force effect was awesome! You just disappeared into the leather covered bucket seats Santa Pod Raceway style and we were off like a rocket!

Why were you on the A74 (M)?

I was wondering if you were going to ask me about that, obviously you've not travelled much outside the Edinburgh/Glasgow area and probably never on an A-Road down around our way! I'd taken that route partly to let them know I was up and running and of course to noise them up at the same time. I could then cut off further down and make my way through Strathaven and on out of

Lanarkshire. Then down through Darvel and just skirt passed Kilmarnock on the A71 then down the A77 home. Or I could cut off over the Graigie Hill down the back road heading for Monkton and Prestwick Airport then I'd cut off before hand into Tarbolton, at the bus terminus turn right at the hill passed the Old Piggery and down the hill on the other side, turn left up and over the Bow Road and into Mossblown at Whiskyhall Housing Estate. I'd almost come a cropper on that A71 a couple of winters previously on really bad Black Ice lying on the double bends on the approach to Strathaven town from the west! Not far from the road-end to Sir Harry Lauder's old house through the trees on the left. Lady luck shone down on all of us all that particular night! Big Ian Miller and the Brothers Morgan (The Fabulous Harlequins) and once again, Wee Jeff Bradley were all in the car at the time, we were headed to yet another show in the Town Hall in of all places Hamilton. Oh and I completely forgot to give a plug for the Peco Big Bore Twin Chrome Exhaust Pipe which I'd fitted on the car also! It used to sing to you especially on a quiet warm breeze, summer mornings just as dawn broke and the birds came out to play. You could hear the sweet hum of those melodic pipes miles away as I negotiated the tight twisting bends taking full advantage of the newly overhauled ZF Gearbox as I made my way rather speedily into leafy commuter belt Ayrshire.

Sounds quite poetic: "And the birds come out to play"

Do you really think so? Well I'd like to lay claim to being the genesis of that Wordsworth like sentence but I'd be lying. Those rather apt pieces of Prose were coined by my wee mate Mr. Jeff Bradley. I used to drop him off usually last thing at his home in the mining hamlet of the already mentioned Mossblown, usually after we'd been involved once again, in a long drive from the back of beyond. As always my car would have been jam backed full with sweaty, tired, sleep filled grapplers most of whom had joined the land of nod moments after getting in and settled comfortably! My Guardian Angel “Sam Taylor” [Real name] never slept he just sat there in the back in the corner rolling the odd hand made fag, then he'd open the widow and light up, he was always very considerate in that regard. It was almost as if he denied himself some rest to make sure I, as tired as I was, stayed focused and alert! He had no need to worry on that score as we were all very well aware; especially after what had gone before when some of our forgetful fraternity in the south had fallen foul of the dreaded veil of Morpheus on occasions whilst tiered, head nodding blissfully at the steering wheel and gone off the road. He used to like to listen to the sound of my distinctive exhaust as he walked the last quarter mile down his street, having stopped for a final roll-up from his self customised Golden Virginia tin before going to bed! That way he once told me later on he could sleep assured and relaxed comfortable in the knowledge that having kept and eye on the timing by counting away the short minutes “One Elephants, Two Elephants” “Three Elephants” etc, until he could no longer hear the trumpeting purr. If it was within a few seconds of Three and a Half to Four Minutes then all was well with the world, because by then as he could no longer hear the purr, he knew I too was home and safe some approximately five miles down the road. Like the song of the birds believe it or not it was possible to distinguish the sound of that particular exhaust on the quiet air of an early morn. He was a good pal I really miss him as he passed away recently after a short and quite sudden illness! Heart attack! He went quickly! Please don't think I'm soft or anything it's just that Sammy wouldn’t want me or indeed any of his pals to remember him in any sad reflective kind of a way. He was always the life and soul of the group and he always had a smile on his face and a word of friendly encouragement for everyone. I still can't understand why he didn't like football though but what the hell! Moving to the mirror to hide his embarrassment Dale wipes away a tear. Eddie Rose one of the Manchester guys I mentioned earlier, he really liked that car! He used to rave about all the time. He even said he'd never seen anything like it but sadly he liked it even more when I wasn't driving it and if I was driving it then he much preferred not to be sitting in it with me. Did you know he once took the bloody train home from a show? Yes, he really did the daft bugger! I'd taken a bunch of lads to Oban for a season summer outing and we'd used the Loch Lomond route. I was driving and it's a crappy road at the best of times, if you've ever driven it I'm sure you'll agree!

Yes it is. It's easily Scotland's worse road! It's been falling into the loch for years and now it needs a lot of work done!

Thank you very much proves my point I think. Anyway, it was the Glasgow Holiday Fortnight and the road was full of slow moving caravans going both ways, it resembled a bloody "Western Movie Wagon Train!" Nose to bloody tail I might add and we needed to get there quick, get the picture? And as usual I got us up there in great time and we've avoided all the traffic hold-ups. Actually we've passed eight or ten cars and vans at a stretch and I might add we missed every bloody one of them! Then after the show, he Eddie who's a really good pal tells me he's booked himself a seat back down on the Flier to Glasgow and can he have the price of the train fair back please. I might add I was shattered, how dare he question my skill with a black leather covered special racing steering wheel!

What did you do blow your top? Did you sack him?

No indeed I did not I'm a reasonable man, well most of the time! I gave him the train fare in his hand in cash and I wished him a safe journey, to which he replied. Likewise!

So weren't you annoyed at him even just a little bit?

No! Not at all! Besides he was perfectly correct if I'd had

Ask him again ref!

the choice I wouldn't be getting in the car with me either!

Why ever not?

The answer to that is quite simple. I'm a Fucking Nut Case!

Clearly you like this Eddie Rose a lot. That's at least twice you've mentioned him now.

Yes, you could say that.

And is there anyone else you hold in such high esteem?

Yes, Joe Critchley stands out in the crowd for me as well, there's nothing I wouldn't do for him, or he for me!

Have you had any other strange experiences? Things you wouldn't normally want to talk about.

No more than most I suppose, but let me tell you about this stranger than fiction situation that happened to another good friend of mine when he was a much youngster.

Total mileage Ayr to Dingwall and back: 296 Miles
Total time taken for the full journey: 8 Hours 52 miles

(Courtesy of Mr A Street)

Miss Linda "Blackfoot Sioux"

Mr Show Business Himself

(Courtesy of Mr A Street)

(3 photos courtesy of Mr A Street) (1 with Bobby Barnes Hell's Angels Tag Team)

The many faces of a real "Super Star" Mr Adrian Street

CHAPTER TWENTYEIGHT

(Every Inch the Wrestler's Wrestler!)

Life can be hard and somewhat bizarre from time to time and it can throw up the unexpected and the cruel. These things are hard to deal with when you're an adult and you have both some experience of life and also the support of a close family unit around you, but when you're a teenager and only just starting out into as they say, "Life's rich tapestry" at the tender age of seventeen, without a strong close family unit things can be devastating in the extreme. One such situation happened to a man whom both I and many, many others have over the years come to admire greatly. He was born and brought up in Yorkshire the youngest in the family and as a youth, sadly he lost his mother. That in itself was bad enough but only a few short weeks later to be told by his father he was moving on and when his son asked "where are were moving to dad?" The short and rather terse reply was that he [the father] was moving elsewhere but his son was now on his tod and would have to learn to survive on his own and that was that! Totally devastated but left with no other option the young lad now found he was in at the deep end with nowhere to rest his head and very little in his pocket. Not surprisingly the priorities were firstly to get a roof over his head and the other was acquiring some form of gainful employment. An old dilapidated and almost totally derelict building was all that was available to him, so for the time being at least he would have to make do. Rather clichéd greatly overused and always overstated by some so called famous folks; "*who were never at anytime dirt poor*" in their well over priced, ghost written memoires containing obligatory phrases like; *"Life just couldn't get any worse for me."* Or *"I just couldn't get any lower."* Or *"All I had at that* time in my life for a table and some chairs were some old wooden *orange boxes!"* Well in this particular unfortunate's case things like this were in actual fact very much the truth.

Although unlike their wimp like moan you'd have been hard pressed to hear anything as negative and defeatist coming from his lips. The rough sleeping arrangements on a welcome pile of cardboard boxes on bare Grey Yorkshire Stone Flags weren't ideal and the one and only gas mantle in the centre of the living room was precious, although how safe it was is anybody's guess! Electricity and running hot water from the one Belfast sink were also a non starter. Luckily there was still a serviceable fireplace but no money to feed it with heat providing coal! So what little warmth it intermittently provided was accrued, care of other materials the origins of which even to this day must forever remain a closely guarded secret. Honest work acquired helping out a local builder was both physical and exhausting and really not the type of job a young lad somewhat smaller in height and stature for his age and most definitely not fully developed muscularly should have been forced to undertake. His academic education had also been suffering long before he left school in the later part of the 1930's and given the non existence of any Welfare State, which wouldn't see the light of day for around another ten years meant no Social Workers, no Social Security as we know it today and little or almost no Charitable Institutions to seek some help from. Even if this proud and stubbornly independent young man had wanted to seek such assistance, apart from the indignity of appealing to the parish for a leg up where else was he going to get any help from anyway? Some much needed support in the form of a local gym owner was already in the pipeline although as far as the now badly in need of a full body wash, dust covered, dirty faced lad was concerned any form of "Fairy God Mother" was something you only read about in children's books or was played out by one of your peers in the school teacher directed Christmas Play. He himself even to this day is still not fully aware who raised some concerns within the community about the plight of this now effectively orphaned boy but nevertheless he has always been very grateful. A benefactor had decided to see if help could be offered, but what kind of assistance and by whom? How to handle this somewhat tricky situation had also to be worked out because it was well recorded that the likeable youngster already displayed a proud and an independent streak. So that's where an idea was formulated to see if he could be engaged by way of making it look as if he, [the lad] would in fact be helping out a local gym owner by accepting his offer to let the youngster use his facilities. "Is there a warm shower?" was at that stage the only thing on the dirty cherubs mind and when he was informed there was and it was hot and steamy, no further encouragement was required. A long and lasting friendship had now been set in stone and the coach not only taught him the rudiments of how to use the weightlifting equipment, likewise it transpired he also took him under his wing showing the local squatter the basic rudiments of the rough and tough sport of amateur wrestling. Thus from that night onward the die had been cast which after a good and hard earned grounding on the mat, the knowledge gained set him off on a long road where only a few short years later this eager pupil eventually broke into the pro-ranks. So with a regular warm wash and some kindly character building, as well as some solid body muscle development secured for three nights in the week, all that was then required was to fill in the gaps with somewhere else where he could enjoy the benefits of more clean running water on the other two nights. Given that Yorkshire is famous for a myriad of sports this task was not the most difficult to achieve now that the fitness bug had bitten him. Another invite to join a local Rugby League Club was eagerly accepted and with a small weekly membership fee dutifully paid regularly on the nail. A hot scrub had now been secured for five nights out of the full week. Things were on the up and life was getting so much better! Much more secure and happier now surrounded by solid friends the fortunate young man moved on from these simple beginnings to become as the years rolled by a very popular, comfortably placed, successful building business owner in his own right. Having made an audacious bid for a local two story building he quickly set about converting it into both a working Builder's Yard and also far more importantly a much more comfortable place to live. This time supported by things we seem to take for granted nowadays, like electricity and gas. He had now become a well respected honest, hard gradting businessman with a reputation for good quality workmanship. He was also becoming noticed and talked about in the pro grappling world and his star was about to rise even higher. A life changing event was on the cards this episode would prove to be a 1967 watershed moment and it would have ramifications that would rock the wrestling world to its very foundation. That once dirty faced young man I'm very proud to say is a good personal friend of mine and of many others as well. He is the very well respected, honest and very loveable Mr Peter Preston.

Total mileage Ayr to Bradford and back: 322 Miles
Total time taken for the full journey: 8 Hours approx

(Courtesy of Mr Peter Preston)

Mr Peter Preston "The Wrestlers Wrestler"

CHAPTER TWENTYNINE

(All quiet at Digbeth City Hall Birmingham)

A strange experiences for me personally was clearly nothing like as traumatic as what happened to Peter but nevertheless it did throw me somewhat at the time. It took place on the first of a series of shows I worked on for Mr Gordon Corbett starting in the Midlands under the auspice of World Wide Promotions. My opponent that night was a really tricky ex-Lightweight Champion called **"Ian St. John"** [Harry Walsh to his pals] All the remaining bouts except for Gordon's I think he was on with Klondyke Jake [Barry Hawkins a truly nice man and a really good pro] were all top rated Asian performers, some of them were even nothing short of legends in all their domestic sporting circles. Needless to say they were the attraction and not Ian, me or the two far bigger men hailing from the Birmingham area. [Sadly Mr Gordon Corbett died in 1985]

The Bill itself is all a bit of a blur now as it's been a few years but I am however quite certain Mr Dara Singh was in the Top Slot. He's a God and he may have shared the lime light with another top Asian worker Mr Syed Saif Shah? The support was along the lines of Ragenar Singh, Amarjit Singh, Majid Ackra plus others although total and complete accuracy as to who were on the actual undercard may well be in question because as I've already stated it was so long ago now. That show was clearly aimed at the population centres which had large Asian communities and it toured several cities UK wide. From the land of Spaghetti Junction it went all the way further north to Manchester and the likes and then on into Scotland. The Halls were packed full every night you just couldn't get a seat! As luck would have it we finished in Glasgow at the Govan Town Hall so it was only a short trip home for me, great stuff. We opened in The Digbeth (Institute) City Halls Birmingham and our bout the Lightweights Warm-ups was first on. Halfway through the first round I was thinking to myself god this is a load of shit we're not that bad surely? We were going at it hammer and tongs and yet we were getting almost no heat whatsoever. You could almost have heard a pin drop for the whole 300 action packed seconds. After the first five minutes the bell rang and we were on our way back to our corners when loud applause nearly took the roof off! Suddenly it was as if Royalty had entered the room, unaccompanied and unannounced it was all very strange. Ian [Harry] hailed from Accrington he was very wiry and very fast and he had a set of big yellow teeth which reminded me of someone eating a handful of salted peanuts. Nevertheless he worked you hard as he had great reserves of energy. [Sadly Ian St John passed away in December 2012. RIP] I'd never worked in The Middle East or on the Indian Sub-Continent then or even now so I'm not all that aware if that's the way it's done over there, especially when World Wrestling Legends from India and Pakistan are appearing on the show. I must confess however it did throw me a bit at the time. I was formally introduced to all those top men later on at a meal arranged in a local restaurant and I had my picture taken with everyone on them. It was a great personal honour for me especially the shots with Dara and Syed Shah. Sadly over the years and a couple of house moves they've disappeared I've no idea what happened to them [Dara Singh the "Wrestling Legend" passed over in July 2012]

And what about the opponents you've like to have fought but haven't. Would you care to give a list?

God, that's a really difficult one but I'll do my best. Do you mean irrespective of the weight difference?

You tell me.

There are lots and they aren't in any particular order but here we go:

Jimmy Breaks, Clayton Thomson, Billy Robinson, (I'm sure I would have learned a lot from any encounter with Big Bill) Tony Charles, Jack Dempsey, Judo Al Hayes, Billy Joyce and Cyril Knowles. [These two men in particular were as hard as nails] Bill McDonald, Peter Maivia, Earl Maynard, [If only to get some muscle definition building tips from him] he was a "Mr Universe" you know. Of course an encounter with Lou Thesz would have I'm sure also proved fruitful he was a long established American star and an Ex-World Champion to boot. I'd of course need to balance all these performers on my wish list against probably the one man I'm kind of glad I have never had to face and that's **"Mr Bert Assirati"** but it's all already been said by many who actually shared a mat with him about just how powerful a man he was, so best to leave it there for the moment.

The London legend **"Mr Joe "Dazzler" Cornelius"** would also I feel have proved a difficult opponent but just to have shared a canvas with the "Dazzler" would have brought me a lot of personal kudos. He's one of the first of the modern era to publish his wrestling memoir only just this year in fact through Star Books it's called "Thumbs Up." Oh and this might be of some further interest to you if you'd managed to get in there first about five years ago now you might have gotten yourself onto an International Wrestling Story Scoop! There's this guy who started training in Florida USA in 1976 called Terry Gene Bollea. Some of the London based heavyweight lads who've worked over in the US regularly have been raving about him for a year or two now. Al Hayes says he's a huge guy in every sense of the word and I read somewhere not long after that Billy Robbo has also been saying good things about him. He [Terry] stands 6Foot 7Inches tall. You'll already have gathered I'm not over the moon about the over hyped element in wrestling in the so called "Land of the Free." But since his pro debut in August 1977 he's been working not only in the States but also in Germany and over in Japan as well in some of the Top Tournaments to get some experience at the highest level against good oversees opponents and in so doing he's becoming more familiar with the different styles and approaches. Again I'm told he's a real trouper and very popular among the other lads as he knows how to work a crowd and he is quite comfortable using the British Style. He was born in Georgia and he looks great, since the huge movie exposure he received after appearing in the Rocky III film his profile and his popularity rating has gone universal in all the entertainment genres. I hear Hollywood is considering him for many more screen roles they seem to think he's got a natural comedic talent. Vince McMahan the billionaire Chairman of the world's most successful TV Wrestling franchise WWF has been building him up over the last two or three years now letting him "Knock-Off" some of the really big names, so he must be fully confident Terry has the where-with-all to be able to handle real mega stardom and if things were different he could even have come over here for a period. If the present breed of promoters in the UK really knew what they were about and were willing to shell out some real money then with that kind of forward thinking he could have improved his overall skill base no end! Terry appearing on our TV screens and also in our Halls the length and breadth of the land for periods of lets say two to three months or more at a time over the next couple of years would also have done wonders for the failing fortunes of our domestic sport which at the moment is slowly going down the toilet. What that would have given us is a real muscle filled, athletic hero for the punters to salivate over and at the same time it would have given a huge shot in the arm to domestic viewing figures. And what do we get instead the exact opposite, namely a very large, non athletic, top hat adorned apparition that headlining our domestic shows and filling our Saturday afternoon screens, huffing and puffing almost constantly. Given what Terry's did over there in America in a very short space of time he could have been really big over here on this side of the pond as well, mark my words he's already love by those in the know in Japan. In the

Ask him again ref!

Land of the Rising Sun "The Catch" and he's most definitely not just your usual posing Yankee type, he's a lot more of a British Style performer, he can and he does use a lot more proper grappling moves whilst still maintaining all of the essential and important characteristics of the Native American Style of Razzmatazz. That's seldom been the case with a lot of their so called stars when they've come over here but clearly he is the exception as he can actually work on the mat! As I've repeatedly said the Yanks in general terms don't do it for me but as well as Hulk Hogan I will concede them at least one more vital element!

And what might that be?

They nearly always bind their elbows up and more importantly their knees in strong elasticised type pads thus holding and supporting the joints and the ligaments in their correct position for when they take a bump! I like a lot of others over here are already beginning to show signs of wear and tear in my knees, so they've clearly got that part correct and sadly we've clearly gotten it very, very wrong!

So his ring name is Hulk Hogan. I remember him in Rocky III but only slightly I was only looking at Sylvester Stallone and no one else. Did you see all those bulging muscles?

Those Pectorals really are things of beauty those and his "Latissimi Dorsi" that's "Lats" to you and me hen!"

They are a lot more than that to me mate!

Sylvester is now big in every way in the movies. But **"Hulk Hogan"** is equally big in Wrestling terms and its popular the world over, even in places Hollywood can't really reach which I will concede are somewhat few and far between. Dale continues whilst attempting to mimic the sound the Hulk makes in the television series Gra.....hhhhhh! "Don't make me angry! You wouldn't like me when I'm angry!"

Ask him again ref!

God I'd love to be there if he ever gets paid short in his brown envelope! He'd been standing there in his torn underwear holding out his big green hand saying. "I think you'll find there's a few dollars short in here buddy!"

OK that's enough. I'm really frightened now. Not!

But I was only just getting started.

Enough! Sorry but I'm getting a slight headache now.

Point made, keep your hair on.

How about injuries? Have you had any over the years?

Total mileage Ayr to East Kilbride and back: 69 Miles
Total time taken for the journey: 1hour 56 Minutes

Herc and Maggie

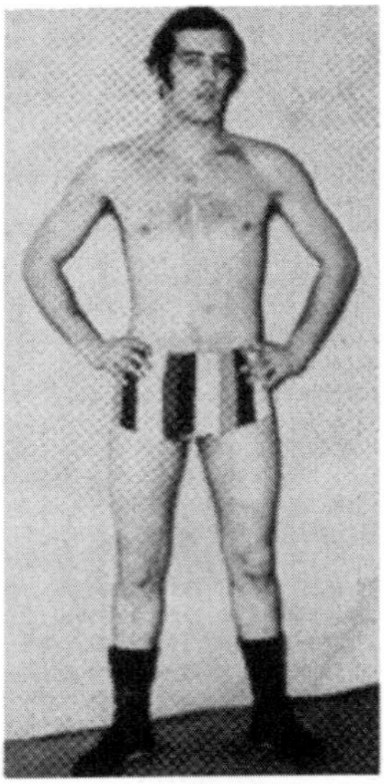

(Courtesy of Mr B Welch)
Bruce Welch

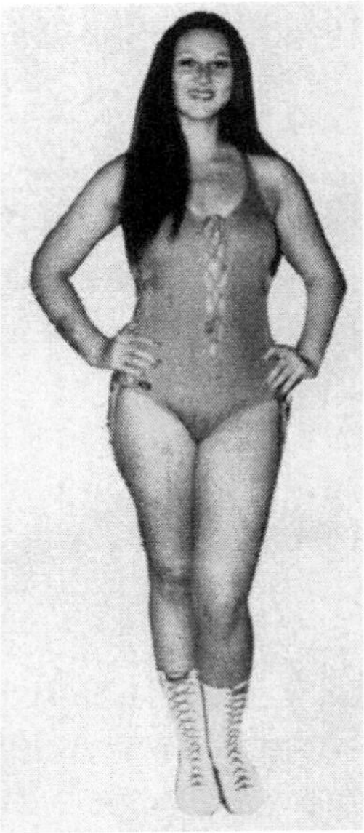

(Courtesy of Ms G Pyne)
Cherokee Princes

Ask him again ref!

CHAPTER THIRTY

(Serious Injuries and Absent Friends)

Personal Injuries good question, actually I've been very fortunate over the years I've never had anything really serious happen to me. Well not yet anyway, I did however get very badly sun burned in Douglas Isle of Man in July 1970 when I was on my honeymoon and like all young folks setting out on such a venture I thought I was invincible! That's OK if the only person you're trying to impress with your manhood, so to speak is your eager young bride but I was there to work as well. I was on the Bill at the Villa Marina Show. I'd managed to wangle the two together to try and save some money! Things were tough and one ferry fare from Ardrossan saved, plus half of one week's Boarding House Lodgings being reimbursed as well from the promoter Orig Williams' now prophet filled bulging pockets meant more cash to spend on the love of my life! And of at the same time I could give all those bikini clad beauties on the sea front the once over as well!

You're winding me up, I hope?

Of course, I am just having a laugh anyway I already had far more than enough for me to handle night or day. We'd actually got married in the January that same year but due to her employment circumstances, Lilian carried out all the office paperwork for both her bosses at the same time. [Strangely they had to hire in two temps to cover whilst she was away] so we'd been unable to take an extended break at that time. Anyway it's cold and it's damp in January almost everywhere in the UK and the Isle of Man in particular is closed. I had refused to go to Spain on holiday till that Fascist Dictator Franco died so it was out! The bout was not till later on in the week so we set about making the most of the island's hospitality. Let me say on a couple of nights we did over indulge on more than a few local cocktails, so much so on the second night the bloody Landlady locked us out of the digs. I've absolutely no idea why as we were never all that late. Midnight is surely not the curfew time on that holiday island, is it?

I wouldn't have thought so but maybe she was religious?

That meant I had to do my athletic James Bond hero type act by jumping over the moat like drop whilst narrowly missing a spiked wrought iron fence where more by luck than judgement the situation saw me grabbling hold of the outcropped brick windowsill. Thankfully avoiding falling around fifteen feet into the basement area! Hanging there by a couple of finger nails I struggled to enlarge the already slightly open widow space from its two inch orifice to a size whereupon I could clamber inside. Needles to say the Aspidistra plant perched proudly on the dark wooded antique pedestal was just as surprised as I was when we both ended up prostrate on the carpet of the chair filled front sitting room. The laughter that followed was really hard to control from both from me inside and also from my new misses outside. So with the plant hurriedly stuffed back into its pot, albeit rather clumsily, its wooden perch restored to almost its exact position and the front door having been opened and then studiously re-bolted we both still giggling feverishly crawled up the winding staircase carpet to our third floor room. Strange to say nothing was mentioned at the breakfast table the next morning, thank God! So relieved to still have a roof over our heads we crabbed our swimming gear and headed for an already busy beach! As the morning ticked away the frolics of the night before started to take their toll and I slowly dropped off to sleep. In so doing I slept the sleep of the both the righteous but also the rather foolish! Having finished her book around half an hour later my good lady joined me for forty winks, only for us both to wake up well over an hour later. In my case at least my skin was now a bright rather tender aching shade of Salmon Pink! Lilian has an entirely different skin make-up from me; she has a much darker pigment and looks every inch the complete Southern European in no time at all, deep rich tans seen to run in her family! Good God was the by word as I was burned to a crisp, but only on my front! My feet and my toes also ached like hell and now I was a disaster on two levels! The first being the fact my legs and my stomach were now as tender as a new babies bum and on the other I was due to step into the ring the very next afternoon! Needless to say my introduction into the ring went ok until the point when I had to remove my gown! Some of the comments from the crowd were hilarious, obviously there were a lot of smart arses on the Island on holiday and most of them had probably arrived from Glasgow! That was not the worse part of it, I had never worked with my opponent before that day and I was only introduced to him minutes before we were given our instructions by the ref! I did however notice he was wearing both padded knee supports and also padded elbow pads. That was unusual in the British Style for most workers as I mentioned previously, it's more the American way of doing things, and yes you've guessed it tender red hot flesh and rough padded supports are not a good mix. Needless to say my skin got scraped off in large part from around my shoulders and my chest. Sandpaper couldn't have done a better job but it was what I deserved, I suppose? There was no way I couldn't blame Liverpool born Bill Kennedy for anything that happened that day. Luckily I did just enough through the pain to get on with securing a victory whilst Billy also did his best after the first swathe of Deltoid covering skin landed on the canvas not to disfigure me further. Things were clearly proving to be just as awkward for him as they were uncomfortable for me! It is after all a contact sport and you do have to grab hold of one another! He lived on the Island and both he himself and his father ran a small wrestling venue in one of the other small towns on the other coastline! So realising I was staying over he asked me if I'd like to fill in as he was a man short for the following night. So after almost another full day spent under a cold shower in the digs, he picked us up at the Boarding House and we made our way out of Douglas down across the bottom of the island towards Port Erin. I felt much more comfortable within myself now and we had a much better bout this time around. As he was not only the local hero but the promoter as well naturally he took the victory going over to jubilant applause, all the adulation was rightly his this time around! Later on when on the way back to the Capital Town we dropped off, invited by a local clearly well off wrestling patron who'd kindly offered us the chance to partake of a few glasses of wine from his rather exclusive collection at his rather expensive looking cliff side villa near by! As the now livening up highly charged impromptu "Party" got up to speed and more and more of the moneyed locals arrived I became strangely aware that we, the only two, non-local young holiday makers types were fast beginning more and more the centre of attraction! My sixth sense had kicked in and in fact it was now working overtime and I was becoming very suspicious of the real reason why it might be we had been invited to this old, rather Gothic looking house in the middle of nowhere and by complete strangers! Panic and paranoia had now taken hold, perhaps wrongly and as far fetched as it may sound now, years later in the cold light of day, that particular island had for a long time a ghostly connection with the world of witches, warlocks and witchcraft rituals from the past! Apparently or so I've read rich middle aged boredom can sometimes manifest itself in the form of Witches and Covens for those so inclined. So just to be on the safe side we made our apologies and then we left, I might add in somewhat of a hurry! The old thumb came in very handy just a few hundred yards down the eerily quiet country road when a very nice older couple stopped to give us a lift back into Douglas. Apparently they'd been paying a retired Vicar fried his weekly visit. Thank god for cups of tea, jam scones and a game of bridge I thought to myself, as we sat in the back sharing a seat with a yappy wee poodle. If our hosts had been planning some sort of secret ceremony in the woods and required a nubile, young virgin lady as their centrepiece they were of course far too late, but then again they were not to know that for sure? Nevertheless these would-be Denis Wheatley fans would now need to get hold of some other sucker to play their little game! When asked by our rescuers, why were walking alone and at night on that lonely road, our explanation was greeted with complete silence, obviously they much preferred a simpler less exciting lifestyle. Getting back to the question you posed at the start my biggest worry regards injury might well not have been in the physical sense. It may well have been much more about me dying on my arse in the ring! That would have been rather harder to live down and as a proud performer that would have injured both me and my pride almost irrevocably, simply because I'd clearly not given my all. Good God I'd very probably have had to lie down in a darkened room for a week if that ever happened to me! Only kidding but you get the picture I'm sure. The real physically of being subjected to a really painful ring injury never enters your head, it can't or you'd never climb in between those ropes again! Actually dying in the ring and I mean quite literally dying is seldom contemplated by most performers and fortunately it has been the exclusive provenance of only a limited and in some ways a chosen few! Please, please don't get me wrong I'm not making light of a thing like that but if you have to go then that's the way some would prefer to leave this world if they had a choice and why not? After all we're all artist so what else would we as performers like more than to go out on a stage under the lights still performing to the crowd! Mr Mal Kirk left this world as a result of his efforts in the ring and that was all very sad for everyone who knew and liked the man and let me add at this point, he was a very popular chap among his peers. The manner of his sad demise must have been particularly devastating for his family but more about Mal later. Another who achieved what some might respectfully refer to as the ultimate was my good friend the late and the great Mr Gordon Lythe. You'd know him better as **"Klondyke Bill."** He was a real star, a really nice man and a truly hard working wonderfully warm hearted performer. He always gave of his best for his army of fans and in so doing finally paid off all of his dues to all who shelled out to place their bum on a ringside seat to watch him. He was a man whom had a lot of time for everybody, he would stand and sign autographs all night long, no matter if there were six or sixty fans waiting and it made no difference to him whether it was chucking it down or the sun was shinning he still signed each and everyone! He was undoubtedly a genuinely good person and a real gentleman! He weighed in at well over 30 stone but in the main he used to carry it well although he had indicated to some close cohorts before that fateful night that he sometimes felt a little unwell, from time to time, both during and after some sessions in the ring! He would often take an unrehearsed break holding onto the ropes just to get a breather trying to fully composing himself until he could carry on. Sadly, he met head on more or less the beginnings of an untimely death in The Dam Park Hall dressing room in Ayr after complaining to colleagues of not being at all well. Orig Williams was the promoter but he wasn't there that particular evening. I'm told Gordon had complained of not feeling all that great that fateful night to fellow performer Adrian Street who was also on the bill. Eventually it became obvious Klondyke was not in any fit state to work so even before the start of his contest Adrian made the announcement that Gordon would not be appearing. Sadly on his return to the dressing room after the conclusion of Ada's own bout Klondyke's condition had deteriorated further so at that point brother Street then called an ambulance. The medical people rushed Gordon to the local Hospital. Ayr County only about quarter of a mile away across the other side of the river from the venue! [Sadly Gordon Lythe never left Hospital after some initial indication of a possible recovery, his condition deteriorated and he passed away on Saturday 14th of July 1979]

Deservedly there was a really big turnout for the funeral service in his native Yorkshire. He is fondly remembered by all those who worked with him. Personally I liked the man a lot, I enjoyed our bouts together. Rest in piece Big Man! Miss you; you were real trooper right to the bitter end!

"Melvin Riss" [Harry Winstanley] copped a really bad double ankle break in the most bizarre circumstances! He's a real flyer, fast and bouncy both in and out of the ring and a very well respected "Catch" man from the Wigan Snake Pit as well. You name it he can do it, he's very clever, anyway I can't remember who he was on with and for the sake of this story it doesn't really matter because his injury was for the most part entirely self inflicted! As always his endeavours were designed to always give the public good value for money and Mel in throwing himself up and over in a back flip to escape an advancing opponent totally misjudged his position relative to the ropes, meaning he travelled out over them and landed on the outside edge of the ring apron on the overhanging lip. Only the balls of his feet actually came to rest on the extended wooden boards and as you can perhaps imagine, his weight was still travelling downward. The sudden impact of the boards stopped his feet but there was still velocity or is that inertia? I always get the two mixed up, in the rest of his body mass, simple schoolboy physics really, so it [the mass] just kept falling at the same rate. As a result the Wee Man shattered both his ankles! God love him it must have been excruciatingly painful. As I already mentioned earlier "Mucky Mal Kirk" also known as King Kong Kirk or Kojak Kirk was a very likeable Yorkshire man and former coal miner. He was a real giant of a man standing around 6foot 1inches and weighing in around 22 to 25 stone. He'd made his name both here in the UK and also in the big European Tournaments of the 1970's in Germany and the likes, where he was one of the main men. He had been a pretty good Rugby League Prop Forward (No 8) in the mid 50's and he played for both Featherstone Rovers and latterly for Doncaster where the regular "Hooker" was another wrestler "Ted Heath" of "The Red Scorpion" fame. Mucky Mal tagged regularly with "Paul Luty" initially [Yet another son of York and a good solid worker, who later on in his career turned his hand to acting] Both Paul and his ring partner Mal were really good company outside the ropes and were very popular among their peers. I worked with Paul often in the 1960's and also with Malcolm's oft time opponent Big Shirley in the same period for promoter and former Army Officer Norman Berry. [Crabtree was in the ring with Malcolm on that fateful day and he too is a big heavy lad but not half the man Kirk was. Mal sadly left us prematurely but at least he went down and out whilst he was performing and no one in this wonderful business of ours would, I feel sure if asked what they wanted from this performance driven business would never have wished to go out on "A Low Ebb" better to leave them [The punters] well satisfied at a job well done. Mal Kirk having been "Belly Flopped" a signature move from Big Daddy during a bout at The Hippodrome Circus Great Yarmouth in Southern England on 24TH August 1987 had tuned an unhealthy colour on his return to the dressing room and an ambulance was called. He was declared dead on arrival at the James Paget Hospital in Gorleston in Norfolk. A subsequent fatal accident inquiry cleared Shirley of any blame citing the fact Mal had a serious heart condition. [He was in his 51st year. Paul Luty has also gone over the vale as well, He only 52nd yea old. In his written Will he left Cancer Research a large sun of money. Condolences go out to both their families and their friends especially Malcolm's daughter Natasha.]

Another top performer and a leading light in the trio of the Belshaw Brothers, Mr Jack Beaumont died in 1963 of a massive coronary aged only 45 years after a bout which took place in The Princess Theatre Club Barlow Moor Road Chorlton Manchester England. When the opportunity of a show stopping high all-be-it one in which there is definitely no chance of any **"Come-Back"** opportunity presents itself unexpectedly and without warning, some might feel themselves blessed on at least one level to have had that headline grabbing opportunity gifted to them to die for the cause. Or is that just too terrible to contemplate?

A bit of both probably. I'm really not qualified to answer.

Then again that self-same opportunity some might say is an empty statement and it may sound more than just a little callous to someone like you who is not in the grappling business, hence your reticence. I can however assure you that o some in the fraternity it is most definitely not a futile set of over the top words. Luckily most injuries are just sprains and grazes, the odd black eye or even a blooded nose. The odd hitch here and there can occur unexpectedly but sometimes in a strange way it can often bring a different dimension to a contest. If the protagonists use their common sense and grab the moment, making every event work for them and for the performance as a whole even if that means some good old fashioned ego bruising gets thrown in for good measure then so be it!

And the Promoters you've worked with? How do they rate?

Total mileage Ayr to Dunfermline and back: 148.2
Total time taken for return journey: 3 Hours 14min

(Courtesy of I Bryden)
Davie Simpson

Mr Eric Taylor is second from left

CHAPTER THIRTYONE

(Our Lords and Masters)

The guys I've worked for so far have all been to a greater or lesser extent generally good promoters of this the sport I love, some are much nicer than others but you get that in all walks of life. As long as I'd recouped my out of pocket fuel expenses and paid the wages I thought I was worth and most importantly, they'd put me on with other professionals who'd looked after my body and who like me wanted to give the paying public good value for their hard earned money, then in the main I had no real complaints. The difficulties arose when you got shoved into the ring with an imposter, a charlatan who quite frankly shouldn't have been in the business in the first place let alone facing me on that particular night! They can be and sadly sometimes are a real danger to your well being and that's when I tend to shut down and go into self preservation mode, not a place you want to be and definitely not the best environment in which to entertain the public. Rather sadly from that moment onward the only thing that really matters is the defence of my continued good health! From a spectator consideration point of view that particular aspect can become second best to making sure I get out of that unwanted situation in one piece, body in tact back to the warmth and the comfort of the wife and the kids, injury free and able to go back to my daytime mortgage paying real work job the very next morning! It's a really horrible feeling and it's totally avoidable but that apart some promoters can still genuinely get it wrong when they match-make and in a quiet moment in the dressing room, if no one else is around they will usually acknowledge that fact. Others do things for some perverted personal enjoyment reasons and not always for their own gratification. On long trips which for them can sometimes be boring it can also be for the enjoyment of the more Neanderthal element on the bill so they of that persuasion can stand in the wings and whilst experiencing some pseudo orgasmic pleasure watch the disintegration of what is supposed to come under the umbrella of entertainment, crudely unfolding whilst falling apart before their very eyes. To give you an example of this stupid moronic practice I for one had the full weight of a tall well built, tights wearing magnificently dyed blonde haired guy whom by the character name he was hiding behind had clearly been around long enough to know an awful lot better. He came down from a great height with the full force of his rather large size wrestling boot right on top of my fully exposed totally unprotected lower spine! God was I in extreme agony and I couldn't get a breath of air either. The pain was so bad I doubled up in the unnatural juxtaposition! So much so, I thought I had bloody Lock-Jaw! I gave the big bastard the benefit of the doubt as I'd never been in the ring with him before and I had only heard or seen his name on the odd Bill. So I had no way of knowing if he was in fact the real thing, rather sadly no dressing room apology was forthcoming when we got back in there. His liberty taking showed a complete lack of respect given both his supposed and my definite years of experience in the business. It most certainly was not a lack of good judgement or indeed distance on his part and I'm pretty confident having analysed the whole bout later, that it had not been done on the orders of the Promoter on that night. On further analysis of that potentially permanent spinal injury blow I've had a lot of time to ponder and I'm now convinced the deed was paid for in advance by a cowardly arse hole, former promoter from my fairly recent past! He [My assailant] only got that one botched chance and that was only because I was on the mat face down and fully trusting in him to take care of my, at that moment very vulnerable body! On reflection I should have taken his pink tights wrapped them round his neck and strangled the twat but I'm not like that in the ring. Well maybe I still should have been this one time? Anyway I then made the fully thought out and conscious decision to let him try and finish the job the next time we met in the ring later on that week. Unlike him I don't need to kick out at a man on his blindside when he's face down and helpless on the mat! Strangely and unexplainably I didn't get the chance to show him what I could do to him if he repeated the ambush because and it still remains a total mystery, he didn't finish the week! He disappeared into the night like the cowardly, failed assassin he undoubtedly was. Bastard! I've never to this day come across his face again but I for one now remain fully convinced why that was. Maybe I should take a moment to further inform the uninitiated as to the bond and the trust you need to have in your contemporaries at all times and here's another example but this time all was ok. The first time I fought Marty Jones was at Dumfries on a **"Mr Jack Atherton"** show, we'd never even shared a dressing room previously as I'd only recently come back over from the Indies again although I was a big fan of the new kid on the block! The very first words Marty ever spoke to me were to say: "I'll give you a point if you manage to get around behind me when we're in there!" An obvious reference to the catch/amateur side of the sport of grappling and the top drawer training he'd received in The Snake Pit Gym in Wigan as a youth. Naturally I had no intention of undermining neither himself nor indeed my gaffer for the night Old Jack so my reply was something alone these lines: "No need for any points scoring here son. I will get behind you but no need to panic as I will be looking after you and your body at all times and I'd really appreciate you making sure you do the same with mine that way we'll both be just fine!" It was my great pleasure to be in the ring with someone of his class and his ability that night and I like to think we had a good entertaining contest. My only disappointment is that I was billed under a bastardised creation not of my making! "Drew Bryson" rather sadly does not quite stand out on any Bill Poster irrespective of the class of the opposition you're up against on any given night! Even more so when the others appearing consisted of the following top class line up!

Ask him again ref!

J A PROMOTIONS
PROUDLY PRESENTS

WRESTLING

Friday 12th January

The Loreburn Drill Hall Dumfries

Kendo Nagasaki V Bobo Matu

....

Marty Jones V (Drew Bryson) Dale Storm

Big Ian Miller V Keith "Bloodboots" Martinelli

....

The Hells Angels V The Judokas.

The Tag Teams were made up of **"Adrian Street & Bobby Barnes"** as the Hells Angels. The Judokas consisted of **"Alf Marquette" and "Tug Wilson"**

But let's get back to my bout and Marty's first words to me that night in the dressing room in South West Scotland. If he [Marty] in a coded sense was telling me that he'd heard some not very good things about some Scottish based grapplers, then that came as no surprise to me, it's a fact I've already eluded to in an earlier chapter. Some Scots were a bit like that but only a few! It's just a pity that he without even knowing me might have had some preconception of what he was going up against! Sadly some workers north of the border did have a bit of a reputation and with some justification for being both "Tight" and far too "Greedy." In as much as their only intention was at every opportunity to be "Putting Themselves Over" at all times. Marty had no need to be concerned on that score as I was quite happy to deal with his point and to take it on board in good faith and in good humour. [Marty Jones went on to become one of British Wrestling all time Greats! Mr Jack Atherton left this world on 21st December 1991 he will be forever fondly remembered RIP Jack and many thanks]

But you must have a favourite promoter and conversely some you're glad not to be working for now?

I'm not going to put them in some order of preference, I'd rather not do that but if you have a problem with something I say and you feel it needs more clarification then that's what I'll do! OK? I'll start at the beginning shall I?

That's great for me, you just carry on!

As I've said earlier Danny Flynn and Freddie Woolley were my early mentors they and the halls they ran are my Alma-Ata. Freddie was a different kind of a man from Danny and early on when we were in the ring he would take some liberties, well at least that was how I saw it at that time but with the passage of time I grew to see things in a completely different light. One example being the incident in Rothesay which demonstrated his total defence and total loyalty to all the lads in his employment and it taught me to think a little differently about the man! If he hit you with a "Forearm Smash" sometimes he really did hit you and bloody hard! Maybe not enough to knock your teeth out or break your jaw but nevertheless he could hit you hard! Maybe he just wanted too toughen me up or maybe just make sure I would "Sell it" properly! Baring in mind I was new and very green as far as the Pro Game was concerned or maybe he was saying to me what others years before had probably said to him when he was trying to gain a foothold in professional wrestling.

....**Things like:**

Ask him again ref!

The business you're about to enter is my business!

If I let you in and I might not!

Don't ever sell the business short, it gives me a living.

Don't get so far up your own backside you think you may now be, a Somebody! Because you're a Nobody!

Always bear in mind nobody and I mean nobody is bigger than this business which you've expressed a wish to join and become part of. It's a craft which requires you to be, at all times true and professional!

At the moment you are just a boy, a journeyman, an apprentice!

You're just a spoke in the wheel of a far larger circle which has some secrets and a language all of its own.

A language not everyone has access to. Only the initiated and the enlightened can enter our realm.

You will have to study it and you will have to learn it.

If you are lucky enough to be given the gift of fame then use it well, it is not assigned for you to abuse.

Because as easily as it can be given to you it can just as easily, be taken away from you again.

Others who share a ring with you will make you look good! It has very little to do with your own abilities.

This, the sport of pro wrestling is not open to everybody it's a closed shop into which you are invited. If you are made of the right stuff that is!

Ask him again ref!

And if you as a new entrant are not made of the right stuff I will find out your weaknesses and very quickly.

And then I am going to kick your arse and throw you out of my profession!

So as I said earlier, don't you ever sell it short and don't you ever take it for granted! And it will give you all the rewards you deserve.

Because like most, you will only get out of it what you put into it!

And don't you ever forget that! As I and others long established shall be watching you constantly.

Freddie was of course perfectly correct and clearly he was just testing me, finding out what I was made of! In all the years thereafter I have always taken the view that this wonderful business needs to be protected from those not really suited to its ideals and its traditions. Sadly some who like me have the luxury of a gym and a squad of trainees have not always exercise their best judgement with some whom they either introduced personally or have let slip through their normally robust vetting processes' and who have done those who depend for a living on wrestling a truly monumental disservice! There is no doubt in my mind that some who were only interested in their own career and not the wellbeing of their fellow professionals and the good name of Grunt and Groan as a whole have already been wrongly initiated. They know who they are and so do the promoters who wrongly use them and perhaps much more importantly, they are also known those of us who truly love this sport and for all the right reasons! Sadly and mark my words this will kill wrestling as we know it in time! Some continue to selfishly use it to further their own star struck American focused careers when they've hardly taken the time to serve even a short professional apprenticeship right here in the UK! Others whom some might say were among the worst workers, especially when it comes right down to being safe, never mind their wrestling ability have been wrongly catapulted to stardom and relative riches only by virtue of nepotism and their wider family connections. Again like me many of my peers feel that too will come back to bite our sport in the arse someday! On a personal level I've had lots of lads through my gym and through my hands and all had some ability and in only a few instances when their application and dedication was not what was demanded and although all were bitterly disappointed, they did not get the chance through me and my gym to join the ranks of the paid pros! Danny Flynn brought many others as well as me through the ranks. I worked with him a lot on a one to one and he taught me almost everything I know and both he and Mr Woolley deserve their place in the sports history. If Danny had lived and oh how I wish he had, there is no doubt in my mind I would have stayed with him and continued to work for him for as long as he wanted me to continue to do so. I'm very loyal to people I like and admire I have always lived my life in that regard it's the way my parents brought up to behave. Danny was not the kind of man to hold you back he wanted only the best for me so he arranged for me to get more pro experience by asking other promoters like Norman Berry and Gordon Corbett to include me on some of their shows as well.

My grandfather on my father's side was a lovely man and a true Christian in every sense of the word! I learned a lot from him when I was growing up, he helped set me out on the road through life with some basic values and he used to say "If you have nothing good to say about a person then do not say anything bad about them either!" Sound advice which I followed faithfully until I was around the age of fifteen or sixteen! Rather sadly you will by now have gathered I've fallen down badly on that score ever since. But I still totally respect those who are of the same mind set. Shortly after Mr Flynn departed us for a better place things started changing. Mr Gordon Corbett, Mr Ben "Thunderbird" Watijesk and Orig Williams contacted me asking me if I wanted to work for them as they were now taking over. As it transpired their consortium was to be very short lived. Given there had only been the briefest passage of time since Danny's passing it was now obvious to me the vultures in a manner of speaking were beginning to circle in the sky. All went well with the new set-up at first Freddie was still there but rather strangely he was only on the periphery or a least it looked that way to me. Gordon and Ben were both very easy to get along with and I'm really pleased to say they seemed to like me as well. Both had spent time at a higher level having previously been employed by Joints as had Freddie and Danny. Gordon was the fist guy I'd seen doing The Boxer verses The Wrestler routine a throwback no doubt to the old Showground Booth Days. Orig on the other hand was a much deeper man and a lot harder to judge or even to get to know properly. I got the impression very early on he had some personal demons, maybe I'm wrong but that's my heartfelt and my honest opinion of the man. It was clear he had not been long in the wrestling promotion business when we first met and his ring persona at that time also lacked some real finesse. Although you'd have been very hard pressed to convince him of that fact! Unlike the other two he had never worked on a Joint Promotions Show although he had or so I'm told been topping some lower level bills on some Independent shows, mostly it would seem in his native homeland! And again at that point he'd never performed prior to that in Scotland either. Apparently he'd had a long career as a professional footballer in the proceeding years with Oldham Athletic and latterly in the Welsh Leagues before making the move into Pro Wrestling. Any early bouts, involving we two, were sadly not the best I've ever had as his ring style lacked breeding mainly because he always insisted on taking the lead and he was hard to follow at times so it never fully flowed. Those shortcomings I feel sure would have been viewed by him as being down to me no doubt! Back then he could just about get away with playing a villain but only just and without a good and more experienced blue eye along side knowing when to make the comeback moves, things could get lost and regularly becoming quite samey and noticeably pedantic. I've no idea which gym he may have attended or who taught him or indeed if he ever stepped onto a mat anywhere with a competent coach. Maybe if he'd studied elsewhere in let's say Wigan or Bolton or even in Scotland in my gym he'd have been far more aware that Soccer and Wrestling are two separate and two completely different genres and never the twain shall meet! If he'd ever been called upon to really "Shoot" he'd have been completely lost, although at his best he was clearly successful on at least one level; he was strangely adept in most instances at hiding his undoubted very limited knowledge from those to whom he paid the wages on a nightly basis. At the end of the day some might say that was what was much more important and they'd probably be correct! It's just that the respect of your peers has always been very important to me and I've always judged others in the same way, I hope that's how they've judged me as well. Real respect has to be earned disrespect is easily achieved! He's always had a tendency to try and intimidate opponents both inside and also outside the ring, apparently he'd had a reputation on the Football Field for being a bit of a bully and disappointingly he brought that attitude into the ring. The saddest part of the whole scenario at that time was the fact that quite a number of those he was employing regularly to fill his bills were new entrants and therefore they didn't know any better. This meant some were prone to flaming the fires of his ever growing and enlarging ego and he did the same for theirs. Lies and untruths were also regularly spread about others, the more experience really seasoned pros knew what was going on but they just chose to turn a blind eye! I would however be less than honest if I didn't mention the fact he did however possess the ability to think on his feet, that tells me that in the Football World he may well have been a defender and obviously an uncompressing one in the tackle! He also clearly had a tendency to learn very quickly and he eventually travelled widely setting up contacts and shows in both Europe and also in the Middle East. I take my hat off to him for that at least although he liked to tell folks he'd worked with all the Indian and Pakistani sub-continent greats. Although I've been informed from those who were actually there at the time that his primary function was as a referee and he never ever put himself forward to "Shoot" like they did, if challenged from outside the ring by a local! Maybe if I'd crawled a little more I too might have been included on trips to foreign climes but then again probably not. Clearly all kinds of foreign ventures must undoubtedly have accrued for him a large degree of monitory success. In principle there is of course nothing wrong with that although he was in my opinion only ever in the business for two reasons, the previously eluded to ego trip and as I've just mentioned the other being a fast and the fairly easy accrued Quid, Franc, Deutschmark, Lebanese Pounds etc! Again that's just my personal opinion but unlike most others I'd been round him fairly regularly over long periods in both the good times and the not so good. So I was therefore fairly ideally placed to make not only an honest, considered and almost totally informed impartial judgement. Some have even alleged, not me I might add, HM Revenue and Customs would have shown a keener interest regards his again alleged Off-Shore earnings accounts had they known about all these other business dealings in foreign climes? Again my old grandmother God Bless her, she once told me I had The Gift but as yet it was not fully developed. She added "You need to learn to use it and use it well!" Her side of the family go back a long way into our Irish heritage background! Personally speaking I hate it! I don't want it gift or not! I've always found it never to be the bringer of good news. Still Orig and I got along ok and for many, many years in fact we even shared the odd laugh or two.

As the months passed working for the trio got stranger and stranger Messer's Corbett and Watijesk seemed to spend more and more time in the south in the Birmingham area and we in Scotland saw less and less of them and more and more of the Welshman born in Ysbyty Ifan. I can honestly say I worked tirelessly for the Williams fellow over the intervening years but still I never felt completely relaxed, comfortable or totally at home around him. I even gave him the pick of my lads in my gym to use as and when he needed them. I didn't do that for everyone else with whom I was also associated back then! And I never at anytime took any commission from any payments, including fuel expenses I secured for my lads! Sadly from the outset I was never fully convinced he ever really appreciated that gesture or the benefits he accrued from that bunch of really good workers! He always seemed to be more and more preoccupied with the fact that I in the past before we first met, had sometimes promoted my own shows. Actually the fact I'd been taught by a real showman and a real professional in the shape of Mr D Flynn was a real bug bear to him. As a native born Scot I and any others like minded felt fully justified, should we so desired to put on some shows in Auld Scotia after all it's a free country and it was our country unlike other less paranoid established promoters he seemed to dislike anyone else building up their own following in Scotland, native born or not! Maybe that would go some way to understanding why he unlike others before and since chose never to allow me any higher up the billing order than an occasional second top spot! Sadly, what transpired years later, regards the Stirling debacle clearly proved my sixth sense gift to be all too accurate. I can tell you honestly and truthfully what transpired given I was a completely innocent party in the matter was a particularly painful and a very bitter pill to have to swallow! On a brighter note not long after the three promoter partnership invasion a former punter now turned referee also appeared out of the blue. He was young, he was cocky and he was genuinely basically honest and he was going places and fast. He the man with the jet in his arse was none other than Mr Brian Dickson and he and I hit it off right away! I really liked him right from the moment I first met him in fact I still do. He was a breath of fresh air in the now changing grappling business, he'd watched and he'd learned all about the business and by the end of the process he really knew how to run a show. He had the blarney, he knew how to talk the Joints stars into coming over to the Indie side. He'd never worked in the ring as a grappler but he'd been around in several other capacities under other promoter's banners, some good and some bad and he'd been very observant throughout the whole process. He'd also done some interviews for magazine write-ups as an even younger lad and I think I'm correct when I say he'd also run a Wrestling Fan Club. Mostly importantly he knew how to pay and he knew how to treat you right! I worked for him for a year maybe two and then almost as suddenly as he first appeared, he too was gone again, just disappeared out of Scotland! I don't really know what brought about his promoting demise in Auld Scotia, well not exactly that is. Some unsubstantiated rumours started to circulate or maybe I'd better say things were alleged but opinions and allegations were once again usually given off camera so to speak and what was being said amounted to the fact he'd been warned off and told "to keep out!" By one or more of the other Indie guys who were promoting in Scotland by this time. I have my own theories and purely because my special gift was by now going loopy as is its want sometimes! I'm not prepared at this time to put any messages I received from another world onto the printed page, suffice to suggest elements of the grappling Celtic Mafia were afoot and they did not represent the interests of Joint Promotions Organisation!

Next we've got Max Crabtree a good solid worker in his own right in the ring when he'd pulled around on the circuit. As a promoter initially he mostly fronted for others in the Joints Group people like George deRelwyskow among others but he's actually a Top Director now. A few years back he also handled some of the Ted Beresford and Norman Morrell stuff as well before they went into liquidation in 1974. Although Joints still use the name and the way things are going its beginning to look more and more like every "Bill Poster" will have the Dale Martin logo on it eventually. There's talk in the camp that Max might well be a Director their as well? Anyway he still continues to do a reasonably good job most of the time with the noted exception of just one or two basic and totally avoidable errors but to be fair oversights like these have usually been few and far between generally speaking although many in the business seldom, if indeed ever, express a good word regards the whole family. His overdressed refereeing brother Brain gets on the nerves of many when he regularly and wrongly elects to attempt to steal the heat from those paid to perform for the public's enjoyment. As opposed to those like him, who get paid predominately to check boots, finger nails and of course to count up to three when required to do so! Luckily due to the fact I was getting more than enough work elsewhere, generally I did not have to work for them. Suffice to say if their big brother is what the TV viewers have to look forward to then it will only be a matter time until someone at the top in ITV pulls the plug! And thereafter dressing room occupants will no longer cringe when being subjected to those now immortal and always totally detested condescending phrases such as: ***"Eh Kid, what wi gonna do wi ye?*** **'Ow we gonna present ye to 'em art theer?"** Honest and heartfelt apologies to all the good folks of Yorkshire for the badly phrased quote and the way it's been delivered on the page. No disrespect intended as I've always felt totally at home in your wonderful Kingdom among its very friendly populous.

Once again you've mentioned whom you consider to be the terrible threesome! Don't you think you're over the top?

You are of course correct I have mentioned them again but

the case against those promoters and flawed performers who do the business a regular disservice, not always the brothers cannot be overstated or overlooked. It is what it is and that's a fact! Sorry I for one will not be glossing over it!

Mr Jack Atherton among those facilitating shows in the UK was a far more experienced person on the mat than most at any level in the UK, he alone among that fraternity is rated as one of the top men by those who've both work with him in the ring and had a wage from him also. His zany methodology constantly applied whilst paying you your cash wages direct into you hand was truly a work of pure comic genius! Given he is standing with you in the middle of a busy dressing room full of other curious performers all of whom equally curious to discover just what money you are actually on! No matter how the other guys tried over the years to break his quirky personal Enigma Code none, I'll wager, have ever even come close. He was the best payer I've ever encountered as well as being a really wonderfully honest and well mannered individual. [Sadly as I've already pointed out earlier the Drill Hall in Dumfries was never ever the same place after this "Master" retired and things moved on]

Another member of The Alliance was Mr George deRelwyskow a true gentleman in my opinion, we should be very thankful that people like him were custodians of our business. I've worked for both in a few places Hamilton, Dumfries, Perth and Kilmarnock in particular on a regular basis and in most of other venues in their portfolio of halls in Scotland and beyond. I've also been billed on shows in Yorkshire and parts of Lancashire again for George Rel. He always gave the new younger guys a chance and they always try to reward him with good solid performances. I particularly remember a bout I had with Jeff Kaye, he's a steady worker if a little languid and I've always found him to be a decent enough guy and safe to work with. He looks after your body and you can go with the flow and give him his head with anything he wants to try, sadly in recent years it's not every opponent whom you'll expose you face, your noise and especially your teeth too without thinking about stepping aside as he cleverly breaks your "Full Nelson" hold steps forward a pace or two and then "Drop Kicks" you backwards! This entails both his feet flying out at you at full speed whilst he is facing away from you! His precision athleticism and timing are always spot-on. Well done to deRelwyskow and his fellow promoter and business partner Mr Green.

Mr Norman Morrell some will tell you was the real brains behind the Joint Promotions concept. It was he who first recognised that if an all encompassing umbrella could be structured then continuity and integrity of performance and hopefully steady employment could then be guaranteed. His brain child was not dissimilar in its basic form to that of Charlie "Lucky" Luciana, when he put in place the Roman type structure to the American Mafia because like that plan Morrell's idea meant all the bosses had to work together for the good and the wellbeing of the whole organisation. The one stand out addition was Television and in particular the new emerging ITV Commercial Cannel which proved to be a godsend, the timing of their business venture could not have come at a better time for The Grunt and Groan as it sought to improve its roughhouse image. ITV was searching for programming to fill time slots and the marriage proved to be very successful for both industries. Sadly I don't recall ever meeting Mr Morrell directly although as I said earlier I did work on many shows over which he had some direct control. My loss I think! At other times I've also appeared on shows run by other top names that have all eventually realised their drawing power potential and turned their hand to operating for themselves. Men like Auchterarder's onetime adopted son Andy Robin. Actually he was born in one of Stirling's Town's rather rough and rather infamous districts know as "The Raploch" housing estate area! Leeds Utd FC and Scotland skipper

Billy Bremner can also lay claim to having lived there as a kid. Andy took a punt tried his hand and he's done well and all credit to him, his heart has always been with his fans who've loved and adored him since his triumphant return to these shores from the Canadian Highland Games Circuit. He did however fall down on one of the basic principles of professional presentation on one of his very first solo promotions. The Grand Hall in Kilmarnock was the chosen venue and someone forgot to place all three ring ropes in the van, or so he said, more than likely himself. We all get it wrong from time to time and clearly he was new to the ring building process, so perhaps he should not be judge to harshly? As was usual I turned up an hour before official Kick-Off to find a ring as expected already set up. Well almost but it had only two ropes fully strung, not the obligatory three, I was quite frankly appalled! Not only did it look very unprofessional it could have been very dangerous for the performers Why he didn't think to send somebody round the corner to the nearest Tesco, which in this particular case was only five minutes away, to purchase two or three cheap clothes lines to fill the space was way beyond belief! It seemed as stupidly remiss to me as it did to the other guys and galls on the bill that night! We couldn't help thinking but for the lack of a very small investment of just two or three pounds this glaring example of substandard workmanship could have been so easily fixed. Presentation verses belligerence was never a true contest and has always been more about narrow mindedness and oversight! These basic facts regards a job done correctly had clearly been sadly lost on Brother Robin! A factor which clearly led months later to a serious and totally avoidable career ending painful disaster!

My good pal Adrian Street has also on odd occasion billed himself as the Headliner on his own shows with supporting bouts usually involving both yours truly and some of the lads based in my gym. Occasionally these were in clubs such as Glasgow's standout "Ashfield" and they usually featured the internationally famous "Mr Glen Daily." He also ran shows in some larger pubs and hotels where they had higher ceiling function suits and also some tried and tested local halls! I particularly remember a venue up in the north near Elgin in Morayshire, not that far from the heart of The Whisky Trail in the Spey Valley. One morning whilst stripping down the ring still suffering slightly from a headache brought on no doubt by far too much of the Amber Nectar. It was interesting to note the clearly recently used, brightly coloured condom which was proudly occupying the centre stage spot right in the middle of the off white ring canvas! Whom, I thought to myself had been responsible for this late-night performance in that lovely little Rosehearty Hotel lounge, your guess is as good as mine mate! Sadly we'll never know but I'll have to reluctantly admit it hadn't been me, bugger! The folks who'd shared its lubricated stem at the time were never boastfully forthcoming! God a dreadful thought has just crossed my mind surely it couldn't have been the end product of a single handed kinky act by an overly frustrated Highland Shepherd, performing some small and personal sexual research on the merits or otherwise of this new fangled, only just discovered by him Durex product, from a never before seen mechanical machine in the toilet area? It would however be so much nicer to think this act of passion may well have been homage to orgasmic and intimate excitements which were initiated by the movements of those Gladiators who had all entered into that self same arena previously, but as I said earlier we'll never know, will we? Adrian like Andy Robin is a treat to work for or indeed work with and he always fills a good bill with various weight divisions and his shows normally also feature his gifted and lovely looking lady wife Miss Linda. Matched against some equally capable big breasted, sex oozing female opponent! I'm thinking particularly of the fully vamped afore mentioned Miss Susan Sexton and the like! Adrian and Linda are both real pros and he in particular has always been fully appreciative and completely understands every aspect of our business! Therefore he always makes sure he does his best to please each and every section of the entrance fee paying crowd both young and old alike! I will always be eternally and humbly grateful to Linda and Adrian for all the friendship they've shown me over the years. It's not all that often you meet really good and genuine people in any branch of entertainment but these two most certainly are. Other happy situations fondly remembered where I've been fortunate to work with other good and genuine people and to whom I dedicate sections of these career memories contain the names of some I've sometimes even broken bread with in my home and sometimes in their homes as well! That list contains the likes of Mr Joe Critchley a true professional and an honest and a good friend. A hard man if he needed to be when working in the travelling booths having served his apprenticeship with Billy Riley. Then there's Mr Eddie Rose our friendship goes back probably a lot longer than most, he too is a good man and a terrific human being. Also Mr Mark Wayne and my other long remembered very colourful buddy, the now sadly departed this earth Mr Ezra Frances. Next the also sadly gone to the Top of the Big Bill Show in the bright sky Mr Jeff Bradley who was of course my revered long-time, much loved and sadly much missed "Guardian Angel" aka Wee Sammy Taylor. Next up, my wonderful wee pal of many, many memorable years Mr Scott Thomson, not forgetting his two biggest fans his talented Church Organ playing devoted wife Margaret and their lovely and equally gifted former wrestler daughter Lorraine-Lynn. The Viking another true pal the hilarious Mr Michael O'Hagan, The Fabulous Harlequins aka The Morgan's sometimes referred to by their original given family name of The Simpson Twins. Then there's Teddy Bear Taylor [No relation to Wee Sammy] and of course the Isdale Brothers Jim and Bobby, not forgetting their other sibling our Ronald [Moon] who along with big brother Bobby also now graces the lists of the fondly remembered deceased. Then there's the always smiling Big Arnold and Our Auntie Betty followed by the Allan Twins, Johnny

Powers, Big John Alexander and both Bill Wilson and Big Jimmy Wilson [Not related] Ian McKay, Bruce Welch, the always deeply suntanned Bill Robertson and young John Leckie and Jim McQuacker whom I worked with in Scotmec Engineering. Then there's the never to be forgotten star performer my younger brother Big Ian Miller. [Brutus to his pals] Jimmy Hughes and his younger brother Brian and all the hard working lads in their Glasgow based troupe. Ronny Archer his talented younger brother Wilf and Ron's pal Big Rae Elliot and the nearly always rebelling Brian McClung aka "Murphy the Surfy!" Last but most certainly not least a very, very special mention for all those shapely goddesses who brightened up all our lives both inside and also outside the ring "The Ladies" who attended and who trained very hard in that rough and ready wee village gymnasium; especially Catherine, Patricia, Mary and the afore-mentioned Lorraine-Lynne Stevenson. Great credit must be given to the man who was probably UK Wrestling's biggest fan Mr David Simpson regularly but lovingly chastised for spending show-time blissfully engrossed in what was happening right in front of him inside the ropes when he should have been fulfilling his duties as the ringside time-keeper. Lastly the referee who officiated on most of my shows was Gerald my younger sibling and he always did a really good job. Sadly his University studies and the living of his young life got in the way so he retired almost before he ever really got started! The Grappling game is all about entertaining and putting on a show and the man from Elgin Mr George McDonald with whom I've shared not only many a laugh and many a dram was a real Showman! We shared some really precious hours where we sat and just talked about how we'd put the world to rights. A better man would be very hard to find either in this life or the other. He listened when it was the right thing to do; he gave advice only when it was prudent to do so and he always saw and heard nothing when it was the correct course of action to take. He was an extremely humble man but his largely unheralded talents knew very few boundaries. His army career was forged in the Gallant 42nd better know perhaps as the "The Black Watch" and his piping skills or so I'm told by those with knowledge in that field were of the highest quality. There's a story that during the time when a particular resident piper at the Edinburgh Military Tattoo was for whatever reason unable to end the famous nightly proceedings in time honoured tradition. Allegedly alcohol was the reason so the iconic television camera captured final moments had been saved when George quite literally stood into the breach perched atop one of the highest battlement outcrops adorned in all his highly polished finery as befits such a truly monumental occasion, highlighted in full colour in the full glare of the arc lights and seen by millions watching in television land. George had been selected and then secretly given the squeaky bum numbing task of rescuing the situation and by all accounts he gave a top notch seamless rendition of the full repertoire to great aplomb. Only to be pulled up by an eagle eyed Senior Officer during his decent through the many stair-wells and passages on his way back down to God's good earth from his wind blown lofty perch. Apparently the giveaway as to the imposter under all that Tartan and the Bearskin Bonnet was the hastily overlooked and unchanged White Military Spats. The type the big man was wearing being of the historically noted 1700's punishment issue when some of the 42nd Regiment had absconded refusing to be sent to Jamaica! The spats in question being of the Square Toed Variety [A regimental punishment for breaking the line in a famous battlefield action] as opposed to the rounded toed more common type normally worn by the ill absentee. I've no idea what punishment may have been handed out to George but bear in mind this was back in the era of the late nineteen fifties early sixties and being the military it must have been in some eyes at least a terrible affront! Not uncommonly when members of the 42ND are around other regiments in some military messes the world over, the reference most often used by those not of The Black Watch Regiment seems to be the derogatory: “There is a distinct smell of sheep around here don’t you think?”

Is there anything else apart from Wrestling you wanted to do but so far you’ve not yet managed?

No not a great deal life so far has been pretty good to me although from my time as a youth of maybe eight or nine, I do have one big regret in that I didn’t take up an offer made by my father for me to learn to play the piano.

The Piano! How strange! Would you care elaborate?

My father a tall hard working, well muscled miner and a God fearing man asked if I’d like to learn to play the piano. Even at that tender age I was fully aware playing that particular instrument in my village environment was considered to be effeminate in the extreme. A slightly nicer word than the street-speak of that time in which I would have been labelled a Poof and regularly thereafter been given a good kicking, enthusiastically administered by the local “Big Boys!” An opportunity sadly missed on my part!

Total mileage Ayr to Bolton and back: 421.6 Miles
Total time taken to complete the journey 7Hours 54Min

Spot the young Mick McManus?

Evan Armstrong

Kath Hellcat Haggetty & Naughty Nancy Barton

Jackie “Mr TV” Pallo

(Courtesy of Robin Christie)

Young Starsky V a Kung Fu copy-cat.

Chic Purvey

CHAPTER THIRTYTWO

(The Metaphor 2 Armageddon: (The Big Finish!)

The internal Tannoy speaker crackles into life. “Right that's it they’ve finished six rounds most of it really boring shit!”

Annoyed at the derogatory and uncalled for comments Dale shouts some abuse at the intercom speaker! Cheeky Bastard! Another electronic message fills the room. “So you've got nothing much to follow, oh and by the way there's been a last minute change to the bill you're now working with local "Blue Eyed Boy" and ultimate ego tripper young Mickey Mackenzie now! The Boss told me to call him he's standing in at short notice the Cowboy's been taken ill again, he'll kill himself the way he goes on his liver's must be bleached white! You've got five minutes. Do yourself a favour, raise your game! These new guys can be a bit **“Tasty!”** [Not an ideal opponent if you want to look good for your public, no give and take! In another context also used to describe those who is really hard, no push over, as tough as old boots! Some in the know, might even use the term “Bloodboots!”] Or am I mixing my metaphors? Although you’d probably say “Stiff!” or useless! [Meaning very clumsy, dangerous, all flying knees and elbows, grabs hold of far too tightly] “He’s another one of new breed who’re really only interested in the promotion of themselves! Good Luck!”

Thanks a million Kid! Bloody metaphors and bloody Mackenzie both in the one night, cocky little bleeder! He's not that long in the bloody business, arsehole! Another back door job! Must have some friends in high bloody places maybe some relation? Father, brother pushing him that’s the way the business has been going for a few years now, it’s all very sad! He's only just moved up to the welterweights as well and he's hardly star material. He’s got no skin colour for a start and he's as thin as a rake, all bloody bones and best described as; a skinny wee "Knight in Shinning White Skin!" Twenty odd years ago they've have put him in a Sanatorium for Rickets or Tuberculosis or something**!..........Why are you looking at me like that?**

Is that a problem you facing this McKenzie chap?

Well yes as a matter of fact it is a problem presentation wise if nothing else. In this particular case seeing will be something you won't necessarily want to believe. He'll never be able to sell it, even if he wanted too and he seldom does. Besides he's far too light for the likes of me!

What's wrong with that every business needs new blood to evolve it's an organic thing, what's wrong with new faces?

I'm repeating myself here but here we go again! I'll tell you exactly what's wrong with it, shall I? They don't work because a lot of them can't work and they don't care about giving the public a real performance! They don't die long enough, sometimes not at all and they don't share the storyline, it's all about them! They're only interested in boosting their own profile, not the show and certainly not the business! They're all elbows and knees, no sense of timing and when it comes to working the crowd they take them up and up till they want to kill somebody, but that's not difficult a monkey could do that! But ask them to bring them back down again to a safe level you've got no chance! Even if they could, which they can't they won't! And ask them to string five or six basic moves together like real mat "Catch" wrestler and some of them are completely lost! However they do have one common thread and that's the biggest nonsense! They've all got a shinny new cheap looking plastic American style Championship Belt and most of them to date have never even won a bloody argument!

Have you ever won any Titles or a Championship then?

Ask him again ref!

Taking the opportunity Dale attempts to emulate Marlon Brando's famous speech in the back of the taxi cab from "On the Waterfront". **"I could've been a contender. I could've been somebody. I could've had class, instead of a bum, which is what I am! Let's face it!"** [A direct quote from the Academy Award Winning movie] Titles! Wrestling Titles is it? Well you can write this down if you've a mind too! The Scottish Lightweight Title! The British Welterweight Title! The European Middleweight Title! At one time I've held both the British Lightweight and European Welterweight Titles all at the same time. I gave up the British one undefeated and I used just the one black leather belt to cover the lot of them and nobody noticed! I struggled to make the weight limits after a time, well I got far more money the closer I got to Heavyweight and that made a lot of sense to me.

That's Five Titles in total! Are you boasting a little here?

Well if that's what you're telling me, you'll be correct! Some of these newer young guys they remind me of most of those Yanks, all muscles and very little real substance! They wouldn't look out of place on a lady-boys revue show with their Blonde Hair, High Heel Shoes Big Plastic Tit Implants! Thank God we don't have that load of crap over here in the UK! The WWF my bloody arse, although we could benefit from some of their organisational skills!..........

Dale's comments are interrupted by yet another Tannoy message: "He's already in there and he's winding up the crowd with all his usual nonsense! Stick your head out the door and have a listen!"

Having opened the dressing room door Dale stands there for a moment ear cocked. Listen to that useless wee shit he's all mouth, his bloody mother should have taken her hand off his backside more often!

Ask him again ref!

The wall mounted electronic commentator tries to encourage Dale to hurry. "You don't want to keep him or them out there waiting for to long they're in one of their funny moods tonight and so is he! Time to go old man! Emshay Bhalla and remember the Gaffer's early finish!

Again Dale shouts at the Tannoy. Aye Right! Hawd the bus I'm getting there, alright, turning apologetically to the reporter. Sorry hen. Right I'm ready now are you coming out to watch this nonsense or are you going to wait here?

I'll probably come out to watch it! How long will it take?

Shouldn't take much, I'll have to carry him for a round or two then I'll finish it in the third most probably!

About ten minutes to fifteen minutes then? OK I'll watch it.

Good let's go. You get the door will you? See you shortly.

Dale and the Reporter leave the dressing room, at the top of the stairs they part company, Dale descends the wooden staircase into the cauldron, the reporter tries to find some standing space among all the biz. She's hot, sweaty and thirsty so she decides to exits the hall.

Dale enters the ring, a noisy, baying for blood crowd express their opinions in a not so gentlemanly fashion. Announcements and the referee's pep talk concluded the ringing bell gets the pantomime underway. The crowd goes wild and so does his young opponent!

Only a few short minutes later Dale re-enters the dressing room area again, he's more than a little disoriented. Close behind although totally unobserved by the now beat up grappler walks a young female reporter. Dale's vest is ripped and blooded; his nose is badly bruised and bleeding! One eye is badly bruised

Ask him again ref!

and already darkening in colour, it's slowly closing. Blood streams from one of his ears. He's a total mess!

(The Genesis: Part Two)

The Reporter re-enters the dressing room from the toilet area.

Good God! Do you realize what that dozy wee Bastard's just done to the already dented image of the business! I did tell you earlier he wasn't safe! Stiff little shit! Didn't I say that earlier? I think I did? Didn't I? I can't remember now, did I say it was a miss-match!? Help me out here will you I'm a little lost, look at the state of me, what did he think he was doing it's not as if he's never seen me working before!

Are you trying to tell me this could be a Seed Change event? Maybe even a Watershed moment?

That's exactly what I'm saying but then again that seems to be the direction this whole business has been headed in!

Cui Bono!

Say again! More bloody Gobbledygook how appropriate!

No it's more Latin! Cui Bono, but you're not far wrong some might refer to it as Gobbledygook and yes it's appropriate it means "Who Benefits?"

Well you got me there girl! Everybody has their own style and their own opening and I always go for a walk around the ring, it really noises up the punters! That's what I do and I've been doing it for years now, ever since I went back to the mantel of Arch Villain! I'm the Bad Guy, the Heal if you prefer and that's what I always do! The punters know it and they expect it. Am I repeating myself here? God what's up with me? Look at the state of my gear stiff it's bloody ruined! I'll kill him! I've never been so bloody humiliated, and I got disqualified into the bargain! That's never happened here at the Eldorado my professional bloody reputation is in tatters! Dale sounds a little lost. Sorry did you say something? I can't bloody hear you now!

I didn't say a thing you're looking pale. Sure you're alright?

No! I'm ill, so I'm not bloody alright, do I look alright? My ear's still ringing it'll probably go Cauli-Bloody Flower! I could finish up looking like a caricature of Jake La Motta!

Jake who?

Sorry, you wouldn't know him he's an American boxer know as The "Brox Bull" a Middleweight he was as hard as nails but even he's taken a few beatings over the years. Bloody Drop-Kicks! Bloody three of them and bloody rapid, one after the bloody other and all before I've even got finished all my posing and preening stuff, how bloody unprofessional! The room falls strangely silent, eventually Dale speaks. What's that you're saying? Sorry ears again!

The referee was correct you left him with little choice!

Oh, is that what you're saying? OK he got it right within the laws he was technically correct. Yes, yes, happy now?

You were well out of order!

I probably was but I was left with very little choice in the matter! I was taught nothing gets in the way of the performance least of all his misplaced bloody ego!

Ego! Well that's rich!

Oh come off it what else could I do?

Ask him again ref!

Maybe not booting him in the Family Jewels for one thing!

Again OK yes, yes! Maybe you're right But he deserved it cocky little Wanker! Did you see that look on his face as he sank to the canvas, real pain! Now you don't see that very often in this game, I really enjoyed that bit! He! He! I take it all back, all that stuff I said earlier he did sell that part and really well too, credit where credit is due! I'll need to stop laughing even although it's cheering my up just a bit. It's just too bloody sore on my cheek bone. Three bloody "Drop-Kicks" he was spot-on with every one of them, the wee shit's been taking some lessons somewhere! One right on the bridge of the nose as well! I think he's bloody broken it! Another to my eye, not bloody funny and one on my ear, my bloody good ear as well! My head bouncing off that metal turnbuckle joint in the corner didn't help it caught my other bloody eye. God it's painful my heads killing me!

Moving to the mirror Dale makes another comment regards his damaged face. Look at the state of my eye it'll be completely closed in the next half hour, he did that intentionally! I'm supposed to be working almost every night next week and on top of all I've got a TV recording in Leeds! It'll be the main support bout on next Saturday's "World of Sport" transmission! What was that? Sorry I'm getting even deafer here, what was it you said?

Why didn't you mention the TV appearance stuff before!

Unlike him, I've really not into all that ego stuff anymore! Actually, I was saving it, it was going to be a surprise for later. I was keeping it till the end of the bout. The Big Finish after the Big Finish so to speak! Obviously I had something different in mind like him sticking to the script maybe!

But how did you know what was to happen in there, no one came near the dressing room.

Ask him again ref!

Easy! The Ref. gave me the script when I got in there. I was "Going Over" in the Forth Round, he was getting nothing after all as I said earlier, he's far too small and beside he's got no hard earned history! He's still got to serve an apprenticeship and know his bloody place! I had to go through all that years ago, nobody in charge really cares anymore it's all bollocks now and all that shit in there has just makes my point for me. It's all just fucked up now!

Try and calm down will you please! Sit down, take some deep breaths! Better now? A trip to Casualty might be a good idea what do you say?

No bloody chance I've already told you, I'm alright!

OK just try to relax, let's change the subject shall we? Tell me more about the television stuff. Who's on etc.

You could come down as my special guest if you're available that is? It's not all that far from here just down the A1. I'm on with Peter Preston and that'll be a cracker he's a really good guy and a great wee worker. No Hanky Panky intended honest to God. You can get the rest of your storyline when you're down there we'll have more time then. It's being filmed on Wednesday night. Can we leave it there for now please? God my heads really hurting now and my eyes beginning to sting even more, maybe we could get a pint once I've had a shower, what do you say?

Well ok but just the one!

Before you say it, you're driving! Glad that's sorted then!

Are we going over the road?

Cousin's bar, no not tonight they'll all be gathering in there, we'll give it a miss! Not with me looking like this, we'll nip along to "Berry's" [One of two main pubs in Leith used by the wrestlers] place instead hopefully it'll be less busy. We can get a seat in the corner away from the television. I'll meet you at your car, where are you parked?

I'm in behind the State Cinema.

Good thinking makes sense, what kind of motor is it? No don't tell me let me tell you! It'll be small and probably Red and White with a Union Flag painted on the top!

How did you know it would be a Mini?

It's not hard to work that out, maybe the retro white Kinky Boots you're wearing were a giveaway? Might even be an Avengers fan, would that be Emma Peel or Tara King?

Actually it's Cathy Gale! An auntie gave me the car, the boots and a Mary Quant Black and White Bag. I spent quite a bit of money on restoration but it's looking great and it turns more than a few heads on Princes Street.

Never! Well that doesn't surprise me so naturally you prefer you're Martini stirred and not shaken? Is that right Miss Money-Penny? This whole scenario reminds me of a scene from a James Bond film. "Do you expect me to talk?" [Direct quote from the film From Russia with Love]

Jumping in the reporter finishes the lines. *"No Mr. Bond I expect you to die!"* [Another direct quote from the script]

Well done that was word perfect.

I've seen all the movies several times so far, I'm a big fan.

If it's a trendy wee Cooper S why don't you try and get hold of one of those 007 number plates. Wouldn't that be great?

Of course it's a Cooper, not sure about the plates though.

Ask him again ref!

They'll be long gone? Anyway that's just a bit over-the-top!

Silly old me you're probably right! OK you shoot off then.

Are you sure you're going to be ok? How's your head now?

Easing a bit, I'll be fine. I'll only be about fifteen or twenty minutes, maybe. Don't suppose you've got any of that foundation make-up stuff in your bag have you?

No self respecting girl travels without her war paint!

Given what I've just been through, that's not the best choice of words but I forgive you. Can I borrow it please? Leave it on the bench when you go. I'm in need of a wee touch up, I'll return it later!

Sure thing! Right I'm off see you! Enjoy your shower!

Oh and don't forget the pain killers as well, remember I asked about them earlier?

Before leaving the room the reporter places the make-up plus a foil containing some headache pills on the bench.

There you are I hope your headache clears soon? See you at the car.

No sooner had the reporter left closing the door when there's another badly timed message from the wall speaker. *"The Gaffer says thanks for the early finish but it wasn't in the Script. You were supposed to give it your all for four rounds then take the win 2 to Zero! You never got out of first gear and the Disqualification was never on! The punters are up in arms it's them who pay all our wages!"*

Dale shouts back at the Tannoy System: And what about the wee bastard that caused the whole bloody mess?

Ask him again ref!

"The Boss is ragging he blames you says you're the experienced man, you should handle it better and for that lack of professionalism you're forfeit a wage reduction!"

Tight Bastard! There was nothing I could do he was the one who went off script, he was the one who didn't let me get my stuff in and he was the one who messed up! I didn't get a bloody chance to turn things around! I was the one who got bloody ambushed mate, and bloody big time!

The second part of the message sings out. *"Your opponent will live thankfully! His "Rumpy-Pumpy" might be curtailed for a day or two but then again knowing the Michael boy as I do, I doubt that very much. By the way he sends his regards asked me to pass on best wishes for your trip down to rural Yorkshire and the Television Show. Says by the time the cameras start rolling you'll be looking like a Million Dollars! As for the damage to your gear his only comment was to add "Well its just one of those things, it happens so get over it!" he recons the punters loved it!*

Thanks for nothing! You're just yet another Smart Bastard!

"Oh just one more thing, the Gaffer has suspended your work indefinitely! Till further notice Brother Mackenzie will now be taking over all your remaining appearance dates!"

Cocky Bastard! Cui Bono! So now we know who benefits! What a bunch of back stabbers!

"Oh and no point appealing at a higher level, anyway the Gaffer's a pal of the Head Bummer as you will already be aware, so it'll be a total waste of time!"

Strewth! That's shot the Fox I never saw that one coming. The announcer signs off on a down note. *"You can pick your money up, what's left of it that it at the Box Office on the way out. They're all over at **"Cousin's"** having a wee* *refreshment. I'm just heading over there myself we probably won't be seeing you there, will we? Well you won't have enough cash left to get your round in. Will you?"*

Your boss must love you, you sycophantic little Bastard! Looking in the mirror, shaking his head in disbelief Dale makes another comment. Unlucky old bastard you too have now become another victim of the clearout. Shafted and Drafted! Double crossed and dumped onto the scrap heap! No wonder the other guys have been jumping ship in droves the job is completely fucked, ruined by those who should know better and a few young upstarts who are so blinkered and driven on by the prospect of a fifteen minute television slot sadly they don't really know any better. Oh and one or two overweight folks who do know a lot better but who just don't seem care about this wonderful business anymore! Well it happens, you're not the first and you certainly won't be the last so get over yourself. Good God you're beginning to sound like that wee schemer Mackenzie. It'll be back over the divide to the Independents for me then. Well that's where you started so it won't be so bad! Shit, who am I kidding? No it'll be OK they're bound to be queuing up to get somebody with my drawing power and ring reputation back on their circuit once the word gets out! The phone will be red hot might even get a call from Brian Dixon we can renew old acquaintances. You've always gotten on well with him, one slight problem area although he's a good payer I'll still have to take a drop in the kind of money I'm on right now and I'll have to travel further afield, in fact all over the bloody place! God, motorway bloody madness and with petrol prices going through the roof I'll have even less spending money in my pocket! Big Lil will definitely be less than pleased what a bloody mess. Worst still no more Saturday Afternoon Television appearances so I'll probably have to put the Boarding House Pension Plan idea on hold for a few more years as well. God I hope this make-up stuff covers these bruises, need to look my best in the pub don't want to spoil my image. Well you never know who might be in there, do you. Placing his hand in his trouser pocket, he takes out what few coins are in there, he studies the contents of his hand before making one final comment. “You poor misguided wee bastard McKenzie what have you and your kind, self-centred egotists the lot of you, done to what used to be a very popular, truly wonderful totally entertaining sport?”

Fin

“Maktub”

مكتوب

[It is written]

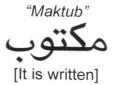

My Personal Hall of Fame

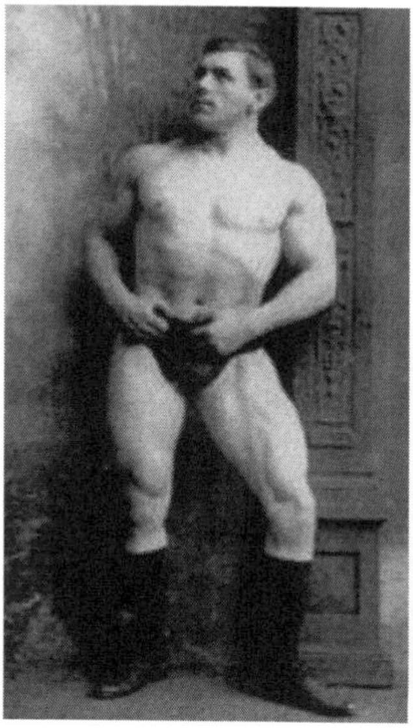

Robinson **Hackenschmidt** **Gordienko**

Three world class Catch Wrestling Icons every one of whom left their own unique mark on its long history.

Thank You Chapter!

(We were not alone, thank God!)

Although we in Scotland had our own domestic circuit run for the most part by smaller local operators and almost entirely manned by native Scots wrestlers. The addition of the odd guest Englishman, Irishman or Welshman to work the crowd and to give the proceedings more of a UK feel by way of there strong regional non Scots accents was a vital ingredient when putting a show together. I was always conscious that we needed more interaction with the crowd in the sense of we were always in danger of becoming a sound-a-like outfit, but unlike some of today's performers the folks who worked for me would never have been allowed (unless instructed to do so) to grab hold of a microphone from out of the hand of the only sensibly equipped person who had anything to say that had any relevance to the show. Egos were definitely not permitted to raise their disruptive head! It was of course always hopefully good for business to have at least one top name on your posters, more so if they were known from being seen on television, although occasionally that idea could backfire when expected ticket sales failed to materialise. The cost of backing the wrong horse so to speak could be a bit of a outlay too far and most of your already tight profit margin could disappear very quickly! People like The Wild Man of Borneo [Gunga Singh] for instance did no extra business on any show of mine. Sadly he just didn't have what it took in charisma terms to put more bums on seats as a so called TV name when I billed him. Although to be fair his appearances on the box had been few and far between. He would of course choose to blame the lack of interest in him as down to some inadequate advertising or the poor footfall position of the venue or the quality of the supporting wrestlers. None of these excuses were of course valid as all the support, myself included, had good performance skills and credible reputations build up in

Scotland over many years. As for the advertising, the "Fly Posting" and the press pre-publicity had all been handled personally by yours truly and I had been taught by the best.

Adrian Street's drawing power was the exact opposite I could have filled even bigger halls had I had even more access to his services, but he was very popular with promoters and public alike and was therefore very busy. He was always in demand although compared to most of those promoting out-with the main Independent Circuit I got shows spots regularly filled by more Big Stars than most.

Jackie Pallo was the same he never failed to add substantial numbers to box office queues. He of course wanted and got what he considered to be his worth in the market place and he was correct I never shared an angry word with Jack in all the time I knew him.

Andy Robin was the same he always filled halls and he always gave the crowd what they'd come to see, although things did not always go to plan and there could be some unforeseen consequences but that's just Andy. Crowds everywhere especially in Scotland loved him to bits and why not. He's an immensely well muscled and very strong individual with a veneer of granite but beneath all that beats a compassionate and a caring heart. I once asked him and a few others if they would care to get involved in a Big Charity Show, the proceeds of which were to go in there entirety, to help fund a medical trip to America for a young girl from Tarbolton Ayrshire suffering from a severely debilitating, life threatening illness. I took the view a successful crowd factor element would be almost guaranteed if I could get him on board. He accepted gladly and we were off and running. A substantial cheque was later gratefully received by her mother for a job well done.

Joe Critchley, Eddie Rose, The Harlequins, Big Ian Miller, Bull Wilson, Bruce Welch, Jeff Bradley the masked duo of

The Viking and The Scorpion all volunteered their services. The Referee was Gerry Carol. Both I and the child's parents will always be grateful for the Christian generosity shown by everyone who gave of their time on that truly magic night in the Ballroom of the Caledonian Hotel in Ayr.

Jack Cassidy especially in the 1960's was always a guaranteed earner. His Cowboy persona; the hat and especially the six guns use to send the crowd wild and when he started to use his ring villainy to effect the punters were up in arms. He had them just where he wanted them.

Eddie Rose one of the most versatile workers anywhere was always able to give you anything you asked of him. He helped me out regularly by adopting some Leon Ares style "Patter" He always gave me lots of his good solid Lancashire accent whether he was playing it straight and clean or as a rule bending bad guy. Over the years Eddie developed quite a following in Scotland among fans and peers alike, a testament to his very friendly interpersonal skills and his wonderfully easy going warm temperament.

Another man hailing from just over the Saddleworth Moor from Eddie in Yorkshire was Sam Betts aka "Dwight J. Ingleburgh" billed almost all his wresting career as an American. He of course had both the height and also the physic to carry it off. Sam boasted a very muscular body and he stood several inches over six feet tall. He worked in Scotland a lot in places like the Eldorado in Leith Edinburgh. Top pro turned promoter George Kidd booked him regularly as did Peter Keenan. He is also up there with only a handful in the UK when in comes to the number of overseas tours he undertook and for he calibre of International opposition he **"Knocked off."** As well as regular European ventures his other treks saw him headlining in the Middle Eastern Tournaments where the opposition could be particularly tough. Sam never backed down and he took on all comers, he's a truly lovely man and a real gentleman. He was born in Barnsley and at one time he worked in the "Booths" the length and breadth of England. He's still a very humble man for all his years of experience and his top class CV. He is however a man who's rightly proud of his strong Yorkshire Coal Mining roots. He was later conscripted into the British Army and given his height he wore the uniform of the Guards with pride but strangely it was in the Irish variety. He also spent sometime in the Merchant Service. Sam had trained as a boxer as a youth before joining the famous "Charley Glover" gym situated round the back of the "Junction Pub." Sadly he never appeared on my shows but nevertheless he graced every canvas he ever worked on. Unless my memory is playing tricks with me I also remember working with another Glover train wrestler name of Harry Bennett during my early years? [Sam regularly attends the Leeds Wrestling Re-Unions every spring and autumn and it's always my great pleasure to talk over old times with him.]

Joe Critchley was another who like Sam Betts worked in both in the mines and also on the Travelling Booths Circuit. He too had honed his skills in a good solid catch gym in Billy Riley's now world famous "Snake Pit" as some of these pages will testify. Joe holds a very special place in both my memory and my heart and I will never forget the debt I owe to both him and memorable times we spent together As well as being one of Wigan's finest he was one of life's real gentlemen. Any show he attended for me was always all the better and all the more professionally staged for him gracing the canvas

Ezra Francis was another about whom I could wax lyrical all day and all night but perhaps given the memories I now carry in my head it really only remains for me to reiterate he was unique. He was a good pal to all, a great character and a wonderful performer. Audiences everywhere warmed to him the minute he entered the ring but no more so than in Scotland. Again in every sense of the word my shows would not have been anything like as colourful had I not recruited his services. Rural areas especially would probably never have had the chance to see and appreciate his very special qualities had he not toured with Spartan.

Mark Wayne "Prince Charming" to his mates and Ian Wilson were and still are good friends from the past both of whom being introduced to me and my set-up by Eddie Rose. Mark was more the showman perhaps where as Ian gave off an aura of a more solid amateur style training regime. Mark worked as an engineer and as well as his pre-arranged appearances for me, occasionally he'd be in Scotland on a maintenance contract brief and would call me to see if I had anything on the go where he could slid in. I always made room for him as I considered him to be not only a good solid performer but a really nice man into the bargain. Ian on the other hand appeared mostly in a red bonnet as one of Les Diablo Rouges aka "The Red Devils" Tag Team. Although not a founder member he took over a year after its formation from Pete Lindberg. He like others who came up to Scotia skirted around the margins between the Indies and Joints thinking they could perhaps operate to some degree unnoticed by the main players in The Joints Organisation and to a large extent they did till they got caught out and were then given the ultimatum which usually meant them immediately falling back into line. Among those fairly regularly chastised were the likes of another good pal Jim Moser, who I first encountered when we both worked for Danny Flynn although at the very least he used to bill him under a cessation of different names to keep him under Joints radar. Jim however hated most of these aliases; handles like "Sugar Ray Dodo" which Ezra Francis worked under as well and "Joe Co-Co" were hardly acceptable back then and would definitely not be allowed nowadays in this now overly controlling PC world. Jim was good for Scotland and again Scotland was good for him but only until he too got found out, yet again and got the warning letter from Joints. Other associated shows featured such greats as Les Kellett, what more could I add to what's already been said many times over about this great son of York. Not a lot except to repeat "I liked the man immensely." Coming from a hard working class environment like he did, I for one can fully appreciate why he might get a little annoyed if he felt someone was letting the business down. He was a very dedicated man, a true professional and to the punters he was just fantastic.

Billy Two Rivers also graced a few of those Bills and he always went down a storm (pun intended) in Scotland and I for one fully accept the fact he was Canadian had a lot to do with it. After all we on this side of the Atlantic clearly feel almost everyone over there must have originated somewhere in Scotland and quite a number obviously did. Although as far as I'm aware we can't really lay any claim to having a Highland based Two Rivers Clan!

Liverpool born Buddy Ward [Alf Woodward] was another frequent visitor to the halls up here in the 1960's. In fact one of my very first contests was against him. I learned a lot from being in the ring with such an outstanding worker.

Johnny Saint was a particularly skilful star with the Indie Promoters for many years in fact long before he ever appeared on our TV screens. Johnny had been introduced to the grappling world and was schooled in the correct manner which always showed anytime he entered the ring.

Ray Glendenning and Mickey Gold were another two who graced our rings and both worked for Joints at one time or another. Mr Gold signed up with Arthur Wright's, Wryton's Promotions early on and spent most of his formative years in the business working for Joints, then he moved to the Indies. Raymond's journey went in the opposite direction and he finished up working for Joints on a more regular basis during the second half of his career after leaving the Indies. [Raymond sadly died in 2007] These two men

made regular visits to both the Central Belt and also the Highlands over the years. Again I worked with both of them regularly. Ray in the 1960's mostly and Mickey in the 70's.
Ian Gilmour and Jeff Kaye who worked together as a Tag Team also made frequent visits to Scotland and in Ian's case it was a bit of a home coming because he was born in Scotia's South West. These two guys worked exclusively for Joints from the start and only after it all started to fall apart in the 1980's did Ian move over almost full-time to the Independents. They had worked constantly for folks like Morrell and Beresford, deRelwyscow and Green and Max. They could be seen in halls as far apart as Ayr, Edinburgh, Kilmarnock, Stirling and Dumfries. Again I pulled round with both these guys for Joints and it goes without saying they'd had the best of training and learned their trade well.

Others who travelled long distances on the shocking sub standard road system in Scotland in the 1950's and 60's have to be specially congratulated for making the effort. People like Danny Flynn, Freddie Woolley, "Gentleman" Jim Lewis, Lord Berti Topham, Pete Lindberg, Bob Sweeney, Jim Armstrong, Bob Sherry, Johnny South and the original British Undertaker, Top Hat Tailcoat and genuine Wooden Coffin in tow, Ian St. John, Johnny Saint, Chief Thunderbird, Gordon Corbett, Dennis Savage, Paul Luty. My old sparing partner John "Gypsy" Kenny, we go back a long, long way now. He's a really nice lad and a great guy to work with as well. Crusher "Butch" Mason, Bobby Graham, Judd Harris, Gordon "Klondyke Bill" Lythe and Barry Hawkins his one time Tag partner "Klondyke Jake" and also tough Yorkshire born and bred submission specialist and all round very, very nice man Mr Eric Taylor.
In the 1970's transport had improved somewhat and we were then visited by father Eric's two sons Steve and Dave and many more far too numerous to mention. Dave "Fit" Finlay also cut some of his early professional teeth on the Scottish circuit long before he went over to Joints and thereafter moving across the Atlantic to continue his career

in the USA. The worse thing for fans in Scotland and of course in the rest of the UK as well was someone billed to appear and then for some reason they failed to show up! On some occasions genuine injury may well have prevented appearances, in a contact sport these things are inevitable but thankfully didn't occur that often. Joints in the main did't resort to billing somebody whom they already knew was not going to be there but sadly the same cannot always be said for some of the Indie guys. One or two were almost incapable of telling the truth on many occasions and they were sometimes less than honest men in other ways some have alleged! One in particular who at one point ran almost everything in the land of the "Heather covered Mountains" and the home of the "Water of Life" was nearly always what we Celts like to refer too as a bit of a rogue and a "Right Chancer!" He was particularly notorious for two things; one regularly exporting our Scottish based "Tennent's Lager" in large quantities in the boot of his car back to the "The land of our Father's" and two; for ripping off those with innovative, very popular new ring personas especially of the mask variety. He then filled these copy costumes with journeymen, overly star struck fakes. The exception to this would probably have been amiable Al Miquet and Leeds based Ian Gilmour who both acted out with some aplomb the Kung Fu character unashamedly stolen from Emerald Islander martial arts mat man and the character's rightful copyright owner Mr Eddie Hamill.

Many Ladies also enhanced the ring north of Hadrian's Wall folks like already mentioned Naughty Nancy Barton, Mitzi Mueller, and Klondike (Jayne) Kate, not forgetting Hell Cat Haggetty and her smaller ever smiling sibling Lolita Loren. The Cherokee Princess, Rita Shillito, Paula Valdez, Susan Sexton, Blackfoot Sioux and Jackie McCann who is one of Britain's best researched and fully informed wrestling historians. Her wide knowledge of the operators of the travelling Showground "Booths" is particularly invaluable. Also Ms Anne Barton who due to an early attack of stage fright missed out on the persona she was originally trained to fill. We north of the border were lucky enough to have inherited one of the best MC's ever in my opinion in the form of Mr Peter G. Baines, an original son of Essex who lived and worked in Renfrewshire and who brightened up all the Shows he ever appeared on. I can't however conclude my list of afore mentioned Ring Goddesses without paying some homage to the Scot's based "Mossblown Gym" trained ladies who graced my shows. Paramount among them is the real "Gaffer" the one and the only Diamond Lil! **Deepest thanks are conveyed to each and everyone, especially those who were not mentioned above. Without you the Scottish Wrestling scene would have been a far less interesting forum.**

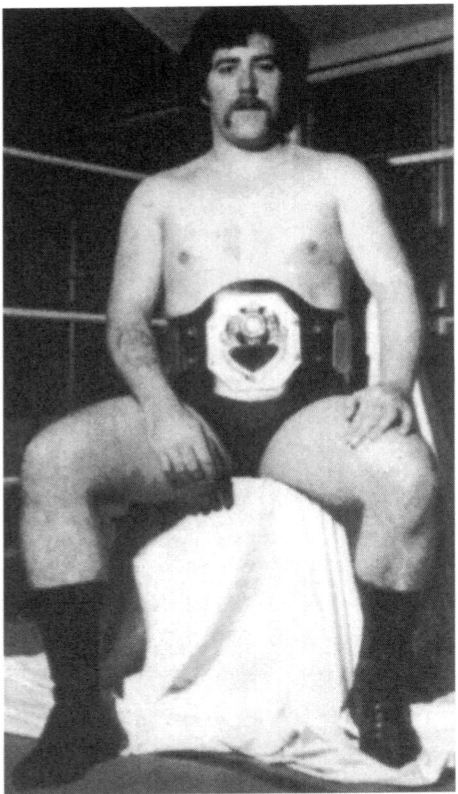

(Courtesy of Andrew Brodie-Frew)

Me the moustache and the title belt

The Epilogue

When I started out on this literary journey I wanted to make it clear to all where my political and my trade union leanings lay. It was my attempt at trying to show why I've always respected my wrestler peers as men and woman. Whether I rated some as performers is entirely another matter. Now that I have almost completed my opus which I hope you'll enjoy I would now like to take this opportunity to further enlighten you. I am not the only wrestler who is or was proud of the fact he'd been a long standing trade union member. I'm honoured to inform you "Michael" William George Mathews "McManus" was also a trade unionist of long standing and in fact he held the distinction of being awarded "Life Membership" status for his long and unbroken service in actors "Equity" I too have held a card in this professional organisation for many a long year now.

Almost as I finished these pages the debate as to whether we in the UK should now be demanding the total return to our halls and possibly our television screens of the proper British Style of Wrestling has raised its head again, led in no small part by some with more than a passing financial interest it its reinstatement! Naturally if it were possible I too would want to see its triumphant resurrection but rather sadly any attempt would be all to no avail and for one very simple reason. The structure that existed UK wide and in the main had operated largely unchanged until the end of the 1970's start of 1980's has long since died a death. There are no longer the large numbers of properly trained workers in any of the regions of Britain as there was back then. Sadly most of those who originally schooled these Grappling Gladiators are almost all, fond but sadly largely distant memories now and most of the better Gyms who taught and who nurtured the traditional British style are now no longer in existence either.

Anyway the true British genre had already started down the

road of a Crossover Hybrid Style becoming far more glitzy and Americanised to some extent by the end of the 1970's. This trend continued to gather pace and it dominated even more in the early to late 1980's. Almost all the new guys who entered the business in that period rather sadly had little or no real knowledge of the old and proper style and worse still, some of those who started teaching during that time scale, especially in the 80's and who have since taken up promoting, once again using the hybrid style had, had little or no real experience of working in our traditional sport's "Golden Era" of 1955 to around1975.

Sadly all that would happen would be a period of initial hype followed by euphoria, followed by a short series of shows featuring those old stagers still in some kind of physical shape. After that initial burst those putting the shows together would very quickly run out of new and different old style trained faces, if any actually exist in the UK today? Who among these usurpers would have the charisma, the story telling ability or the screen presence of an Adrian Street or a Jackie Pallo or indeed the ability of most of the many regulars who had at one time graced all our TV screens and our high equally popular live wrestling shows! Only to be posted missing for most of the 1980's having felt it necessary to leave Joints, the original television franchise owners clearly openly frustrated by the way the business was being run and being equally badly projected by some sadly second-rate ring-men at that time.

Of the rather negative points raised in the previous paragraph the most important one must surely be the "Story Telling Element" a basic and essential ingredient which is sadly lacking in almost all of the bouts I have personally witnessed from the British New-Wave regime!

Changing the focus slightly, rather inexplicably three standout common denominators present in most of the better workers of yesteryear which now seems to have been overlooked by many others were: Membership of the Royal Air Force, a Mechanical Engineering qualification or a Coal Mining background. I've no idea why? How many I wonder of those who might "Pull Round" for our enjoyment on the small screen in this the digital age would be able to claim ownership of any of these elements? Rather reluctantly I would have to say the debate although always welcome is a bit of a waste of time as it would prove impossible to truly resurrect something that died well over 30 years ago now. Far better we who were actually there content ourselves with our fond memories of a distant past.

This Grappling Game Opus is dedicated to the memory of three of the best men it's been my great pleasure to know. One is my original mentor and employer Mr Danny Flynn. The second is my good friend and sometimes mentor, a true, a good and an honest man. Elgin Town's Big George McDonald! The other is a fellow gladiator; he was a really nice man who was always a really good friend to me as well as being a former Scottish Lightweight Champion. He too was an honest man who taught me a lot about many, many aspects of both the business and also the men who controlled it. He was quite simply one of Auld Scotia's favourite grappling sons Mr Jimmy McKenzie. Among other comrades who also deserve a mention; a fourth walks among us and he is still very much alive, thank God. His name is Eddie Rose and he is quite simply the nicest person I've ever met in Wrestling. The others are Mr Alan "Hack" Bamber of the (Wrestling Heritage site) another is his fellow administrator (Simon) Anglo-Italian. Without whose help and encouragement I very much doubt this memoir would ever have seen the light of day. Deepest, grateful and heart felt thanks for all your help, your selfless devotion to wrestling and its history and your treasured friendship....................Regards Dale Storm

My career was finally brought to an abrupt and somewhat painful conclusion in late 1980 on a show promoted by one of Scotland's finest and strongest performers "The Bear Man" Andy Robin. There is perhaps another story yet to be written in there somewhere but its best left for another time and another place and almost certainly another author?

It was just one of those things but nevertheless it was a totally avoidable accident. Had we been living in the litigious world of today things might have been a lot different? The person responsible for building the ring that fateful night got it wrong Big Time! Lax construction when laying down the one inch thick plywood ring boards caused one of them to spring up. Invariably this meant the unfortunate formation of a rock solid bone crushing ridge! Consequently a usually safe throw routinely executed hundreds of times previously without any fear of injury, on this one unfortunate occasion resulted in some severe spinal damage requiring major surgery. [**Dale has been in almost constant pain ever since but being a true pro he holds no ill will and holds no one responsible**]

(Courtesy of Robin Christie)

Andy Robin applying the Power-Lock

My Conclusions

With the benefit of hindsight if such a long and varied career had to finish better it ended in the presence of a real gentleman, a wonderful worker and a true professional not some overweight, huffing and puffing jumped up usurper. The venue was one of my favourite halls where on that night as always the large crowds were vocally supportive and very appreciative, just like they'd always been in the Hamilton Town Hall. Although my career came to a finish the business UK wide was still fairly healthy and buoyant at that time. Shortly thereafter however the expansion of satellite broadcaster Sky and its total introduction of the American style with its extravaganza of performance known at that time as WWF, along with the decision of the head of Independent Television Sport to axe the still reasonably popular Saturday wrestling slot, were two huge body blows from which our industry was doomed never to recover its glory days! Perhaps if Mr Jackie Pallo had succeeded in his bid to secure the television franchise from under the noses of those who were taking it nowhere then our wonderful sport could have been saved to emerge hopefully even stronger than it had been just a few years previously. Destined once again to become a real staging post for proper, clever wrestlers who entertained as opposed to the overweight nonsense that had slowly and predictably strangled the skill and real performance values which ultimately proved to be wrestling's eventual undoing. This folly is now widely acknowledged by most former ring men as the real cause behind grappling's premature and sad demise, done to death and maybe mercilessly put out of its self imposed misery by the former working class lad now New Labour Supporter "Who had done good for himself" in the world of TV broadcasting and who is now widely regarded by many real socialist and real wrestlers alike as the opportunistic, ladder climbing non-socialist back stabbing New Labour supporter Gregory Dyke.

On 9th November 1955 when the ring lights were first switched on in The West Ham Baths and British Traditional Wrestling was first aired under the ATV Weekend Programming Franchise and Francis St. Clair Gregory faced Mike Marino flowed by Cliff Beaumont aka (Belshaw) verses Bert Royal who would have thought our sport would take off and generate some of the biggest audience figures ever seen, week after week in the history of British Television Broadcasting!

It must be noted however and sadly this fact has been overlooked by many writers and commentators and not commonly known by most of the fans of Joints. **"Not all the best British wrestling performers appeared on TV!"** Even the great Johnny Saint who started out with the same mentors as I did in the late1950's was for many years a top Independent draw. He did not suddenly improve out of all recognition when he moved to Joints but their production values most definitely did. He was always a good guy and a great worker, he just got more exposure. Mike Marino also worked for Independent promoters most notably Paul Lincoln. [He died in August1981 returning from Folkestone]

Wrestlers are Entertainers: Actors, Acrobats and Comedians and as in all these other show-business genres we've always borrowed from each other. Folks in wrestling have always had a tendency to copy new, innovative and creative holds and that's always been perfectly acceptable. The difficulty arises however not when someone can do it better, like "Mike Eagers" out-bridging "Adrian Street" live on Saturday afternoon television and the crowd going crazy. It only becomes a problem when those who steal a trick or a move you had previously borrowed from someone else and you can do it really well, because you've worked on it night after night in the gym to perfect it, you might even have improved it slightly. Things start to go wrong when the usurpers are not good at the execution of a

stolen move, but still they continue to use it. Thus they bring down the long term standards established over many, many years. Sadly when that happens and boring rapidity sets in the public are then liable to be turned off by the low skill repetitiveness being displayed by some members of the genre. What I observe in a lot of the modern Anglo/American Crossover Style is this very factor. Far too often the bouts are all the same, they share the same time frame, the same constant nonsense microphone garble and almost always repeated identical moves inevitably performed in the same order. Apart from occasionally spectacularly executed, flying sequences everything else is very disappointing and very boring!

Sadly the demise or retirement of almost all the Joint Promotions "Old Guard" in such a relatively short space of time meant real disappoint for many wrestlers who through their hard work had helped make their family fortunes. The fact there was no real will among our former gaffer's offspring to carry on with what had for many, many years previously been successful family business ventures, their total capitulation and their blatant acceptance of "The Thirty Pieces of Silver" meant they'd sold out their hard working, faithful grappling workforce completely! Meaning the future and hopefully the continued popularity of TV's Grunt & Groan was now under the stewardship of Max Crabtree, his younger brother Brian and what was even more worrying their now "Top Hat" wearing entirely rebranded but still not entirely peer rated, failed former Independent performer older brother Shirley! The senior sibling had now assume a new identity as "Big Daddy" becoming in the process the totally manufactured hero of the kids in the main although some of their parents became totally brainwashed also. Unfortunately the passage of time meant many began to see through the over the top hype and the lack of any real wrestling ability and decided to vote with not only their feet and far more importantly with their TV Remote buttons as they tuned their television sets over to another channel! What's even sadder is the fact none of the siblings then in charge shared to any extent any of the talent, the expertise or the vision of men like: **Billy Sandow**, **Ed "Strangler" Lewis** or **"Toots" Mont"** better known collectively in the world wide recorded history of wrestling industry as the now famous **"Gold Dust Trio!"**

The book which features this now famous threesome "Fall Guys" also uses the rather apt phrase "The Barnum's of Bounce" to describe those who were the grapping stars of their day in what was, even in those early years a very successful, financially strong part of the US entertainment business. Barnum was of course one of the globe's first and most successful Travelling Circus owners. Recognised the world over as a master of the psychology of being able to produce and promote a product the thrill seeking public were happy to pay their hard earned cash to come and see. These were the men who in the mid 1920's in the STATES were among the first of the eventual worldwide cartels to realise the full potential of putting together a format and an organisation structure in order to control wresting in a large, profit making business sense. Even in today's market place in the USA it still maintains huge sport and entertainment sector profits. Much more about these American pioneers can be gleaned from this very well informed, well crafted publication written by Marcus Griffin and published by Reilly & Lee Co Chicago in 1937. Originally out of print it is now available on line from Argos Classic Reprints.

Before closing this opus it's appropriate I think to mention some of the modern **"Catch"** exponents who graced our rings in Britain. **Billy Robinson** is one and again it goes without saying he was trained by the legendary Billy Riley in Wigan's Snake Pit Gym. He was one of the toughest all-time "Shooters" ever to grace UK mats. His record either as a pro exponent or in the armature style stands up to scrutiny on any level. He has gone on to train several freestyle champions over the years. He is still vey well regarded all over the world, especially in Japan. Another European born individual only mentioned briefly [Photo included at the bottom of page 38 was another of the world class grapplers who also trained with Billy Riley in Lancashire] A name change saw him enter the pro ranks as "**Karl Gotch.**" Born Karl Istaz in Antwerp Belgium in 1924 He grew up in Hungary although he represented Belgium when wrestling in London's Olympics in 1948. Thereafter determined to make it big as a pro he sought the help of the master Mr Riley. Gotch trained in Wigan for a period in the 1950's and from there the new persona of "Karl Krauser" emerged to take on the elite of Europe, where he was a feared as a very competent submission hold specialist. [Karl Gotch passed away in 2007] The last man in the trio has been deliberately left to the end quite simply because although many would argue the merits of the aforementioned duo as being giants in their field none were physically as big or as potentially capable as **George Gordienko**. He was born in Winnipeg Manitoba Canada on January 7th 1928. He was trained in Minneapolis USA by another well respected shooter "Joe Pazandak" George toured the world and fought in Germany, Iran, India and Saudi Arabia against the likes of the Bohlus Brothers and also Dara Singh, he also visited Australia. He was resident in London for many years and graced many British rings. During this time he developed a love of painting, he was a devoted follower of Picasso and he painted in the styles of the Cubists and the Surrealists and like his hero his paintings are now highly prized fetching large sums at auction. A fellow pro once told me they'd shared a car on the journey from London down to Southampton, George had asked if it was ok to go a bit earlier as he wanted to catch the light. All was revealed when they stopped at a very scenic viewpoint where the big Canadian set up his easel and quickly mapped out a scene which incorporated some Poplar trees. Those briefest of moments standing watching the fine brushwork being applied by those huge hands convinced his passenger he too should give it a go. His name was Peter Preston and he's become quite an accomplished artist himself ever since. I'm very glad to say I have two of his works hanging proudly in my home both presents from my good friend. On leaving the UK George moved to northern Italy and lived there for many years with the love of his life Christina Tassou, a stunningly good looking lady descended from Greek aristocracy whom he'd met years before in Athens. In later years he returned home to his beloved scenic Canada. [George Gordienko died in 2002 in Victoria British Columbia] Another connection shared by all three grapplers is they all wrestled as crowd pulling headliners in the USA. Robinson and Gotch later took up permanent residency in America. [Billy Robinson lectured worldwide until his sad demise at home in Little Rock, Arkansas USA in Spring 2014 aged 75 RIP]

Without "Catch" Pro Wrestling would never have been possible and a great entertainment opportunity lost!

Some Snake Pit members, Billy Riley dark suit front row right. Joe Critchley four from the right on the very top row.

My opponent on that fateful night which effectively ended my career was in no way to blame for the incident and due to the pain delay factor, a natural consequence of warm and supple muscles still to experience the cooling down process, he [the man in the other corner] had showered and dressed in the adjacent changing room and had already left the now empty auditorium totally unaware anything was untoward. This was long before my now washed and aching body had revealed to me the fact that I had sustained a potentially very serious, physical injury. He [my opponent] was at that time and he still remains to this day a really good friend. He is none other than "Mr Peter Preston" a true and a dedicated professional to whom I definitely attribute no blame whatsoever.

This opus has been written about the British Style of Professional Wrestling and the people who practiced it faithfully. It's full of memories of my twenty, mostly happy years spent entertaining a grateful and an enthusiastic public who were happy to buy a ticket to watch me performing and in so doing they helped to support both myself and my family. For that gesture I shall always be eternally grateful. I've tried to give you a feel for the times I spent both in the ring and also in the company of good friends and clever colleagues. In as much as I might wish for the return of those heady days they have now been consigned to sporting history never to return. I always gave of my best I only hope it was good enough. Thank you for reading my literary work I truly only hope you enjoyed this two decade journey through a memorable part of my life.

A List of popular Scottish Wrestling Venues

Aberdeen (Music Hall) **Airdrie** (Town Hall) **Alloa** (Town Hall) **Arbroath** (Town Hall) **Ardrossan** (Civic Centre, **Annan** (Town Hall) **Avimore** (The Centre) **Ayr** (Ice Rink. The Dam Park Hall. Butlin's Camp) **Banff** (Town Hall) **Barrhead** (Town Hall) **Bathgate** (Town Hall) **Beith (**Town Hall) **Biggar** (Town Hall) **Brechin** (Town Hall) **Buckhaven** (Town Hall) **Buckie** (Town Hall) **Campbeltown** (Town Hall) **Castle Douglas** (Town Hall) **Clydebank** (Town Hall) **Coldstream** (Town Hall) **Couper Angus** (Town Hall) **Cowdenbeath** (Town Hall) **Cumbernauld** (Civic Centre) **Dalkeith** (Town Hall) **Dingwall** (Town Hall) **Dumfries** (Drill Hall) **Dundee** (Caird Hall) **Dunfermline** (Carnegie Hall) **Dunbar** (Town Hall) **Dunoon** (Town Hall) **East Kilbride** (Civic Centre) **Edinburgh** (Corn Exchange) **Elgin** (Town Hall) **Ellon** (Town Hall) **Eyemouth** (Town Hall) **Falkirk** (Town Hall, Ice Rink) **Forfar** (Town Hall) **Fort William** (Town Hall) **Fraserburgh** (Town Hall) **Girvan** (Picture House. Beach Pavilion) **Galashiels** (Town Hall) **Gartcosh** (Social Club) **Glasgow** (Kelvin Sports Arena,) **Glenrothes** (Town Hall) **Gourock** (Town Hall) **Govan** (Town Hall) **Greenock** (Town Hall) **Haddington** (Corn Exchange) **Hamilton** (Town Hall) **Hawick** (Town Hall) **Helensburgh** (Town Hall) **Huntly** (Town Hall) **Inverness** (Town Hall) **Invergordon** (Town Hall) **Inverurie** (Town Hall) **Irvine** (Drill Hall. Magnum Centre) **Paisley** (The Ice Rink, Town Hall) **Jedburgh** (Town Hall) **Kelso** (Town Hall) **Kilmarnock** (The Grand Hall) **Kirkcaldy** (Town Hall) **Lanark** (Town Hall) **Larbert** (Town Hall) **Largs** (Barrfield's Pavilion) **Leith** (The Eldorado) **Livingston** (Town Hall) **Lockerbie** (Town Hall) **Lossiemouth** (Town Hall) **Maybole** (Town Hall) **McDuff** (Town Hall) **Moffat** (Town Hall) **Montrose** (Town Hall) **Motherwell** (Town Hall) **Mussleburgh** (Brunton Theatre) **North Berwick** (Town Hall) **Newton Stewart** (Town Hall) **Oban** (Corran Hall) **Paisley** (Ice Rink) **Peebles** (Town Hall) **Peterhead** (Town Hall) **Penicuik** (Town Hall) **Perth** (Ice Rink. City Hall) **Port Glasgow** (Town Hall) **Port Seaton** (Pond Hall) **Renfrew** (Normandy Hotel) **Rothesay** (Pavilion) **Rosyth** (Town Hall) **Saltcoats** (Town Hall) **Selkirk** (Town Hall) **Stirling** (Albert Hall) **St. Andrews** (Town Hall) **Strathaven** (Town Hall) **Stranraer** (Picture House) **Tain** (Town Hall) **Thurso** (Town Hall) **Troon** (Walker Hall) **Wick** (Town Hall) and **Wishaw** (The Civic Centre)

A Small Selection of Old Wrestling Posters

(Courtesy of JA, WFGB, Relwyskow & Green, Cape, Spartan and Mr S Betts)

"It's a skilful sport of that there is no doubt. If you watch the good wrestlers you can see they have true skill and ability. I hope the time never comes when all that isn't there anymore and we are then left with only the gimmick stuff. We must avoid that day at all cost, because there can only one loser in that bout and that will be the very popular sport of pro wrestling!"

Kent Walton 1979

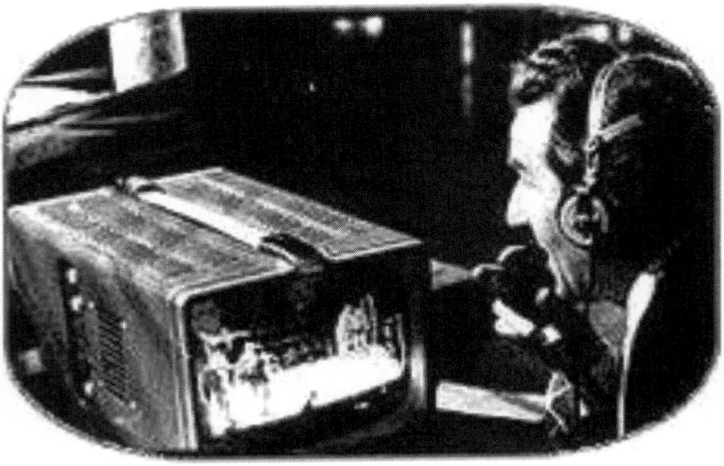

Dum Spero Spiro
(While I Breath I Hope)

Rear Cover: (main pictures courtesy of Mr Robin Christie)
Three smaller photos of the continuation of the contest with Joe Critchley plus a larger picture featuring the winning fall. Below them from left to right: A picture of Hack and Anglo-Italian both of whom run the Wrestling Heritage site. Next to them is Greg Dyke the man responsible for ending television wrestling and next to him a picture of the author Dale Storm as he looks today, plus both his parents. The Poster dates from a show in the Drill Hall Dumfries in the late 1970's.

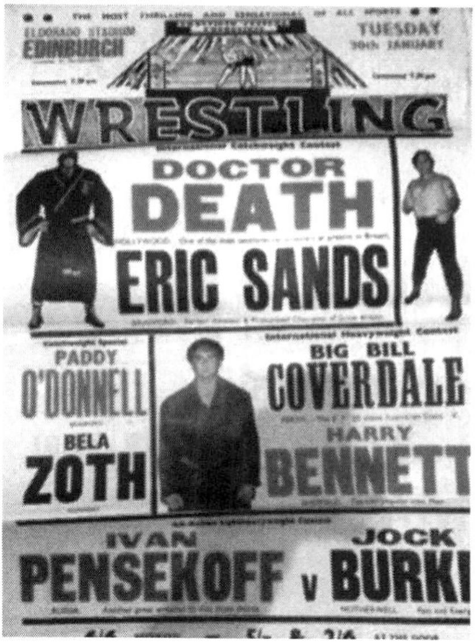

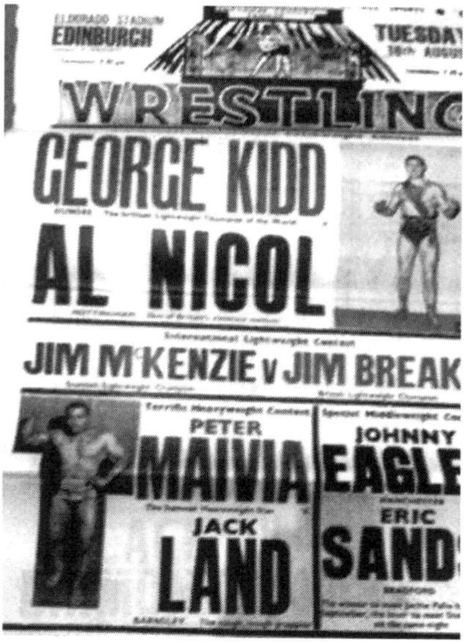

Early 1960's Eldorado Stadium Posters

(Courtesy of Mr S Betts)

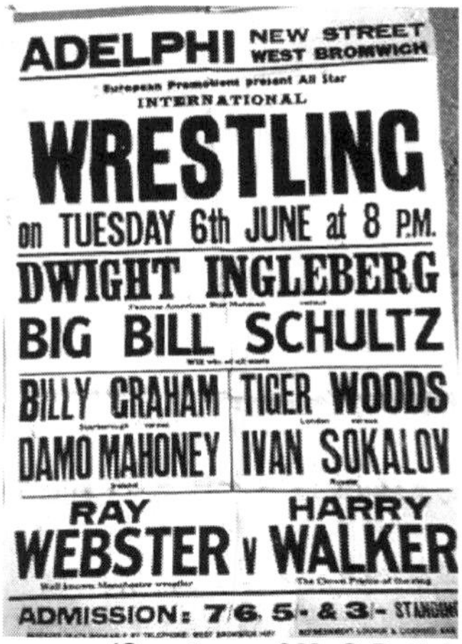

(Courtesy of Mr S Betts)

Fred Hill [moustache, short hair] with Sam Betts. Sam appeared at the Eldorado Stadium regularly as his alter ego American persona named: Dwight J Ingleburgh.

The Eldorado Stadium Leith in its heyday!

(Courtesy of both Lyndsey Mason and Natasha Kirk)

Crusher Mason & Mal Kirk God bless and keep them.

Even the TV Soaps benefitted from Wrestling's Fame!

Big Ian Campbell is brought to his knee by a Dragon in the form of top Soap Villain "Corrie's" infamous hair net wearing, milk stout drinking Ena Sharples!

The Village where I was born and spent my youth

(Courtesy of Andrew Brodie-Frew)

Early 1970's Ayr Utd Squad Picture. Ollie Reed's Chair.

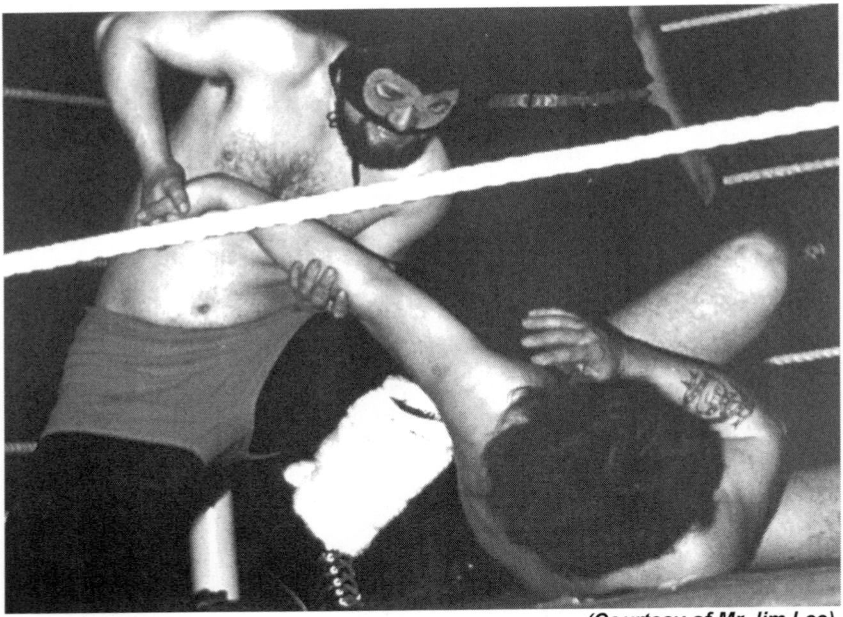

(Courtesy of Mr Jim Lee)

The Viking applies an arm-lock on me!

....(Courtesy of Mr J Critchley)

Joe Critchley in a blonde wig & Dave Morgan at Butlins

Ask him again ref!

The 1984 Miner's Trade Union Struggle

(Courtesy of the National Union of Mine Workers)

Leading politicians and The National Union of Mine Workers Leadership march to keep the Pits Open.

The <u>Brutal</u> and the <u>Unacceptable</u> face of <u>Thatcherism!</u>

*** National archive papers released in early 2014 now prove Arthur Scargill's claim. There actually was a Pit Closures "Hit List" by Thatcher's Tory Government ***

(Courtesy of Andrew Brodie-Frew)

A break from filming with James Cosmo & KT Tunstall.

(Courtesy of Andrew Brodie-Frew)

Billy Connolly playing Queen Victoria's Scottish man servant John Brown and me as an Upstairs Butler.

(Courtesy of Andrew Brodie-Frew)

Graham McTavish right, Roger Moore's daughter Deborah one in, Fiona Kempin and yours truly.

(Courtesy of Ms Diamond Lil)

And finally my minder and myself on holiday in my favourite Mediterranean country Greece.

Ask him again ref!

(Courtesy of Scott Lomax and David O' Connor)

"Ode to the Golden Era of the Grappling Gladiators"

And now the show has ended, the appointed Victors have all taken their bow and for those of us less privileged and driving home, it's back to the drawing board for now. The MC made his announcements, the Ring Seconds towelled them down, the Referee was quite correct when he gave the Villain a "Public Warning" for which he wore a frown! The Crowd were getting restless their "Hero" was trailing one fall to nil. Old Les forever smiling slapped their faces and almost always at his will! As for cocky Jackie Pallo "Ask him now ref!" was his well rehearsed refrain and oriental masked man Nagasaki ever apologetic, indicated with a nod he wouldn't break the rules again! George Kidd he tied them all in knots and seldom, if ever he broke sweat. Jim Breaks spat out the Dummy and Boscik as usual he took the pet. John Cortez was the consummate entertaining flier and Vic Faulkner unlike Bert, he'd got some pace. Sam Betts, Peter Preston and Al Marshall no longer tour. Ezra's gone, Mal Kirk, Crusher Mason, Jim McKenzie, Eric Taylor and Romeo Joe our world's a poorer place. But Eddie Rose still writes thank God! Although in the past it was under a different name. Latterly "The Business" was on a slippery slope. Far too much flab around, the more things change the more they stay the same, only this time under another name. Denials all round and still no one accepts the blame! Mr Show Business Adrian Street outshone almost everyone as a flamboyant legend of the ring well draped with bulging muscles and dyed blonde hair he was such a pretty thing! Sadly those halcyon days are long gone now, just a sometimes fading memory of great times of long ago. When at four o'clock we'd all sit down, me and my Gran and Mum and my Dad to watch the World of Sport all-star Saturday afternoon all-action ITV 4pm Wrestling Show. © *Dale Storm*

Ask him again ref!

In loving memory of
Ms Eily Morton
1934-2014

7390116R00258

Printed in Great Britain
by Amazon.co.uk, Ltd.,
Marston Gate.